Everyday Ethics

Making Hard Choices in a Complex World

*A companion to the
Gnomengen Group Ethics Game®

Karin,
Thanks for letting
your passion meet
the world's greatest
need!
Peace,
[illegible]

Catharyn A. Baird

Tendril Press

Denver, CO
2005

Liability Disclosure
All names, characters, places and incidents in this book are entirely fictional and any resemblance is coincidental. CB Resources, LLC, and the author take no responsibility for any liability, injury, loss, or risk, which is incurred directly or indirectly as a result of the information contained in this book.

EVERYDAY ETHICS: MAKING HARD CHOICES IN A COMPLEX WORLD
A companion to the Gnomengen Group Ethics Game

ISBN:0-9763706-1-1 Hardback
ISBN:0-9763706-0-3 Paperback

10 9 8 7 6 5 4 3 2 First Publishing: March, 2005

Printed on acid free paper in the United States of America by:
Sheridan Books, Ann Arbor, MI
734.662.3291

Published and distributed by
CB Resources, LLC,
7027 South Chapparal Circle West
Centennial, Colorado 80016
303.489.6835
cbaird@cbpresents.com

Book Design, Web Site Design, Marketing and Art Direction by:

A. J. Images Inc.
Graphic & Communication Design
www.ajimagesinc.com — 303•696•9227
info@ajimagesinc.com

For educational and individual sales information, call CB Resources, LLC, 303.489.6835
Visit our web site at: http://www.cbpresents.com

Order ID: 105-7925923-0267457

Thank you for buying from Cen10ialbooks on Amazon Marketplace.

Shipping Address: Tina Fantozzi 5519 N ARTESIAN AVE APT 1 CHICAGO, IL 60625-2200	Order Date: May 23, 2009 Shipping Service: Standard Buyer Name: Tina M Fantozzi Seller Name: Cen10ialbooks

Quantity	Product Details
1	**Everyday Ethics: Making Hard Choices in a Complex World [Unabridged] [Paperback** **Merchant SKU:** 8H-ZX51-A9L1 **ASIN:** 0976370603 **Listing ID:** 0522EK53NHJ **Order-Item ID:** 51909120954322 **Condition:** Used - Like New **Comments:** Inscription/autograph by author. Gold sticker on front states autographed 1st edition. Bindng is tight, Pages are clean, crisp and unmarked. Cover has no visible shelfwear.

Thanks for buying on Amazon Marketplace. To provide feedback for the seller please visit www.amazon.com/feedback. To contact the seller, please visit Amazon.com and click on "Your Account" at the top of any page. In Your Account, go to the "Where's My Stuff" section and click on the link "Leave seller feedback". Select the order or click on the "View Order" button. Click on the "seller profile" under the appropriate product. On the lower right side of the page under "Seller Help", click on "Contact this seller".

Thank you!

To my parents
who helped me frame the original question:
Is it possible to be compassionate and spiritual
while being effective and ethical?

To my students
who journeyed with me through the
thickets of learning to make
good ethical decisions.

To the memory of
Princess Juana, S.J.,
the first and only woman Jesuit.

The GG Ethics Game

This text is designed to be used with The GG Ethics Game, a web-based simulation, which allows participants to assume leadership roles in a fictitious organization or company. The leadership teams must solve a set of problems which are typical of those facing people in management structures in the United States and around the world. These choices have both intended and unintended financial and social consequences, mirroring the sometime randomness of our lives.

The thesis of this book and the accompanying simulation is that the vast majority of people want to become effective ethical agents. However, they are rarely given either the opportunity to examine their beliefs or training in how to develop their ethical skills. The pedagogy of the simulation is based on educational research which demonstrates that with thought, training and practice, we can avoid ethical pitfalls and learn to make better decisions.

Research indicates that in order to become ethically mature, we have to integrate both ethical theory and ongoing practice in decision making. This text provides a theoretical base for a learner-focused approach to ethics and assists in practical mastery of concrete problems. The simulation is designed to imitate life by allowing participants to try unfamiliar decision making models and receive feedback — while having a bit of fun. As they work through a series of dilemmas, participants increase both their self-knowledge as well as understanding of their community. In the process each may even acquire a tad more wisdom, a carefully honed sense of what behavior is appropriate in a given situation.

The simulation may be used as part of a traditional undergraduate or graduate ethics class or to facilitate a company's leadership or ethics training. And, because individuals may not have an opportunity to participate in a formal setting, the CBPresents team is making the simulation available to individuals and informal social groups. For more information about the simulation or to register for a game, please go to our website, cbpresents.com.

Table of Contents

Dedication iii
About the GG Ethics Game iv
Table of Charts ix
A Parable x
Preface xi

Part 1 The Perennial Question: How Should We Live?

Chapter 1 Exploring Ethical Decision Making 3

- An Historical Perspective 4
- Becoming a Responsible Ethical Agent 8
- Bernard Lonergan's Method 10
- Formation of Belief Systems 13
- Source of Information for Belief Systems 22
- Conclusion 34
- Continuing the Conversation 35

Chapter 2 The person-in-community 37

Building Blocks of the Common Good 40
Core Values and Economics 50
Core Values and Law 59
Conclusion 67
Continuing the Conversation 67

Chapter 3 Stepping Stones and Safety Nets 69

Core Beliefs and Manifestations 71
Implications for Ethics and Public Policy 84
The Excluded Middle 87
Conclusion 90
Continuing the Conversation 91

Chapter 4 Foundations for Decision-Making 93

Step 1 ~ Be Attentive: Consider What Works — or Doesn't .. 94
Step 2 ~ Be Intelligent: Sort through the Data 103
Conclusion 117
Continuing the Conversation 117

Chapter 5 Strategies for Decision-Making 119

Step 3 ~ Be Reasonable: Evaluate the Options 122
Step 4 ~ Be Responsible: Choose to Act 129
Step 5 ~ Return to Awareness 139
Conclusion 141
Continuing the Conversation 143

Part 2 Making Hard Choices in a Complex World

Chapter 6 The Path to Maturity 147

Charting the Conversation 148
Core Contextual Questions 152
The Ethical Map 157
The Moral Map 160
The Crucible of Spirit 164

The Opportunity for Maturity 168
Conclusion 171
Continuing the Conversation 171

Chapter 7 Rights/Responsibility Lens 173

Characteristics of Rights/Responsibility Lens 175
Using the Rights/Responsibility Lens 179
Conclusion 200
Continuing the Conversation 201

Chapter 8 Results Lens 203

Characteristics of Results Lens 205
Using the Results Lens 210
Conclusion 224
Continuing the Conversation 224

Chapter 9 Relationship Lens 227

Characteristics of Relationship Lens 229
Using the Relationship Lens 234
Conclusion 253
Continuing the Conversation 253

Chapter 10 Reputation Lens 255

Characteristics of Reputation Lens 257
Using the Reputation Lens 260
Conclusion 288
Continuing the Conversation 289

Chapter 11 Life with Integrity and Grace 291

Can't We Just Return to the Good old Days? 299
Embracing Complexity 301
Conclusion 303
Continuing the Conversation 305

Appendices 307
Appendix A: Core Ethical Frameworks 309
Appendix B: From Ethics to Law 325
Appendix C: Rational and Relational Ethics 331
Appendix D: Excellence and Efficiency 337

Notes 339

Works Cited 355

Index 361

About the CB Resources 373

Table of Charts

Core Ethical Frameworks 2

Perennial Organizing Questions 36

Matrix of Approaches to Justice 68

Applying Lonergan's Method, Part 1 92

Applying Lonergan's Method, Part 2 118

Path to Maturity 146

The Rules/Relationship Lens 172

The Results Lens 202

The Relationship Lens 226

The Reputation Lens 254

A Parable

A little girl was watching her mother prepare a ham for Easter dinner. As she looked on, the mother sliced both ends off the ham before she placed it in the roasting pan. "Why are you doing that?" asked the little girl.

Her mother thought for a moment and admitted, "I don't know. It's what my mother always did. Maybe you should go and ask Grandma."

The little girl found her Grandma and asked, "Grammy, why did you cut the ends off of hams?"

Her Grandma though for a moment and confessed, "I don't know. It's what my mother always did. You should ask Great Grandma."

Off went the little girl to Great Grandma to whom she posed the question. Great Grandma smiled and with a twinkle in her eye said, "Well, I can't speak for your mother or grandmother, but I always cut the ends off of the ham so it would fit into the pan."

Preface

People have fussed over the relationship of ethics and business for as long as organizations have existed. The first person who cheated his neighbor or lied about a product triggered a conversation designed to resolve questions such as "how does our community define what is fair?" and "what is the right way to do business?" Over many years, stakeholders in for-profit and nonprofit business enterprises — owners, employees, customers, suppliers, and the community — have asked perennial questions such as:

- *What is a fair price for this particular product or service?*
- *What is a fair wage?*
- *What is the proper way to treat people?*
- *What are customers' responsibilities when they purchase goods or services?*
- *Who should bear the risk for the failure of a company or the safety of a product?*
- *What responsibility does this company have to the larger community and the environment?*

Depending on the time, place, and society, the specific answers to the perennial questions are different. But we are often like the mother with the ham: we use the tools and understandings of the past to solve the problems of the present, sometimes without understanding why we do what we do. As technology advances and distances between our global neighbors shrink, the answers of the past are frequently inadequate. Further, because professional ethics is applied ethics, each situation has subtle nuances that require thoughtfulness. Culture and our understanding of ourselves are always in flux. Relating individual and community norms to specific business issues requires thought and discretion, because what a community or an individual accepts as an ethical result is often peculiar to that culture and time.

The upshot is that over the centuries, our understanding of what is considered fair, just, and ethical behavior in business has changed. In developed Western countries, the methods used to assure compliance with ethical norms have evolved from shunning or marginalizing someone, to an ever-changing legal system which now not only includes the opportunity for redress after injury but also seeks to prevent harm through a regulatory system. Nevertheless, whatever the system, the core questions are the same.

On the threshold of the technological age, members of the industrialized world community ponder the implications of a global economy while confronted with the economic fallout caused by corrupt behavior at the very top of highly respected corporations. The stories which punctuate the business pages of the press as our community transitions between the 20th and 21st centuries rock the confidence of the whole community — investors, employees and consumers. Overwhelmed by business shenanigans, people are demanding new solutions for a new era.

Participants in the American and global economies are not satisfied with "cutting off the ends of the ham" just because that is how business has "made things fit" for centuries. Rather, we want better ways to articulate and practice traditional values. Lacking confidence in historic approaches to business ethics, leaders are searching for new methods and constructs for evaluating problems, reasoning about appropriate solutions, and fashioning behaviors which will bring out the best in each person and build a thriving economy.

Distinctive Features of this Text

This text, which is designed to be used with an accompanying ethics simulation or other learner-centered approach to business ethics, provides a refreshing method for solving today's questions. Rather than futilely focusing on finding the right results, this approach focuses on asking the right questions while accomplishing the following:

Gives readers the tools to sharpen ethical decision-making skills

Children learn the fundamentals of ethics in their family and immediate community. As adults, our responsibilities increase and we need more than the rudiments of ethical decision making to be successful. We need to acquire finely honed skills to assist us in resolving hard problems in a complex world.

This text walks through four specific approaches to evaluating ethical questions: what are our rights and responsibilities; what results do we want; what relationships should we honor; and what is our reputation and character. The learner-focused approach also gives us an opportunity to practice decision making using a variety of templates. As we learn to analyze issues using these four ethical frameworks, situations which were fuzzy and unintelligible will come into focus and decision-making will be easier.

Addresses the emerging issues of a postmodern world

Over the past several decades, scientists and philosophers have articulated new theories about the formation of knowledge. Realizing that trying to identify core ethical principles which meet the rigors of modern scientific analysis is futile, philosophers (particularly those who study applied ethics) are coming to terms with what it means to live in a contingent world. Each person has limited knowledge; none of us can ever know all there is to know. Further, our ideas and values are personal and cultural. These individual differences are magnified in a diverse community where people embrace the beliefs of different cultures and religious teachings. Thus, universal agreement about what particular action is ethical becomes impossible.

The study and pedagogy of applied ethics, the discipline that addresses the question of how a particular person is to live in a particular community, must change its course. The search for timeless philosophical or theological foundations, which promise to ground specific ethical decisions in universal principles and values, is problematic. Rather, in community, people are given the opportunity to ask questions, find the best answers given limited knowledge, and act in a way that moves the community towards the greater good and the individual towards ethical maturity.

Embraces values-based management and corporate social responsibility

A key lesson learned from the scandals of the 1990s is that individuals alone cannot be responsible for the ethics of an organization. The culture of the organization itself mediates the values that are held by individuals, expected by the community, and practiced by an organization. A newly-emerging conversation considers the scope of corporate social responsibility as companies decide how best to be members of their communities. The emerging consensus is that organizations must not only meet the best interests of their shareholders, but also must consider other stakeholders (employees, consumers, suppliers), and the community as a whole as decisions are made. Today's leaders need a new set of tools to meet the expected triple-bottom line — economic growth, ethical behavior, and environmental sustainability.

Explores leadership opportunities to pace progress to ethical excellence

Organizations cannot develop and sustain an ethical culture without ethical leaders. As leaders face their personal psychological shadow, acknowledge individual weaknesses, and explore their own mixed motives for acting, they will see more clearly the problems in their company. As managers contemplate the implications of people having a mixture of honorable and suspect motives and behaviors, they will need creative strategies for encouraging organizations to be more ethical while managing the bottom line. Leaders who are able to meet both economic and ethical objectives will be able to pace the ethical development of their organization's culture and their personal quest for excellence.

As we are each part of the ongoing conversation, we have the privilege and responsibility to determine for ourselves what essential ideas of past traditions need to be brought forward and re-appropriated. As we use experience and imagination to explore rights and responsibilities, choose preferred results, nurture relationships, and protect our reputation, we each can determine how best to be an individual in community while fashioning a world where all — our own and future generations — can live and thrive.

Acknowledgments

This work could not have been done without the wonderful students at Regis University in Denver, Colorado. Exploring Jesuit pedagogy, with its commitment to participatory learning and justice for those without power, has informed my understanding of the obligation and opportunity for those who work in a variety of organizations to model ethical behavior in a fiscally and socially responsible manner. My students have constantly challenged me to "walk the talk" and have thus profoundly shaped my thinking.

I am also indebted to my friends at Regis, especially my writing partner Aimee Wheaton, who was relentless in her encouragement. My compatriots in the Colleagues in Jesuit Business Education, a consortium of faculty members from the business schools of Jesuit universities, and my colleagues in the Academy of Legal Studies in Business, buoyed me when I was floundering. My editing team, Genevieve Baird, Anisa Divine, Kerry McCaig, Jeanne Peterson, Connie Talmage, and Aimee Wheaton wielded their red pencils to make the writing crisp and intelligible. My book editor and designer, Karin Hoffman, provided an exquisite layout. All errors are my responsibility alone.

The idea for the simulation came from my son, Thor Nelson, who remains an ardent gamer. Embracing the family vocation of teaching as an affiliate faculty member in the MBA program at Regis University, he invited me to consider how to engage today's generation of students into strategies of ethical decision-making. The structure evolved in conversations with my sister, Jeannine Niacaris, a human resources expert *extraordinaire* who assured that the project reflected real life. As the simulation evolved over several years, I am grateful for students who provided valuable insight and critique.

My husband, Bob Russell, has been unswavering in his support — even when he scowled and told me to get my fingers flying on the computer keyboard. My daughter, Jeanne Peterson and her husband, Lee, provided invaluable legal and financial research support, to get this project off the ground.

I have been blessed in my vocation. This book is my offering to the community to further the conversation about how we all can be more effective in our work, which is an essential part of being human. As we endeavor to live out our heart's desires and provide quality goods and services at an appropriate price which enhances the world community — in short as we learn to be effective and ethical — we can provide another link in the chain of civilization. And, perhaps, together we can make this astonishing world a little bit better.

Peace,

CB

Catharyn A. Baird, J.D.

Part 1

The Perennial Question: How Should We Live

Chapter 1 Exploring Ethical Decision-Making 3

Chapter 2 The Person in Community 37

Chapter 3 Stepping Stones and Safety Nets 69

Chapter 4 Foundations for Decision-Making 93

Chapter 5 Strategies for Decision-Making 119

Core Ethical Frameworks*

Community
(Rationality)

Reflection
(Autonomy)

Action
(Equality)

Reputation Lens Teleological Tradition (MacIntyre — Virtue/character focus) An ethical action is one which is consistent with good character.	Relationship Lens Deontological Tradition (Justice/systems focus — Rawls) An ethical action is one which sustains integrity-building, just environments.
Rights/Responsibility Lens Deontological Tradition (Kant — Rights/duties focus) An ethical action is one where one does one's duty and follows ethical standards of action.	Results Lens Teleological Tradition (Goal/ends focus — Mill) An ethical action is one where the goal is to create the greatest good for the greatest number.

Individual
(Sensibility)

Key Definitions

Deontology (deon=duty + logos=words): conversations about duty

Teleology (teleos=ends, goals + logos=words): conversations about goals and ultimate ends

*Adapted from Petrick and Quinn, *Management Ethics: Integrity at Work* and Ken Wilber, *Sex, Ecology, and Spirituality*

"...the world we live in, our
view of it and the values we attach to it,
is shaped by what we know.
And when what we know changes,
the world changes and with it, everything.

James Burke[1]

Chapter 1

Exploring Ethical Decision-Making

The study of ethics concerns the rules and relationships which govern individuals living in a community. Throughout history, conversations about the rights and responsibilities of people, both as individuals and as members of a community, have centered around a set of core values: rationality, sensibility, autonomy, and equality. Over history, diverse communities have had varying expectations for the appropriate balance among these four core values. Different communities also have had widely disparate notions about what constitutes ethical or unethical behavior. However, even though the specific content of the ethical standards may change (what specific behavior is considered ethical), the conversation and the core vocabulary remains relatively constant because all communities must come to terms with how to balance the rights of individuals against the claims of the community.

As seen by the chart on the preceding page, one thread of the conversation focuses on the rights of individuals *(autonomy)* in opposition to the demands of the community *(equality)*. This dialogue asks when individuals should be able to assert their prerogative to live their lives as they see fit, and when their behavior should be modified by the expectations and constraints of community norms. A second thread focuses on when individual reflection and societal expectations will provide the lodestar for what is right and wrong by setting predictable criteria for behavior *(rationality)*, and when our actions are appropriately guided by changing circumstances and emerging goals *(sensibility)*.[2]

Each of the core ethical frameworks answers the question slightly differently. The Rights/Responsibility Lens (deontological tradition with a rights/duty focus) emphasizes the right of individuals to determine the principles which govern how they should best live. The Results Lens (teleological tradition with a goals focus) centers on individuals choosing goals which will make them happy in light of changing needs and desires. The Relationship Lens (deontological tradition with a justice/systems focus) is concerned with when and how community interests should take priority over individual interests in the name of justice. The Reputation Lens (teleological tradition with a virtue/character focus) helps us ask how character is shaped as individuals respond to community expectations.

An Historical Perspective

A glance at the history of ethics in the Western world shows that from Plato forward the various frameworks have come in and out of prominence in a relatively predictable sequence. Given that each of the approaches balances the excess of another, the pendulum swings as intemperate behavior in the name of one particular theory is corrected by the opposite theory coming into vogue. Current theorists advocate tempering the seeming over-emphasis of the two individual frameworks which have held sway since the 1600s and reasserting a concern for the community. During the past thirty years, we have seen correction within the teleological tradition. The guiding principle of utilitarianism, finding the act which will provide the greatest good for the greatest number, is being moderated as virtue ethics has moved to center stage. The current emphasis on character (*Reputation Lens*) seeks to correct the excesses of the utilitarian (*Results Lens*) frame which put the goals of the individual above the needs of the community. During the same time frame, the deontological tradition

(*Rights/Responsibility Lens*) has also been calibrated as justice theories (*Relationship Lens*) are offered to offset the perceived selfishness and isolation which comes from overemphasizing individual rights.

From the Modern to the Postmodern Era

But we're getting ahead of the story. Let's go back to the beginning of what is called the Age of Enlightenment and see how we got to this kaleidoscope of opportunities and challenges which define the beginning of the 21st century. While change happens gradually, the watershed years which moved us from what is known as the Medieval Age to the Modern Age (the Age of Reason) are the 1500s, with the birth of the scientific method and the Protestant Reformation. The new idea which emerged from the monastic laboratories was that through reason and research we could find out how the physical world worked.[3] The scientific method was then applied to what came to be known as the social sciences. Theorists asserted that the underlying principles and rules for ethics, economics, and politics could be discovered through reason and research rather than through revelation in scripture or traditional teaching.

Philosophers and theologians set themselves to the task of identifying the universal principles that undergird all moral action. Using the tools of the Age of Reason — a scientific, rational approach — the question was whether universal ethical principles could be identified and then made the basis of human action. The spokesman for the deontological tradition, Immanuel Kant [1724-1804], offered what he called the categorical imperatives which could be used to determine the universal principles to guide ethical decision-making. Kant believed that, after determining the principles which delineated our rights and responsibilities, we would be able to choose appropriate goals for our lives.

The spokesman for the teleological tradition, John Stuart Mill [1806-1873], asserted that the goal was to find what course of action would result in the greatest happiness for the greatest number of people. Mill believed that after determining what goals or ultimate ends would make us happy, we would be able to identify the core principles of ethical behavior which could guide individuals and policy makers. Conversations about which of these approaches was correct (and variations on the themes) dominated the discourse about ethics until the last quarter of the 20th century.

Mid-twentieth century scholars began to suspect that the project to find universal principles was going to fail. The implications of the new physics — in particular Albert Einstein's *Theory of Relativity* and Warren Heisenberg's *Uncertainty Principle* — shook the certain foundations of science. As Einstein demonstrated that everything — even time — is relative to the observer, the belief that science could provide facts which were independent of the observer faltered. Then Heisenberg demonstrated that the very process of science was subject to bias. For example, when one conducts experiments to determine the nature of light, if one asks questions about light particles, one sees particles, and if one asks questions about light waves, one sees waves. In other words, one sees what one looks for. Thus, everything we believe that we know is limited by the very questions we ask and the methods we use in seeking the knowledge.[3]

Sociologist Peter Berger continued the conversation in the social sciences by demonstrating that every person's knowledge of reality, our convictions about what is real in our world, is constructed from our beliefs. As we walk through life, our world view is shaped by an elegant intersection of the authorities we find persuasive, the traditions we consider important, how we learn and what we know, as well as our personal experience.[4]

In response to Berger's work (and that of other sociologists, philosophers, and linguists), a broad category of concepts named postmodernism challenged the underlying premise of the modern era: if we sought objective knowledge using the tools of scientific inquiry, we could with certainty find and verify "The Truth." The promise was that by identifying the truth, people could find universal, and thus certain, foundations for ethical actions which would withstand the test of time. The expectation was that these truths would be obvious to people who used the same analytical processes which were based in the scientific method.

As noted by the postmodern thinkers, the understanding that individual and community questions, assumptions, and resulting beliefs shape a person and a culture posited an interesting conundrum for those who were part of the classical school of thought. If the theorists were right that the matrix from which ethical decisions arise is personal and communal, the Enlightenment Project of finding timeless foundations was doomed. The insight of the postmodernists was that the world view of individuals and the community (the sum total of their beliefs) provides the foundation for understanding how to live in community, not timeless rules grounded in universal ideals.

Postmodernism also provided a way out of the dead end of dualism where every act is either right or wrong by providing a more holistic approach to life, one which includes the excluded middle and legitimizes the grey shades of both/and as we seek the good, the better, and the best.

Emergence of Postmodern Thought

The postmodern conversation thus requires that philosophers, theologians and ethicists redefine their task. If, in fact, the rational foundations for the universal truths do not hold, the question becomes whether the appropriate quest is to seek the ultimate truth. The other option for ethicists (and persons in community who want to act ethically) is to attend to the perennial questions as they seek better answers to today's problems. These questions have no pretense of giving us unshakable foundations for the right answers. However, carefully crafted questions can guide the discussion as well as help us clarify our beliefs and prioritize our core values and the resulting virtues.

As the notion of postmodern thought has just emerged in the past thirty years, the definition is still under construction. Most philosophers now acknowledge that all truth, everything that we as humans know, is contingent — based upon our very best understanding of what is and what should be. As we seek knowledge and wisdom, we take the pieces of our experience that do not make sense, given what we believe, and seek more complete answers to the emerging questions. Postmodernism actually makes intuitive sense for those in the trenches who have to apply ethical theory to the practice of every day living. Rather than straining to find agreed upon universal principles by which to live our lives, we can entertain the perennial questions. By using the analytical frameworks which have informed ethical thought throughout history, we can find the best possible solutions to difficult situations. The task of ethics thus changes from a preoccupation with correctly applying the right rules to using a thoughtful process for finding the best available answers.

In the process of working through a problem, we may find that two solutions are both ethical as the different frameworks emphasize different values. The traditional approach is to say that one value must take priority over the other, an either/or approach. But now we have the opportunity to harmonize the conflicting values by using a both/and approach.

For example, we believe that employers should provide a safe workplace for employees. We also believe that employees are responsible for avoiding injury on the job. Traditionally, when deciding whether enhanced requirements for safety should be made law, such as requiring that employers provide their employees state-of-the-art ergonomic equipment, we have tried to decide whether the value of a safe workplace (even if it will increase the cost of goods and services to the community) should be given priority over that of employees assuming the risk of injury. In that case, the value we (either as an individual or as a community) believe is most important will determine both what we do and what we will require others to do. A holistic approach would determine where employer and employee responsibility converge and from there implement a nuanced policy.

As we take responsibility for creatively solving today's problems, we are encouraged to help fashion a world which provides greater dignity to all humans and allows communities to thrive. The ethical agent gets to ask, "what is the best way to approach ethical decision-making if I want to make sense of my life and continue in my quest to 'be all that [I] can be' while building a healthy community?"[5] In the process of asking questions, we can each take responsibility for the decisions we make rather than being content with having our choices validated by other people or beliefs.

As we engage in this new quest, contemporary philosophers and ethicists remind us that we construct our own lives by the way we tell our stories, contextualize our experience, and determine what is meaningful.[6] We can embrace the privilege of becoming fully functioning adults as we use our mind and imagination to make sense of our place in this world and take responsibility for our choices and actions. In the process we develop the skills needed to become mature ethical agents in an emerging technological age — the ability to be effective while assuring that in the future we have a planet and community for our children.[7]

Becoming a Responsible Ethical Agent

While the implications in theory and practice for this new way of looking at our world are not all known, the immediate question is whether all ethics boils down to radical relativity — we all get to do what we want — or whether we can identify some constraints for unrestrained individualism. A responsible inquiry-based method of resolving ethical issues does not allow us to rely only on our own unreflective personal preferences but demands that we also ask what will serve the community as a whole. History seems to teach that when either the community ignores the legitimate needs of individuals or when individuals abuse their prerogatives, both suffer. The study of ethics invites us to balance the claims of individuals and the community as well as seek balance between the personal and work aspects of our own lives. In the process we learn when to act in our own enlightened self interest and when to overcome our biases and fears to act for the good of the community. We also learn when we need to take a stand against community expectations that seemingly require us to violate our own sense of what is right. In short, we can learn how to be an ethical and effective person-in-community.[8]

The thesis of this book is that whether we call it being ethical or moral, the vast majority of us want to be good individuals and citizens. Researchers in ethics find that all of us seem to have a desire to be ethical and/or to be perceived as ethical.[9] As we look for patterns in the stories of those who have breached the ethical norms of the community, often the problem is that they may not have had either the knowledge or the skill to make effective ethical decisions. Thus, to restore confidence in our individual ability to make good decisions and to create an ethical culture, we need opportunities to stretch and move beyond our childhood understandings of ethics and become ethically mature.

One of the difficulties in ethics texts is that theorists have not agreed on the definitions of ethics and morality. In common usage, an ethical person is one who acts from a set of ethical principles, and a moral person is one who follows the standards of conduct expected in the community.[10] Another interesting distinction is that morality defines how we as humans use our freedom, and ethics is how we think about and reflect on the appropriate use of freedom. The conversations also distinguish between individual acts which can be considered ethical and the formation of a moral character.[11]

While this usage may be contested, for purposes of this book a distinction is made between ethics, which focuses on our use of reason to find appropriate rules, and morality, which considers how we blend our reason with our emotional resources and skills. Those who use the term morality as distinguished from ethics tend to emphasize factors such as caring for the other person (*e.g.*, Nel Noddings[12]), developing our conscience (*e.g.,* Charles Shelton[13]), or enhancing our emotional maturity (*e.g.,* Daniel Goleman[14]). In reality, the distinction between ethics and morality is not as tidy as portrayed in this book. However, highlighting the difference in this way allows us to explore the tangle of reason and emotion which forms the matrix for our decisions, whether labeled ethical or moral.

Bernard Lonergan's Method

One contemporary philosopher who carefully engaged the question of how to find better answers in a contingent world was Bernard Lonergan [1904-1984], a 20th century Jesuit philosopher who asked how we could be responsible agents in light of our incomplete knowledge and the uncertainty of life. Using scientific inquiry as his starting point, Lonergan noted that given everything we know is contingent, our most complete knowledge is still based on our best, current information. Lonergan observed that as we continue to live and work in this world, we see that pieces of our knowledge and experience do not fit our existing notions about the world, leaving us with unanswered questions. Lonergan asserted that every person's core desire is to make sense of the world and to make the pieces fit, which he called our unrestricted desire to know. While his work (like that of all good philosophers) is dense, requiring much study to begin to understand all of the implications, he articulated a four step decision-making process. His clear method provides an excellent concept map for those seeking to be responsible while making hard choices in a complex world.[15]

Step 1: Be Attentive

The hardest part of being fully present in the world is paying attention to what is happening around us, attending to human affairs as we live in our fragile world. The attention that Lonergan envisions involves not only attending to the facts and situations outside of ourselves, but also the process of knowing ourselves, our motives and nature, inclinations and foibles — our very identity. Another facet of being attentive is finding out what we do not know. When we see a fact or hear an assertion, we need to check whether we can attest to that piece of data or whether we need more information. We also need to ask what information is missing, what details have been ignored. Thus, the first step of effective ethical decision-making is identifying the ethical agent, attending to the various stakeholders in the situation who have varying interests and expectations, and setting the context of the decision.

Step 2: Be Intelligent

The process of being intelligent requires that we inquire about what is going on. What is the true state of affairs? What is happening around us? What are the most reliable data that we have? In this stage of inquiry, we seek to learn the best available information about how to live well in this world. As we work through this phase, we do not put our heads in the proverbial sand, refusing to see what is about us, even if the information is disquieting.

Being intelligent as we work to make effective decisions requires that we carefully articulate the issue before us. This task demands that the ethical agent have well-developed moral sensibilities and be able to see ethical issues even though flashing neon lights do not boldly announce their presence. The next task is to carefully consider the values in conflict. Ethical issues are always about competing good solutions. The crux of decision-making is identifying the competing individual and/or community values which underlie the ethical conflict. The final task is to craft possible options for action.

Step 3: Be Reasonable

As human beings we must judge among many goods and goals. We must choose among competing values. We must assess the truth or falsity of another's statements as we discern for ourselves what is as well as what we prefer. Those who do not learn to discern truth are at the mercy of the last book they read or the last polemic they heard. Being reasonable includes analyzing what will or will not work, what is or is not feasible. For this step, Lonergan invites us to move towards the greater good, to find the best result given what we know about the world and the humans who inhabit it.

Being reasonable requires that the ethical agent work to hone critical thinking skills. We must look carefully at all facets of the problem. Then we can explore the ramifications of action by synthesizing two or more of the ethical and moral frameworks. The more complex the problem, the more valuable a multifaceted and synergistic approach becomes.

Step 4: Be Responsible

A telling critique of many ethics classes is that we discuss endlessly without helping people learn to come to resolution. Yet, every day each of us makes a multitude of small ethical decisions. We decide among competing rights and responsibilities. We choose one set of goals over another. We decide to give up our own prerogatives (or not) in order to maintain relationships with those who are important in our lives. We consider our reputations and what is essential to us. All of these choices are ethical choices. Lonergan challenges us not to wander mindlessly through life but to be intentional and responsible as we decide what to believe and what to do.

Therefore, as we choose to act, we need to correct for personal bias and attend to the common good, a holistic world view which considers and balances the needs and privileges of both the one and the many. Because each of us has blind spots and tends to be selfish, the notion of ethics carries with it the expectation that we will become self-reflective and self-regulating persons who can temper our choices to correct for personal preference and cultural bias.

As we act responsibly, we can seek an answer which most elegantly balances the competing values and the resulting virtues in the community. For instance, the lessons of the 20th century teach that we are all connected both economically and ecologically. The phenomenon known as the butterfly effect, which states that the flutter of a butterfly's wing changes wind patterns across the globe, reminds us that the business decisions of people in organizations impact an entire economy. The decisions also affect the physical well being of our planet. We attend to the common good by finding the decision that will benefit not only ourselves but those around us.

Step 5: Return to Awareness — A Reprise

The method articulated by Lonergan provides a useful structure for making decisions. After we act, we have an opportunity to notice again the intended and unintended results. As we move in the world, others decide what our actions mean and the context in which they want to hold the event. We also get to learn about ourselves, our strengths and weaknesses. The process of self-regulation lets us see where our actions fail to match our expectations for ourselves and thus demand change. Self-discipline requires noting where we need to restrain our desires and inclinations to reach the goals we have set.

Thus our world views intersect with each other in a lacework of fractals — seemingly random events that create exquisite patterns of life.

Formation of Belief Systems

The reflective process which Lonergan outlines mirrors the process by which we each create our belief system, the world view which we form in childhood and modify as adults. This outlook becomes the lens through which we look at the world — our belief window. Thus, a belief system is the totality of a person's ideas. We go through life and things happen — neutral events from which we get knowledge and experiences, what we call ideas. As we name these neutral events, we come to hold certain truths about ourselves, our community, and our work. We then interpret these events based on what we believe and know to be true. From our "truth" we make fresh choices which give new results and additional explanations about life.

Some would argue that no such thing as neutral events exist. Even the very act of noticing something requires judgment and evaluation. However, the mental discipline of stripping away as much as possible of our preconceived notions, which come from biases embedded in our culture and from our personal history, helps us open possibilities for recontextualizing an event and giving it a different meaning. We can then respond differently than we may have originally anticipated.

For example, those of us who were born and raised in the United States tend to see everything first through a individualistic, market economy lens. Thus, the arrangements that Europeans make for caring for the sick and elderly do not make sense to us. Europeans who tend to see through a communitarian, social-democratic economic lens find our arrangements for health care similarly mystifying. If we try seeing with another lens, we as Americans may find ourselves becoming more generous than we originally thought as we distribute health care resources.

Knowing how we remember, retell and contextualize the experiences of life (the Heisenberg principle of "when we look for light waves, we see light waves" in action) makes understanding the dynamics of the workplace much easier. If we believe that most people are out to cheat the system, what we see in the vast majority of cases is people cheating the system. If we believe that most people are basically honest, what we see as we look around are people being honest.A perplexing question is how do each of us decide what to believe? What, exactly, is truth?

Forming Belief Systems

The process of observation, reflection and action informs the structure of our belief system. From the moment of our birth, we collect information about how we fit in the world. While our first information comes before we learn how to reason, through trial and error we learn how to see and evaluate our surroundings. We first notice something. Then we make a decision about whether that something really exists, in the sense of whether it has an anticipated particular structure, value, or meaning. From that decision we choose a course of action. That action results in intended and unintended (anticipated and unanticipated) events.As the cycle is repeated, we form a set of beliefs about ourselves, others, and our world. Our total set of beliefs is our world view.[16]

A poignant example of the first step of the process of deciding what truly exists comes from the popular movie *A Beautiful Mind*.The main character, John Nash, suffers from paranoid-schizophrenia. At a critical point in the movie he has to determine whether his companions are real or not. He determines that they do not really exist because over the years the little girl has never gotten older. Nash has to rework his belief system to reflect that his companions — both good and evil — are not real. We may not have imaginary friends, but we all have beliefs which may not be grounded in truth.

Interestingly, biologists tell us that the action of the brain mirrors the philosophers' teachings about how belief systems are formed. According to Andrew Newberg, M.D., who has exhaustively studied the way the brain processes information, the first step of perception occurs when the primary receptive areas which are dedicated to the five sensory systems receive unprocessed data. Then the perceptions move to the association area where the data are matched with the memory and emotional centers as the brain organizes the information. The finished image only becomes accessible to the conscious mind when the image combines with memory and emotion. These steps give the image context and meaning. The final stage comes as the image is assimilated and processed through the visual association area, where it is then correlated with information from other parts of the brain.[17]

Daniel Goleman indicates that sometimes information gets to the emotional circuitry before it goes through either the long-term or short-term memory centers. Sometimes information is scrambled on the way to the memory centers. This scrambling may result in a person responding inappropriately to the data, such as the tragic circumstances where a father kills his child wandering around the house at night. The emotional center registers "unknown noise ➤ intruder ➤ danger" before the parent can note that the wanderer is a child.[18] This research reminds us that we need to pay attention to both rational and emotional data to assure that we respond properly to environmental cues.

Noticing Neutral Events

The choreography is fascinating. The dance begins when we notice something happening in our world. Through our senses we apprehend a flower, a sunset, a tone of voice. Many philosophers assert that these events have no meaning in themselves: they are neutral events. Nothing that we see, hear, or feel has by itself any intrinsic meaning. All events are interpreted either through our cultural and/or personal context. For example, the exact same event in a divergent time or an alternate place may take on another meaning. When I survey my lawn, a dandelion is a pest to be eradicated. When my five-year-old grandson brings a dandelion to his Grammy, the dandelion becomes an act of love. Same flower/weed, different context — totally new interpretation.

Because so much data are available, we only see (hear, feel, touch) that which we have named or expect to see. During the late 1800s when publishing his seminal work on bacteria and disease, Louis Pasteur was ridiculed by the medical establishment for asserting that disease was transmitted by contaminated hands and instruments. Given that a status symbol in the medical community was how much blood was on an apron, his colleagues contended that, because the microbes could not be seen, they did not exist. By demonstrating that microbes caused infection, Pasteur changed "the way we frame disease and what we can do about. From this point forward, disease would be framed in terms of specific living causes, an idea that was called the *germ theory of disease*."[19] The practice of medicine changed as a result of Pasteur's recontextualizing of disease "because what is done about the sick person depends on the conception of what is wrong with him or her."[20]

Those in every other profession have experienced the shift in world view which heralded the birth of scientific medicine. Some embrace the reframing of their professions while others are skeptical. Thus, the human tendency to see only what we expect to see gets replayed in the business world as we make decisions based on what we have previously named. As one pundit says, we drive with our eyes on the rearview mirror. That is, we look for what we have seen previously; then we respond to current events based on information stored in our personal historical archives.

One of the primary tasks of an attentive person is to be willing to see what is not expected and thus what is not named. While we may never be able to be free from our cultural understanding of the world, the act of trying to see as clearly as possible helps us lessen the dangers of myopia. For example, when women began naming their experience of being treated as sexual objects in the workplace as harassment, because the culture did not have a category called "sexual harassment on the job," the women's experiences were initially trivialized. However, once we knew what to see and decided that the behavior was not acceptable, people noticed occurrences of sexual harassment everywhere and began pressing for behavioral change. The difficulty with newly named unethical behavior is that actions which are not sexual harassment may be labeled as such. The challenge is to notice what others do not see and to evaluate that particular event in light of itself and not be quick to judge in light of past labels or choices — either positive or negative.

The second task is learning to see without judgment, with no value added. This ability to see events as neutral allows us to see what does not seem to fit or make sense, to change context quickly, and to respond to change. Newspapers are filled with tragic results which come from people not being able to change behavior when they receive new information or are confronted with a unique problem. A stark example of this pattern was seen in Colorado when two young gunmen entered Columbine High School, shot students and faculty, and then killed themselves.

The members of the SWAT team were trained to move very slowly, making sure that the gunmen, whom they expected were holding hostages, did not kill any others. Even though the reports transmitted via cell phones from inside the high school indicated that the gunmen were dead, the police stayed with tried and true procedures. The claim is that some who were wounded died as a result of the delay. Should the police be faulted for following established procedure? Should they have been trained to respond to the crisis at hand rather than acting from a script? Everyone who has put in place processes and protocols for action knows the difficulty of that choice. On one hand, fidelity is essential for uniform action and results. On the other hand, we want employees to respond creatively to an emerging, new situation. Being trained to see an event as neutral — without inherent meaning or value — and respond from a rich repertoire of actions tends to get better results than acting from prejudged bias or habit.

The final step in evaluating neutral events is to notice that all events are apprehended in two ways: with our emotions and with our mind. The emotional response is our first indicator of danger or safety — to fight, flee, or stay for dinner. For much of modern business history, we have been told to ignore our emotions and pay attention only to our minds. The popular wisdom is that emotions are unpredictable and unstable, even though people talk about following their gut instincts.

At the end of the 20th century, psychologists began exploring the realm of the emotions, especially as they affected ethical behavior. Goleman, who coined the phrase "emotional intelligence," says that impulse is the "medium of emotion and those who are at the mercy of their impulses, who lack self-control, are morally deficient."[21] Emerging research indicates that the ability to notice and manage our emotional response to an event is a critical skill. Those who cannot manage themselves are often unable to be ethical in their business dealings. To be ethical, one needs both the skill of self-awareness as well as self-regulation: doing the right thing even when no one is watching and no one will ever notice the difference.

Naming the Neutral Event

The mind, the intellect, knows and names the event and gives it being. As we find ourselves in new situations we are given the responsibility of naming what is going on in that

> **1 — Noticing a Neutral Event**
>
> She was asked to give a presentation on spirituality and work at a law school. As she walked in the door a sign indicated that she was speaking on ethics. Two different groups of people appeared to be vying for exactly the same space for their meeting. Her stomach tightened. A sense of panic came over her.

situation. The naming includes both the activities of the event as well as our own response to the stimuli. The gift of naming is one of the most important processes that we as humans have. It is no mistake that in Genesis, the first book in the Jewish/Christian canon, after God created the world, Adam and Eve were instructed to name all the plants and animals. Through the gift of naming, Adam and Eve were given power over all creation — and themselves. Because of the power of naming, some cultures give every person a secret name so strangers do not have power over them.

> 2 — Does this event exist?
>
> She recognized all the books and saw that students were milling around just as she had in law school some thirty years ago. She could have chosen to ignore the panic but remembered it as an old friend — the panic she felt in class, then again in front of a judge and jury during her first felony trial, and then again when she argued a case in front of the State Supreme Court.

Naming an event involves three decisions: (a) does this event exist; (b) what is the value of this event; and (c) what is the meaning of this event. The first choice is to give the event life, to determine whether or not what we see really exists. The naming is arbitrary, based on the intersection of our mind and physical being. From the moment of birth we continuously compile a personal directory of experience with corresponding judgments about those experiences. These judgments form a data bank for all we know. Each new event becomes a version of the game "one of these things is not like the other." As we compare and contrast our current experience with previous data, we put the new experience into an existing pigeon hole, sometimes jamming it into the conceptual box to make it fit. Then we decide how to value the emerging event.

Putting a value on events is also highly personal. We evaluate an event as good or bad/useful or not useful based on the context in which we place the event and on personal expectations and roles. Some thrive on the adrenaline rush of excitement and chaos and so find highly challenging events good. Others prefer a much more ordered life with little risk and so embrace much more tempered events. Some also tend to see the world through the proverbial "glass half full" lens while others take a darker view of what is going on around them.

> 3 — How should this event be valued?
>
> Now, how was this panic like or not like those other times when she was panic stricken? Was this panic good or bad?
> What to make of the sign? She thought she was speaking on spirituality; was it ethics? How about the confusion?
> Was anyone in charge? Should she do something?

Because what we seek out and how we name what happens to us depends on how we contextualize the information we have received about our world, we need to attend to our own core personal biases.

Thus, the way we value events depends on our temperament and native abilities, characteristics we have had since birth, as well as the cumulation of our life experiences. Current research indicates that about 40% of who we are is hard wired, the way we are born, and about 60% is soft-wired, a result of our choices and responses to life.[22] What we call instinct is often those gifts with which we were born. Our beginning palette of skills, whether it be mental acuity, empathy, or spiritual awareness, provides the oils and pigments with which we start to paint the picture called our life.

Interestingly, research indicates that "nature can only act via nurture."[23] Our genetic inheritance can only be activated as the gifts are nurtured through the choices we make and the opportunities we have growing up. The most malleable time is when we are children. By the time we are adults where our inherited genes have predisposed us to experience our environment in certain ways, our "intelligence is like personality: mostly inherited, partly influenced by factors unique to the individual, and very little affected by the family" into which we were born.[24]

Thus a person who is born cautious with a skeptical approach to life (the 40% hard wired part) will tend to be risk adverse and so avoid risky ventures as well as evaluate events as more intimidating than one who is born adventurous and thus embraces challenges. Because who we are is a combination of both aptitude and appetite, what we prefer influences what we choose to do and believe which then reinforces what we prefer.[25] We can learn to change our response to life (the 60% soft wired part) through making a conscious choice to become more aware and walk new paths as we intentionally change our belief system and actions. The cycle continues over an entire life, not just during the first few years. If we are not aware, we mindlessly reinforce existing beliefs and learned bias. If instead we discipline ourselves to see with fresh

4 — What is the meaning of this event?

As she entered the classroom, she began to examine her panic. First, she was not going to be in the student section and therefore would not be expected to answer esoteric questions nor was any particular case going to hang on her ability to articulate the points of law. However, she did not want to embarrass the student who invited her. Was she qualified enough to make the presentation?

eyes, we can evaluate our world more carefully. Through education and practice, change is always possible.

5 — What are earlier, similar events?

She remembered another day when she was to make a presentation on the relationship between one's beliefs and one's ethics in the practice of law. Some ten years earlier she was invited back to her alma mater, her home law school. She was nowhere as confident in the content of the presentation. Then the Dean sat in the front row and fell asleep while she talked. Panic did overcome her and she forgot to give her presentation with humor and "presence." Would the same thing happen this April day?

The last decision involves giving the event meaning. What are the cause and effect relationships which are alive and well in this situation? How does this event fit within the fabric of our own lives? We all want to make sense out of our life and experience. We are often tempted to ignore events that do not seem to fit within our belief system. However, if we are attentive, we can evaluate the event and clarify our own world view, thus giving the data meaning and enriching our belief system.

At this point, the strong tendency (which needs to be resisted) is to place the information in a context that makes our own established world view correct. The most important lesson to learn from this section is that *we choose meanings that make us right, to validate our own preferred world view — even when we may be wrong*. Thus when we see an event — something which could be interpreted two different ways — we interpret the event to fit what we already believe to be true about the world even though a different, competing interpretation of the event would be more useful and give us a better result.

This bias towards making our world view correct even in the face of data to the contrary has caused untold misery in our community. Whether one is a Galileo who had the temerity to suggest that the world revolved around the sun and so found himself in the middle of the Inquisition or a scientist who notes that the O ring on a space shuttle needs attention and finds himself testifying before a Senate sub-committee, those in positions of power do not like to admit that they may be wrong — often with disastrous results. We replicate

6 — Deciding about the event.

As she looked out at the students, she knew that she was a gifted teacher. She was prepared (always an antidote for panic) and had confidence in the content of the talk. She believed that what she had to say had value. The only benefit in treating the panic as real was to make sure that she did not let her guard down and ignore subtle signals of her audience. Having a mind that was just a bit unusual, she thanked Panic for showing up and invited it to welcome two close cousins, Excitement and Enthusiasm, to the party. She then suggested that her friend Panic take a seat in the back where it could raise its hand again and speak if the students' attention began drifting.

that error in smaller ways in our every day life. For example, when we have a conflict at work that could be either attributed to our misunderstanding of the situation or to someone setting us up to fail, we tend to believe that someone else is responsible and we are blameless.

A person needs a great deal of integrity and discipline to interpret a problem as a flawed personal belief system. Given that the stakes are very high if we interpret the world around us incorrectly, having a world view that is as accurate as possible is critical. Every situation, every neutral event, emerges from the intersection of at least two sets of beliefs and actions. To both acquire wisdom and be effective in our community, we must be willing to admit errors of interpretation and continually modify our beliefs.

Responding to the Neutral Event

After we name the experience, we formulate a set of possible responses to the event. The options range from ignoring the stimulus to the full engagement of our mind and body. When our children were little, my husband and I quickly learned the difference between naming unidentified noise as a problem to be solved or children at play. We agreed that the first person who noticed that something was amiss with the kids had to address the situation. As intervention required work that we could not pass off to the other, we became skilled in differentiating between sibling bickering and emergencies which required parental involvement. In the process, we encouraged our children to become responsible for themselves while we discharged our parental obligations.

In choosing among the options, our ideas about ourselves and our dreams for the future play an important role in the selection of a preferred mode of being and acting. By using our imagination, we can explore different potential choices and begin to determine which result will be the best for us and fulfill our own dreams. In evaluating our action, if we are thoughtful, we will also include the possible reaction and reasons for action of the others who are involved. The final step is to consider what options will benefit those who will be affected by the choice.

> 7 — Responding to the neutral event.
>
> Remembering her own intimidation with the raised platforms and steeply banked seats, she neutralized the situation by sitting on the table at the edge of the platform and meeting the eyes of each student, seeing them as individuals who were trying to make sense of their belief systems and how those beliefs would intersect with the requirements of the legal profession. She also remembered how to neutralize her own panic, through breathing and speaking slowly and surely with a smile.

The cycle begins again. Each action results in a response and another action. The results will be both anticipated and unanticipated. Because those who react to our actions will make their own choices based on their belief systems, we can never really predict what someone will do. In any event, we have new information for our belief system, information which will either confirm our world view or require us to adjust it. The next time we act, we will make new choices about what to believe and what to do through the filter of our current belief system and the lens of our core beliefs.

> 8 — A new neutral event.
>
> As the presentation unfolded, the students actually did not care about either ethics or spirituality, as broadly defined. What they wanted to know was how to reconcile their responsibilities as Christians against their responsibilities as lawyers: how could one defend a person whom one knew was guilty? Fortunately, she had an answer to those questions and so plunged into unanticipated territory. All was well — and the audience was satisfied.

Sources of Information for Belief Systems

We have four sources of information for our belief systems which correspond to the four core contextual questions that provide the foundations for the inquiry-based method of ethical decision-making: reason, experience, authority, and tradition. When we use the tool of reason, we look within ourselves to determine whether the information we receive is accurate. When we use experience, we use personal action and life events as a test case for our ideas. The tool of authority helps us choose whether or not to accept the ideas of others. Finally, with tradition, we see what others have taught as truth, both in the theory of what is true and the practice of how to be in community.

Component 1 — Reason

The primary source of information about our belief system is our reason — what we choose to believe.[26] Reason is the first source because we all make choices regarding what we notice and how to interpret the data. As children we get information first through our emotions. As adults, we use complex emotional information to interpret events while using our

Who am I? Tradition	How do I fit? Authority
Reason Why this choice?	Experience What should I choose?

reason to interpret the data. We use reason in two ways. First, we have the *process* of reasoning itself. Learning the tools of critical thinking helps us reason more effectively. As we practice the skill of critical analysis, we make better ethical decisions. Second, we have the *content* of reason, what we know and believe to be true. As we learn more about our world through study and research, we have more information available with which to make decisions.

People who did not know that the Black Plague was caused by rats carrying the disease blamed the deaths on sinful people who brought down the wrath of God. Today, faced with an epidemic, science tells us what agent and process are responsible for the illness. We can then change behavior (such as washing our hands) to stop the spread of disease. Reason is key, as the gift and curse of being human is the ability to think with the attendant responsibility of free will. To responsibly exercise our prerogatives of freedom and action, we must assess rational and emotional information. While we use authority, tradition and experience, at the end of the day our minds determine what data we consider persuasive and what we will do.

Component 2 — Experience

Wending our way through this world, we create a data bank of experience from which to evaluate life. As our primary goal is survival, we look at past experiences to let us know whether a particular course of action will keep us alive. This practice is useful as we learn that fire is hot and driving recklessly may endanger our lives. This tendency may be detrimental if the conditions have changed which make past action no longer valid or if we have additional skills with which to navigate the danger.

Experience helps us expand our world view. After developing relationships with people from different religious or ethnic backgrounds, those who were previously biased may find their prejudices dissolving. People who have never been poor have a very different world view of poverty after spending a day or two with someone trying to raise a family on minimum wage. People who have always been healthy have a whole new world view after becoming sick or sitting with someone during a critical illness. Abstract concepts such as sick leave, health insurance, and co-payments become concrete when faced with a medical bill from an industrial accident. In using our experience as a touchstone, we must be careful not to generalize all situations based on our interpretation of a prior series of events. Because of the limitations of our own experience, we may interpret an event incorrectly. For example, we may see someone making what we think is an absolutely incorrect business decision. However, with more experience or more data, we may see that the choice is, in fact, correct.

We must also be careful not to discount the experience of others. Those who came of age during the Civil Rights Movement of the 1960s have a very different experience of discrimination than those who entered the job market in a time of more equality. A pundit once said that one knows that progress is made when, instead of hitting the glass ceiling at 25, women do not hit it until 35 or 40. Thus, when young women or minorities do not get as passionate about "the movement" as their parents, we have to understand that their experience of the world of equal opportunity in school and athletics translates to an expectation of equal opportunity in employment.

Finally, we must continuously evaluate the naming of our experience. This process can be easier if we are careful about our use of emotion-laden words. One way we socialize children is by telling them that certain actions are bad and wrong while others are good. Hitting other children is bad; sharing toys is good. Often the words come with a disapproving tone of voice or punishment, which makes us feel shame or guilt. As we become adults, we carry the emotional imprint of that early conditioning. Thus, as we decide that certain actions are "good" or "bad," we may also have an emotional response to the naming. Sometimes evaluating a course of action becomes easier if we name the events as "useful" or "not useful." So, deciding to always keep our promises is not only "good" because that is what we were taught, but it is also "useful" in building relationships and trust. A belief that self-assertion is "bad" because we need to be seen as modest and gentle may not be "useful" if we want to be an effective advocate for justice. Thus, we may choose to change our beliefs through experiencing ourselves as brave and strong.

If we are to become effective ethical leaders, we must be willing to see ourselves as responsible adults who use personal and corporate power wisely. If a decision we made about ourselves and our abilities is no longer useful, then we must discard it. Sometimes we have a set of failures which we attribute to our own shortcomings. Sometimes those events have nothing to do with us. In those circumstances, labeling ourselves as failures is not appropriate. Sometimes we think we are being effective using a strategy that worked for us before, even though we are no longer getting desired results. Through the continuous mindful evaluation and reevaluation of our experiences, we can set ourselves on a course for maturity.

Component 3 — Authority

Our first source of information about life comes from our parents in the first five to seven years. They teach us their truths of the world, including religious and political views. Their understandings of work shape what we believe is possible for us. Early on we learn what tasks are appropriate for men and women, for people of different races, and for people in our family. One particular biological family may relish eccentricities and value those who are neither pretentious nor evaluate people based on appearances. Thus, each generation of that family recounts with pride stories of their grandfather, dressed in his overalls, ready to pay cash for a car: if a person would not serve him based on how he was dressed, that person did not get the sale.

As we progress through school, we are exposed to other sources of information which we might find persuasive. One of the tasks of becoming an adult is to critically consider the information we received about the world from our parents and our birth community. Over the years, we gather knowledge and consider ideas which are very different than those with which we were raised. At some point we have to evaluate whether to accept these new world views into our own belief system. The difficulty is that we all tend not to evaluate authorities carefully when we agree with them and to be super-critical if we disagree with the premises. Learning to listen to authorities in terms of the soundness of their information, care of reasoning, and implications for the ideas is difficult.

One strategy is to "try on" the new information and see what difference the new way of looking at the world would make. A colleague described his journey from a closed, Protestant community to being comfortable in a predominately Catholic environment. He found his childhood notions of the world comforting but not useful for being an aware adult in a complex world. The biases against Catholics which he had learned growing up in a blue-collar, prejudiced neighborhood were not going to be useful if he was going to teach at a Catholic university. He had to critically evaluate his belief that all Catholics needed to convert "to true Christianity" and "to be born again." He also had to decide whether what he was taught about other religions, their ethical structure and their legitimacy in the community, was true. After study and soul searching, he "tried on the idea" that tolerance of other faith traditions made sense because none of us can really claim to have a corner on the truth. He found that the new idea supported his sense of himself and helped him be an effective teacher. That decision also opened the door to exploring the possibility of celebrating the gifts of other religious traditions. Although the full shift in understanding took time, each new instance of experiencing the value of other traditions strengthened his new world view. After a while the new way of thinking was habitual, and he could not remember thinking any other way. The change also had a bitter-sweet result. His children adopted his new way of thinking, taking for granted the value of religious plurality and tolerance, and not placing the same value on organized religion as he did. That which was important to him was not valued by his children. Every change in beliefs results in multi-layered changes, some of which are neither foreseen nor intended.

We have three primary sources of authority which inform our belief systems and which give us plenty of new ideas to "try on."

▸ *Philosophical and religious sources*

For many, religion and philosophy are the most important sources of information about the world and form the foundations of "right" and "wrong." Because the United States was formed in religious diversity, we embraced the notion of separation of church and state. However, from the beginning, many of the communities were tightly homogenous, and so we did not have to learn to live effectively with diversity. To honor the right of each person to choose which ideas to believe, because our ideas are precious and because we think of religion as private and business and government as public, we are reluctant to tell people about the religious views we cherish and which deeply inform our sense of self, others, and the world.[27]

As we have become more diverse, the illusion of agreement is dissolving. At the same time people want to reclaim some sense of grounding their personal and professional life in their religious beliefs. Since the late 1990s, a new area of study, spirituality in the workplace, has been accepted by the Academy of Management. This research explores what difference our faith and longing for wholeness makes in how we do our work as well as how we treat other people. The research indicates that as we attend to our spirits, minds, and bodies, we tend to be more effective in our work and more content. As people increasingly demand that their work be meaningful and fulfilling, conversations about faith and religion crop up around water coolers and in employee lunchrooms.

A corresponding concern about giving religion or philosophy too much preeminence in the workplace is that our faith or philosophical ideologies will impel us to a particular action which we might then force on others. Sometimes the choice has good results, such as the owners of Chick-fil-A® deciding to keep their restaurants closed on Sunday to honor the Christian first day. Other policies come from a desire to honor the sacred dignity of each human person, such as making sure privacy policies concerning Internet and computer use are the same for all employees. Other decisions are more problematic. We scowl when those in authority prominently display a sacred text, which implies that the successful employee is one who embraces that text, or demand that all participate in specific religious services. Wisdom and discretion are needed to discern between using our beliefs appropriately to inform actions and the inappropriate use of personal or corporate power to impose those beliefs or requirements for action on others.

The study of ethics explores the conversation among people of different beliefs and experience to see how they come to a shared understanding about how best to live in community. The study of ethics also provides individuals and groups with the foundations for asserting that certain actions are appropriate or inappropriate. To fully appreciate the interplay between conversation and convention, we must remember that our faith (whether in God, the Sacred, or in humans[28]) and our philosophy provide the strongest grounding for our actions. Being aware of our own beliefs and those of others helps us negotiate the dialogue.

For example, if we do not accept the authority of a particular scripture, we know that the text will not be persuasive for us in informing our belief or action. This truism is often lost. I experienced the narrowness that can come with righteous ideological purity while standing in line in the San Francisco Airport. I struck up a conversation with the gentleman in front of me, and we talked of our work. When I said that I was a lawyer who taught ethics, he burst out laughing. Then he said that people did not need to be taught ethics, they just needed to follow the Ten Commandments. When I asked about those who were neither Christian nor Jewish, his retort was that they just needed to convert.

In attending to our world, we can certainly find those who share our beliefs. If we are courageous, we will also listen to those with different beliefs without demanding that they convert to our world view. The saving grace is that often the same behavior is indicated by different religious and philosophical convictions. So in the every day world we can agree on what to do even when we may not agree on why we are doing it.

The Enlightenment Project, the quest to ground ethical beliefs in reason rather than revelation, was envisioned as a way around the contested authority and meaning of religious texts. As Protestants and Catholics disagreed to the death about the meaning of the Bible and whose authority and interpretation was binding, the notion was that if people could use their reason to find the rules of life, we could reach a common understanding about what we should do. In the intervening 200 or more years since Kant wrote *A Critique of Practical Reason,* which posited universal foundations for ethical action, we have become more comfortable with the idea that philosophical traditions are just as contested as the religious ones.

Our philosophical beliefs are also shaped by what we understand about the nature of humans, the purpose of property and the proper use of power. As inheritors of Cartesian dualism, the Western community has two competing notions of human beings: one is that we are all deeply flawed and thus need to be tightly managed to avoid making mistakes; the other is that we are basically good and thus as we are guided by friends and colleagues with whom we are in relationship, we can be directed to do the right thing. We also have competing notions of property: one is that it is to be used for the good of humans; the other is that it is to be conserved for future generations. Finally, we have competing notions of power: one is that people need external constraints to keep from abusing power; the other is that as we are in relationship we will learn how to use power appropriately. Each of these positions has a corresponding ethical set of beliefs.[29]

After centuries of debate and contemplation, no agreement on these three seminal understandings of the world is on the horizon. Philosophers have different understandings of the core questions, which often mirror the view of the theologians. So the two primary strands of dualistic ethics, deontology and teleology, contain representatives from both philosophy and theology. The postmodern twist works to move from dualism to a holistic ethical monism. No matter which approach we find persuasive, as an individual in community, our knowledge, beliefs, and dreams continue to set the trajectory for our actions.

▶ *Social sciences*

The second source of authority comes from the social sciences like economics, psychology, history, sociology, anthropology, and political theory. Through use of the scientific method borrowed from the hard sciences, these disciplines explore the nature of being human, how we use property, and the use and abuse of power. Based on their underlying beliefs about the nature of humans and society (informed by theology and philosophy), scholars have put forward theories about how we behave and have offered norms, or rules, for how we should live.

Each school of thought offers a description of the human condition based on its observations and experience and predicts how people will behave in the future. As with any study, the questions we ask and the emphasis we place on the data drive the conclusions. In economics, if we focus on how people who are in charge of their own destiny seem to be more proactive and productive in their work, an argument can be made for an unrestricted free market. If we focus on how people abuse power or how those without access to financial resources may not be able to take charge of their destiny, an argument can be made for an economic system which provides resources to those without. Different ways of organizing our political life will have corresponding strengths and weaknesses. Just like theology and philosophy, the social sciences have not provided any certain answers for how we should live which will satisfy all persons in varying circumstances.

▶ *Natural sciences*

The natural sciences provide two important sources of information. The first is data about what is. Medical science made tremendous gains when microscopes revealed a teeming world of microbes which profoundly affected our ideas about health. Technology put copper refineries out of business as we discovered that fiber optics were much more effective at transmitting data than copper wires. The experiments and insights of our scientists provide the building blocks of our enterprises. As we get new information about what is, we dream about what can be. The hard sciences also let us know what we can know. The modern quest, informed by a Newtonian world view, sought to understand the nature of things, to find the quintessential qualities which are the same for all people. Scientists worked to find the physical properties of matter which were not dependent on the observer but on the nature of matter itself.

As scientists began noticing at the quantum level, the person watching the experiment changed the results, they put forth the idea that we could never with certainty identify physical properties of matter. All of our knowledge about our world is dependent in some small way upon the observer. The promise of Newtonian physics, which would give us certainty about our physical universe, could not be kept. Rather, quantum physics must deal with probabilities. Thus, the work of scientists subtly shifted.

While scientists still seek to find universal truth, they know that the structure of the world also involves uncertainty. Our understanding of the world is now colored by the fact that knowledge is contingent. As scientists are always bringing forth new information and data, we cannot definitively know the unchanging *nature* of the world. We can only know its current *state* — our best understanding of its condition right now.[30]

Component 4 — Tradition

Culture is transmitted from generation to generation as we adopt the traditions of the community into which we are born or which we join. The earliest traditions come from our families and our national community. Cultural traditions are also part of every business and profession. We can recognize tradition when we hear someone say, "we have always..." An interesting exercise is to ask ten people what makes Thanksgiving for them. Many begin by saying, "we have a traditional meal of..." and the differences begin. Starting with varying methods of preparing the turkey or goose to selecting all the side dishes and continuing on to acceptable dress, family activities (*exactly* how much football?), and the guest list, tradition is multifaceted indeed. The links to the past which are established through tradition provide continuity not only for families but also for professions, businesses and communities as a whole.

As humans we yearn to belong to a group and to know our place in that community. As we adopt the traditions of our chosen peer groups, we know that we belong. The difficulty with tradition is knowing when the customs need to be changed to adapt to new needs and situations or when the habits are destructive and impede progress. Often tension emerges between tradition and knowledge: what can be changed as the culture evolves and what practices are essential to the identity and maintenance of the community. Sorting through the questions provides communities an opportunity to continually redefine themselves.

▶ *Who belongs*

Controlling membership is a key method for maintaining a community. Whether the criteria are ethnic (Sons of Norway), economic (being able to pay the initiation fee), or testing (passing the bar exam to become an attorney), those who are part of the group determine the requirements for membership. Particularly for professional and business membership, a certain threshold of knowledge and experience is required to do the job. However, because we like to do business with those we know and with whom we are comfortable, businesses are challenged to assure that belonging is somehow tied to competence rather than our social circles.

A current conversation about belonging centers around whether universities should admit legacies, the children of graduates, even if they have lower test scores and/or grades than other admittees. The question is pertinent when programs such as affirmative action to assure that people of color, an underrepresented gender, or those of lesser economic means, are well represented in academe have been rejected. The difference between accepting someone because they are knowledgeable or because they networked effectively and packaged themselves well is subtle.

▶ *What behavior is acceptable*

While secret handshakes are parodied, every business and profession has a set of acceptable behaviors which may or may not be shared with the newly admitted member. In academics, each discipline has a carefully nuanced set of protocols for writing papers, presenting at conferences, and critiquing each other's work. The professions and businesses have their own barriers to entry. A former student recounts that on his first day on the job he cheerfully greeted everyone and introduced himself. He did not know that the unspoken (but disliked) rule was that the newbie did not speak until spoken to. The CEO was so impressed that he took the new hire under his wing and showed him the ropes, much to the chagrin of his colleagues. If we are lucky, when we take a new position, an established member of the group will help us sort through the protocols, and we will be able to understand and implement the suggested course of action. If we do not have a mentor, we must be very attentive to the unspoken traditions of an organization and make judicious choices about when to push the edges of acceptable behavior.

▸ *What protocols must be maintained*

Many of the judicial systems in countries that were part of the British empire maintain the protocol of lawyers and judges wearing wigs. Each different style of wig signifies appointment to a different level of court with the more ornate wigs signaling increasing levels of respect being due. American judges and lawyers do not wear wigs, but no-one ever calls a judge by his or her first name unless one is either also a judge or related to a judge. In universities, an interesting protocol is how long a class must wait for a tardy professor. Traditionally, the higher the rank of the professor, the longer the wait. With an emerging sense of egalitarianism between students and professors, that protocol is slipping. Many lament the informality as a loss of respect; others find the changing protocols refreshing. Again, discerning between essential and non-essential (but sometimes wonderful) protocols to maintain the integrity of the practice requires gentle wisdom.

The same wisdom is needed in deciding how to begin new traditions or translate old ones. One of my cousins delivered the first dollar from the tooth fairy to his daughter, complete with a personalized certificate of achievement. A few days later, he did not have time to do the same thing with the second tooth. The following morning he had to scurry to placate a distraught seven-year-old who wanted to know why the tooth fairy hadn't left the certificate. The next night the certificate appeared, complete with an apology. In the business world, attention must be given to traditions such as welcome and farewell events, award ceremonies and other community building activities. If someone anticipates a certain ritual upon a rite of passage and the ritual is skipped, that employee will be upset, defeating the purpose of the traditions.

▸ *What beliefs and knowledge must be adopted*

Traditions also have a set of accepted beliefs and knowledge. For example, in order to be part of a religious group, one must attest to a certain set of beliefs about that faith. In order to be an art conservator rather than a repair-person, one must not only be technically competent but also agree to certain beliefs about how to best preserve the historical past. Conservators have lively conversations about whether a patron should be able to see where a piece of art has been treated. For some, the integrity of the art demands that the difference between the original art and the intervention be clear. Others believe that good conservation requires as little distinction between the original art and the treatment as possible. Those in the latter school believe that with good conservation the patron cannot tell where the repair has been made.

In general the rule is that we must be accepted into the tradition before we can change that tradition. Sometimes meeting this requirement is difficult if we are a member of a group that cannot gain access to a tradition. A solution may be to appeal to reason and experience to get people to change their attachments. As the Civil Rights Movement took hold, many who were part of the white-male establishment were persuaded that people of color and women should be granted access to all of the schools and professions (and we rose up and called these white-male pioneers blessed). Thus, they worked within the system to help those outside gain access to economic and political power in the United States.

Sometimes those who are excluded start their own traditions. Thus, women and minorities who were not welcomed into the existing power structures started their own businesses, social clubs, and networking opportunities to find occasions to excel. These groups also made the argument that as they struggled to survive in a hostile environment, they should be given certain considerations to be able to get contracts and other employment. Their lack of inclusion gave rise to affirmative action and minority set-aside programs, which have always been resisted and are now under increasing scrutiny.

Another impetus for changing tradition is slow death or irrelevance. As young people refuse to participate in a group or tradition, those who are part of that tradition find that they must change or become increasingly irrelevant. For example, we currently see a trend where young men *and* women are changing professional traditions as they demand that their work include flexibility to allow then to be part of their children's lives. The story is told of a partner in a New York law firm who was arguing against making a young attorney a partner. Even though the requirements of partnership had been met, the partner asserted that the young man was not committed enough. The partner continued by saying "I gave this firm three marriages. I'm not sure that he will do the same." Others in the room gently asked whether the criteria for partnership should include a willingness to get one divorce, let alone three. The young man was accepted for partner.

Conclusion

Learning how to make ethical decisions in a contingent world requires a slight but very significant shift of perspective and a willingness to engage in the task of shaping ourselves and our community. The recursive design of the decision-making templates allows us to engage in the process of reflective action, learning to identify the best knowledge available about both the nature of the world and its current state. We have an occasion to look at our personal beliefs as well as the beliefs and values of the community in which we work. We have the opportunity to examine the world of organizational ethics to see what works and does not work, what fits and does not fit. We also have an opening to explore a variety of problems using different ethical lenses and asking different questions, to see how the vantage point changes with a new focus. Then, we get to act again and see what happens.

Because we make these decisions in relationship with others, we also learn to negotiate among competing values and visions. As we practice, we not only learn to attend to the formation of our belief system, but also the belief systems of others and the whole community. With practice we also learn to make better decisions and more effectively communicate our values and commitments to others. As we dance the minuet of life together, the community's culture — its underlying beliefs and assumptions — change as well, for good or ill.

This chapter began with a quote from Burke who asserts that "when what we know changes, the world changes and with it, everything."[31] If the physicists who study matter and light are right that what they know is shaped by the questions, experience, and context of the observer, then our world has changed. The implications for those who study ethics is profound: given our understanding of the contingency of knowledge, the focus of ethics must shift. Rather than searching for the absolute truth which determines the rules which guide our actions, we must turn to the study of the individual ethical agent. How can we each — individually and as groups — better decide the best course of action given our contingent world which is subject to uncertainty? The process of knowing becomes as important — if not more important — than what is known. Given that each of us is shaped by what we notice, how we name that event, and then how we respond, learning to become skilled knowers will help us become mature, ethical persons-in-community.

Continuing the Conversation

1. Find an article in your local paper or a news magazine which deals with a current ethical situation. Read the article using the steps of Lonergan: (1) As you pay attention, what assertions are made by the author? What information is missing? What viewpoints are not present? (2) Be intelligent. How trustworthy are the data? How does what the article asserts fit with your own knowledge and experience? (3) Be reasonable. How do these assertions fit with your value systems? What are the implications of the options which are presented? (4) Be responsible: If you had to make a responsible decision, what would it be and why? Compare notes with colleagues to find similarities and differences.

2. Find a neutral event in your life — something as simple as a flat tire on the freeway. See how many meanings you can give the event: how can you change the context to make the event good, bad, the best thing that happened that day, an absolute tragedy?

3. Interview someone you respect and ask them how they formed their beliefs about business ethics. How did they use the four components of a belief system to shape their ideas about ethics? (1) What values are important? (2) What experiences have they had? (3) What authorities are important to them in deciding what is right and wrong? (4) What traditions are essential?

4. Write a brief description of your own beliefs about business ethics. Again, use the four components. Particularly attend to how your family and birth community have shaped your ethical belief system.

Perennial Organizing Questions

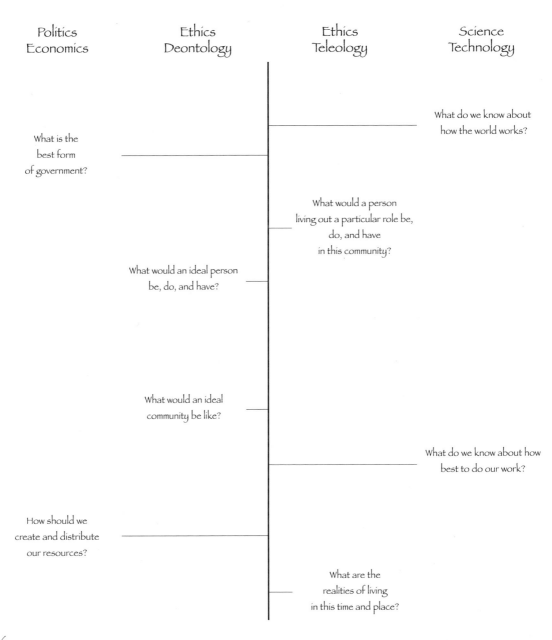

Politics Economics	Ethics Deontology	Ethics Teleology	Science Technology
			What do we know about how the world works?
What is the best form of government?			
		What would a person living out a particular role be, do, and have in this community?	
	What would an ideal person be, do, and have?		
	What would an ideal community be like?		
			What do we know about how best to do our work?
How should we create and distribute our resources?			
		What are the realities of living in this time and place?	

So it is the process of learning
that breaks the vicious circle.
Judgment on the correctness of insights...
occur(s) within a self-correcting process in which
the shortcomings of insight provoke further
questions to yield complementary insights.

Bernard Lonergan[1]

Chapter 2

The Person-in-Community

Imagine a community where all persons with an education are killed. Every accountant, artisan, doctor, entrepreneur, judge, teacher, nurse — anyone who has any skill or knowledge — is murdered. A leader has come into power who believes that those with education and professional skills are the cause of all the problems of the community. This leader believes — and convinces others — that by having a society comprised of people who are neither corrupted by education nor blinded by initiative, the innocence of an earlier agricultural age, a time more simple and seemingly more pure, can be regained. Because of his ruthless personal power and charisma, within four years, two generations of wisdom and knowledge evaporate as approximately 1.7 million people lose their lives, 21% of the country's population.[2]

During the bloody years, the people learn to trust no one. With the deaths of the skilled and educated adults, the history of the community is gone. All of the cultural knowledge and wisdom that is held and transmitted by an educated population and the elders is buried. All of the memory of how the infrastructure of the community operates is missing. All of the information about how to establish a business and conduct commerce with the wider community is forgotten. Now, the people only know terror and fear — and that they no longer want to live this way.

Now, imagine that you are part of a project to reestablish the community. Your job is to work with the people determine how they are to live together, how to find and balance their very human needs for autonomy and equality as well as fidelity and sensibility. Where will you begin? Because you know about the needs of persons-in-community, you have perplexing questions.

- *How will you participate in reweaving the fabric of a community which does not know how to articulate the values or inculcate the virtues necessary to establish a culture which supports persons-in-community?* [3]

- *How will you interact with others to replace the reality of fear and violence with beliefs and experiences that will allow them live together and rebuild a safe community and stable economy?*

- *How will you teach people to create, maintain and be faithful to the ethical and legal systems required for individuals and communities to flourish and thrive?*

- *How will you convince them to follow shared ethical norms and rules, the law, so the community has a measure of fidelity and safety, rather than the radical individualism which leads to anarchy and chaos?*

- *How will you describe the beliefs which are foundational for a respect for the human person?*

- *How will you talk about the value of private property and balance that against the needs of the community?*

- *What principles of ethics will you teach? What goals will be valued? What virtues will be extolled?*

- *How will you convince people that the foundations for those ethics are secure enough that the virtues should be embraced?*

▶ *How will you help people trust each other and the institutions of their community while being aware that they also need to protect themselves?*

Judge Juanita Rice, a District Court Judge in Centennial, Colorado, tells of working in such a community — Cambodia. From 1975 to 1979, the Khmer Rouge regime, headed by Pol Pot, "combined extremist ideology with ethnic animosity and a diabolical disregard for human life to produce repression, misery, and murder on a massive scale."[4] After Pol Pot was deposed and exiled, the people struggled to rebuild their community but lacked the essential building blocks of a civilization — the knowledge transmitted from person to person and institution to institution through education and continuity of community.

Many members of the global community went to Cambodia to help. One such project was the Cambodian Court Training Project. Judge Rice spent two years, from 1995 to 1997, working in Cambodia as part of a team tasked with rebuilding the judicial system. The team was not only trying to recreate an infrastructure (processes for filing papers and keeping records) but also dealing with corruption (judges were paid by the party who won the lawsuit because state resources were not sufficient to guarantee salaries) and with ignorance, as the rationale for the values and ethics of a legal system were not part of the shared memory.

As Judge Rice experienced the difficulty of rebuilding a community, she began to have a deep appreciation for a vibrant culture and healthy country which provides a matrix in which individuals can thrive. At the conclusion of her presentations about Cambodia, Judge Rice emphasizes that all persons, no matter how insignificant their life and work may seem, are links to the past, a foundation for the present, and a trajectory toward the future. As each individual chooses how to work and be in community, that person helps or hinders everyone else from reaching their goals and dreams. The community building seems doable when we focus on our small community; as we focus on larger segments of our country, the problems often seem intractable.

The lesson of Cambodia is that each of us contributes to the embodiment or destruction of society's shared values and virtues. The task is to not only be a responsible adult but also live so that we support the institutions which provide the threads for the fabric of our civilization. Accomplishing the goal of balancing the prerogatives of individualism with the demands of community requires rethinking the very assumptions which have governed us since the 1600s. As we examine the core values which shape our community and the resulting public policies and economic structure which come from those core values, we can begin to make sense of the problems which face us. At the threshold of a technological age which is marked by a global economy, we need new strategies for answering perplexing questions in our very complex, pluralistic world.

The Building Blocks of the Common Good

From the first moment that more than one person inhabited the planet, communities evolved and participants debated about how to treat people, the right use of property, and the proper use of power. The book of Genesis recounts the creation of social systems in light of the core values of the community. The first hierarchy (or partnership, depending on how one reads the text) emerged when Eve was created. Further, Adam and Eve were given responsibility for the animals and the land. In fact, many a current environmental debate turns on the interpretation of God giving "dominion over the land" to the new inhabitants of the Garden of Eden.[5]

That story is followed closely by the first murder, when Cain killed Abel. Cain's rejection of personal responsibility is articulated in the haunting phrase "Am I my brother's keeper?"[6] The writer recounts that God was not impressed with Cain's dissembling and imposed the sentence of exile without death.[7] Other cultures have similar creation myths which articulate the relationships and responsibilities among persons-in-community. These myths were followed closely by narratives which taught people to respect and follow the teachings of those in authority and schooled them on the rules and responsibilities, goals, and dreams of the community.

The stories which embody the expectations and rules of a community are transmitted through the religion, ethical norms, and legal structures of the society. These narratives provide a context for technological developments which energize the creation and distribution of resources and legitimize governments. While the oral and written traditions which shape people's expectations differ across communities, the task remains the same: to assure that societal institutions, such as family, church, business and government, are both constrained and agile enough so that individuals and the community as a whole can thrive. Over the history of civilization, societies perennially tinkered with their ethics and laws to find and maintain a proper balance between autonomy and equality, as well as between sensibility and rationality, so that individuals can effectively function in a strong and healthy community.

As we look for the patterns of ethics and public policy across the sweep of history, we notice that each community must determine the balance to be struck between protecting individual freedom — *autonomy* — and assuring that all members of the community receive comparable treatment — *equality*. Communities must also decide how people know what to do. By identifying universal rules that apply to all people, we use the tools of *rationality* to create the structures we need to make sure that people are treated fairly and are faithful to the community norms. By noticing that particular people have specific needs, we use the tools of *sensibility* to allow for flexibility and generosity. The arrangement of these core values in a community provides the building blocks for the common good. Just as varying configurations of brick and stone create different buildings, public policies and ethical norms which tilt the balance toward one core value over another will result in divergent cultures and different societies.

Building Blocks of the Common Good

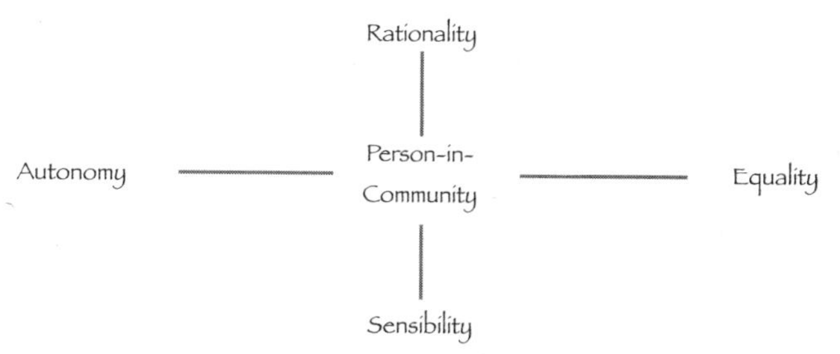

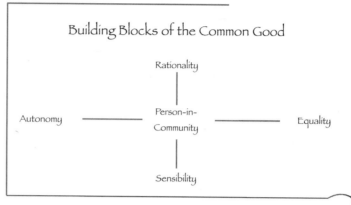

The four core values are overarching concepts. In our lives, we approach our ethical decisions through a set of principles (rules) or goals which we hold as persons-in-community. Through this process, we manifest virtues, specific moral qualities regarded as good or meritorious by individuals and their community, associated with each core value. As the conversation about living out the virtues has continued over the course of history, those who believe that the way to develop the virtues is through finding universal principles (rules) are part of the deontological tradition. Those who believe that the way to acquire the appropriate virtues is through specific goals are part of the teleological tradition.

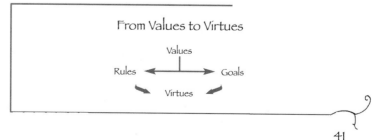

From Values to Virtues

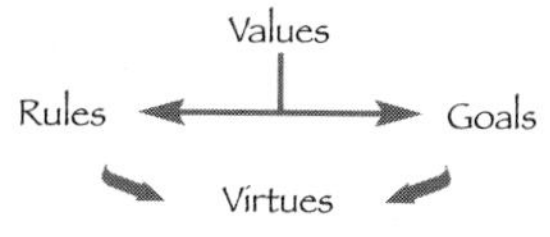

As people work together to determine the restrictions and opportunities of their society, they consciously or unconsciously determine the appropriate tradeoffs and balance among the competing core values and resulting virtues. The goal of the balancing act is to provide an environment where, given the realities of the community in a particular time and place in history, an individual living in association with other individuals, a person-in-community, can thrive.[8] Given that community is created as people come together to share a common set of traditions, values, and narratives, each person and each generation has the task of understanding, mending, and then transforming the existing society.[9]

Each person also participates with others of his or her generation to weave a new segment of the civic fabric. People begin by picking up the threads of the environment into which they are born. They then creatively integrate their individual and shared experience as well as their dreams for the future as they create the next portion of the tapestry for their children.

Virtues Associated with Autonomy

Free — Diligent — Authoritative — Meritorious
Self-controlled — Dutiful — Independent
Accountable — Responsible

Despite frequent failure, the task of a person-in-community is to strive for what may be called the common good, a community where people can live, work, raise families and become whole persons.[10] In the process of community building, people experiment with new societal forms and negotiate with each other while engaging in the perennial question: how do we assure that the four core value sets — autonomy, equality, rationality, and sensibility: the building blocks of the common good — are balanced and harmonized so that the foundations of the community are strong. Thus personal and organizational ethics, as well as public policy decisions, require a continuous calibration to find that perfect tension which creates balance. Let's look at each foundational block in detail.

Virtues associated with the core value *Autonomy* give people incentives to become resourceful and skilled as they embrace their rights and corresponding responsibilities.[11] The gift of freedom, which is bestowed on adults, carries the expectation that individuals will not become unduly dependent on others to care for them. The value of rationality, the privilege of each person to choose how best he or she is to live, emanates from autonomy.

Conversations about ethics explore the privileges people can claim against others by virtue of being human. What rights of ownership can we demand from our labor, from our property, and our bodies to give us the tools of equality and resources for safety? This value cluster also carries with it the notion of self-control and accountability. As we embrace our individual rights we also agree to take on personal responsibility for ourselves as well as our community.

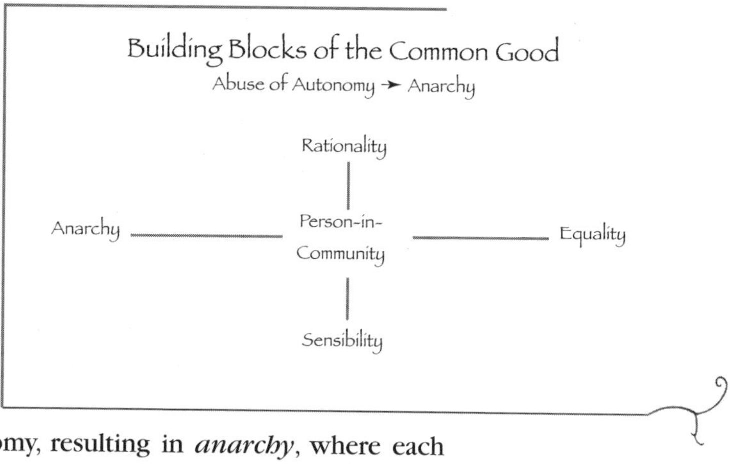

Abuse of autonomy occurs when either the community allows or an individual demands too much autonomy, resulting in *anarchy*, where each person does only what is right in his or her own eyes without regard for others. If people do not have enough autonomy, they either do not or cannot become fully functioning adults. The tension is to recognize the uniqueness of each human person while also acknowledging real differences in need or ability.[12] A society may limit autonomy by not treating a member as a full person with a mind and free will. For instance, some communities have not considered women or certain minorities capable of becoming fully adult and thus have limited their opportunities. Loss of autonomy may result from the strictures of the society which limit individual choices, such as denying access to certain jobs or schools based on criteria other than whether one can do the required tasks. Individuals can also choose to restrict their autonomy through believing they are powerless, refusing to embrace the responsibilities of adulthood, or choosing to give up personal rights for the good of the community.

Virtues associated with the core value *Equality,* which is always in tension with autonomy, allows individuals to thrive as people take responsibility for themselves and their own well being. Equality reminds us to provide a measure of fairness in distribution of resources as well as assistance for those who are not always able to care of themselves. This core value helps to assure that all in the

> **Virtues Associated with Equality**
>
> Fair — Just — Equitable
> Proper — Evenhanded — Impartial
> Unselfish — Balanced – Restrained

community have sufficient resources to survive. For a person to thrive in community, society must provide both access to economic resources and the opportunity to participate meaningfully in the political structure. The value of solidarity, individuals banding together to share communal burdens and benefits, flows from valuing equality.

Conversations about ethics explore the two ways that the community can choose to limit the autonomy of individuals while expanding opportunities for those who are not privileged. The first approach focuses on redistribution of resources. Through taxation or charity we can provide resources of money or opportunity, thus assuring that all members share in the basic goods of the community — food, shelter, education, health care. This strategy emphasizes equality of result. The second approach provides people with access to the institutions and resources of the community like education, employment, and capital. This strategy emphasizes equality of opportunity as members of the community need certain resources to move safely towards self-sufficiency. If a community demands too much equality, the result is *apathy*. If people believe that the incentives for working or consequences for not working are insufficient, they will not exert themselves. If people expect too much equality, they may not take enough initiative to assure that the community has the resources it needs.

One source of unevenness is our difference in ability to provide for our own needs. This inequality may come because of physical restrictions, illness or disability. Persons with physical or mental limitations may not be fully employable and thus not be capable of earning sufficient money to provide for themselves. A second source of unevenness may result from inadequate access to resources such as education, information, capital, or power. If a person does not get a basic education or information, that person will not have the tools to function effectively in a community.

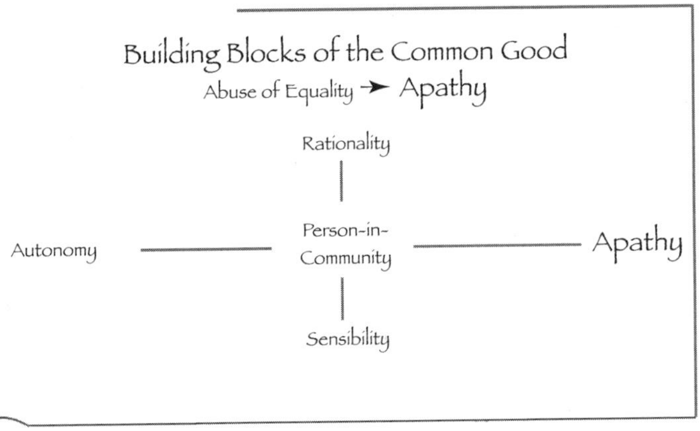

Inequality may also result from systems that prohibit people from fully participating in the community. Racism and sexism have often limited people from access to good jobs and resources. If people in power believe that certain categories of people are not qualified for particular jobs or positions, a society constructs implicit or explicit institutional barriers. People who encounter those barriers may give up and not even try to become part of the community or they may go "underground" and create a separate society of their own.

Many experiments in communal living (as well as group projects) fail because people do not take personal responsibility for assuring the tasks are completed. On the other hand, without equality of opportunity or resources, people may not have the tools to become independent adults. The conundrum of equality emerges as we seek fair treatment while we remember that each person is unique and not a "fused self with others in a single totality."[13] Even though we have similar needs, we are not all alike. Each person has different dreams and goals, different abilities, strengths, and weaknesses. We all need sufficient breathing room to be individuals at the same time that we make sure that everyone in the community has a sufficient supply of basic resources to thrive.

Virtues associated with the core value *Rationality* let us plan for the future and live with a modicum of safety because we know that the moral conditions which are necessary for individuals to thrive, even if they are not in the same physical or economic group, will be met. Rather than treating people differently based on their particular circumstances or giving favorable consideration to those whom we know, we can use our reason to determine universal rules that all should follow. By sharing a commitment to the same rules, we can have a community which has some sense of ethical obligations to each other even though we are strangers.[14] Because our global community is diverse and we are not bound together by family or even national obligations, we need to have some sense of the expected community norms and rules, so that we know what behavior is required. When we are able to connect with strangers in a chat room with the click of a mouse, the relationships which both define and guide us are certainly more dispersed than when our best friends lived right around the corner.

Virtues Associated with Rationality

Loyal — Faithful — High principled — Pure — Inviolate — Predictable
Honorable — Scrupulous — Upright — Trustworthy
Incorruptible — Consistent – Entitled

The discipline of rationality allows us to faithfully follow norms and laws of the community. The image I use to hold the concept of rationality and fidelity comes from the Dr. Seuss' children's story *Horton Hatches an Egg*. Horton promised Maize, the flighty Mom, that he would sit on her egg until she returned. As the weather turned bad and the days turned into months, Horton's refrain was "I meant what said, and I said what I meant! An elephant's faithful, one-hundred percent!"[15]

Rationally determining which rules we will scrupulously embrace regardless of the nature of our relationship to others in the community is critical for a well-functioning society. In legal language, because of his promise, Horton had a fiduciary duty to Maize which transcended his personal preferences or family obligations. Once having promised, his duty was to honor the promise and be true to his word regardless of the personal cost. As rationality is valued in a society and we adopt the norm of the rule of law, we know what is accepted behavior, what will not be tolerated, and what will result in punishment.[16] The more consistent the punishment for breaking the rules, the more effective the norm will be for modifying behavior of the individuals in that community.

The second gift of rationality is security. The claim of those who emphasize reason as the road to ethical behavior is that if we as members of a society are faithful to one another, regardless of our blood, cultural, or geographic ties, we will also put appropriate safety nets in place which protect individuals who are not part of our group from the financial uncertainty of disasters such as a flood or unemployment as well as from the violence of those who would destroy the community. Thus, each person gives up some degree of autonomy and flexibility in order to have a community with physical as well as economic safety.

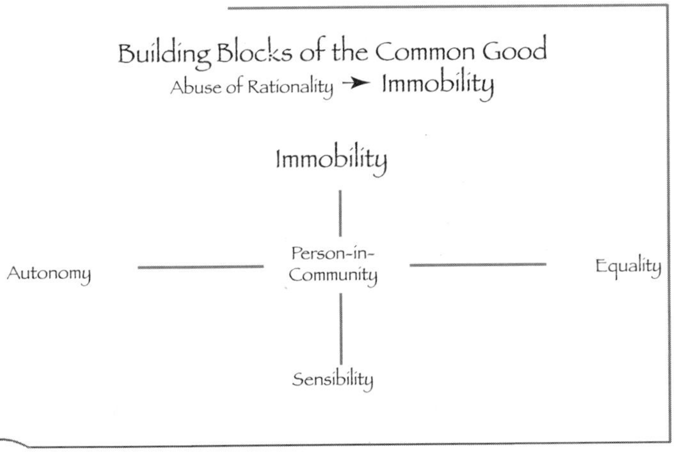

To provide a safe community, people must give up some personal liberty and share some resources to create the infrastructures of sanctuary. These infrastructures include police and military protection, the legal system, and pension and health care plans. Conversations about ethics explore the claims individuals and the community make on each other to assure essential military, police, and fire protection as well as to protect us from the greed of others in the community. An ongoing question is what individual freedoms should be relinquished and what resources should be shared to preserve autonomy and assure equality?

If a society or its people rely too heavily on rationality, the result is *immobility*, as people become restricted and cannot innovate or respond to changing conditions. If a community or its people demand too much security, the richness of intermingling cultures, people, and ideas is lost, which diminishes our ability to meet all of our physical and economic needs. If people cannot get to their work because of physical barriers, their ability to provide for themselves is limited. When people cannot depend on others to honor the rules, members of the community may choose not to be responsible for themselves or others because of fear for their lives or because they know that whatever they do today might be destroyed.

This conundrum is seen in the continuing tension between the Palestinian and Israeli communities on the West Bank of Israel. The Palestinian community finds its economic health decaying as people cannot go to work on the West Bank because the Israelis deny the Palestinians access to the places of employment in the attempt to insure the security of the Israelis. However, the greater the physical barriers and the more the economic health of the Palestinian community deteriorates, the more likely the Palestinians are to risk everything. Their desperation contributes to a devolving spiral of physical and economic insecurity.

Individuals and communities have always vied for resources, most commonly land, labor, capital, and the hearts and minds of people. Through war and violence, people seize for themselves power and assets. The history of civilization is strewn with the bloody and broken remnants of communities waging war on each other to garner for themselves desirable resources. A black strand of history also embroiders the tales of those who embrace violence and war for the sake of power, greed, or a belief that their way of life demands that others either embrace the conqueror's culture or suffer the penalty of annihilation. Another dark thread traces the shenanigans of business leaders who betrayed the trust of their constituents and caused loss of money and the demise of companies. A key task of ethics and law is to restrain greed and abuse of power so that individuals and the community as a whole can thrive.

Virtues associated with the core value *sensibility* are held in tension with rationality. Because the values associated with moral sensibility are contextual rather than universal, we can embrace kindness and tolerance as needed, which allows people to change in response to emerging events as well as new opportunities and challenges. Gracious flexibility allows us to adjust to the changes in our community. We explore new concepts about the nature of the person-in-community (philosophy), at the same time that we accept new and innovative ways to build society (technology). Compassion allows us to quickly respond appropriately to the specific misfortunes of life such as floods, famine, and other natural or human-caused events.

Virtues Associated with Sensibility

Charitable — Prudent — Courteous — Respectful
Moderate — Temperate — Measured — Benevolent
Beneficent — Kind — Generous — Merciful
Compassionate- Grateful — Flexible

One of the historical strengths of the United States is that it embraces the core value of sensibility, both in terms of financial generosity and the liberal acceptance of diversity and quirky individualism. Ironically, sensibility was bifurcated by role: men were expected to respond rationally to impersonal needs (poor-houses and orphanages) while women were responsible for meeting personal needs as a corollary to the running of the households.

Even though the theorists of the Scottish Enlightenment (David Hume, Adam Smith, and Francis Hutcheson) extolled the value of moral sensibilities which responded to particular contextual needs and circumstances, that value was marginalized as people tried to make sense of the emerging philosophical and political notions of individual freedom and social contract. In light of the challenges of the increased mobility of humans and resulting loosening of the societal connections, rationality became the norm and province of men while sensibility was tolerated and became the province of women.[17] The consequences of this split, with a corresponding call for unity that is nourished by self-reflection and is not role dependent, is seen in the novels of Jane Austin such as *Sense and Sensibility.* According to Alisdair MacIntyre, Austin underscores

> ...[that] just as patience necessarily involved a recognition of the character of the world, of a kind which courage does not necessarily require, so constancy requires a recognition of a particular kind of threat to the integrity of the personality in the peculiarly modern social world, a recognition which patience does not necessarily require.[18]

As the roots of dualism grew deeper into our culture, we denigrated sensibility as mere emotivism where all moral judgments are "nothing but expressions of preference, expressions of attitude or feeling, insofar as they are moral or evaluative in character."[19] Many fretted that relying on emotions to make the hard decisions at best makes us soft or at worst leads to no foundations for a moral community. However, charity of spirit is always in conflict with fundamentalism — whether it be political, religious, or corporate. Thus, many advocate holding tightly to the fundamentals of our beliefs to assure that we are not being contaminated by the new-fangled ideas planted by those who advocate tolerance and flexibility. The tension becomes, as Austin noted, knowing when constancy is required to counteract the corrupting tendencies of our society and when charity is useful as we explore new ways of living together and honoring the uniqueness of each person.

In the business sphere, this tension may become evident as conflicts arise about how much risk-taking is appropriate, which is a key feature of flexibility and tolerance. Different persons and cultures have varying threshold tolerances for risk-taking, or in management terms "uncertainty avoidance." Those persons with a high risk threshold find themselves in sales or entrepreneurship. Those cultures who embrace risk tend to value equality of *opportunity* over equality of *result* in allocating rewards. However, those who are risk adverse or do not have as many resources to hedge against losing (either opportunity or money) may prefer a system which favors equality of result or a helping hand in the face of failure.

The United States, whose central myth celebrates those who embraced the risk of taming the wilderness, has policy and financial structures which reward risk-taking and innovation — equality of opportunity. Europeans, whose central myth celebrates national identity and continuity of community, have policy and financial structures which result in much more equality of result. Thus, a core question for ethics becomes what minimum safety nets — what resources — should be in place for community members and businesses so they are

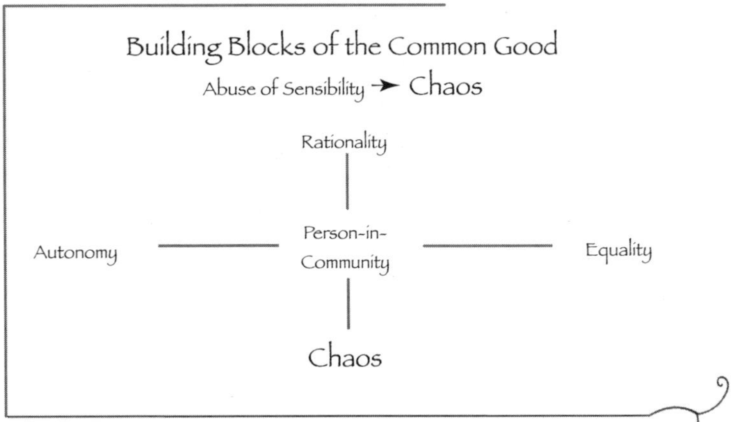

protected against the vagaries of life at the same time that initiative is encouraged and nourished through well-placed stepping-stones to individual success.

If a community or its people rely too much on sensibility with its resulting flexibility, the result is *chaos.* A key critique of situational ethics is that people can rationalize any activity based on the fact that in this time and in this place, that decision seems the best. Thus, the behavior of others is never predictable. Without the restraints provided by the value of rationality, none of us knows how to gauge the risks for any venture. Without the structure of accepted norms or a legal system, subtle forms of favoritism, which at the extreme result in discrimination and bribery, creep into the system.

Also, if people demand unrestricted permission to do whatever they want, fraud and charlatans are tolerated and the common good becomes shredded. In a macro-sense, with too much sensibility the social tapestry becomes moth-eaten from environmental degradation as businesses demand the right to pump anything into the air or dump anything into the water they want. In a micro-sense, the cloth becomes frayed when people, either individually or collectively, use personal and political power to demand unfair bargains from workers (low wages and no benefits) or consumers (shoddy goods and no service).

This drama is played out every year when Congress determines who will get tax dollars for local transportation projects. One such project, a two million dollar bridge to connect a handful of citizens on an island off of the mainland of Alaska, was justified by the Representative by stating that his job was to "bring home the bacon" for his constituents.[20] Thus, the restraint that is provided by rationality as the needs of the whole are considered in light of limited resources falls to the siren call of sensibility where local benefits translate into votes for reelection. Intentionally weaving sensibility through the warp of rationality assures a strong social fabric which holds individual desires and preferences in perfect tension with the needs of the community of as a whole.

Core Values and Economics

All conversations about business ethics explore the dynamic between ethics, doing good, and economics, doing well. According to the dictionary, economics is "the science that deals with the production, distribution, and consumption of wealth and with the various related problems of labor, finance, taxation, etc."[21] Thus, the continual conversation about the relationship between doing good and doing well depends on whether economics and ethics are seen as being in competition or partnership. For most of our history, economics and ethics were seen as partners. In fact, economics has a role in each of the four core values. Because people are careful about the use of their resources, they value *rationality,* since the security of the individual and the community depends on having sufficient resources to sustain them during difficult times. This value manifests as a sense of entitlement as people struggle to differentiate between their needs and their wants.

One of the prairie farmers' key lessons was that in times of scarcity, they never ate the seed. Without seeds, no crop could be planted the following year, a recipe for community extinction. Part of this conversation requires determining what kinds of resources a individuals in a community need. If we all need water to live, the community must find ways to provide that essential good to which all members of the community are entitled. These kinds of questions underlie the current conversation where Coca-Cola purchased water rights in Kerala, India. One could praise Coca-Cola for providing clean water and products for the citizens or vilify them for quickly depleting the aquifer and selling what was previously a free resource.[22]

Embracing *sensibility* allows dreamers to develop new products, services, and processes to capitalize on emerging scientific and technological developments. The notion is that people will develop their own personal capabilities in order to adjust to emerging societal situations. Kant asserted, for example, that we each have a duty of self-improvement. Thus, our community well-being depends on each of us becoming more effective ethical agents.[23] Further, the market forces, where people choose how they will spend their time and money, guarantees tolerance that is not constrained by government regulation. Thus, if people want to choose from among fifty varieties of cereals, the market provides the opportunities.

As *autonomy* increased in importance, the concept of private property was extended. Enlightenment philosophers provided a rationale for claiming individual rights, so people began to assert their prerogative to use their property as they liked and to exercise their legitimate personal power to gain more wealth. The full understanding of private property which operates in the Western world today is relatively new (1700s). For most of our history, people were expected to restrict their personal appropriation of property in favor of community use and need. However, as the individualism of the Protestant Reformation moved from the church to the marketplace, and as the values of personal effort and ingenuity took hold, people asserted that they should receive in salary and lands that which they personally earned based on their merit. Thus, people have a right to use their resources any way they choose as they make their way through this world.

Equality is advanced by the notion that all members of a community have the right to share in some basic goods and services. Whether through the voices of the Old Testament prophets who called Israel to accountability for proper use of wealth and caring for the widows or orphans, or Karl Marx championing a radical reorganization of wealth, the claims of the community compel us to look at fairness in distribution of resources. We all have some sense that all people who are part of the community need and deserve certain threshold goods to survive — food, shelter, education, and health care. One thread of ethics explores what claim members of the community can have on the wealth of others based on their very presence.

History tells us that a strong community is one in which all members have a chance to share in the opportunities and wealth. This belief is played out in the Western commitment to a strong, fluid middle class which allows people to move into positions of wealth based on merit and effort rather than pedigree. Equality of opportunity provides this movement. What we also know is that when the perceived discrepancy between the "haves" and the "have nots" gets too great, the community fractures into lawlessness or revolution. Equality of result reduces the disparity between those who began with many gifts and resources and those who were thrust into this world with many fewer choices.[24]

In common parlance, we have a sense of the balance between economics and ethics being maintained if an action is deemed fair. However, as Michael Walzer in *Spheres of Justice* notes, we have different criteria for determining whether an allocation of resources is fair and just. One criterion is merit, that which we have earned, which parallels autonomy. Another criterion is just deserts, that which we deserve because we are a part of the community, which parallels equality. The last criterion, which embraces both rationality and sensibility, is the market: we can get what we can purchase with our personal resources.[25] The market moves between regulation (which provides rationality and safety) and freedom of contract (which provides charity and tolerance) as we make choices which then, in the words of Smith, provide the invisible hand of the market.[26]

This arrangement masks the role of inheritance, where the original position of all members of the community is not the same. Thus, some inherit wealth or ability which, by definition, results in inequality of opportunity. Since we do not all begin at the same place on the racetrack of life, whether the rules governing the distribution of goods are seen as acceptable depends on the core values one advances and whether the members of the community believe the results are fundamentally fair.

Merit is the notion that each person/group earns whatever they are worth and can use their earnings to purchase whatever they desire for whatever price they are willing to pay. Thus, if a company can only get the CEO that it wants for $4.5 million dollars a year but can get a cashier for $14,000 per year, under the criterion of merit, those wages and allocation of a firm's resources are perfectly acceptable. The notion of *just deserts* is the notion that members of a community deserve certain threshold goods and services simply by being part of the community. Those conversations focus on *who* is in the community (*e.g.,* citizens, resident non-citizens, or undocumented workers) and *how much* of the basic resources they can claim.

Thus, if a company provides health care for the members of its community, the question arises how many hours a person must work in that society to be considered a member. For some employers, the magic number is 32 (which is why so many people are offered part-time employment). For others, who have strong feelings about making benefits available to part-time workers regardless of what the law requires, the threshold number is ten. In making an ethical evaluation of a company, we might say that the company that cuts off benefits at 32 hours is meeting the requirements of the law but is not being ethical (*e.g.*, assuring equal access to the resources provided to all members of the community).

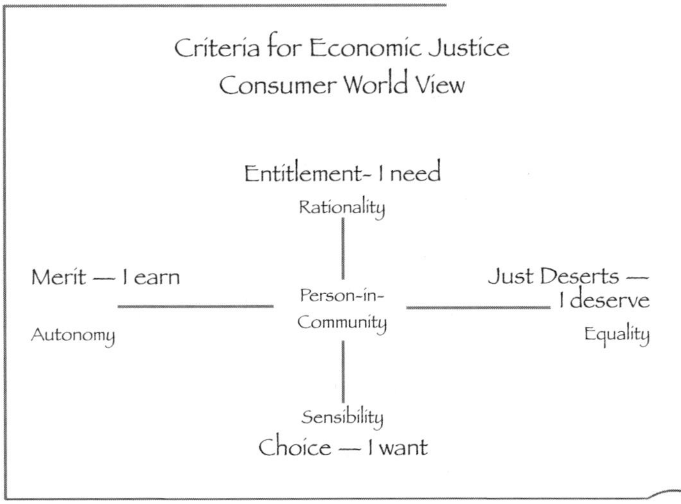

In fact, William Greider asserts that the willingness of employers to pay a higher premium for temporary workers because they are expendable not only demoralizes workers but also leads to the weakening of democracy. When participants in the market economy have unequal power, our economic structures teach both passivity and powerlessness while restricting human dignity, equity, and self-worth because the ability to actually make effective economic choices is limited. This passivity also leads to apathy in voting and lack of participation in our political processes.[27]

Entitlement is the notion that each person and group needs certain resources, including being treated as fully human and assuring that the bargains they make (sanctity of contract) are honored. Because each person and group has a right to survive and thrive, people should get access to resources and be paid a sufficient amount to be secure and not dependent on others. *Choice* is the notion that each of us gets to determine how we will use our core resources, our time, our talents, and our money to get what we want. Thus, those for whom time is valuable may choose to be in a job that does not pay top dollar but allows a great deal of flexibility and reduced hours.

Many who review the above core value sets would assert that two concepts are missing — efficiency and growth — which are key goals of corporations. A prior threshold question is whether efficiency and growth are means to achieving the core values or are essential values in their own right. The first claim of this book is that efficiency is a means to reaching the core values of rationality, autonomy and equality. The second claim is that growth is a function both of efficiency and the ability of the firm to meet the fluctuating needs of the community and is thus related to the core value of sensibility.

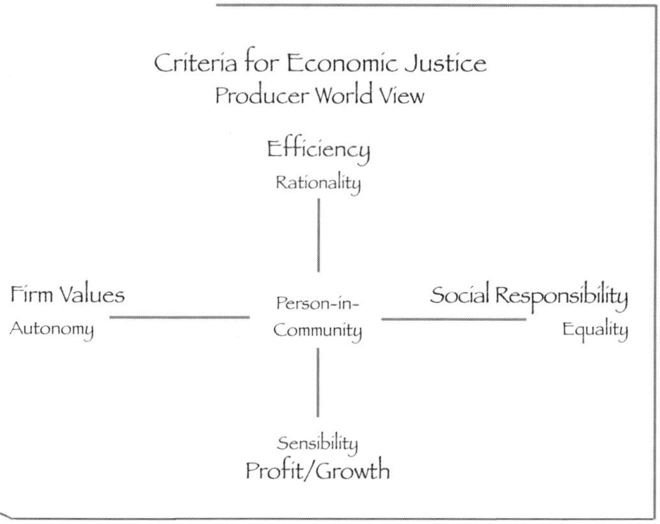

Thus, companies will find themselves in continual flux, waxing and waning, depending on the wisdom and skill of the team members and the vagaries of the economy. By tracking the twin indicators of efficiency and growth, leaders can assess the trajectory of the company. However, if efficiency and growth are primary goals, the core values of the company and community which provide the underpinnings for the company may be neglected or ignored, which may ultimately be a very high cost. While rationality and sensibility are needed for an economy to grow, even Smith knew that rationality and sensibility could only be secured in a political system which assured justice, defense, and maintenance of public systems, which were needed but might not be profitable, such as roads and education.[28]

The economic term for careful use of resources is efficiency, the ability to reach a desired goal with a minimum of effort, expense, or waste.[29] Deborah Stone, in *Policy Paradox,* asserts that efficiency is a means to the other four core values. Even so, she notes that many people treat efficiency as a value in itself.[30] However, if ethics and economics are not to be set in conflict with each other, efficiency — using resources wisely — must be a handmaiden to the other core goals. If efficiency is seen as a primary goal, then the other core values may be sacrificed as abuse of power and greed come into play.

Embracing the value of autonomy, individuals and companies claim the right to use their market power to gather for themselves the goods that they want. In the process they may get more of a particular good than may be healthy for the balance of power between individuals and the community. As one group has more of a particular good than needed, others who need access to that good may be kept from getting what they need. Greed corrupts the community as people keep for themselves more resources than are needed for security, for no other reason than just to have more. As business leaders embrace the perspective of scholars such as Robert Greenleaf, who wrote *Servant Leadership,* leaders will rearticulate their roles in light of stewardship, assuring the well being of the company rather than gathering for themselves power and money.[31] Thus the core value of equality manifests as companies explore the parameters of social responsibility. Then the core values of individuals as well as those of the organization as a whole will drive the economic decisions, not the reverse.

Another way of looking at the intersection of economics and ethics comes from William C. Frederick in *Values, Nature, and Culture in the American Corporation.*[32] Frederick asserts that the business community has traditionally had three core values: *growth,* which depends on following one's gut while embracing flexibility, resulting in more successful economizing by the firm; *systemic integrity*, which brings the firm together as a whole through the autonomy of the firm to develop its own culture and values; and *economizing*, where success and failure are measured in monetary profit and loss and thus parallels rationality.[33]

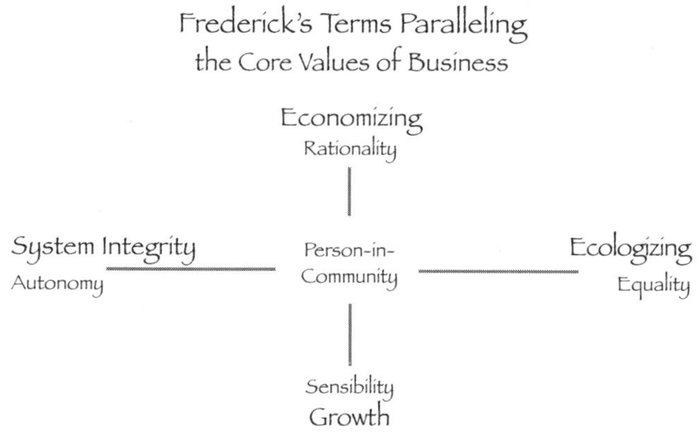

Healthy growth would indicate that a firm is both efficient (using its resources effectively) and attentive (appropriately responding to the community by producing the goods and services which members of the society want). Thus, healthy growth requires a firm to be flexible to meet changing and emerging market preferences. *Systemic integrity* supports autonomy: the organization is seen as a whole as the company becomes the autonomous actor and members of the firm work together. Finally, the value of *economizing* (efficiently using resources to stay in business) is essential to the financial well being of a company. It does not serve a company well to either squander resources on perks for the employees or to provide benefits which result in the company going out of business.

Frederick asserts that corporations have ignored the core value of equality, which he names as the value of *ecologizing*, defined as embracing those life-conserving values which build and maintain community.[34] Frederick further states that the ethical as well as the financial health of the corporation can only be maintained through working with other firms, both in sharing resources, such as information and effort, and in being part of a healthy community. Thus, in the economic life of a company, leadership's antennae must be out for two different variables.

First, we must attend to the careful use of the company's resources to assure they are used appropriately to balance among the values of rationality and sensibility as well as autonomy and equality within the firm and in the life of the stakeholders to which the firm has responsibility. Second, we must respond to changes in available resources and needs in the community: when fewer resources are available or when priorities of the community change, the growth and efficiency of a company will change.

Classically, the question of the allocation of community resources is described as a "guns or butter" conversation. Those monies which are put into the military, industries which provide military supplies, and agricultural subsidies to assure an adequate supply of food for the community during war (whether invasion or siege) are seen as supporting the goal of national or community security, in shorthand "guns." Those monies which are put into education, health care, housing, or food for the poor are seen as supporting the goal of equality, in shorthand "butter." The notion is that economic growth comes from the efforts of autonomous individuals and corporations who share their resources through taxes or direct charity to provide security or equality, guns or butter"

In a time of a threat to national security, firms which make weapons will experience growth as community resources are put into guns at the same time that firms which provide consumer goods might shrink as resources are withdrawn from butter. In a time of expanding wealth, the community resources might be put into increasing health care, day care, education or any other number of services for those who may have less access to individual resources. Those companies which provide such services and goods will thus experience growth as the community buys butter.

Clearly, times of imbalance and transition are times of great uncertainty. In the months following the September 11, 2001 attack on the World Trade Center, American firms scrambled as resources were reallocated from butter to guns. The increased interest in security coincided with three other tumultuous shifts which had a profound effect on the economic structure of American society and demonstrated deep ethical flaws.

The first began in the early 1990s, where, as prosperity grew, people felt a need to emphasize autonomy, by keeping their resources for personal use and making those who use services pay for them. Charity (especially in the narrow sense of almsgiving which was seen through efforts to privatize services which had previously been delivered by the government) was favored by minimizing government interference in the running of businesses which manifested as a flurry of legislation designed to reduce regulation. This shift was at the expense of equality, reducing those taxes which provided resources for goods and services for all regardless of individual ability to pay. The shift to less regulation was also at the expense of rationality which assured that external governmental controls were in place to militate against corporations' unbridled economic power. Even as the prosperity of the country faltered, the United States Congress passed more tax cuts to stimulate the economy which favored autonomy and sensibility, while authorizing greater military spending and commercial protections for security which favored the value of rationality.[35]

Ironically, those changes were made during the second seismic shift, the bursting of the technology bubble with its economic ramifications. The third shift was the revelation of illegal and unethical actions which had led to an unprecedented increase of wealth for a few at the expense of the many. As these events sank into the collective consciousness, the stock market plunged, resulting in increased unemployment and fewer opportunities for firms. The ethical crisis exacerbated the economic crisis, which led to fewer individual resources available for purchasing goods and services. Then when people did not have sufficient individual resources to buy goods and services, they had a greater need for a community safety net, which had been dismantled. As the resources of the community shrink, the question is which of the core values needs attention: which of the core values are so out of balance that we need to recalibrate?

As we evaluate whether a company or individuals are appropriately using resources, society tends to find those companies ethical which, within the constraints of available economic resources, maintain a balance among the four core value clusters. Stakeholders in a company do not expect raises, increases in benefits, or dividends at a time when the security of a company is threatened. However, stakeholders do expect some level of equality in sharing the burden of shrinking resources. Thus, the executives at Enron would not have been vilified in the press if they had taken their financial lumps in terms of reduction of share value with all of the other employees. Cries of foul play were heard when the executives abused their power by exempting themselves from the downward slide of profit while either not informing the other stockholders of the economic problems or not allowing the other stockholders to move their money to minimize their own personal financial loss.[36] Martha Stewart was pilloried because she was perceived to have received an advantage through information not available to the rest of the community as she took her money from one company and put her resources in another.[37]

Economists are fond of saying that economics is value-free. The implication is that Western rationality results in decisions that are value neutral. This assumption overlooks the fact that all of our decisions are in fact driven by our values. If economic theory is used to describe what is currently in place, economics is in fact value free, a description of what is. However, as soon as economists move into the realm of predicting what change in resource allocation will cause what results, they enter the world of ethics: any change in resource allocation is in fact a value judgment about the best way to balance among the competing interests of the core values of the firm and the community.[38]

As Lynn Sharp Paine in *Value Shift* asserts, leaders and managers of companies must begin to see their task as maximizing both the ethical and economic well-being of the firm.[39] Thus, ethics should not be seen as an added bonus, to be considered only if the company is doing well financially. Rather, the goal of the firm is to assure that the core values of the company, which themselves are often in conflict, remain in balance as the financial fortunes of the company fluctuate. Then the company can attend to the triple bottom line — ethics, economics, and the environment.

Core Values and Law

Ethics and law mediate among the core value sets and help assure their balance both in individual and corporate action. Personal ethics provide an individual foundation for moderating behavior. Our conscience provides internal structure, directing us as we decide what is the right thing to do. Community norms provide external pressure to conform to the expectations of parents and other members of the society. The mild punishments for violating our personal ethics or community norms range from reproach to guilt. Being removed from the community, shunning, is the greatest threat.

Each of us is complex: a mixture of good and bad. We generally know what is right to do and we work to be good, virtuous citizens. We also are interested in assuring that in our corner of the world we maximize our power and wealth. Even in institutions whose mission is to help the downtrodden and mediate the presence of God to the people, leaders get caught by the desire to accumulate power and privilege, a desire often at cross-purposes with their organization's mission. Thus, we need both carrots and sticks: rewards for doing well and threats of punishment to keep us in line.

Political Structures

Political structures, whether in families, organizations, or nations, provide webs of accountability which help us maximize our tendencies to be good and minimize the temptations to transgress. Webs of accountability, whether informal peer groups or formal rules and regulations, provide us with early warnings that we are about to go astray when we have been blinded by our own hubris or blind-sided by our naiveté or ignorance. In a rapidly shrinking world where the current primary social organization is nation-states, the first question is the shape of the political structure of the country. Three different models exist across the globe. The first one is the liberal market economic model, which values a free market. The second is neo-mercantile, which values nation building and security. The third is social democracy, which values equality in sharing the social burdens and benefits.[40]

The United States is modeled on a market economy. In its pure form, the liberal economic model has a commitment to individualism, the free market, and private property. Proponents of this political and economic school of thought advocate an unregulated market. The belief is that because people are rational, economic persons, as they make their choices, the market will continuously recalibrate itself in accordance with its own internal logic. According to Robert Gilpin, "[t]he rationale for a market system is that it increases economic efficiency, maximizes economic growth, and thereby improves human welfare...the primary objective of economic activity is to benefit individual consumers.[41] The notion is that a market economy will move, over the long term, toward equilibrium and inherent stability.

Manuel Velasquez reminds us that this system is ethical in three respects: (1) because buyers and sellers are free to enter or leave the market when they wish, a market economy embodies "the negative right of freedom of opportunity;" (2) because no one is forced to buy or sell that which they do not wish to buy or sell, including their labor, a market economy embodies "the negative right of freedom of consent;" and (3) because power is shared among many firms, no one firm will be able to so dominate the market that it will be able to force others to accept its terms, thus a market economy embodies "the negative right of freedom from coercion."[42]

However, a cursory look at the world around us shows some of the serious flaws with a purely unregulated market. First, as anyone who has ever tried to start a micro-enterprise will tell you, entering and leaving the market is neither inexpensive nor easy. The overwhelming majority of new businesses fail in the first year. Second, as those who are watching their jobs leave the United States and go to other countries will tell you, employees do not have the same market power as employers. Finally, although some may argue that Microsoft simply had a "better mousetrap," the antitrust litigation against Microsoft indicates that it used its market power to dominate the economy. When faced with true competition from Linux, and lax enforcement of anti-piracy laws, even Microsoft blinked and offered its programs to Thailand at a lower price to assure that the next generation of consumers is raised on Windows.[43] Thus, while a market economy may establish a capitalist form of justice, maximize utility, and protect the negative rights of buyers and sellers, other important core values and forms of justice are not met, particularly those based on rationality (entitlement) or equality (just deserts).[44]

A common response to the problems of distributive justice in a market economy is social democracy as seen in the policies of Europe and other communities which strive to assure that people in their communities receive sufficient resources to provide basic needs. These communities may provide benefits in the form of vacations and pensions or may tax themselves to provide for health care, housing, and other human needs. Thus, in our mixed economy, those who favor transfer of resources for butter tend to favor tilting the balance toward social democracy. Many countries respond to the problems of a market economy inadequately providing for national security by imposing taxes to pay for national defense, moving toward a neo-mercantile model. An example is the People's Republic of China which has the second largest defense spending behind the United States, even though many of its people live in dire poverty. In our mixed economy, those who favor transfer of resources for guns are said to favor tilting the economic structures toward neo-mercantilism.

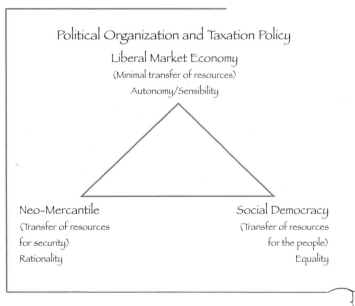

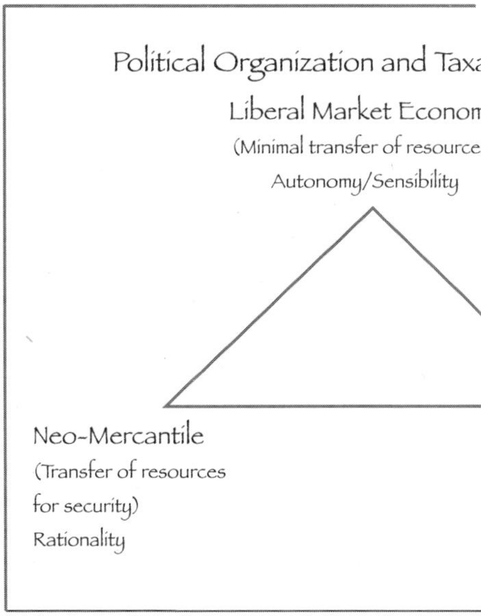

When using personal ethics as a standard for public policy and law, a key variable is that we have to find some way to mediate the competing world views of individuals and organizations in the community. The more homogeneous the community, the less likely that a legal structure is needed. So, the People's Republic of China has a minimal legal system because culturally its citizens are expected to fit in and follow the societal norms. If the religious or cultural structures of the community either formally or informally enforce an ethical code, governments do not need to pass laws to insure the approved behavior.

Legal Structures

The multi-cultural United States, which values individuality, relies on its legal system to resolve differences. When people have competing notions about what is or is not ethical behavior because of religious or cultural differences, or when the church or dominant culture is no longer able to enforce behavior, laws become necessary to mediate competing personal and community world views. When members of the community do not agree upon the purpose for which resources should be transferred through taxation, public policy debates erupt which are couched in ethical language and claim legitimacy through appealing to the core values of the community. In these contested situations, law tends to become codified ethics.

Law and ethics are seen as synonymous at the edges, and litigation becomes the means to enforce these ethics. Further, as the norms of the community are contested resulting in the undermining of the dominant authority, or as the society becomes so diverse that the religious or cultural world view is no longer compelling enough to assure compliance with an informal ethical code, communities pass laws with appropriate penalties to coerce behavior. A society's legal and ethical structures use both persuasion to enhance responsibility and coercion to enforce accountability to balance the four core values: autonomy, equality, rationality, and sensibility. Paradoxically, autonomy is enhanced through self-regulation when people choose to live by ethical codes.[45] Autonomy is also accepted when people have a high level of trust in each other. In those instances people do not need laws to do the right thing.

- ***As individuals seek to respect all persons, esteem both communal and private property, and then responsibly use power, virtues associated with the core values like integrity, honesty, and compassion emerge.***

- ***As businesses and other organizations articulate the core values and virtues which govern their economic strategies and are willing to hold themselves to a higher ethical standard than the law, trust in business evolves and transactional costs are reduced.***

- ***As companies assure that all qualified applicants have access to jobs and that the benefits of the company (such as salaries, vacations and other perks) are fairly distributed, those companies will be respected and may minimize their exposure to lawsuits and regulatory oversight.***

However, if people or businesses do not embrace the ethical values of the community on their own or do not trust each other to keep their word, laws must be passed to define the norms (rationality) and to provide a method of enforcement (equality). Equality is enhanced through the laws which enforce our contracts and mete out punishments such as fines or confinement for violations of societal norms that are found in the common law or in the regulatory scheme. The actions of the law in these situations are reactive, after the fact. Thus one who has violated the laws and expectations of the community is subject to court action.

For litigation to be effective at regulating behavior, enforcement must either be frequent with low penalties (the chances of getting caught are high and the fines are low) or infrequent with high penalties (the chances of getting caught are low but the penalties are high, such as triple damages, large fines, jail time, and one's name all over the front pages of the paper). If enforcement is inconsistent or infrequent with low penalties, people will consider fines a cost of doing business, take the risk of getting caught, and continue engaging in illegal or unethical behavior.

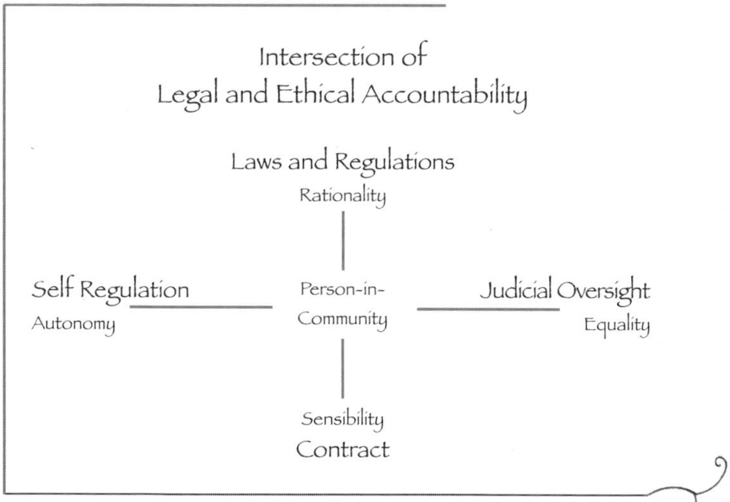

Our laws and legal systems also reinforce equality by determining what redistribution of resources is required. This could happen through a tax system where property tax and income tax are used to provide education for all members of the community, or housing, food, and health care for those who are without money. Businesses may also be asked to absorb some of the social costs through requirements such as providing health care, worker's compensation, or family medical leave. The trick is to assure that our demands for equality and rationality do not stifle autonomy and sensibility manifested as innovation and initiative.

The law supports tolerance and flexibility which enable people to negotiate contracts which embody the risk and the responsibilities they agree to undertake — whatever goods and services they want for whatever price their fancy desires. As long as people accept both the benefits and the burdens of those contracts, the community is strengthened. However, if the consumer wants the benefit of a contract (such as being able to engage in dangerous activities like white water rafting), without assuming the burden (possible death without compensation), the community will restrict their ability to choose. Many of us seem to want to decide how we want to live but then expect the community to pick up the pieces when the gamble goes sour.

During the 1980s, many savings and loans institutions failed because of risky investments. Some people had more than $100,000 in their favorite Savings & Loan institution. When the banks failed they lost any investment greater than the federal guarantee. Many wanted to maximize their return on investment and had not noticed that the community only guarantees a loss up to $100,000 through federal insurance. Those who expected more than the guarantee were very upset that they could not recover all their loss, even though they made the decision to make deposits exceeding the federal guarantee. The public policy tension is finding the right balance between risk and protection of investments. Through our legislators, we balance the cost of protecting people from the risks inherent in sensibility with rationality manifesting as limitations on autonomy to assure survival of the community as a whole. The amount of the federal guarantee represents the balance Congress struck.

Rationality is accomplished as legislatures pass laws and administrative agencies promulgate regulations which let people know their obligations to the community. Laws which are proscriptive (such as emissions standards to reduce environmental pollution or requirements for labeling packages) tend to promote rationality because they put businesses on an equal playing field. Carefully considered regulations can reduce the economic pressure which the market (both producers and consumers) places on companies to inappropriately minimize expenses and maximize profits. This pressure is felt by companies such as WalMart where owners want to maximize their return and consumers want to pay rock bottom prices. By having every business absorb the same social costs (such as minimum wage and requirements to provide health care) which move toward equality as part of their social responsibility of doing business, employees, consumers and the environment can be protected while companies thrive.

Rationality is also enhanced through a redistribution of resources such as taxes or through voluntary behavior which restricts individual liberty in order to provide a safe environment. Pooled resources and taxes pay for military and police protection as well as provide subsidies to companies that manufacture goods which are essential to the well being of the community (such as steel and airplanes in wartime). Businesses and individuals are also expected to use personal resources for safety, whether through keeping sidewalks free from snow and ice or paying to create safe environments for employees. They are also expected to not poison the common environment such as air and water. Ultimately, we want to evenly enforce the laws while not requiring too much redistribution of revenue. We want to preserve the incentives for personal responsibility and accountability while assuring that the resources for equality are not shortchanged.

Because a community is always in flux regarding the allocation of scarce resources, maintaining the proper balance among the core values, individual and community ethics, and the law is imperfect.[46] A member of the community who believes that the law is unethical can force society to reevaluate its stance. Dr. Kervorkian invited the United States into a conversation about the ethics of assisted suicide in the face of terminal illness. Oregon chose to modify its law to allow physicians and patients to make a decision about ending life. After considering this difficult situation, citizens of other states made other choices.

The reverse can also happen. The community can determine that a particular ethical value can no longer be tolerated and thus change the law to coerced a change of behavior. People are fond of saying that morality cannot be legislated, which is true: laws alone cannot change a person's heart. However, the law can force people to act differently. The Civil Rights Movement and the resulting legislation forced many

Relationship of Law and Ethics: an act may be...

Legal and ethical	Not legal but ethical
Legal but not ethical	Not legal and not ethical

people to stop overt behavior of discrimination. In the thirty years since the passage of The Civil Rights Act (Title VII), a new generation has come of age which takes as given that we do not discriminate based on race, religion, or national origin. Personal and communal ethics have changed in response to the requirements of the law.

In the 1990s, Dr. Kervorkian appealed to the core principle of autonomy, the right of each person to choose how to live — and how to die. Currently, the conversation about assisted suicide hinges on assuring that people who choose to die are in fact making the choice freely rather than being forced into a choice just to save health care resources. The Civil Rights Movement appealed to the core principle of equality, the right of each person to have access to the goods and benefits of the community. One question concerning the persistent remnants of inequality is whether individuals who have historically been disadvantaged are exercising sufficient autonomy, making choices which will assure that they maximize their potential as humans, or whether barriers to equality still exist.

In reaction to the destruction of the World Trade Center, the United States Congress passed sweeping new legislation, The Patriot Act, which in the name of national security severely limits the rights of privacy and citizen access to public venues. The question remains is whether the security gained from the new law is sufficient to justify the tradeoffs in autonomy and equality.

The impetus behind privatization of government services and deregulation of segments of the economy is to encourage economic flexibility. In continuing conversations, voices in the community speak to persuade others that the ethics and/or law are not adequately balancing the four building blocks, and thus the rules, or even the underlying assumptions of capitalism, must be changed. This fluid dialogue requires everyone's participation, as new situations and understandings of what it means to be a person-in-community are brought forward for critique and evaluation.

Conclusion

The perennial organizing questions which opened the chapter — questions concerning politics and economics, ethics, and technology — are answered differently in various communities, depending on which of the four core values are seen to be out of balance and what preferred solutions make sense to the people. As each of us identifies our preferred stance on these issues, we can enter into conversation to fashion the best public policies to solve the emerging problems. However, because the claims of each point on the political triangle are persuasive and have both benefits and burdens, we are often conflicted. We want low taxes and a secure community. Or we want low taxes and safety nets for the poor and disenfranchised. Or we want low taxes and shared social goods such roads and national parks.

Unfortunately, because resources are limited, solutions do not come neatly tied up in the above packages. We must make hard choices as we discern how best to provide for the individual in community. These choices are often driven by our fundamental understanding of the nature of human beings and our role in the community. Thus, our basic religious and ethical convictions drive our preferred ethics and public policy. Understanding this basic truth and knowing our own positions helps us mediate among competing values in order to make more consistent public policy decisions.

Continuing the Conversation

1. Find an article in your local paper or a news magazine which discusses both sides of a public policy question, such as minimum wage, moving jobs off-shore, or providing health care. See if you can identify which core values each side invokes.

2. Identify an ethical or public policy issue which is present either in your professional life or in the public eye. Try to formulate the arguments for and against a particular solution in terms of the three public policy models — liberal market economy, social democracy, or neo-mercantile.

3. Interview two people — one on each side of the debate. Interview a person who would tilt toward social democracy (often a liberal Democrat) and one person who would tilt toward neo-mercantile (often a conservative Republican). Ask them why they favor one school of thought over the others. Also ask them how they begin to fashion compromises when faced with a public policy decision.

Matrix of Traditional Western Approaches to Justice

Organizing Question	Deontological (duty) Politically Conservative	↔	Teleological (goals) Politically Liberal
Our relationship to the sacred is	God is Transcendent seek to recreate the ideal (heaven).	↔ so we	God is Immanent celebrate the real in the here and now.
Human beings are	Flawed (sinful) rules to avoid punishment.	↔ so will respond to	Basically good (misguided) relationship to assure respect.
Individuals should embrace	Individualism through autonomy we can each creatively find the best way to live.	↔ so that	Communitarianism through consensus we can respectfully share a good life together.
Private property is	Necessary for peace be able to accumulate wealth and control its use and distribution.	↔ so individuals should	Instrument of progress be encouraged to share wealth and be a good steward for all.
Our community should be structured to emphasize	Independence egalitarian and admit people based on merit.	↔ which means that we are	Interdependence hierarchal and admit people based on birth or embracing our beliefs.
Our government should therefore be	A democracy with a tilt to neo-mercantile provide security to enhance autonomy.	↔ so resources are transferred from individuals to	A democracy with a tilt to social-democrat provide opportunity to enhance equality.
Our global relationships should also emphasize	Independence Individual agreements with countries or companies.	↔ with agreements that assure	Interdependence Inclusive considerations for the people in the countries.
Our relationship to the earth should encourage	Development individuals have resources to create wealth and thrive.	↔ to assure that	Conservation the planet is left intact for our children and grandchildren.

Give a man a fish,
and you feed him for a day.
Teach a man to fish,
and you feed him for a lifetime.

Chinese Proverb

Chapter 3

Stepping Stones and Safety Nets

Beliefs about which core value should take precedence over another have evolved over the course of our civilization. Reviewing the trajectory of history shows that one thread of the conversation remains constant: seeking to understand the nature of the human person and the human condition, how we live our lives in community. As our life together moves through time, the two core traditions (deontological and teleological) about people and life are continually rearticulated against technological innovations and scientific breakthroughs which drive changes in political and economic structures. Our core beliefs about humans and their condition (good or flawed) thus provide the underpinnings for our beliefs about ethics and justice (deontological or teleological) which inform our public policy and laws.

Throughout history, two primary traditions have prevailed. Deontology, asserts that to determine the right thing to do, we should identify the duties and responsibilities of humans and assure procedural justice to protect individual rights. Teleology (also known as consequentialism), asserts that we should focus on the goals and character of humans. Each tradition is grounded in very different understandings of humanity which then lead to very different policies about the treatment of people and use of property. As they lay out their theories, philosophers address the implications of their theories for our personal life — *ethics*, and for our shared life of politics, economics, and business — *justice*. While philosophers place themselves in a particular tradition, they also demonstrate how their theory has relevance to the problems of the day.

Representative Theorists

Deontological Tradition		Teleological Tradition
Plato	(400-300 BC)	Aristotle
St. Augustine	(300-1300 AD)	Thomas Aquinas
Martin Luther	(1500-1700 AD)	Isaac Newton
Immanuel Kant	(1700-1850 AD)	John Stuart Mill
Charles Darwin	(1800-1950 AD)	John Dewey
John Rawls	(1950 - AD)	Alisdair MacIntyre

As the dust was settling in the 16th century after the Protestant Reformation, Kant (deontology) and Mill (teleology) explored how we could move from an ethic grounded in revelation and mediated through the church to an ethic grounded in reason and mediated by individuals. They were deeply informed by Descartes' dualism where "the soul is understood as mind, and human awareness as distinctively that of the thinker."[1] As Richard Tarnas notes, this understanding of the universe was a shift from the vibrance of the Medieval mind where the universe was alive, to a belief that the universe was composed of "nonvital atomistic matter" which could be understood in mechanistic terms. Tarnas continues,

> Descartes enthroned human reason as the supreme authority in matters of knowledge, capable of distinguishing certain metaphysical truth and of achieving certain scientific understanding of the material world. Infallibility, once ascribed only to Holy Scripture or the supreme pontiff, was now transferred to human reason alone.[2]

Once the religious authority for social organization was undermined, the work of seminal political philosophers such as Thomas Hobbes [1588-1679] gave rise to the notion of social contract, where citizens agree on the system of governance by which they will be bound. The logical conclusion for the Enlightenment notions of self-governance was democracy and an liberal market economy, which is unregulated in its pure form.

In the 20th century with the advent of the Industrial Revolution, social reformers highlighted the unintended consequences and problems of an liberal market economy. Reflecting on the labor unrest of the early 1900s and the Great Depression, John Rawls (deontology) explored how attention to procedural justice could mitigate the myopia caused by a focus on individual goals (teleology). Alasdair MacIntyre (teleology) turned our attention to our character to mitigate the shortsightedness caused by a focus on individual rights (deontology). These theories were the underpinnings of a political shift towards a regulated economy with statutory protections for workers, consumers, and investors.

> As humans, we are born into a family that tends to favor one tradition over the other. Whether considered in terms of religious or political preferences, our parents have a set of core commitments which they wish us to adopt as well. These core commitments define us and have the potential to energize and transform the self, the family, and the community. As we wend our way through life, we have the opportunity to first identify the salient elements of our birth tradition and then either reaffirm that tradition, change traditions, or nuance our beliefs by a thoughtful synthesis of the two.

In each case, the theorists who identified with one or the other tradition began with shared assumptions. Getting an overview of the core differences in the traditions helps us make sense out of the deeply held convictions of people in our community and the solutions that are then advocated for the problems which face us. While the following discussion sketches tendencies in very broad strokes, if we think of the various positions as points along a continuum, our own world view, the sum total of our core beliefs, comes into relief.

Core Beliefs and Value Manifestations

Robert H. Nelson, in *Reaching for Heaven on Earth: The Theological Meaning of Economics,* charted the different sets of assumptions which profoundly inform these two traditions. Nelson asserts that core beliefs about the human person, our relationship to the sacred, and our life with each other provide foundations our ethics and also convictions about economics, law, and government. From a bird's-eye view, these core beliefs, whether conscious or unconscious, manifest as favored political and economic structures as well as public policy preferences. With a modicum of consistency, the assumptions we hold about the sacred and human nature will also establish our theoretical grounding for business ethics and public policy.

While the representative theorists are placed in a particular tradition (deontological or teleological) either through self-identification or based on their body of writing, Nelson notes that none of them fit squarely within a given school of thought. Over the course of their lives, each one may have grappled with weaknesses in their own tradition or appropriated ideas from the other. However, the two traditions are a good place to start in charting our own belief systems.[3]

Our belief systems depend on which core values inform our actions, define how we should treat each other (ethics), and determine our policy preferences for society (justice). Many of us believe that if the other person just saw life the way we do, all this fussing and bickering would stop. However, each tradition has strengths and weaknesses, so we can make a persuasive argument for policies which flow from either. Those who favor the deontological tradition, what one student called "D-people," tend to favor what I call "*stepping stone*" policies. They believe that the best public policy provides incentives and structures for people to care for themselves, which they can use — or not. If one slips off and gets wet in the stream, it is the problem of the individual. Those who favor the teleological tradition, "T-people," tend to favor what I call "*safety net*" policies. They believe that the best public policy provides a safe haven for people to regroup after a difficult time complete with access to the resources they need to move forward, and requires people to wear helmets when they ride their bikes.

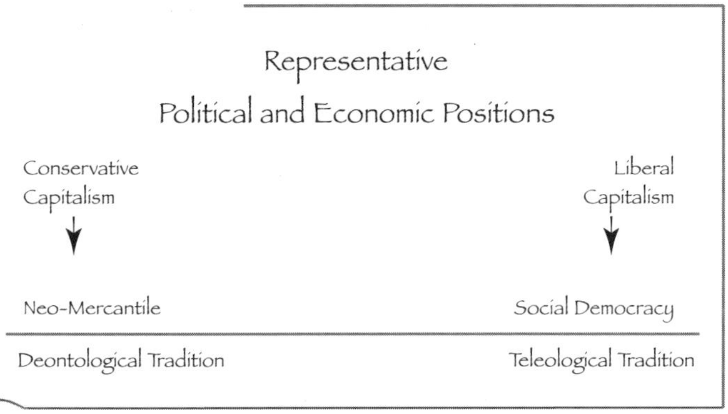

The saving grace is that in ethics and public policy, we often agree on *what* to do even if we do not agree on *why*. Usually the best solutions are a blend of the two traditions, providing both safety nets and stepping stones — giving a woman a fish while she is taking fishing lessons. Of course, the question is always *how many* fish and *how long* the lessons should take to learn. Thus, the best public policy is hammered out when one group does not have a monopoly on power but shares power with other groups holding different beliefs.

The following listings are the representative core beliefs of people in the two traditions. It is useful to consider each tradition as the end points on a continuum with many gradations in between. In addition, we each hold some of our beliefs very strongly and others more tenuously, which also impacts our action. Because each position contains some truth, we may try to reach a both/and position and thus mix and match beliefs. We have to carefully discern when the mixing results in a judicious balance rather than schizophrenic behavior caused by choosing a position which favors us this time and then moving to a different position when we would receive the benefit of the policy. However, surveying the big picture, helps us situate ourselves in the ongoing conversation about the state of the world and understand our response to it.[4]

Nelson asserts that our world view is grounded in our beliefs about the transcendent, our relationship to the sacred.[5] Thus, we begin our survey by exploring the fundamental nature of what is considered sacred and the nature of humans. Then we will explore our understanding of community and our relationship to each other. Whether acknowledged or not, these beliefs define how our core values are choreographed together in elegant if-then dance steps. These values manifest as our choices and actions, our ethics. As our dance evolves, we see whether we favor soloing in our own break-dance or participating in a line dance with others. In any event, whether we acknowledge our partners or not, all of us dance together in this amazing performance we call life.

Relationship of Individuals to the Sacred

The foundation for all of our beliefs is our understanding of the sacred as either transcendent or immanent. Those in theistic traditions name this presence God. Those in non-theistic traditions, such as Buddhism, may articulate some sense of the presence of Spirit and speak of that which connects all of us. Those in the humanist tradition, who assert that human understanding and reason are sufficient for us to know what to do, speak of matters spiritual without invoking a deity, but find the Spirit within each person. While we may not agree on what "It" is, every tradition speaks of something which is beyond each of us individually.

	God Is...	
Transcendent		Immanent
	so we	
seek to recreate the ideal (heaven)		celebrate the real (the here and now)
Deontological Tradition		Teleological Tradition

- *Deontological tradition*

  - Core belief: God is believed to be primarily Transcendent, separate from creation. A persistent image for those in this tradition is that of Orseme [1325-82] who described God as the great watchmaker who created the universe as a clock and then withdrew to let history unwind. In this view, God and/or Nature is seen as capricious and impersonal. Humans are powerless in the face of a predetermined destiny.

  - Manifestation: People in this tradition are often pessimistic idealists because they see the goal of life as recreating the ideal which is beyond us, but despair of actually being able to reach our goal. Plato's *Allegory of the Cave* presents the image of humans chained to a cave who see reality in flickering shadows. Plato asserts that we can free ourselves as we individually come to understand Truth. This individual change may lead, when necessary, to a radical reorganization of society. This theme of radical change is threaded through the writings of the idealists. Responsibility for facilitating change resides in the hands of the chosen enlightened leadership.

- *Teleological tradition*

  - Core belief: God is believed to be primarily Immanent, active in history and human affairs and can be partially known through reason. Humans are seen as being able to work with God and/or Nature in shaping our common destiny. People in this tradition often see themselves in conversation with God or Spirit as they choose how to live and shape community.

  - Manifestation: People in this tradition are often optimistic realists because they see the goal of life as creating heaven on earth. In theological language, the realists seek to usher in the "Reign of God" through appealing to the reasonableness of humans as they celebrate and embrace the sacred nature of each person. Responsibility for change resides in the hands and hearts of each person who lives out their birthright of sharing in the divine ideals.

State of Human Nature

The next conversation concerns the nature of humanity: are we essentially flawed or good? Our concept of the state of human nature determines what interventions we see as useful for assuring that individuals behave well and follow the norms of our community — rules to keep us in shape or relationships to guide us through love and respect. The point is well made in a cartoon which shows two school children giving each other a "high five." The boy tells the girl, "Wow! You only got an 'I'm disappointed in you.' I thought you were going to get punished!"

▶ *Deontological tradition*

▹ *<u>Core belief:</u>* Idealists believe that human beings are flawed and by ourselves we can do little to change that situation. As articulated by the Protestant reformers, the separation from God which comes from original sin can only be corrected by God's grace — which may or may not be given. Because even our minds are tinged with the stain of separation, reason is not useful in making us better persons.

Human Beings Are...	
Flawed (sinful)	Basically good (misguided)
so will respond to...	
rules to avoid punishment.	relationship to assure respect.
Deontological Tradition	Teleological Tradition

In the Evangelical Christian tradition, the antidote to the essential separation is being born again, signaling God's intervention in the human condition and the healing of the breach caused by original sin, the condition in which all are born. Humanists who believe in the flawed nature of humans find that a striking life experience may become a catalyst for change. Thus, those who unexpectedly experience discrimination may see that their beliefs about the differences among humans are not accurate and begin to work for change.

▹ *<u>Manifestation:</u>* Given that Idealists believe that change comes either through radical metamorphosis of belief or transforming experiences, people in this tradition tend to be pessimistic about the future of individuals and society. Because reason cannot be trusted to keep us on the straight and narrow, Idealists favor rules so all know what is expected. The threat of punishment keeps folks in line.

- ***Teleological tradition***

  - <u>*Core belief:*</u> Realists believe that humans are basically good. As articulated by Roman Catholic and liberal Protestant theologians, through reason and being in relationship with others who are good, we can learn how to be ethical persons. The notion is that because we desire to stay in relationship with those who are important to us, we will modify our behavior to stay in their good graces.

  - <u>*Manifestation:*</u> Because Realists believe that through reason we can determine the best way to live and imagine possibilities which enhance human existence, people in this tradition tend to be optimistic about individuals and society. "Agreeing to disagree" becomes their mantra as preserving relationships is important. Shame and the threat of exclusion from the community are used to keep people in line. We recognize someone in this tradition when to discipline us they sigh deeply and say, "I'm disappointed in you."

Relationship of Individuals to the Ideal

A persistent question in philosophy is whether we can achieve an ideal state on earth — whether we can find or create Nirvana or any of many other utopian visions on this earth or if we must wait until we enter another plane to find our ideal.

- ***Deontological tradition***

  - <u>*Core belief:*</u> Idealists do not see any possibility of creating "heaven on earth." Because we are separated from God by sin, we must escape this plane and go to another world to evade pain, selfishness, and greed. In one popular version, our life on earth is a dress-rehearsal for the real play, which will be heaven.

  - <u>*Manifestation:*</u> Idealists tend towards asceticism as they see this world and its gifts as inherently evil. The Puritan heritage of the United States which

The Ideal can be reached...

Only after death		On this earth
	so we should...	
work to minimize the effects of sin.		work to make the the world better.
Deontological Tradition		Teleological Tradition

historically has distrusted displays of opulence and expected people to not trust the experience of physical pleasure, calls us to live simply and not seek comfortable living. The money raised by one's effort goes back into the business or the community. Warren Buffett, a multi-millionaire, would be a contemporary example of the value of simplicity as he still lives modestly in his first home in Omaha, Nebraska.

- *Teleological tradition*
  - *Core belief:* Realists are committed to creating "heaven on earth." Because we have reason, we can choose to act in a way which will make this world a better place. Realists believe that compassion for others and imagining a better world will solve our problems.
  - *Manifestation:* Realists tend towards hedonism as they embrace the gifts of this world and expect people to enjoy them. Thus, the "good life" is to be celebrated, and the joys of good food, drink, and friends are to be savored. Because Realists believe that we can all work together to make this world a better place, they value signs of progress and change which enhance the lot of our lives together.

Condition of Human Society

Once we know the nature of the Deity, human beings, and our relationship to the Ideal, we determine the shape of our lives together, how we build community. With the deontological tradition we work to assure that we resist corruption, with the teleological we trust ourselves and others. This belief determines how we structure and interact with various social institutions.

- *Deontological tradition*
  - *Core belief:* Because God does not intervene in history and people are flawed, Idealists find human existence harsh and cruel. In Jewish and Christian thought, the primal separation began with God evicting Adam and Eve from

Human existence is...

Deontological Tradition	Teleological Tradition
Short and brutish	Fundamentally good
thus we should...	thus we should...
resist corrupting institutions.	calibrate evolving institutions.

the Garden of Eden and condemning them to live their lives weeping and toiling. In the words of Thomas Hobbes, unless we constantly strive to maintain the civilizing structures of community, life is "harsh, brutish, and short" as we are alienated from the sacred, ourselves, and each other.[6] Those who historians name as the protesters of history, from Martin Luther to Martin Luther King, Jr., have railed against corrupt institutions and demanded that leaders be held accountable for their actions or lose their legitimacy.

- *Manifestation:* As each of us is responsible for finding our own truth, Idealists favor autonomy and personal responsibility. Idealists, ironically, are also pessimists because they have little faith in humans. They ask us to evaluate the evidence, make our own choices about life, and then accept responsibility for the outcome. Idealists also value creativity and innovation. Because each of us has the potential for greatness, those who march to a different drummer are tolerated, and brilliant eccentrics are revered. However, a persistent question is drawing the line between individualism and anti-social behavior or insubordination.

- *Teleological tradition*

  - *Core belief:* Because God is active in history and we have reason, Realists believe that many of us can experience the good life. When recounting the creation stories, Realists emphasize that even though Adam and Eve disobeyed God, because people are created in the image of God, as we discover our true identity we can work together and fashion a world where all people can thrive. People in this tradition value change within existing structures rather than wholesale reform.

  - *Manifestation:* As truth is revealed in community, Realists favor trusting the wisdom of authority and tradition in determining how to live. Optimists by nature, Realists believe that we can come together and debate the issues and then agree to live by the ethical guidelines which emerge in that conversation. Because community is valued over individuals, change is tolerated within carefully constructed guidelines, and the loyal worker who mirrors the company values is venerated. A persistent question for this tradition is drawing the line between loyalty and mindless allegiance.

Given the limitations of human understanding, we can never conclusively prove which of these sets of core assumptions is true — and in fact "The Truth" may contain threads of both traditions. However, because we have to make choices in this world, each of us has a world view (either articulated or unarticulated) which informs our actions while we strive to get closer to "The Truth." Ultimately, each must take Soren Kierkegaard's proverbial "leap of faith" when reason alone cannot provide the "answers to life's persistent questions."[7]

The existentialists who wrote during the early 20th century and whose work provided important foundations for the postmodern movement claimed that, in the face of uncertainty, humans have a profound responsibility to determine truth for themselves. As Kierkegaard says, "It is the duty of the human understanding to understand that there are things which it cannot understand, and what those things are."[8] Though it sounds trite, as we wake each morning we each get to choose how best we will live that day. Acting in light of our best understandings, we set the trajectory for our lives together. Because civilization requires that we learn how to live together, we use our core beliefs as a foundation to establish governments, pass laws, and develop economic structures.

Role of Law and Government

From earliest civilization, people have codified the rules by which they agree to live and the punishments for their infractions. These statutes act as both carrot and stick, promising respect if one is seen as a good, law-abiding citizen and threatening punishment for violations of community norms.

▸ *Deontological tradition*

- <u>*Core belief:*</u> Idealists who embrace rationality see the law as necessary to keep us from destroying both ourselves and others. Because we cannot know the truth by reason, human law is a rough approximation of divine mandates which are revealed to us and the inspired leaders. Thus, even

Law Is...

Corrupted product of humans	Noble embodiment of civilization
so government should be...	
limited to provide safety.	expanded to provide opportunity.
Deontological Tradition	Teleological Tradition

though human law is a "corrupt product of human weakness and frail reason," law is needed to keep our selfish self-interest from leading us to "theft, lying, cruelty, and oppression."[9] Government, too, assists in keeping us in line by assuring that our base natures do not take over to the detriment of the community. The primary function of government is to assure the safety and well-being of individuals and to protect us from invasion.

- *Manifestation:* Idealists favor limited government because institutions are subject to being corrupted. Contracts are favored over governmental regulation so that people can choose the conditions under which they want to be bound. The law should be restricted to that which is necessary to keep greed and abuse in check. The government should only be able to marshal resources to guarantee individual safety and to keep the nation safe. Punishment is the primary vehicle for enforcing infractions and assuring that people follow the rules.

- *Teleological tradition*

  - *Core belief:* Realists embrace the notion of natural law, those precepts which are written on the conscience and consciousness of all humans. Because the law of God is imprinted in all humans, the true law can be discovered through reason. So the laws we have are the "noble embodiment of accumulated human wisdom [and put] diverse people under one rule of reason."[10] The American notion of fidelity to the rule of law, where we agree to follow the laws of the community without external coercion even if we disagree with them, flows from a commitment to the notion of natural law.[11] Government becomes the way that we organize our energies to assure the common good and monitor the distribution of resources.

  - *Manifestation:* Realists tend to see government as the way that the goods of the community can be given to all. The modern welfare state, which provides education, housing, shelter, and food to those without, is founded on the core belief of a strong government caring for the weaker members of the community. Given that Realists believe that people will not violate the law if they have sufficient education and resources, access to adequate assets is seen as the way to assure that people follow the community norms. Rehabilitation is the preferred method of intervention after a member violates the law.

Private and Common Property

The proper use of personal property and land is an ongoing conversation in economics and law. The right to develop property for personal gain is in tension with preserving and caring for/conserving that which is held in common for the benefit of all. Protection of private property undergirds capitalism and the market economy. Without Adam Smith's notion of creating wealth by adding labor and creativity to raw materials, our world would be very different. Yet, as we face environmental deterioration, we know that no one really owns water or air. Deeds cannot keep water in aquifers and air pollution does not stop at property lines.

▸ *Deontological tradition*

- ▹ <u>*Core belief:*</u> Idealists believe that private property is necessary to keep us from quarreling amongst ourselves. However, people should not accumulate property for self-aggrandizement, rather they should live simply and avoid excesses of human pleasure. Ironically, Calvinism threw a weird twist into the conversation. John Calvin and his successors taught that since we cannot know if we are "saved," one marker of being part of the "elect" is financial success in the world. However, *enjoying* the wealth is suspect. Thus, one should give away one's wealth to the community in the form of charity. The early Puritans also had a bias against people inheriting property as each was to show his or her mettle alone. The Protestant work ethic which infuses the American ethos states that one is to work diligently to assure salvation but live simply because the world and its riches are tainted.[12]

- ▹ <u>*Manifestation:*</u> Because government is corrupt, it cannot be trusted with either the care of wealth or its distribution. Given that wealth and private property are the result of individual hard work, Idealists believe that we should be able to control our own wealth and property. Those who want wealth should

Private Property Is...

Necessary for peace	Instrument of progress
so individuals should	
be able to accumulate wealth and control its use and distribution.	be encouraged to share wealth and be a good steward for all.
Deontological Tradition	Teleological Tradition

work hard to earn it, especially in a land where each of us has permission to make our own way. While the tenets of Calvinism no longer hold sway as they did at the founding of our country, this core belief is the source of the deep distrust of material wealth that has marked much of the history of the United States.

- *Teleological tradition:*
  - *Core belief:* Realists believe that private property should be used as an instrument for a better life for the community as a whole. As people care for their property and use it to increase wealth, all members of society can benefit. As people seek to increase their wealth through enlightened self-interest, we can move from scarcity to satisfaction.
  - *Manifestation:* Because wealth comes through the efforts of many, not just one, Realists assert that private property is to be shared for the common good. Community efforts such as parks, national forests, roads open to all, health care and public schools benefit the entire community as we share our resources through taxation and redistribution of wealth. All persons who are part of the community should have an opportunity to share in the good life. Thus, people in this tradition favor pooling wealth to protect and sustain the common good.

Historically, we have believed that our country is well served with a strong middle class and few very wealthy or very poor citizens. Thus, our laws encourage individuals to earn as much money as possible, but wealth is taxed upon death to put the resources back into the society for the next generation. The current conversations about the "death tax," the abolition of which would be grounded in the right of people upon death to give all of their wealth to their children, challenge this world view. Also, with the erosion of labor unions and the growth of two-income professional families, current economic policies lead to a strengthening of the upper class, a diminishing of the middle class, a growing lower class and, and increasing poverty.[13]

Self-interest and the Poor

The last set of core beliefs which helps us make sense of our assumptions about business and economics concerns the role of self-interest and the poor. Our ideas about working conditions, wages, distribution of wealth, and the role of government or other institutions to assure a fair sharing of resources flow from our ideas about personal responsibility in community.

- *Deontological tradition*
  - *Core belief:* Because we are each to work out our own salvation, and because we are supposed to be able to tell whether we are in God's graces by our economic well being, those who do not do well financially just need to work harder and improve themselves.[14] Because individuals are responsible for their own well-being, any lack is due to their own choices, not systemic problems in distribution of wealth and opportunities to gain it. Individual charity is the best way to deal with poverty. Thus, we can choose who deserves help and who does not.
  - *Manifestation:* Idealists have little sympathy for idleness and sloth. Those who are poor get what they deserve for not applying themselves. Charles Dickens' Scrooge caricatures this attitude as he says to the Christmas Ghost when confronted with his miserliness in paying wages, "Are there no poor-houses?"[15] The current debate about a minimum wage versus a living wage highlights the tension inherent in this value. Idealists tend to believe that the minimum wage is a more than satisfactory beginning point. People in this group tend to believe that if people want to have more money and greater resources, they should improve their skills and work harder and that the economic system will expand to accommodate their diligence.
- *Teleological tradition*
  - *Core belief:* Realists have an empathetic view toward the poor. Aware of the differences in ability and distribution of resources which are an accident of birth, theorists in this tradition assert that we have an obligation to help the poor by working to change the systems which create and sustain poverty.
  - *Manifestation:* Realists value systems which assure that all have an opportunity to share the "goodies" of the community.

The Poor...

Get what they deserve	Are unfortunate
and thus we have...	
no obligation to help.	an obligation to help systematically.
Deontological Tradition	Teleological Tradition

They believe that the government should intervene to assure that those with wealth and power do not take advantage of those without power or privilege. Citing the imbalance of power between employers and employees, this tradition asserts that those who work should be paid appropriately, not the lowest wage possible. Realists were the primary movers behind the labor revolution in the late 19th and early 20th centuries, resulting in the right to collective bargaining and improved work conditions. Realists also provided the impetus behind the Civil Rights Movement which resulted in the passage of Title VII, The Civil Rights Act in 1964. Those currently arguing for a living wage for all workers and holding owners of businesses accountable for work conditions tend to be part of this tradition.

This very brief overview of the core beliefs and how they manifest illumines the source of the debates about business ethics and public policy. Different people and varying groups have divergent ideas about life. Our core beliefs define what we consider to be ethical behavior. Our core convictions determine how we define justice, that which we are convinced is required for fundamental fairness in the larger business and political arenas. Yet in spite of all these differences, we are supposed to live and work together with some semblance of harmony.

Implications for Ethics and Public Policy

Over the past several decades, we have seen vitriolic policy debates about what are proper business ethics as well as about the correct government response. These discussions generate much heat but little light. To the degree that we can not figure out ways to honor the beliefs of those with whom we disagree and we do not want to be seen as waffling on the topics, we position ourselves near the ends of the political continuum and proclaim our positions as the truth. In the process we lose the ability to find meaningful solutions which incorporate the strengths while ameliorating the weaknesses of our positions.

Our Community Should Emphasize...

Independence		Interdependence
	which means that we are...	
egalitarian and admit people based on merit alone.		hierarchal and admit people based on birth and/or belief.
Deontological Tradition		Teleological Tradition

The policy debate about access to jobs and education highlights such differences well. Those who favor independence believe we should follow the rules and hire people based on merit, considering only whether they have job skills that we need and thus are the best persons for the job. For example, this group of people believe we should admit young people into universities based on their proven ability (grades) or potential (test scores). Those who favor interdependence believe we should admit young people into top schools based on birth (being the child of a graduate, or a "legacy admittee") or belief (assuring that people ascribe to a set of principles).

Another difficulty comes when we want to use merit for one category of people (women and minorities) and prerogative of birth for a second category (our own children). We risk being at best schizophrenic or at worst hypocritical and selfish. A similar conundrum is seen in the current debate about non-documented workers. Because they are not admitted through the formal processes of immigration law, they are not given legitimate social status. Yet, using our market power we hire them to do our work while simultaneously denying them both the protection of the law which would come with legal status and the protection of the community which would come with belonging.

A next logical question becomes the right use and regulation of community resources. Those who tilt toward the neo-mercantile side believe that since private property needs to be in the hands of individuals who can use it as they wish, our taxing policies should be designed to transfer wealth only for national security. Thus, tax incentives which protect business, particularly industry and agriculture, are permissible. Because government structures can not be trusted, we should have as few regulations as possible.

Those who tilt toward social democracy assert that we need to assure that children, and by extension their families, need food, shelter, health care, and education. They believe our resources should be transferred to provide these building blocks of opportunity. Further, we need regulation to prevent the abuse of power by individuals seeking to maximize their own self-interest.

Our Government Should Tilt Toward...

Neo-mercantile	Social Democracy
so that resources are transferred	
to provide security for the community to enhance autonomy.	to provide opportunity for individuals to enhance equality.
Deontological Tradition	Teleological Tradition

As we now seek to make sense out of a global economy, another set of priorities appears. The conversation which is played out in the domestic arena is replayed on the global stage. Those who favor independence believe that companies can make whatever agreements they want with other companies and/or individuals in the global economy. If people choose to work for a few cents a day, that is their prerogative; if they do not choose individually to bargain for decent work conditions, that is their choice. Those who favor interdependence look more carefully at a balance of power and assert that those of us with greater market power need to attend to the common good of those in other communities as well.

Global Relationships Should Emphasize...	
Independence	Interdependence
with agreements that assure	
individual agreements with companies.	inclusive considerations for the people in the countries.
Deontological Tradition	Teleological Tradition

The final, and in fact the most difficult conversation, requires that we sort out our relationship to our Mother — the earth. Historically, we were exhorted to use and exploit our natural resources to create wealth. Because we want to have access to inexpensive oil, we find ways to drill on national parks and in the wilderness. Because we see a better life created by individual homes on the desert, we divert water from our rivers. Because we love nature, we build our homes on the edge of the national forests and complain about fire. But mostly, because the danger does not seem real, we do not restrain our own desires to assure that our children will have resources for their lives.

When the earth seemed huge and the supplies unlimited, these policies made sense. However, we now know that resources are not limitless. We know that our earth is fragile, and we are responsible for our planet. While young people may disagree on other areas of public policy, those under thirty often agree on environmental policy. Those who see themselves as staunch political and fiscal conservatives have questions about global warming and the politics of drilling in the Arctic. They are also clear that

We Should Encourage The...	
Use of natural resources	Conservation of natural resources
to assure that...	
individuals have resources to create wealth and thrive.	the planet is left intact for our children and grandchildren.
Deontological Tradition	Teleological Tradition

the intertwined policies of enhanced production to build healthy, growing businesses and patterns of unrestrained personal consumption contribute to the problem. Because many have the niggling thought that we must completely revamp our assumptions for politics, economics, and business in order to address the ecological problems, people are increasingly willing to set aside closely held ideas to find imaginative or creative solutions.

Interestingly a new movement is beginning, environmental peacemaking. Across the globe, "hostile countries that share borders are working together to save their common environments."[16] Because the stakes are high, countries are learning to cooperate to solve problems from jellyfish that are taking over the Caspian Sea to peace parks which are "created in transboundary areas with ecological significance" such as the Cordillera del Condor Peace Transborder Reserve in a section of rain forest between Peru and Ecuador.[17] This thoughtful humility allows for innovative local answers to environmental problems.

The Excluded Middle

As long as the task is seen as finding the right answers, the debate will continue endlessly. If the postmodern theorists are right and reason will never provide a definitive answer, the only resolution would seem to be radical relativism, where each of us gets to choose knowing that we do not have any provable criteria for determining what is good or better. However, that resolution does not bring comfort either. Many assert that the problem with the 1990s was a lack of guidelines so that greed was able to have its day to the detriment of many of those without power. In their heart of hearts, many know that mindless relativism will not solve the problems of a global economy or environmental deterioration.

From Answers to Questions

As the postmodern debate matured, the existentialists demonstrated that all we know is our own existence, which takes us to nihilism — the doctrine that all is pointless and absurd.[18] The Phenomenologists focused on the role of language in shaping our understanding and experience of the world. Because reality can only be known through the concepts and the words we choose, everything depends on language and individual interpretation, at which point any shared understanding seems impossible.[19] While the academic case made for existentialism and phenomenology is persuasive, they do not offer much hope to those trying to practice applied ethics.

Some ethicists, to escape the conundrum of trying to find foundations for ethical action when the pillars of the temple melted into unfathomable muck, acknowledged that the bulwarks of truth were contested and then chose to pretend that the dissolved foundations were in fact essential for coherent ethical analysis.[20] However, that approach is not very satisfactory either. We cannot learn how to live with contingent truth (the best that we know now) and constructed reality (individuals contextualizing their own lives) by pretending that the foundations for Truth are at best, unknowable or, at worst, illusory.

Another set of theorists, whom some call constructive postmodernists, sought a systemic and holistic way to move out of the box of rationalism (the use of reason to find ultimate truth), and foundationalism (the use of texts or theories to ascertain ultimate truth).[21] These theorists found that to make sense of our current knowledge, we had to move beyond reason to include emotions which give us empathy, and spirit which impels humans to transcend the limitations of our narrow, often selfish, thinking. We had to find ways to synthesize the right-brain, external understanding of the world with the left-brain, internal understanding of the self.[22] We had to find a way to neutralize the belief that reason was the territory of strong, rational men while emotions was the purview of soft, illogical women. We needed both an ethic of reason and an ethic of care.[23]

This task has emerged in the United States during the last half of the twentieth century. For about the first two-hundred years of our existence, Americans had what Robert Wuthnow calls the unitary self. We did not have to worry about sorting through our core beliefs to know who we were because we were born into a family and culture which had firmly established religious and political beliefs.[24] Those beliefs provided the foundations for our morals and the religious institutions reinforced our ethics. Because everyone participated in a religious community, even if nominally, the church was the location for teaching morals and ethics. In tightly knit communities, the values were monolithic and minimally contested.

Since the 1960s the foundations of the monolithic traditions have been challenged. People are exploring wide varieties of traditions and becoming, what some pundits call, "cafeteria believers," taking morsels from many philosophical and religious traditions and practices to put together a syncretic meal of personal beliefs from which to act. This exploration makes perfect sense in the postmodern world where we have the privilege and responsibility of constructing our own reality. The result is the creation of what Wuthnow calls a "dispersed self...whose being is defined in a wide variety of encounters and experiences, including moments of interaction with sacred objects, such as trees and automobiles"[25] Thus, we not only have to determine our place in the world, but we also have to construct ourselves — to determine who we are and work out what behaviors are important, while finding meaning for both our personal and professional lives.

Feminist philosophers such as Carol Gillian, Adrien Rich, Norma Haan, and Sandra Harding began exploring the disconnect between an ethic of reason which focused on rules, and an ethic of care which focused on relationship. The gauntlet of the postmodern challenge was also taken up by theologians such as Lonergan, who as a constructive postmodernist rejected the course of nihilism and phenomenology to chart a more promising passageway through the treacherous waters of radical relativism.

What Lonergan proposed was that we not focus on trying to agree on the Truth with a capital "T" but rather asserted that all knowledge is contested. His solution was to change the perspective: we can ask *good questions* rather than focus on *right answers*. Lonergan stated that all human beings have an "unrestricted desire to know" which manifests in our trying to make sense out of that which does not make sense. He claimed that we can discern between good and better, and that in fact we have that responsibility as humans. If Lonergan is right, then rather than trying to decide between the two traditions, we can use the wisdom of both traditions. Instead of fixating on either-or, we can approach the problems with a both-and approach which includes the excluded middle of dualism. As we ask questions together, we may not find the Answer, but we may discover better answers.[26]

Conclusion

After hearing the litany of differences described in this chapter, many people assert that the way to harmony is to resist being placed in neat categories or boxes. Practical experience teaches that many in fact use a blend of the ideas of both traditions in making ethical decisions. As we attend to our world, we can see that from the smallest unit of community, the family, to the largest nation-state, multi-national corporation, or multi-national association, the culture of these units is determined by the overall world view, the sum total of the core beliefs held by the individuals and institutions which are involved. We also know that those core beliefs are multi-faceted, and thus we resist one-dimensional answers or solutions to complex dilemmas.

By asking questions, we see the implications of each position. We also see that each tradition has some truth and, if taken to excess, problems. By not being overly attached to our positions, we seek the balance found in a well strung loom where both the warp and the weft are maintained in perfect tension, and find better answers. With this insight, as we weave the tapestry of our life, we hold in tension the truths of both traditions as we define our individual core beliefs and those held by the various communities in which we live and work.

As individuals assess situations and choose courses of action, they have the opportunity to hold in balance the prerogatives of individuals against the claims of the community. Faced with choices, people learn to look at the dilemma from as many angles as possible to discern the best answer. As one person described it, rather than thinking in terms of taking positions at the ends of a teeter-totter, we can think of the process as assuring that the compact disk is balanced so it can play. Thus, our reason (our heads) can be informed by our emotions (our hearts). Then both can be balanced in the crucible of spirituality so that we intentionally and compassionately work together. In the process we come to know when to use stepping stone policies and when to use safety net policies so all members of our global community can thrive.

Continuing the Conversation

1. As you reflect on your own belief system, see if you can locate your place along the various continuua which are part of this chapter. What are your core beliefs in each of the areas? Do you see yourself advocating consistency in how you expect yourself to navigate through this world and in the policies you advocate in both private and public settings?

2. How are your beliefs the same or different from those of your parents? How is your world view different from that of your parents or birth community? What knowledge and/or experience have caused those changes?

3. Find an article in your local paper or a news magazine which deals with a current ethical situation. Does the article give the positions of both traditions? If not, which position is articulated? Are the reasons given for embracing a particular position clearly stated or are they inferred?

4. Read several articles about a current ethical problem or public policy debate. Write two op ed pieces for a local paper. For one piece use the lens of the deontological tradition for both identifying the reasons for the problem and for fashioning a solution. Write the second piece with the lens of the teleological tradition. Which one was easier? Which one do you find more persuasive? How did you address the concerns of the other tradition in the process? Did you find yourself taking a middle ground to address the assumptions of both traditions?

Applying Lonergan's Method
(Part 1)

Be Attentive

- *Identify the actor*
- *Determine the stakeholders*
- *Attend to the context*

Be Intelligent

- *Pinpoint the issue*
- *Explore values in conflict*
- *Identify options for action*

"Cheshire-Puss," she began, "Would you tell me please, which way I ought to go from here?"

"That depends a good deal on where you want to get to," said the Cat.

"I don't much care where — ," said Alice.

"Then it doesn't matter which way you go," said the Cat.

Lewis Carroll[1]

Chapter 4

Foundations for Decision-Making

Most of us give little attention to the strategies we use to make ethical decisions. Relying on habit, we do not seem to consider that effective decision-making requires thoughtfulness on two fronts. We first need to explore what process we should use to resolve our thorny problems. We then need to ask what criteria should be applied to determine what actions are or are not ethical. Using undeveloped tools of reason and emotion, we hone our instincts as children while being socialized by our parents. Our nascent awareness of ethics gives each of us a rough sense of right and wrong.

Even though our embryonic principles or rules of good behavior are usually inadequate for the task, we often use our childhood norms as touchstones when we make complex decisions in a rapidly changing world. Then, when we find ourselves in a surreal environment where no one appears to be behaving in ethical ways, we feel like Alice — we are not sure where we want to go and we do not know if we can get there.

Making effective ethical decisions requires the use of strategies as precise as any other rigorous investigation for truth. Over the past two hundred years, those seeking better answers to difficult questions developed methods of critical analysis. These processes not only unlocked the mysteries of the earth but also assisted in studying the wonders of individuals, communities, and culture. Using the same tools of critical analysis as the scientists, philosophers and theologians strove to identify the criteria for norms — the principles and goals — which must be followed if we want to be ethical persons. Even though these scholars ultimately could establish neither foundations for a universal set of norms nor standard criteria by which the norms should be prioritized, the questions they asked and the world they envisioned help all of us to become more thoughtful ethical agents. As we learn to habitually exercise the tools of science which philosophers use to explore and explicate key principles and goals, each of us becomes better equipped to be an ethical person-in-community"

Becoming an effective decision maker requires practice. A learner-centered approach to ethics encourages participants to use the four step process articulated by Lonergan along with at least two of the four different ethical lenses. This chapter presents the first two steps which help frame the problem. The next chapter discusses the final steps in which the decision is made. Together these two chapters provide an effective process for making hard choices in a complex world.

Step 1 Be Attentive: Consider What Works — or Doesn't

The first task we have as decision makers is to relax, step back, and notice all of the wonderful and not so wonderful things in our world. To navigate the certainties and uncertainties of life, we look at our world, examine the received teachings about our physical home, and begin to ask "what if." Often questions arise because the traditional explanations do not provide adequate answers for what we know or experience. We might have new information or notice that the offered interpretation does not match our experience.

Every new idea that we embrace impels us to action. Every action has both intended (those we desired) and unintended outcomes as well as expected (those we anticipated) and unexpected results. We note what happens, see what pieces of the puzzle fall into place and which ones still have not found a home in the picture — and continue with the next question. When we get an insight, when the pieces of the puzzle that did not fit suddenly do, we see order emerge from the seeming chaos. Thus, as when running through a field of thistles, to avoid the prickles we need to attend to our own world view as well as the details of the particular problem before us, ever watching for the unexpected sticklers.

Attending to Our Own World View

Our personal journey begins as we are born into a community and learn how to negotiate in this world through the received wisdom of our elders. While learning how to think and speak as toddlers, we also absorb our parents' understanding of the world. We learn how to communicate, and, more importantly, we learn to identify what, according to our parents, is real and what is not real as we make sense of the physical world. Part of the task of becoming an adult is reevaluating the truths our parents taught to assure that our perceptions are not clouded by their biases. The Peter, Paul, and Mary classic *Puff, the Magic Dragon* is poignant for we each remember when our magic dragons were sent away and we had learn to deal with another level of reality.

The first exile happens with our shift into the literal world of seven- and eight-year-olds when our pretend friends were permanently sent to camp. The more difficult transition is to critically examine what we were taught by our families and community. From time to time we need to banish some of the comfortable prejudices that we inherited from our birth families. People who are raised with racism may have to learn that people from different ethnic groups are no better nor worse than themselves. People who are raised believing that a particular religious truth is the only way, may have to learn that other faiths have elements of truth. For many, sorting out their inherited beliefs is a difficult but liberating process. Many of the beliefs may be reclaimed, but only after thoughtful consideration.

The interests and beliefs of our biological family also open doors in this marvelous, opportunity-rich world. One family may value the arts, so the children are introduced to music at a very early age and encouraged to develop their talents in that arena. Music and literature set the trajectory for their careers. Another family may teach their children how to look at the physical world carefully and critically.

Biology, ecology, and attention to detail prime them to become scientists. Those early years bend the twig and establish the shape for growth.

Because we build on the knowledge and experience of our families and the information available when we were born, each generation has a different understanding of the world. People born on the threshold of the Great Depression have a fear and respect for scarcity which is different from the expectation of abundance that Baby Boomers take for granted. Those who fought for racial and gender equality are hyper-sensitive to individual and systemic discrimination. Those born after the anti-discrimination laws were well implemented expect that people in the workplace will be rewarded according to competence not by the privilege of race or gender. As we grow to adulthood, we are profoundly molded by our family and our culture.

Our world view includes an understanding of ethics — how to live as a person-in-community with others. We, the children of each generation, accept the ideas of the elders as a given. Then we identify the next set of problems and seek solutions to situations that our parents just accepted as what is and cannot be changed. At some point, every generation questions the received wisdom and world views of their forebears. We begin to determine, both as individuals and as societies, whether what we were told about ourselves, others, and the world in fact matches our experience and understanding. For example, we may ask whether one economic or political system is really that much better than another. We may wonder whether acting only in our own self-interest without considering the environment or other people really makes sense.

The dance which forms a person-in-community unfolds in an intricate set of if-then steps. We say, "if this is true ... then this should follow." When we note that our expected result does not follow, we have questions. Why is this result different? What else do I need to know? What am I not seeing clearly? Is the explanation that I've been given for the state of the world really true? Like Hansel and Gretel, we begin to follow the crumbs of insight, hoping to find our way to a home where all makes sense.

> **Received Wisdom about Ethics**
>
> If one properly reflects and is trained, one right answer will emerge as the correct ethical answer in a given situation.

As we walk the path attentively, we learn to ask, what about our life is not working? What explanations of our world do not make sense? When a new idea appears, we consider whether it is worthy of adoption. As individuals and their community test new concepts, we learn whether our notions are grounded in some sense of truth. Once we get preliminary answers, we ask whether we are willing to change our world view, to follow our dreams based on new data. A pitfall would be to get stuck in a romanticized but inaccurate version of reality and not embrace new opportunities.

Evaluating Received Wisdom

If with reflection and training one right answer will emerge, then we should not have so many differences of opinion and approach to ethical issues
Why the differences?

A final question we ask is "what difference would it make for us to accept this new idea?" The difference can be in our understanding of ourselves, our knowledge of science or society, or in the action that might be required. Given that our sense of ourself and our world is shaped by the beliefs we hold, the new ideas can be terrifying, exhilarating — or both. Like parasailing over the ocean, adopting new ideas and choosing a new trajectory for life — embracing a new world view — gives us an expanded and slightly scary vantage from which to observe and enjoy life.

Working through ethical problems with others helps us identify our own ethical world view, our core beliefs and core commitments. Core beliefs are those ideas which structure our understanding of ourselves and our world. Core commitments are beliefs which are held with passion and compel us to action. As we become skilled at ethical decision-making, we come to terms with our complex world. Thus, we learn how to be true to our own commitments and beliefs, while understanding that they are provisional — at best, all we know at the time. At the same time we strive to effectively work with others who hold different beliefs and commitments, learning from them as we share the best of our knowledge of the world.

New Ideas

What if multiple ways of doing ethics were equally valid depending on one's vision of a good life and one's understanding of the person-in-community?

How can the community accept many different views without having all of ethics devolve into nothing more than egoistic preference instead of common truths?

What change is needed in our understanding of people and business to adequately balance the desires and needs of individuals against the desires and needs of the community?

Embracing a cycle of tension and resolution, the hallmark of mature ethical decision-making, helps us to live peacefully and effectively as a person-in-community. As we become comfortable with the uncertainties of life, we can feel secure in the process of the continuous improvement of our belief system, and celebrate the idea that all of the world is seen and constructed through our personal world view. Taking up the challenge of noticing just how we construct our world, we can enjoy the habit of paying attention rather than avoiding truly seeing just because we are afraid that new information might threaten us. We learn to attend to our environment, committed to seeing that which we do not expect and noticing that which we may not want to see.

Given that we tend to interpret the events in our life to enhance our own vision of the world, and given that all of us want to see ourselves as ethical, we must make sure that our vision is clear. Those who find themselves in a world where the goal is to acquire as many material toys as possible are particularly susceptible to flawed vision. Focusing on the material world, they tend to ignore the spiritual realm which emphasizes mindfulness and humility. Cultivating the habit of awareness helps us carefully ask questions, seek answers, and consider our own biases. To be effective ethical agents, we need to develop our ethical sensibilities — recognizing when either our own or the community's core values are in conflict. As we become more attentive to the ethical values which are held individually and by members of our community, we can make more effective decisions.

All philosophers as well as spiritual teachers caution that we must examine our own selves with as much thoughtfulness as we do the world around us. What are our motives, our goals? What are our fears, our weaknesses? The temptation for each of us is to interpret the world around us — and to make ourselves right. Learning to give up our attachment to being right in order to build and support an effective organization, requires thought and commitment. In fact, giving up our attachment to being right and to promoting ourselves is the most difficult task of ethical decision-making. Often we would rather face failure than admit that we are wrong.

Many of us are like the characters in the classic movie *The War of the Roses* where the husband and wife, in the middle of a nasty divorce, refuse to compromise, preferring to die together swinging on a chandelier. Many a company has gone bankrupt because the owners were more concerned about being right, amassing personal fortune, and exercising privilege than being a responsible steward of the stakeholders' resources. Many employees have been fired because of their attachment to doing a job in a particular way rather than seeing where they could, with integrity, do the work as instructed.

As we practice the discipline of awareness, of paying attention, we must learn to tell the truth about ourselves, others, and the situation itself.

Analytic Elements of Step 1 — Pay Attention

As we frame ethical questions, three preliminary tasks set the parameters of the problem: (1) identify the ethical agent and the situation; (2) determine the stakeholders; and (3) attend to the context of the problem. These steps resemble gathering all of the ingredients before starting to cook a meal. As more care is given to the preparatory stages, the cooking itself becomes pleasurable and less frenetic, which results in a delectable dinner when the process is complete. If the role of the ethical actor is not clearly delineated, then someone may be charged with making a decision who does not have the authority. If the stakeholders are not correctly named, essential constituents may be overlooked. Finally, if facts of the context are ignored, the answer may be incomplete or incorrect.

► *Who is the ethical actor?*

Every ethical decision has someone or some organization responsible for carrying out the action. The temptation is to look at the ethical act either in a vacuum or from an omniscient point of view. However, people and organizations make decisions in particular places and times which affect specific sets of persons. Those people and organizations never have full information about the consequences of their choices and are limited by their knowledge and their best predictions about the results of their choices. Thus, ethical agents must place the problem in the context of their own information and belief systems. Ethical decisions are always contextual: they are made in light of the ethical actor's understanding of the culture, expectations of society, and the actor's own sense of what is right or wrong in a given situation.

In identifying the ethical actor, we must attend to who has the authority to act. From time to time, sending the decision to another desk is important. If the person confronting the problem does not have the proper authority, then consulting an ethics committee or sending the

> Be Attentive
>
> - Identify the ethical actor
> - Determine the stakeholders
> - Attend to the context

issue to a supervisor may be appropriate. At that point, the person referring the problem is not making an ethical decision but rather a managerial one. After consulting with the appropriate stakeholders, the final ethical decision needs to be made by a person with the authority to choose a course of action.

▸ *Who are the stakeholders in this conflict?*

All ethical decisions are relational, because varying parties are directly affected by the choice. Thus, the next step is to identify the stakeholders. Be sure to include those who have to carry out the decision, those directly affected by the decision, and those whose interests are to be protected. We need to be remember that Monday morning quarter-backing by members of the organization and the community accompanies any important ethical decision. As such, if we do not have the buy-in of the core stakeholders, then the right action may be ignored or subverted. Thus the context into which the decision will play out and the potential response of stakeholders in the community are always factors in the strategy.

Lynn Sharp Paine, in *Value Shift,* reminds us that every problem has four different tiers of stakeholders who are impacted by the choices of the organization and who have interests in the decision.[2] In considering all levels of stakeholders, we determine who will be impacted by a decision and decide who has a legitimate claim to celebrate or critique the organization's actions. As we discipline ourselves to identify all tiers of interested parties, we can tune our social antennae. While the claims of all stakeholders may not be equal, all must be considered.

During the last half of the 20th century, a shareholder theory of management emerged. That theory asserts that shareholders and owners are the only stakeholders with a direct interest in the ethical acts of the company's agents, and thus are the only interests to be considered. The belief is that the financial interests of these stakeholders should never be compromised by the ethical decisions of leadership. One weakness of this theory is that historically those who own shares in a company do not exercise control over the operations but vote with their feet by selling their stock when they do not like what a company is doing.

That trend is changing as large pension funds have started to exercise more control by pressuring boards of directors to take action. A recent example is the California State Teachers Retirement System (CalSTRS), the third largest pension fund in the United States, joining with others to force Michael Eisner,

President and CEO of the Disney Corporation, to shed some of his leadership role in the Disney Corporation. CalSTRS also recommended that the investors form a committee to hold Disney accountable for the changes.[3]

> **Stakeholders**
>
> Tier 1: Shareholders
> Tier 2: Employees and customers
> Tier 3: Competitors and vendors
> Tier 4: Interested community members

Finding the shareholder theory inadequate because the interests of the employees and other constituents were often shortchanged, theorists offered a stakeholder theory of management. This theory posits that, to assure the financial and ethical health of the firm, the ethical agent must consider all stakeholders in the decision. The first tier of stakeholders is the shareholders, those whose financial investment and ownership in the company will be directly impacted by the ethical acts of leadership and other employees. The second tier includes those immediately impacted by a company decision, including employees, customers, and suppliers. The third tier lists constituents such as competitors and vendors.

The final tier addresses the concerns of the larger community which may be affected (for example by a company's labor or environmental policies). Those in the final tier may not be directly impacted by the decision but may have persuasive power in the community. As these fourth tier constituents clearly articulate their concerns, they may impact policy. For example, a person may care about whether a particular company uses child labor in Asia. If that person is not employed by the company, does not own stock in the company, and does not buy the company's products, the policy may not have any direct personal impact. However, as Nike and others learned the hard way when the movement against sweatshops brought the issues to the forefront, a group of people who care passionately about a situation can force change. Companies therefore must be responsive to changing community expectations about acceptable corporate behavior.[4] A company's policies toward community constituents fall under the rubric of Corporate Social Responsibility.

While considering the constituents, we need to also consider the role of these groups. For example, a legislative body or administrative agency might represent its own interest or it might be charged with representing the interest of the community as a whole. Thus, if the legislature is a constituent, we need to determine whether it is acting on behalf of itself or if it represents the people in the community. We should also look at the role of the persons involved because someone might represent the interests of another, such as an advocate or a formal agent.

▶ *What are the facts of the situation?*

Finally, ethical decisions require rationality. As people consider ethical questions, each person brings different information and assumptions to the conversation. The facts which are present, the context in which those facts are placed, and the assumptions of the ethical agent determine the way the problem is both approached and solved. We need to determine what biases we have in the framing of ethical problems. A careful description of the facts of the situation is crucial. Thus, we must make every effort not to prejudge the situation but use language which is as value neutral as possible. Thus, the words should be descriptive (*e.g.,* a table; a policy; a person) rather than normative (*e.g.,* an old, decrepit table; a selfish, self-serving policy; a thoughtful, altruistic person). By using value-neutral language, we avoid the temptation to use emotion-laden words to bias the result. While all of ethics is ultimately subjective, we can have controlled subjectivity by being as objective as possible in defining the problem.

The context provides an eagle's eye view of the problem where details can be clearly seen. A brief description of the situation's history is useful. What are the relationships, the expectations of the primary players? Exploring the various approaches to the problem and the concerns of those who are part of the decision may help clarify the primary conflicts. Again, as practical ethics always require application of abstract ideas to specific situations, we should make the description of the context complete enough to give us a sense of the problem at hand but brief enough that the reader will not be overwhelmed with extraneous details.

In describing the situation, we must always acknowledge that our world view is both limited in information and colored by our own closely held values and perceptions. In framing the question, talking with others can assist us in widening our world view. We also need to notice that different facts will be important depending on the ethical lens we choose. The essential elements of the context are contingent on the information needed to investigate a problem using a particular lens. As we get clarity about the contours of a problem, we begin to see the way that ethical beliefs both join and divide a group. These biases may be because of personal experience (surviving the

Holocaust), particular knowledge (training as an accountant), or personal weakness (tending to see everything as a personal threat to well being).

Step 2 — Be Intelligent: Sort Through the Data

As we learn to pay attention to the world around us, we must begin to sort through the data. We begin the process by being intelligent — working to understand what we see, expressing what we believe to be true, and considering the implications of our knowledge.[5] Being intelligent involves not only attending to our own world view but also being sensitive to the values of others as well as cultural and community expectations. Being aware requires that we listen to other voices and explore a variety of experiences to move beyond our own, always limited, world view. As we engage in this phase, three questions will help us intelligently explore the ethical question so the best decision can emerge.

> **Be Intelligent**
>
> - Pinpoint the issue
> - Explore values-in-conflict
> - Identify options for action

First, we ask about the issue, the specific dilemma which must be resolved. Next we ask what core values are in conflict. The tricky part of working through an ethical analysis is identifying the core values and seeing how they are in tension with each other. A good resolution involves fashioning a solution which addresses the underlying concerns associated with the core values. This requires that we find ways to honor conflicting values rather than devolving into polarization. Ethical dilemmas are problems because two or more equally good values are in conflict. The temptation is to give only one priority rather than trying to harmonize them. Finally, we must ask about the options for action. Often this step requires thinking imaginatively or creatively about multiple possibilities, rather than simply doing what has been done before.

Pinpointing the Ethical Issue

Framing the ethical issue involves two distinct phases. The first is determining whether the problem at hand is in fact an ethical issue. We need to distinguish among technical questions, aesthetic preferences, and true ethical issues. The second phase is to frame the question precisely to highlight the conflict.

Framing an ethical problem as a question to be answered is very useful. As discussed previously, we must make sure that the problem is not a technical question (how to best accomplish this goal) or an aesthetic question (what are my preferences in getting this task finished). As the most important part of any analysis is the way the question is asked, we must carefully select the language of the problem. The process involves both individual assessment of the conflict as well as the communal process of checking with others to assure that we are seeing the problem correctly.

► *Is this an ethical question?*

Gordon Kaufman in his book *In Face of Mystery: A Constructive Approach to Theology* presents an elegant construct for determining whether an ethical issue exists.[6] Kaufman notes that for most of our lives we are unaware, acting out of habit and instinct. Then something happens which disrupts the flow of action: something is not quite right, and we have to make a decision about what to do.

One kind of decision Kaufman calls expedient reflection. This kind of thought is concerned with choosing the action that will promote a specific goal and discerning the best technique for accomplishing that goal. A nurse who is to give inoculations needs to be technically competent so that patients do not pass out from fear or suffer through clumsy work. Similarly, accountants need to know the rules of GAAP (generally accepted accounting principles) if they are going to competently complete an audit of a company.

Another kind of decision involves aesthetic reflection. For this decision, the issue is elegance of process and outcome. How can the action be carried forward in a way which is aesthetically pleasing? Many of the decisions that upset us as humans are matters of personal preference. Learning to do our work elegantly is important. However, when we find ourselves fussing over the layout of an office, the typeface on a report, or the form of a project, we need to remember that these issues are not quite as important as those considered ethical decisions.

The final kind of decision involves moral reflection. Kaufman notes that as we attend to ethical issues, we must take responsibility for and be concerned with acts as elements and "shapers of an ongoing web of action (morality)."[7] This conversation involves exploring appropriate action to promote goodness, right action, and justice. Ethical issues raise questions about the proper definitions of rights and responsibilities, appropriate ways to reach a goal, and/or any tension between individual and community obligations. At the center, each controversy is a conflict about how the virtues associated with the core values should be prioritized.

▶ *For this question, what is the very specific issue to be resolved?*

An ethical question will present a set of conflicts. The clash may be between competing rights (*e.g.,* the right of an employee vs. the right of an employer). The dissension may be between competing goals (*e.g.,* the goal of efficiency vs. the goal of having a reputation for absolute honesty). The dispute may also be between competing notions of justice (*e.g.,* the obligation of a corporation to distribute maximum return to shareholders and the obligation to pay employees a fair, living wage with appropriate benefits). The conflict may also be about which virtues are most important in a particular role (*e.g.*, integrity in telling the truth about a situation or loyalty to the company). The question will often involve not only competing values but a question about how to harmonize and balance the values in this particular situation. Because ethics is about choosing a course of action, the first task is to frame the issue as accurately as possible so that the conflict may be clearly seen.

Exploring the Values-in-Conflict

Before we can identify and orchestrate the values for a particular situation, we must become aware of the competing values in the various segments of the culture in which we live. As individuals living in community, overlapping sets of values come into play for any problem. While we have four broad categories of values (core values), the specific content of those value sets, the virtues, is inherited and adopted from our family of origin. Each family has its own beliefs about what kind of autonomy a person should have or what constitutes fairness or equality. These ideas, which are ultimately passed on to us, are shaped by the religious and philosophical commitments of our forebears.

We get additional knowledge about what kinds of actions are ethical from the community in which we live. The more diverse the community, the more varied and disputed are the values in play. Someone who has not paid attention to the amount of privilege they have had (such as having parents who can make a large down payment on their house) may not see that those who do not come from that kind of wealth may define fair as the ability to get affordable housing. Thus, to be effective we must attend to the similarities and differences between personal and community views. A third source of values is found in the culture of the organization where we work and is articulated by the leadership. If we are very lucky, the actions that are expected and rewarded in the company are the same values stated in the mission statement of the organization.

As seen in Chapter 2, the values of the community can be in broad categories (the core values) which conflict with or are in tension with each other. One set of tensions is between equality (assuring that members of the community are treated fairly) and autonomy (assuring that each person has a chance to determine how best to live). The second set of tensions is between rationality (where people know the rules and what others will probably do in a situation regardless of the specificities of the situation) and sensibility (where people consider the uniqueness of the situation and thus have tolerance and flexibility as they move and make choices in light of change and emerging conditions). As stated before, our task is often difficult because we believe that we have to choose between two good results, emphasizing one and excluding the other. However, as we make ethical decisions, we have the opportunity to fashion a solution which weaves together competing values.

The task is complicated even more when personal values conflict with the prevailing values in the community. Mediating the differences among people, communities, and cultures involves identifying the weight and priority that have been given to the different values. The underlying core values themselves are the same for each community, so the *conversation* about core values is similar across cultures. Thus, each culture (whether individual, organizational, national, or international) has to make its own choice about how to balance conflicting core values. For example, in the United States we claim that we value those who hold companies accountable for ethical behavior, whistle blowers. But research which tracks the history of whistle blowers shows that those who reveal corruption in a company are often vilified and fired or marginalized.[8] These incidents teach that loyalty to a company is in fact valued more than ethical transparency, no matter what the rhetoric. Which values are given priority in a situation to produce the best resolution will depend on individual beliefs and commitments as they are worked out in agreement and/or in tension with community beliefs and commitments.

As we engage the conversation, one criterion for rationality is the defensibility of the reasons that we use for the decision. Thus, if the reasons which are given are acceptable in a complex community, then the decision tends to pass muster. Another criterion is the authority underlying the action, be that legal (such as state statutes) or ideological (such as a particular theological or philosophical view).

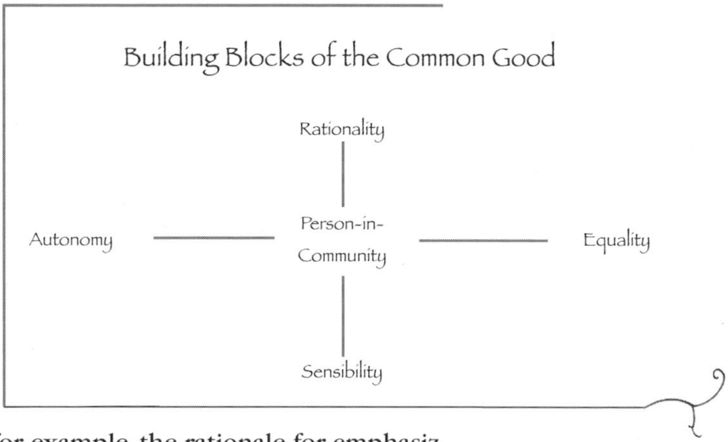

As we consider the virtues which are associated with the core values, any two or more of which may be in tension or conflict, we must clearly articulate the reason for the priority (for example, the rationale for emphasizing autonomy over rationality) and explicate our authority for acting (for example the U.S. Constitution rather than a conflicting local law).

The economics of the situation is also a factor. One element of the financial picture is what is called a boundary condition — we only have so much money in the bank and only certain available resources. Thus, within the financial constraints of the company, we have to make the most ethical decision possible. A second element has to do with how the resources of the company are distributed. In this regard, each four core value exhibits an economic factor which must be balanced along with the non-economic factors. We need to be sure not to bankrupt the company while doing good work. The goal is to do well while we are doing good.

Another complicating factor is that, as we balance these conflicting values, we must consider the organization as an entity in addition to the individuals within the organization and the members of the community. The balancing act involves not only the well-being of the company, but also the well-being of its employees. We are also invited to attend to the common good, to determine which actions will strengthen the community as a whole. The goal is to find that delicate balance between individual as well as community rights and goals so all persons can thrive and become whole.

Taken in isolation the names of the core values and the two traditions which are historically the paths to maturity may not have much intrinsic meaning.

Moving down to the final conceptual level in which the virtues are named gives us a more concrete picture of what kinds of issues are present in each of these categories. As Steven Winter reminds us in *A Clearing in the Forest*, we tend to articulate meta-categories which do not evoke any images or emotions.[9] As we identify the specific actions or items which are part of the meta-category, we can wrap our minds around the more abstract notions. Autonomy as a concept may not have much meaning; however the concrete right to spend our money the way we choose or say whatever we desire, even if it annoys people, strikes a visceral chord.

> Category Levels
>
> Meta-category — value (no specific image)
> Next conceptual level — rules and goals (proto-type image)
> Next conceptual level — virtues (concrete)

Identifying Common Value Clusters

To help identify how the core values — rationality, sensibility, equality, and autonomy — might manifest as virtues in an organizational setting, a number of concrete situations and their attendant virtues and commitments are described below. We can use these examples to help us develop our ethical awareness as we explore which virtues flow from the core values which are present in every culture. While the following lists are by no means exhaustive, they represent the most common expressions of the virtues which appear in organizational ethics. As we work through various ethical problems, the first step is to identify which core values are in conflict. Referring back to these lists might help in the quest.

The listing for each core value is divided into three categories: (a) organizational concerns which address issues facing the organization or company; (b) individual concerns which are the most often articulated in the Western community; and (c) stakeholder concerns which help identify how others will be affected by the decision. The individual is separated from the organization to remind us that while we work for various organizations, we are members of more than one interest group. Therefore, our interests as employees may not be synonymous with those of our employers.

▶ *Rationality: safeguarding expectations, and rules of the game*

This core value focuses on making sure that we have some sense of the rules of the game and that people will follow those rules. None of us likes to be surprised. Thus, even though we may not like the rule, we want to know what the members of our community expect of us. We want to know that agreements will be honored and contracts kept. We also want to be safe, both physically and financially. We want some assurance that we will not be injured and that we will get paid for our work.

- *Organizational concerns:*

  - *Staying in business:* If revenues are down or a policy would break the bank, hard decisions have to be made. For example, as the cost of health care increases, companies which previously provided very comprehensive packages might find they cannot afford to offer the same level care.

  - *Fiduciary duties:* Employees are expected to put the concerns of the company ahead of their own interests. So profit taking or information sharing which puts the company at risk is a security issue. Thus, a key value is loyalty, where one avoids conflicts of interest. In management literature this characteristic is called "attitudinal commitment."

  - *Minimizing waste:* As a company needs to gain the maximum return while using the fewest possible resources, waste of time or resources is a concern. Whether avoiding abuse of telephones, the Internet, or office supplies, employers expect employees to put the interest of the company ahead of personal gain. The values in this cluster are efficiency and productivity.

- *Individual concerns:*

  - *Physical safety:* The company is expected to provide a safe workplace. Safety includes the physical plant itself — stairs, ventilation systems, and machinery — as well as protection against fellow employees — harassment or violence.

  - *Financial security:* We expect companies to assist employees in reaching economic security, having sufficient resources to care for themselves and their families. Minimum wage laws, laws about hours and conditions, and requirements for other benefits are some of the ways that companies are expected to help each person find financial security.

- *Stakeholder concerns:* Stakeholders also have an interest in security. They want to assure that the value of their investment is both preserved and returns a fair profit, so that neither they nor the company is put at financial risk because of bad management decisions, and to assure that the company stays solvent so it is able to employ people in the community.

- *Sensibility: safeguarding the ability to nimbly move with emerging circumstances — flexibility, tolerance, and freedom*

This core values is in tension with from rationality. We are given much freedom to experiment and innovate, thus evoking an expansive notion of sensibility as we tolerate various organizational structures and strategies. A hallmark of American business is that we are expected to move with change. Thus, going out of business may not of itself be a bad thing if we are able to embrace new technology or opportunities to move ahead. We want to assure that all have the ability to change as needed to be more effective and efficient.

- *Organizational concerns:*

  - *Staying in business:* Companies must be able to change product lines, move locations, and reconfigure workforces. Thus, being locked into long-term contracts or expectations of stability may hamper the ability of the company to rapidly adapt to change.

  - *Fiduciary duties:* Granting the ability to respond quickly to the market often means that stakeholders should have little expectation that a firm will be particularly loyal to them. One question is whether the change is arbitrary and capricious or a careful response to changing circumstances. Another issue is whether the company has given adequate notice to the affected stakeholders or met the cultural expectations before implementing change. A value in this setting would be due process, assuring fundamental fairness.

  - *Risk taking:* Companies are often rewarded for taking risk. Different individuals, companies, and cultures have varying tolerances for risk taking. A person who is risk adverse would probably be well suited for government work rather than a seat on the stock exchange. America, as a whole, tends to be more risk friendly than other cultures.

- *Individual concerns:*

  - *Physical safety:* People are expected to be alert, take responsibility for themselves, and protect themselves in workplace settings.

  - *Financial security:* Employees want the ability to move, rather than to get locked into long-term arrangements. The ability to make choices, move within or out of an industry, and take personal risks is carefully guarded.

- *Stakeholder concerns:* Stakeholders want the benefits of moving quickly from a difficult situation in order to restore the company to health. The question often involves leaders determining what is appropriate notice of the decision as well as making choices that will not put the stakeholders at more risk than they have willingly embraced.

- *Autonomy: the ability to choose for one's self how best to live, both in terms of rights and responsibilities*

This core value is deeply embedded in the American psyche. Born in the image of the rugged individual escaping the oppression of a community which did not provide freedom of religion, speech, or economic opportunity, the hallmark of America is its commitment to individual choice and its protection of individual rights.

- *Organizational concerns:* Companies get to choose what products they want to produce or sell, how they want to market those products, and what strategies they will embrace to insure success. If leadership is unskilled and makes ill-informed choices, no one is expected to bail the company out of financial problems.

- *Employee concerns:* Employees care about being able to retain as many of their privileges as independent persons as possible. Being treated as a person helps employees find meaning at work.

  - *Personal lives:* Employees' right to privacy ensures minimal interference with their personal lives (*e.g.*, drug and alcohol restrictions, leisure activities). If a company resists a patriarchal approach to work, the leadership will embrace the notion that as employees give employers a fair day's work for a fair wage, what they do when they are off the clock should not matter.

- ▷ *Professional lives:* Employees expect minimal interference with their professional lives (*e.g.,* cell phone or Internet use, clocking in or out, or being required to do personal tasks for a superior). This value is described as the right to respect, appreciation, and being treated as an adult with inherent dignity.

- ▷ *Balance of power:* While it is true that employees can either take a contract or leave it, most employees do not have great mobility. Thus, employees fear that they cannot easily say no to requests from superiors which may conflict with the employee's personal ethics. Watching the professional lives of whistle blowers crumble, colleagues fear that demanding that their employers be ethical will cost them their jobs. When people manifest the virtue of courage, we are reminded to neither abuse power nor be overbearing.

- ▶ *Stakeholder concerns:* Stakeholders want enough information to make good choices.

  - ▷ *Shareholders and investors:* The company's financial partners expect transparency in the financial documents.

  - ▷ *Consumers:* Those who buy the goods and services expect sufficient information about the product to assess the risks and benefits, as well as the quality of the product.

  - ▷ *Community:* The members of the community expect the company to be a good neighbor and not abuse its power. Whether demanding tax benefits or polluting the environment, a company's exercise of autonomy is not expected to put the the community at risk.

▶ *Equality: fairness in sharing the burdens and benefits*

This core value is in direct tension with the values in autonomy. Those who value equality expect individuals to restrain their use of individual prerogatives in order to attend to the common good. As we structure our community, we want to assure that all persons have both equality of opportunity for living out their dreams as well as some rough equality of result in the distribution of benefits and burdens — the economic and political goods of the community.

- *Organizational concerns:*
  - *Sharing burdens:* The organization wishes to be treated fairly, in the same way as every other organization in the community. Thus, it does not expect to be taxed more or have higher safety or environmental requirements than other companies.
  - *Sharing benefits:* Organizations expect equal opportunity to bid for business with other companies. Issues related to not giving benefits based on personal preferences, not inappropriately granting or withholding change orders, and fair treatment of stakeholders manifest under the core value of equality. An ongoing question is when companies should be treated as a person by the communities in which they are situated. Sometimes the law gives companies the rights of individuals and treats them as a person; other times they are treated as organizations with no inherent rights.
- *Employee concerns:*
  - *Sharing burdens:* Employees are concerned with workload issues, safety risks, and treatment of differently situated persons (*e.g.*, someone with child care issues, someone who has special medical needs, or someone who needs accommodations in the workplace environment). Making sure people are equally treated while real differences are acknowledged is always a balancing act.
  - *Sharing benefits:* Fair access to profits, salaries, and benefits – such as vacation, health care, child care, and pensions and/or retirement funds – is a major issue for employees. One rule of thumb adopted by companies considered ethical is that the highest paid employee receives no more than 30x the lowest paid employee.
- *Stakeholder concerns:*
  - *Sharing burdens:* Every community has formal or informal structures in place to help those who are less fortunate. Organizations whose primary goal is to deliver quality goods and services at appropriate

prices find that balancing their social responsibility to help disadvantaged members of the community while remaining profitable requires careful thought and discretion. The community expects companies to pay their fair share of the burdens through taxes as well as employment; thus, issues of off-shore tax filings or moving employment opportunities to foreign countries becomes germane when determining what is fair.

▷ *Sharing benefits:* Companies often come to a community because of quality of life features such as schools, affordable cost of living, and access to recreation. Stakeholders need to be sensitive to the fact that companies should not expect to be treated differently than other folks. Conversations about tax subsidies offered to companies to induce them to relocate are particularly touchy as members of the community are torn between wanting the benefits that a company can bring while expecting the company to shoulder its fair share.

As we explore and articulate the different commitments in the community, it quickly becomes obvious that various people give different priority to the core values. We are all asked to discern which specific virtues which manifest from the core values represent strongly held commitments and which would be nice if we could make them work. Each of us has a different tolerance for balancing tensions that arise between the core values of rationality and sensibility, and those that arise between autonomy and equality. For example, someone may see loyalty as being critical for an organization where another may more highly prize individualism and independence. We all need to determine for ourselves what the appropriate balance is among the competing values and then negotiate that balance with other members of the community.

Determine the Specific Values in Conflict in the Problem at Hand

The above cataloguing of how core values manifest as specific virtues in a business setting is meant to enhance ethical awareness. If we do not know what is prized in the culture, we may unintentionally violate the ethical norms. As we increase our sensitivity to the ethical nuances of action, we can carefully identify the commitments in question and evaluate the consequences. Many times we do not notice when values are in conflict. Ethical dilemmas do not generally announce their presence in Siren tones. Rather, problems creep up when we least expect them. Much like Brer Rabbit's Tar Baby, the dilemmas are often hidden, as complicated situations have ethical questions buried in the facts, and then catch us in their sticky mess when we least expect it.

As stated earlier, an ethical question will usually present a choice between two or more competing good actions. We must attend to conflicts among competing values in individuals, the organization, and the community. Does the person or the organization desire economizing behaviors, assuring the best productivity and return on investment, more or less than ecologizing behaviors, assuring that people, relationships, and the environment are preserved?[10] Another set of questions would have us ask whether the individual rights of employees or customers are more or less important than the prerogatives of the organization. This conflict might play out in organizational decisions about compensation, leave time, or other benefits. Identifying the specific values in conflict helps us sort out the possible options for action.

Ethical decisions do not usually involve determining whether or not to break the law. In our community, many people equate ethical action with following the law. However a core assertion of this book is that following the law is a secondary conversation. The primary conversation concerns discerning what values and norms should be part of the community. Then we can work towards the goal of having the law match the norms of the community.

When an ethical standard is in dispute, people may choose to violate the law and engage in civil disobedience. Using civil disobedience to draw attention to a disputed standard or unjust law is very different from playing the edges and hoping not to get caught. Because many of us like to get as close to the edge as possible to get an economic advantage, laws are passed to both define the playing field as well as arbitrate among competing ethical norms. Laws may be used to set the rules, if one uses the metaphor of business as a game. Laws may also provide clarification when standards are in dispute or being used to implement enforcement strategies when people do not follow the ethical norms of the community. Discerning when a law is setting the parameters of the playing field and when it reflects a core value of the community will help leaders know when to play the edge and when to be squeaky clean. Practicing making decisions with hypothetical situations such as The GG Ethics Game helps us notice and evaluate our world view concerning the core ethical commitments which are part of our community. As we resolve various ethical problems, we can notice both what values are in conflict and which ideals are given a place of priority.

Identify Options for Action

In Step 2, after pinpointing the issue and exploring the values-in-conflict, we must identify options for action. Applied ethical decision-making is about choosing among competing possibilities for action, including options that we believe are unethical. Many times we need to know why a particular choice does not pass ethical muster. Often an option, which at first blush appears unethical, may in fact be the most ethical course of action. An option for action may include doing nothing, *i.e.,* allowing the existing policy or course of action or inaction to continue. The best options for action emerge after investigation and consultation. While research can never be complete, the final option for action is not more research. We also must assure that we have consulted with all appropriate stakeholders to identify the best possible options. However, at some point a decision needs to be made.

Finally, good ethical decisions are creative solutions which elegantly harmonize competing interests and values. Knowing what different members of the community prefer helps us think imaginatively and creatively outside of the box. For example, a company recently decided that it needed all employees to have ID tags to assure security. One of the long-time employees was a Muslim woman who came to work veiled. The question was how to respect her right of autonomy while respecting the right of the company for security. The solution was to have one ID card with the woman in a veil and another one with her face. The photograph for the second ID card was taken by a woman; in the event of a question, she was promised that only a female security officer would check the identity. With a bit of care, the needs of both groups were met. As a bonus, the morale of the entire company went up as employees realized that they were valued as individuals.[11]

Conclusion

Many times people make bad decisions because they have not taken the time to carefully set up the problem. While going through the step of being attentive and the step of being intelligent may feel tedious and redundant, failing to carefully evaluate the context and the details of the problem will lead to an inferior decision. Finding the core values-in-conflict requires that we become very aware of the context. Often in the United States, minorities and women are more aware of the values-in-conflict in an organization because they are trying to make sense of the system and learn how to move ahead. Anne Wilson Schaef noted that those who are in power in a situation tend not to notice the different elements of the context. Those who are working to fit into a system which is hostile or indifferent know all of the spoken and unspoken rules.[12]

Accurately evaluating the context also requires that we know ourselves very well. This knowledge should include an awareness of where we cannot see clearly because of our own biases and our need to protect our own power base. We all have a fear of failure and a sense of inadequacy. Listening to those who do not just tell us how wonderful we are requires courage and integrity — integral qualities of respected leaders. In the process we will be able to see how we can meet the triple bottom line of our organizations — economic success, ethical action, and environmental concern.

Continuing the Conversation

1. Reflect on your own belief system and review the list of how the core values manifest in a business setting. What values are the most important to you in a business setting? How have you either chosen an employer or shaped your work setting to make sure that those values are part of your work?

2. Find an article or an op ed piece in your local paper or a news magazine which deals with a current ethical situation. See if you can identify the reasons which were given for the decisions. What did the author use to justify the position that was taken? Were you persuaded? Why or why not?

3. Identify an ethical dilemma that you are facing or have seen in your work place. Following the steps of this chapter, in a page or less, describe the context and details of the problem. Now, what do you notice about both what you chose to include and what facts you decided were not relevant? Was the process easy or hard? What did you learn about yourself?

Applying Lonergan's Method
(Part 2)

Be Reasonable

- *Hone critical thinking skills*
- *Apply ethical content*
- *Overlay moral content*

Be Responsible

- *Correct for bias*
- *Attend to the common good*
- *Act with courage*

Return to Awareness

- *Continuous improvement*
- *The Crucible of Spirit*

I shall be telling this with a sigh
Somewhere ages and ages hence:
Two roads diverged in a wood, and I —
I took the one less traveled by,
And that has made all the difference.

Robert Frost[1]

Chapter 5

Strategies for Decision-Making

In the 1960s, the popular culture spawned the human potential movement. Replete with self-help books and seminars, the promise has been that as we learn to take responsibility for ourselves and the way that we live in this world, we can gain control over our lives and find meaning and happiness. Many have speculated about the reason for this surge of interest in pop psychology. Whatever the cause, the result has been that many individuals have spent thousands of dollars and hundreds of hours to learn more about themselves and how they can be effective and happy at work and at play. Lonergan describes this drive to understand ourselves and our world as the common to all humans, the "detached, disinterested, unrestricted desire to know."[2] Lonergan asserts that this characteristic of people drives us not only to understand the physical world but also to seek the good — the good for ourselves and other people as well as the good of our institutions such as the economy, the family, and of our earth.

The desire to know manifests first as relentless questioning. As we gather information about the world, we ask more questions. One set of questions is about the material world itself, one aspect of which is how do markets work? What processes will help me make my product and services better? How can I develop a product which will solve a particular problem? Another set of questions explores what Lonergan calls the spiritual, leading to those questions about the ordering of values in our community.

Free will is the ability to choose how to live. While arguably we may not be able to choose the circumstances of our birth, each of us gets to decide what we will do with the life we were given. Part of questioning includes inquiry about the probable outcomes of our choices, our motives, and which values we will consider important. Theologians and philosophers call this ability to choose the gift of free will. Thus, we can ask questions, contemplate results, and still choose either to do that which will create greater good or that which will not. Because developing rational self-consciousness is an ongoing process, we have the opportunity over and over again to choose to act in light of our best understanding of the world and its consequences or to choose to act in a way that actually causes harm to our self, others, and the environment.

Psychologists call embracing the privilege and responsibility of choosing how to live "self-efficacy." Albert Bandura defines self-efficacy as "a judgment of one's ability to organize and execute given types of performances."[3] Bandura's research demonstrates that those who have a strong belief in their own self-efficacy will be more motivated and proactive in the choices that they make about life than those who do not believe that they are effective. People who have high self-efficacy and high outcome expectancies tend to be productive and satisfied with their lives. Those with high self-efficacy and low outcome expectancies protest and engage in social activism. However, those who have low-self efficacy will be despondent, if they think they have some power over their circumstances, or resigned, if they feel powerless.[4]

Bandura's research also shows that the more accurate our self-assessments and our assessment of the world around us, the more likely we are to have high self-efficacy. As we combine Lonergan's method of learning about ourselves and our community with our knowledge and experience of the business world, our self-efficacy will increase. In the process we become more effective ethical agents while finding meaning and satisfaction in our work. By asking questions (making sure we continually look for data that do not match our expectations in the world around us), while we subject our own motives and desires to the same grilling, we increase our self-efficacy, our ability to believe that we have control over our lives and our work. Fortuitously, as our self-efficacy grows we also increase the actual control we have over ourselves and others and what happens in our professional and personal life.

William Greider asserts that our work situations can create apathy and cynicism rather than the meaning that we all crave, resulting in low self-efficacy in our professional lives. Whether we are on the floor of a manufacturing plant where we have power over only a part of the process or we are part of a system where we do not know whom we are serving and thus are not connected to our customers, even in a time of great surplus we may believe that we have little control over our economic lives and that we are powerless to affect either our personal work situation or the firms which employ us.[5]

The conversation about how to be an ethical person in business presumes that we believe that who we are and what we do make a difference. If we believe that we have no control over the people or the systems in which we find ourselves, we stop questioning and resign ourselves to our world. Much like the government workers in Nazi Germany who took responsibility only for their tasks, it is often easier not to ask what our actions do to help or hinder the greater good. The way that officials in Nazi Germany managed to get good people to buy into the horrors of the Holocaust was by asking them only to do their small, bureaucratic part. Thus, when members of the Jewish community were sent to the concentration camps, all of the bills of lading (a legal document which lets people know what cargo is being shipped) were properly filled out, the fees for transporting "goods" were paid, and no one asked what impact those small bureaucratic acts had on the fabric of the community and the lives of millions.[6]

From time to time in American business, good people find themselves part of a system which does not create good for many people. While we the evil we create may not be on the scale of the Holocaust, when we actually look at the wealth that has been lost through unethical practices causing the collapse of major American corporations or the lives disrupted through employment practices, we must place the responsibility somewhere. An unexpected consequence of the self-help movement may be that people are beginning to have the tools as well as the desire to stop their unknowing participation in systems which deaden their souls and lead to the destruction of the fabric of our community. As we choose to be as responsible and proactive at work as we are in our personal lives, the shape of business will be transformed.

After being *attentive* in identifying the problem and *intelligent* in exploring options, Steps 3 and 4 in the decision-making process demonstrate how to be *reasonable* in solving the dilemmas and then *responsible* in our decisions. By focusing on the perennial organizing questions (see p. 36), we learn to see that which we otherwise would ignore. By subjecting difficult questions to the core ethical frameworks (see p. 3), we get a much more complete picture of not only the problems but also the strengths and weaknesses of potential options for acting. Step 4 of the decision-making process also reminds us that we must act, and that not acting is in fact an action.

As we move our focus from narrowly considering only our own well being, to a wider concern for those around us, and finally to systems — the institutions which provide the structure for our lives — we also become ethically mature and wiser. Often these choices involve taking the road less traveled, the road that asks us to give to others out of our abundance, cheerfully subordinating personal interest to support the common good. Many who have taken the other road find, as in the words of Robert Frost, that it *has* made all the difference.

Step 3 Be Reasonable: Evaluate the Options

Ethics and morality are not just about determining the right course of action but rather are about choosing the best course of action and persuading others that the action is right. All of us must determine for ourselves how best to live. This knowledge emerges through conversation with our friends and co-workers in our community. We are shaped by our own dreams and the community's expectations of us, as others either embrace or critique our world view. The dialogue forms and informs us and our community as we listen and strive to understand and accommodate each other. As we intentionally engage in conversations about the balance between *autonomy*, doing what we believe is best, and *equality*, assuring that everyone else gets the same options, the boundaries between

> Be Reasonable
>
> - Hone critical thinking skills
> - Apply ethical content
> - Overlay moral content

appropriate self-care and selfishness are provisionally set. Many vigorous exchanges explore when individual prerogatives need to be curtailed in favor of the company's financial well-being or security. Such dialogues determine both the content of what is ethical and its application in specific situations.

After exploring the context and determining the options for action, we evaluate the options. Even though an ethical decision is ultimately subjective, we want to be as objective as possible: we want to reach conscious subjectivity. Being a responsible ethical agent requires the application of three intersecting bodies of knowledge. First, what are the analytical rules which will give the best result? Second, what is the ethical content which provides the basis of the decision? Third, what are the moral considerations which provide an essential filter? Answering these questions helps us fairly evaluate our options and determine which ethical and moral criteria to use to judge the rightness of a particular course of action.

Hone Critical Thinking Skills

As we begin to identify values-in-conflict and work toward a resolution, a host of skills is available to assist us in the process. After we experience the situation and become aware of the problem and our own response, the next step becomes to understand and judge the situation and come up with the best response possible. The disciplines of philosophy and law, as well as science and engineering, have specific tools which help in both framing and analyzing problems. Time-tested tools of critical thinking can help us hone our analytical skills. Manuel Velasquez in his text *Business Ethics: Concepts and Cases,* 5th ed. summarizes the skills necessary for ethical decision making. Meticulously attending to these rules helps us find the best possible answer.[7]

- ► *The logic of the argument needs to be rigorously examined; all of the unspoken moral and factual assumptions in the claims need to be displayed and critiqued.*

Each section of an author's outline will contain an *assertion* which supports the primary thesis. Sometimes the author has made an *assumption* in the writing which is veiled. In economics the underlying assumption might be that capitalism or socialism is the preferred system. In theology the assertion might be that Christianity is superior to all the other world religions. Both the above assumption and assertion are contested, meaning that people disagree with them. Be sensitive to the assumptions, both individual and cultural, behind the assertions as you work the problem. The assertions that we make might lose their appeal if others find the underlying assumptions flawed.

Many times we mask flawed assumptions by failing to clarify ambiguity in our statements. The most common cause of ambiguity is difference in definition. Many times we avoid clarifying our definitions because we do not want conflict. However, as all communication depends on assuring that people receive the same message, if we want to resolve the problem, being clear about the definition is crucial. We can clearly see an example of this process by examining the conversation of a group exploring the morality of abortion. If one person in the group assumes that a fetus is a human being (or even potential human being) upon the first division of cells, the preferred ethical act (and underlying analysis) will be very different than for the person who assumes that a fetus does not become a human being until some later point in the maturation process, such as the traditional legal definition of life which is taking the first breath out of the womb.

Analytical Pitfalls

- Circular arguments: Make sure that you do not argue one point by using the same point as validation.
- Ad hominem arguments: Do not attack a person (or their mental skills). Evaluate the argument itself.
- Diversions: Do not go off on tangents or use glittering generalities to hide the reasoning or assumptions or to stir emotions.
- False dilemma: Do not set up the problem so others are forced into believing that only two choices are available.

However, very few people engage in this difficult issue by listening to each other carefully enough to identify the underlying core assumptions about what makes a human. Often as we identify differences in assumptions, the resolution of the problem becomes clear. Sometimes clarity means that we respectfully disagree on the core definitions. As we get better information, we note that which does not fit, enlightened by the beliefs and experiences of those with whom we have talked. In the process we exercise the gift of civility rather than shouting at and denigrating each other. Many fear that unless we learn to respect each other and search for the highest common ground we will destroy our community.

- ***The factual information cited in support of a person's judgment must be accurate, relevant, and complete.***

Doing sufficient research to test our assumptions is time consuming; we usually prefer to go with our biases or with data that seem to support our ideas. Whether we are looking at data about salaries, job mobility, discrimination in the workforce, or a myriad of other topics, we need to carefully check the sources of the data and ask how they were compiled. We also need to be careful about our own use of data as we move forward with our closely-held opinions. Carefully looking to see if our cherished notions can be supported rather than putting a spin on data to support our preferred vision of the world requires intellectual maturity.

Verification for Belief Systems

Anecdotes Tradition	Other authorities Authority
Reason Statistics	Experience Author's expertise

Authors will use many different sources of evidence to support their assertions. The following are sources which are traditionally used to establish credibility.

- ▸ *Statistics:* Many authors use numbers to support their ideas. As we review statistics, we must be aware of the underlying data and the questions which were asked in obtaining the results. Statistics may be descriptive and tell us what is, such as census data. Other statistics are predictive and tell us what is forecasted, such as what the economy may do in the upcoming months. The difference between the two approaches radically affects decision-making.

- ▸ *Other authorities:* Other authors or works can be used to support the ideas of the author. Two questions are important. First, we validate the expertise of the author. Next, we ask whether the author's statement is based on expertise or whether the writing is really just opinion.

- ▸ *Anecdotes:* Authors give examples to support their point. People often use a poster child for an argument, which may depict the worst possible case of the point being made. This poster child may represent only a small percentage of those in a particular category, the statistical extreme, rather than the case which falls within an expected range of results. We need to notice and/or avoid false generalizations.

- ▸ *Author's expertise:* Sometimes an author will rely on the persuasiveness of the argument and/or the author's own reputation as an authority in the field as evidence for the argument. Careful evaluation requires identification of the credentials, assumptions, and commitments of the author.

As each of us evaluates the premises used to support a claim, we judge them as credible or not credible. As we evaluate the evidence, we determine whether we tend to believe it as presented or whether we are skeptical and want further proof before we buy the argument. One professor calls this process being careful whose voices I allow to get into my head. The evaluation and belief continuum might look like this:

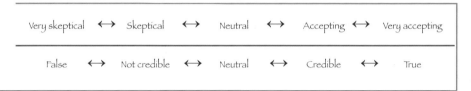

Very skeptical	↔	Skeptical	↔	Neutral	↔	Accepting	↔	Very accepting
False	↔	Not credible	↔	Neutral	↔	Credible	↔	True

Some of us accept information without challenge if our own knowledge is sparse. Others want multiple sources of verification. Some of us have favorite authorities — we always trust the writing of certain authors while distrusting others. Some of us have favorite viewpoints — we always trust someone who basically agrees with us while distrusting another who disagrees. We are usually neutral if the evidence has no impact on us at all.

Through the process of careful evaluation, we begin identifying our own strengths and weaknesses in a subject area as well as our own inclinations. As each of us learns how we evaluate evidence, we begin to see where we are gullible and/or hypercritical. Through evaluation we also learn how to better structure our own writing and thinking to be clear and persuasive.

- *The ethical and moral standards involved in our reasoning must be internally consistent as well as consistent over time.*

The hardest task of ethical decision making is to be consistent in applying the principles and values which form our belief system and rationale for action. For example, a student wrote a set of papers evaluating whether non-documented workers should receive free health care. She was adamant that every human being is entitled to health care, regardless of ability to pay or citizenship and thus kept getting low scores because her position did not seem tenable. Finally the teacher told her that he would revise her grade if she assured him that any homeless person who showed up at her doorstep would be welcome, no matter how long the person wanted to stay or what resources he might need. The student had a shocked look on her face as she told her professor, "I can not afford that." The teacher then rejoined that maybe the United States could not afford to pay for health care for everyone in the world. The issue of access to health care wasn't resolved. However, the student became clear that her reasoning would not be considered consistent while she advocated one set of behavior for the government without being willing to embrace that same behavior herself.

Whether we are evaluating someone else's work or constructing an argument, the quality of our ethical analysis depends on the rigor with which we use our analytical tools. As we become more skilled in critical thinking, we become more effective participants in the business world as well as more persuasive leaders.

Apply Ethical Principles and Values

Once our critical thinking skills are polished, we are ready to evaluate the problem against our core ethical principles and values. One definition of ethics is disciplining the mind, using the tools of reason, to determine the rules of life. Using our critical thinking skills, we apply ethical principles and criteria to a problem to help us select the most ethical act.

> **The World of Ethics**
>
> Disciplining the mind through reason to find the rules of life.

Over the course of history, ethicists have tried to determine whether we have a set of principles from which we live (deontology) or whether the goals of our lives determine our choices (teleology). The two approaches to ethics have been in conversation for thousands of years with no resolution in sight. The theories that underlie these two traditions will be examined more fully in Part Two, illustrating that those who engage in the field of applied ethics — taking abstract principles and goals and applying them to concrete situations — find that the criteria of either tradition can give a good result.

Each of us uses a preferred tradition when making decisions. We recognize our favorite perspective because the process feels intuitive and is easy. The focus we least prefer is the one with which we struggle: we can not believe that anyone could possibly use that approach for making decisions. In particularly difficult situations, we should use the vantage point of the less comfortable traditions, so that we can check ourselves for bias or blind spots. As we become skilled in describing the landscape of multiple traditions, we are able to interact with those whose primary tradition is not our own and avoid confusion while moving toward agreement or consensus.

To become skilled in decision-making, we can practice examining ethical problems using four different lenses. Two of the lenses come from the duty-based — *deontological* — tradition. The first is the Rights/Responsibility Lens which focuses on the question "what should I do?" Kant is the representative theorist. The second is the Relationship Lens which asks "how do I fit into the community?" Rawls is the representative theorist. When used together, these two lenses allow us to harmonize our autonomy, our individual rights and duties, with the community's claim for justice and fairness.

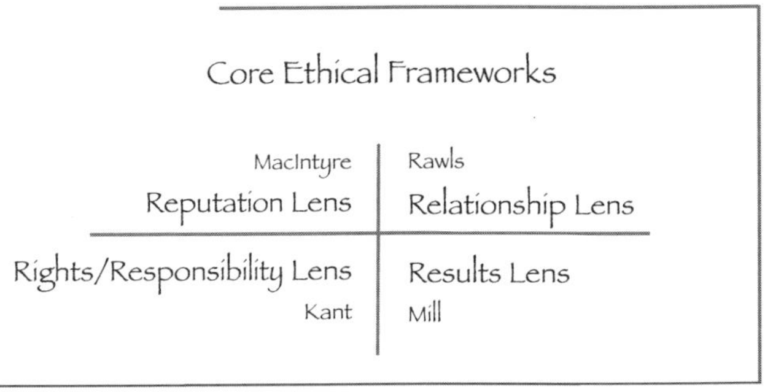

The other two lenses come from the goal-based — *teleological* — tradition. The first, the Results Lens, asks the question "what do I want?" and is represented by Mill. The second, the Reputation Lens, asks the question "who am I?" and is represented by MacIntyre. When used together, these two lenses allow us to harmonize our individual goals with the virtues and character we embody, which is how we are seen and judged by the community.

The difficulty in any problem is in clearly articulating which principles or goals are in conflict and then determining which should be given priority in the given situation. Our ideas about the proper balance among the virtues which are associated with the four core values will determine what we finally decide is the appropriate ethical action given a particular problem — conscious subjectivity.

Overlay Moral Principles and Values

As stated earlier, ethics focuses on principles, rules, and goals. Morality involves emotion and the role of empathy to provide essential information about how best to act in community. Three threads connect those who write about morality. The first is *method.* While we can know the right thing to do, the way in which we carry out the ethical act is as important as the act itself. For example, we can either fire people or terminate their employment in a respectful way that preserves the relationship. The second thread is *responsibility*. All theorists who study how we behave in a complex world assert that ethics is a matter of the head and morality is a matter of the heart — and both must be used responsibly for us to be effective ethical actors. The third thread is *imagination*. As science cannot answer the question how best we should live, we must use our imaginations to envision a world in which the perennial tensions are balanced. Then we can work toward our imagined ideal, knowing that, while we may never reach it, we can get ever closer.

> **The World of Morality**
>
> Disciplining the emotions through empathy to nourish relationships.

For these authors, self-awareness and self-management are key to being moral. Self-awareness includes being sensitive to our strengths and weaknesses, our gifts as well as our blind spots or proclivities for deception. Self-management involves virtues such as emotional self-control, transparency and adaptability.[8] Thus, as we consider how to be moral, we discipline our emotions through empathy to nourish relationships. An ethically mature person will use both the rational considerations as well as the emotional implications for the key relationships before adopting any course of action. The assertion is that the more we develop our moral muscle, the more effective we are as leaders, whatever our positions in an organization.

Step 4 Be Responsible: Choose to Act

Having completed the first three steps, being attentive, being intelligent, and being reasonable, we are ready for the penultimate step, being responsible. To act responsibly, we must have two final filters before we take action. First, we need to be aware of and correct for our own and others' personal bias, the way in which we engage the problem and what we bring to the table in terms of skills

> **Be Responsible**
>
> - Correct for bias
> - Attend to the common good
> - Act with courage

and expectations. Second, because the stakes can be so high for any action given our technological prowess and our ability to profoundly affect the quality of the environment and community, many ethicists are calling for us to attend to the common good. As stated before, each of us is a person-in-community, so the crux of being ethical is balancing the rights and responsibilities of the individual against the claims and prerogatives of the community and to balance the results we desire against the reputation we seek in the community.

Correct for Bias: Become Ethically Mature

Many assert that all we need to know about ethics we learned in kindergarten — and that trying to teach any of us how to make better ethical decisions is foolhardy. Yet, research indicates that we can all grow in ethical, moral, and spiritual maturity. In the final analysis, we evidence maturity by responsibly evaluating courses of action, making choices and carrying out our decisions.[9]

As various researchers have mapped the path of human development, different stages have been named and categorized. While the details differ, the theorist agree that as we embrace habits of growth, we realize our potential to grow and develop into fully functioning, responsible adult humans. The theorists also agree that our maturity can be determined by noticing the meaning that we give to the events of our lives and the choices that we make. As we become ethically mature, we discern that both people and society are multifaceted and complex. Thus, while the decisions that are made may be the same for people at different ethical levels, the reasons given will be very different.

▸ *Ethical Maturity Through the Four Lenses*

One universal life goal is for each person is to become a fully functioning adult — living responsibly while nurturing and being nurtured by the larger community. Researchers who study the criteria which define adulthood have identified benchmarks and defined the stages of ethical maturity. Intriguingly, a theoretical school of thought parallels the key focus of each of the four ethical lenses.

As we use the conceptual tools of the lens, we can also use criteria of maturity to move from acting only to protect ourselves to considering the wider view of the community and looking toward systemic solutions to problems. The research about why people in business do unethical things indicates that often individuals have high ethical standards but find that the system either encourages or rewards unethical behavior.[10] If a person is rewarded for padding sales, the personal value of transparency in recording sales may lose out. Thus, personal values may be subordinated to company values, resulting in unethical behavior.

- *Rights-focused ethics: learning to use reason effectively.* The theorist who studied our ability to effectively use reason is Lawrence Kohlberg.[11] Kohlberg's research focuses on identifying the strategies we use for ethical decisions. He identifies stages of maturity which enhance our ability to find the principles of life through ever more sophisticated reasoning ability and careful use of the universal ethical principles.

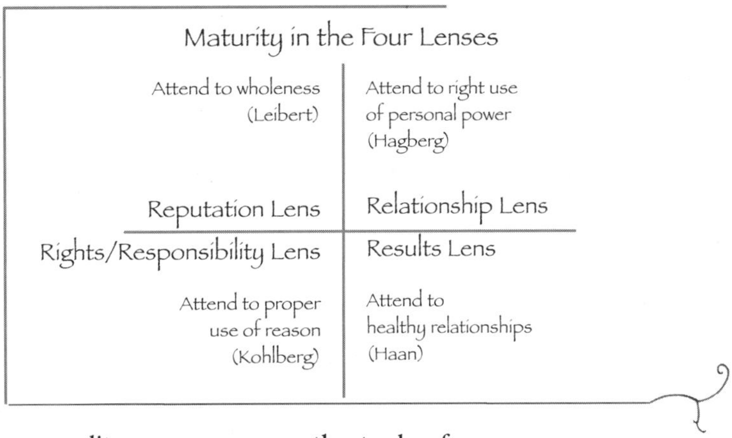

- *Results-focused ethics: striving to nourish relationships.* When acting morality, a person uses the tools of empathy to build relationships. A thoughtful theorist in this arena is Norma Haan who charts the motivations and choices of those for whom maintaining relationships is key.[12] Haan asserts that as we focus on relationships that strengthen the reciprocity between the individual and the community, we become effective actors in the community.

- *Relationship-focused ethics: assuring a proper use of power.* As we move toward both doing the ethical act (ethics) and becoming an ethical person (morality), we increase our personal power. When the question is what acts are not only ethical but just, the way people use their personal and organizational power is important. Janet Hagberg tracks the steps of personal power which parallel the steps of ethical and moral maturity and gives insight into our use of power as we seek justice and fundamental fairness. Hagberg asserts that as we move from powerlessness to getting our power from a self-determined purpose in life we become confident and compassionate members of the community.[13]

- *Reputation-focused ethics: attending to wholeness.* Spirituality is a term which has many different meanings. Elizabeth Liebert, who traces the development of persons in terms of spiritual development, defines spirituality as that which drives us to wholeness. Her approach to wholeness includes the notion of a pacer, one who models ethical behavior and thus encourages others toward maturity.[14]

Contemporary examples of pacers include Martin Luther King, Jr., who challenged the United States to fully live out the ideals of the Declaration of Independence that all persons have a right to life, liberty and pursuit of happiness and Mother Theresa, who modeled selfless care for the least advantaged members of a community. As we consider the virtues which we wish to embody and think about how we want to be known in the world, we attend to ourselves as whole, not partitioned into work, family and friends. A mark of maturity is the ability to exhibit the same personality and characteristics in all settings; thus, the reputation lens encourages us to know all of our self, both the public and the private self, our light and shadow sides.

- *Benchmarks of Ethical Maturity.* Jane Loevenger mapped the developmental stages identified by various theorists and harmonized many of the traditions.[15] We will begin with the young adult, the stage of most high school students and college freshmen and move through to the highest stage to which most adults in our culture ascend.

  - *Characteristics of the Pre-Conformist Stage.* The pre-conformist stage is marked by allegiance to our peer group. At this stage, we are just beginning to differentiate between ourselves and others. A key task of young adults is to evaluate the belief systems — the world view — of their family and friends and then decide for themselves which pieces of that system to reaffirm or reject. Clearly, moving through this stage can be disquieting, both for teens and their parents.

    - *Attending to Reason:* Kohlberg asserts that people at this stage find that the right action is literal obedience to rules and authority. People want to avoid punishment and not do physical harm to others.

    - *Attending to Relationships:* Haan finds that people at this level of maturity will interpret experiences to validate their own self-interests. In terms of action, they will vacillate between compliance and thwarting, believing that others force them to act and that they can force others to their will.

- ▷ *Attending to Power:* Hagberg finds that people in this stage get their power from powerlessness, as they get others to take care of them. These people are dependent with low self-esteem. They are uninformed — helpless but not hopeless.

- ▷ *Attending to Wholeness:* Liebert finds that people in this stage are impulsive, with a fear of retaliation even while they try to exploit others.

- ▷ *Trajectory for change:* As people begin to develop self-esteem and manage their fear of change and the world in general, they are ready to move to the conformist stage.

▶ *Characteristics of the Conformist Stage.* We enter the conformist stage when we accept personal responsibility for our own actions. However, the responsibility is still grounded in and affirmed by an external authority and will be supported by the approval of our significant others.

- ▷ *Attending to Reason:* Kohlberg asserts that people at this stage find that the right action is serving their own or other's needs and making fair deals in terms of concrete exchange.

- ▷ *Attending to Relationships:* Haan finds that people at this level of maturity will accommodate the interests of others when forced. They will trade to get what they want while they recognize that sometimes others must get what they want. The basic orientation is assuring that others get what they want and individuals get what they deserve.

- ▷ *Attending to Power:* Hagberg finds that people in this stage get their personal power by association. They find another person and learn the ropes as they figure out the culture. They are dependent on a leader or mentor as they begin to experience new self-awareness.

- ▷ *Attending to Wholeness:* Liebert finds that people in this stage have a fear of being caught and externalize blame. They are wary, manipulative, and exploitative.

- ▷ *Trajectory for change:* As we develop confidence, we move beyond worrying about the approval of others and the need for security and begin to develop our own ethical compass. We also take responsibility for our self and move into the conscientious-conformist stage.

- *Characteristics of the Conscientious-Conformist Stage.* According to all of our theorists, the conscientious-conformist stage is the stage of most adults. As we begin to take responsibility for ourselves, we realize that because of unthinking adherence to an inherited world view, we have abdicated personal responsibility. Thus, we begin to consider the source of our beliefs and form our own ideas about what is or is not ethical. However, even with attending to our own beliefs, most of us adopt our community's norms and do not seriously challenge the status-quo.

  - *Attending to Reason:* Kohlberg finds that people at this stage believe that the right action is to play a good (nice) role, being concerned about other people and their feelings. Being loyal and keeping trust with others are key. People follow the rules but do not consider the system perspective.

  - *Attending to Relationships:* Haan finds that people at this level of maturity identify their self-interest as the same as the others' interest, thus identifying a common interest. The emphasis is on exchanges based on sustaining good faith. People compromise to include good other persons and reject bad other persons. A person at this stage of development will try to be good so they deserve to receive good from others.

  - *Attending to Power:* Hagberg finds that people in this stage get personal power by the symbols in their lives, such as degrees, cars, money, or position. People at this level are egocentric, realistic, and competitive. As experts, they are ambitious and charismatic.

  - *Attending to Wholeness:* Liebert finds that people in this stage conform to external rules. They feel shame or guilt for breaking the rules. As they mature, they differentiate between norms and goals that are imposed by the community and those that are self-imposed. These people are aware of themselves as persons-in-community and strive to belong.

  - *Trajectory for change:* The crisis for most people at this stage is personal integrity. Most people in America operate at this stage because they do not know they are stuck. At some point they have a personal or professional crisis which leads them to restructure their life according to their own understanding of the world and move to the conscientious stage.

- *Characteristics of the Conscientious Stage.* The crises which propel us into the conscientious stage are never fun. Often we are abandoned by family and friends whom we expected to provide validation for our world view. At this point we begin to take responsibility for ourselves and our world rather than to have unbending commitment to our previously considered principles. A persistent question (which is unsettling) is whether we are being rebellious in making our own way or whether in fact we have moved to a higher level of maturity by taking a more systemic approach to the problem, even if it means going against the norms of community. Finding a mentor at this point can help us sort through that question.

  - *Attending to Reason:* Kohlberg asserts that people at this stage find that the right action is doing their duty in society, upholding the social order, and maintaining the welfare of the society. Persons at this stage consider their individual relationships in terms of their own place in the system.

  - *Attending to Relationships:* Haan finds that people at this level of maturity accommodate their self-interest to meet common interests. They embrace a systematized, structural exchange based on the understanding that all persons can fall from grace. They make conscious compromises, where a person commits to the shared agreements and rules of the community, and believes that he should have the same considerations and privileges as others.

  - *Attending to Power:* Hagberg finds that people in this stage get their power from reflection and are competent, reflective, and strong. They are comfortable with their personal style, are skilled at mentoring, and show true leadership.

  - *Attending to Wholeness:* Liebert finds that people in this stage live by self-evaluated standards and monitor their own behavior by self-criticism and measuring action against long-term goals and ideals. People respect the community and are concerned about maintaining it, as well as striving for justice and caring for others.

- *Trajectory for change:* As people begin to mellow and learn to let go of their own ego, they become ready to make the final move to the compassionate inter-individual stage.

- *Characteristics of the Compassionate Inter-Individual Stage*. Driven to define the purpose for our life, when we move to this stage, we become willing to expand our belief systems beyond ourselves to find ultimate meaning. We are willing to embrace the world view of others and see that the world is gloriously pluralistic in outlook and opportunities. When we reach this stage, we still have intense commitments, but the actions we take to support those commitments are more realistic and more tempered. We become more gentle with ourselves and with others as we accept inner conflict and the complexity of reality.

  - *Attending to Reason:* Kohlberg asserts that people at this stage find that the right action is upholding the basic rights, values, and legal contracts of a society, even when they conflict with the concrete rules and laws of the group.

  - *Attending to Relationship:* Haan finds that people at this level of maturity assimilate their self-interests into others' mutual interests to achieve personally and situationally specific balances. The belief is that one is a moral agent among other moral agents. Thus, people are responsible to themselves, others, and to their mutual interests. People at this stage realize that we are all connected to each other and thus part of each other's existence.

  - *Attending to Power:* Hagberg finds that people in this stage get their power from their purpose in life. People accept themselves and are calm and humble. As visionaries, they are confident of their life purpose and generously empower other people.

  - *Attending to Wholeness:* Liebert finds that people in this stage are tolerant as well as able to cope with conflicting inner needs. They respect autonomy and interdependence.

  - *Trajectory for change:* Most theorists who look at personal development assert that one more level of development is possible. However, none are able to find examples of this next stage except perhaps the very greatest of moral leaders such as Jesus Christ, Mohammad, and Buddha. Thus, the final stage is called the cosmic stage.

As we mature and begin to make sense of the world around us, we move through these various stages of ethical maturity. Our theorists agree that to move on from the conscientious-conformist stage requires great intentionality because our Western culture hands out most of the rewards to people in that stage. We also must remember that rather than predictably moving lockstep through the stages, when we are threatened, frightened, or confused, we may operate at a lower stage of ethical maturity. Because we have free will, we can either choose to make decisions at our highest level of ethical maturity or at a lower stage to protect ourself or others.

As we become self-aware, we accurately assess our ethical maturity and make conscious decisions to become more mature A common fault is that we place ourselves further along the trajectory than we actually are, thus becoming blind to the opportunities for growth that are present. As we learn to correct for the bias which is inherent in the ethical lenses as well as the bias which is present because of our level of ethical maturity, we make better ethical decisions.

Attend to the Common Good

Mid-twentieth century, two images seared the consciousness of the Western world. The first was the mushroom cloud which filled the sky after the nuclear bombing of Hiroshima. That image starkly underscored the realization that we could destroy our earth. The second image was captured by the astronauts in outer space, a luminous blue globe, our earth, with land, clouds, and water — with nary a national border or delineation. Leonard Shlain in *The Alphabet and the Goddess: The Conflict Between Word and Image* asserts that those images changed the trajectory of human existence.[16] For the first time in human history our actions were not local and restricted in time. We realized that the actions of any one of us could have implications for generations, consequences that we could not foresee. As the full impact of the technological revolution was felt in the last half of the 20th century, many from all disciplines and walks of life began to question whether the commitment that the Western community has to individualism could in fact result in the destruction of civilization. In response, a call for a sustainable economy or community arose from many sectors.

Voices from every discipline — including economics, philosophy, theology, sociology, and ecology — suggested that we need to expand our horizons to explore the impact of individual action on the common good. The move towards considering the global community and not just ourselves, our community, or our nation, is gaining ever more acceptance. As Hans Jonas reminds us, we cannot look only to our own desires and preferences, because our acts have the potential of affecting people and generations far removed from us.[17]

The most insistent examples of our interconnectedness are the global economy and the environmental movement. First, as goods and jobs move seamlessly across the globe, we are called to pay attention to economic and social conditions in countries other than our own, particularly those with second and third world states. Second, all of us are affected by existing and emerging issues such as global warming, scarce water, and air pollution. Traditional ethical notions of organizations attending only to their own bottom line will not meet the firm's responsibility to the larger community. In the corporate world, from an organizational perspective, attending to the common good falls broadly under the rubric Corporate Social Responsibility (CSR). Proponents of CSR offer new criteria for determining the ethical behavior of a company, such as attending to the triple bottom line which measures and reports "corporate performance against economic, social and environmental parameters."[18] A telling feature of the value of socially-aware companies is that during the recent economic downturn, those companies identified as socially conscious kept their value much better than those which were not identified as being concerned with the common good.

Theorists predict that in the very near future, companies will not be judged only on how much profit they return to their stockholders, but will also be expected to assure that the interests of all stakeholders are considered in their choices. We are each asked then to give from our abundance, to the degree that we have resources and personal power. As we give of ourselves and our resources, we then assure that others with fewer resources and less power can themselves become fully functioning adults in a world that is safe, clean, and sustainable for humankind.

Act with Courage

No one ever has enough information. No one ever knows all the ramifications of action. Yet, each of us must make choices. Acting with courage requires being as thoughtful as possible in evaluating the situation and then acting, knowing that more information will come forward and the results will be imperfect. As stated before, choosing not to act *is* acting. Thus, each of us is called to make the best decision that we can in the situation at hand, knowing that we are fallible human beings operating in an ever-changing world.

Step 5 Return to Awareness: A Reprise

After we act, we are returned to the process of reflection and awareness. As we intentionally engage in the cycle, the promise is that change — growth — becomes reality.

Continuous Improvement

Lonergan asserts that every new action brings another set of questions. As we move from reflection to action and back again, we can see what results were good and which we want to correct or avoid. We also see which rules or principles were appropriate and which need to be reframed and nuanced in light of emerging knowledge. Thus, we transform ourselves by becoming ever more effective as ethical agents as well as more mature humans. We see this approach in the contemporary management theories of continuous quality improvement (CQI), pioneered by W. Edwards Deming. This movement helps organizations continually attend to their management processes in order to become ever more effective in delivering goods and services. Rather than assuming that bad apples are responsible for failure, CQI initiatives ask where the system unintentionally supported the undesirable result and how the process can be changed to get better results.

An example of CQI in action can be seen as hospitals are working to find ways to reduce mortality rates caused by lack of quality control. One physician noticed that after seeing several patients on a given day as he made hospital rounds, he prescribed a particular set of treatments based on the symptom the patient mentioned first. He further observed that after hearing one or two symptoms out of a list of several indicators, he stopped listening and made a judgment about the appropriate treatment for each patient. Because patients seldom listed the symptoms in the same order, he then realized that this habit led to different treatments for the same illness, which in medical language is called treatment variations. To minimize treatment variations, he designed a process in which he used a hand-held computer to enter all of the information that was given to him by the patient before making a diagnosis. This new process resulted in more uniformity of treatment. He found that his results were better and the quality of care improved. However, many other physicians have resisted adopting this practice because they believe that the using computer takes all of the personal touch and art out of caring for their patients. [19] As this physician demonstrated, working through hypothetical problems helps facilitate the same sort of process of improvement in ethical maturity by helping us develop the habit of reflection and action.

The Crucible of Spirit

During the past decade, interest in spirituality at work and in every other facet of our lives has dramatically increased. Robert Wuthnow, writing about spirituality in America, states that "[a]t its core, spirituality consists of all the beliefs and activities by which individuals attempt to relate their lives to God or to a divine being or some other conception of a transcendent reality."[20] Wuthnow finds that spirituality is both an individual quest for meaning and is shaped by the larger community context. Thus, during the current times when ideas about ethics and morality are in flux, ideas about spirituality are also malleable. Just as no one philosophical approach fits all, we may find that no single religious or spiritual framework meets all needs.

> The Crucible of Spirit
>
> Discipline of the soul through love to achieve integration.

Daniel Helminiak, a Lonergan scholar, says that spirituality is that drive to become a whole human being, marked by four characteristics. The first is accepting that the human spirit has an intrinsic drive which will take us beyond ourselves and our preferences into a search for values which include other persons and ultimately society and the sacred, however defined. The second quality is being open to embracing that drive to move beyond considering only ourselves in decisions.

A third characteristic is movement toward personal integrity and wholeness. The final characteristic is that spirituality is a move to adulthood — thinking and weighing evidence for ourselves, judging and deciding for ourselves what we will do and so become.[21] Thus, spirituality is not tied to any one particular religious tradition and for some may be independent of any formal religious tradition or practice.

Key in this process is learning to love ourselves and others. Balancing the four core values, if we look at our world with eyes of love we learn to discern which virtue is appropriate. For example, to be loving in a particular situation may require assuring that justice is done and the rules are enforced (rationality) to help a person become a fully functioning responsible adult. To be loving in another situation may require that we show mercy (sensibility) and not enforce the rules. As we love ourselves we can determine when being responsible for ourselves and asserting our rights (autonomy) is appropriate and when we need to ask for help. Other times we may notice that as we love others in our community, subordinating our rights to assure that others thrive (equality) is desired. Wisdom guides us as we discern which value should take precedence in a situation and which virtue should emerge.

As we go through life, we need to periodically stop and see whether we are moving toward wholeness. Are we in fact attending to our mind, nurturing our heart, and cultivating our spirit? Lonergan's method helps us correct for error and reinforce success. As we increase our self-efficacy, we have the potential to find meaning in our lives and joy in our work. As we continue to pay attention, explore our own response intelligently, judge soundly among competing understandings of ourselves and the world, and act responsibly, we can be ever more effective persons-in-community. If something does not work well, we can correct the action. As we get more information, we can change course. Honoring the innate drive within us which desires the good and seeks knowledge, we can become authentic human beings who are not just drifting through life. In the process we can also help create an ethical and effective organizational culture.

Conclusion

As you work through ethical dilemmas, attend not only to the choices that you make but also your internal responses — your gut reactions and your reaction to colleagues. As one acts bravely, the self-knowledge which is gained marks the difference between an effective ethical agent and the one who chooses the other road — the well-worn path of obliviousness. The good news is that, as we learn to habitually act only after reflection, the decisions become easier. As we use the five decision-making steps and strive for ethical maturity, we become more effective leaders in our community and more complete human beings.

Michael Stebbins, a business ethicist at Gonzaga University, asserts that as we engage in the process of ethical attention, we will be able to embrace and achieve the virtues of the authentic person and grow in spiritual wisdom.[22]

- *Attentiveness:* As we learn to pay attention in framing the context and identifying the ethical agent; we will
  - *discipline* ourselves not to wear blinders;
  - *be alert* to all relevant data, no matter what the source;
  - *consider* both the forest — our long term goals and objects — as well as the trees — the short term implications of what we are seeing;
  - *expect change*; and
  - *step away* from the noise to notice what is happening rather than getting distracted by the chatter around us.
- *Understanding:* As we seek to explore intelligently the interests of the stakeholders and the complexities of the issues; we will
  - *look* for connections that explain the data;
  - *probe* what we are seeing for root causes;
  - *consider* new ideas or insights, even those from unexpected or untraditional sources;
  - *keep asking* "why?" when we see information or data that we do not understand; and
  - *be patient*.
- *Discernment:* As we learn to judge soundly while identifying options for action, explore the conflicts, and prioritize the values; we will

  - ▹ _test_ our explanations to see if they are correct;
  - ▹ _not jump_ to conclusions;
  - ▹ _not withhold judgment_ when the evidence is in; and
  - ▹ _be dissatisfied_ with anything less than the best available answer.

- ▸ *Responsibility:* As we act responsibly through becoming ethically mature and applying the tests of the various lenses; we will
  - ▹ _choose_ the greater good;
  - ▹ _be actively concerned_ for those affected by our actions;
  - ▹ _follow through_ with courage and intelligence, and
  - ▹ _be willing_ to admit and correct our mistakes.

Continuing the Conversation

1. As you reflect on your own ethical decision making, how do you balance among ethical, moral, and spiritual concerns? How do you adjust for imbalance between rationalism and your emotionalism? On which side do you tend to fall in a difficult situation?

2. Find an article or an op ed piece in your local paper or a news magazine which deals with a current ethical situation. See if you can identify the reasons which were given for the decisions. What did the author use to justify the position that was taken? Were you persuaded? Why or why not?

3. Identify an ethical dilemma that you have faced and resolved. Following the steps of this chapter, in a page or less, describe the criteria you used to resolve the problem. What did you use to justify your position? What do you notice about both what information you chose to include and what you deemed irrelevant? Was the process easy or hard? What did you learn about yourself?

Part 2

Making Hard Choices in a Complex World

Chapter 6 The Path to Maturity 147

Chapter 7 Rights/Responsibility Lens 173

Chapter 8 Results Lens 203

Chapter 9 Relationship Lens 227

Chapter 10 Reputation Lens 255

Chapter 11 Strategies for Success 291

Path to Maturity

CRUCIBLE OF SPIRIT

Sacred Essence
"I am special...just like everyone else!"

Sacred Creation
"I am part of all that is."

WORLD OF MORALITY

Ethics of the Heart
What is a compassionate person?
"I am moral."

Ethics of Community
What is a connected person?
"I am part of the community."

WORLD OF ETHICS

Virtue Ethics
What is good character?
"I am ethical."

Justice Ethics
What is a fair system?
"I am part of the system."

Who am I?

How do I fit?

CULTURAL CONTEXT

Why this choice?

What do I want?

Deontology
What are my rights and responsibilities?
"I am responsible."

Teleology
What are my goals, my good results?
"I have choices."

MIND

Ethics of Care
What is a caring person?
"I am caring."

Ethics of Mutuality
What achieves moral balance?
"I am consistent."

EMOTIONS

Sacred Will
"I delight in my work."

Sacred Imagination
"I am co-creator of all that is."

SOUL

Personality is only ripe
when a man
has made the truth his own.

Soren Kierkegaard [1]

Chapter 6

Path to Maturity

After completing an ethics class and considering the approaches of the various theorists, students often ask "which ethical theory is right?" The answer is all of them and none of them. Just as Heisenberg demonstrated that looking for particles means that we find particles, *i.e.*, we find what we are looking for, all ethical theorists have a question which focuses their attention and shapes what they see. As theorists are both situated within their own historical context and respond to perennial questions (p. 36), their writing is best understood as the next discussion in an ongoing conversation about how best to live in particular time.

Philosophers and theologians who write about ethics and justice respond to the prevalent world view of their time.[2] In addition, each broad historical period has a primary spokesman from each of the two major ethical traditions.[3] Thus, each theorist *responds* to the inadequacies of the prevailing world view and those in the other tradition, *addresses challenges* presented by excesses and abuses of the existing leaders and power structures, and *incorporates new information* about our world and humans which comes through science and technology.[4]

Charting the Conversation

The first task of philosophers is to answer the critiques and expose the weaknesses of currently accepted theories. Because historically the theorists tend to move between traditions, they show how all or part of their predecessor's world view is flawed. In the process, a theorist might accept some of the writing of a colleague and reject other portions of the scholarship or tradition.

Although each generation of philosophers writes during a particular historical time, with the specific circumstances of that time and place coloring their work, they tend to place themselves within a larger tradition based on their core beliefs. In the process of situating themselves in the conversation, theorists reappropriate the themes of their preferred school of thought in light of the problems and emerging knowledge of their generation. Thus, Rawls places himself in the tradition of Kant. Rawls asserts that his work is supplementing Kant's categorical imperatives by adding a process by which those imperatives can be used in today's society. MacIntyre claims that he is rearticulating the work of Aristotle (see p. 70) by recovering a theory of virtue which is needed to make sense of ethics today.

The challenge for us is to determine an overall approach which makes the most sense for us and then live consistently within that tradition while working with people who may embrace the other ethical tradition. A central thesis of this book is that if we continue to try to determine which of the core beliefs are the truth, we will never get unity of thought let alone consensus for action. Further, we will believe that the only resolution for diverse ethical beliefs is relativism where no particular statement about what is the right thing to do can trump another understanding of what is right. However, most of us know that the more complex answers to ethical dilemmas are often better than the simpler ones. The question is how to get to the better and, perhaps, the best solution. One approach is to harmonize the theories rather than holding them in opposition. The claim is that as we learn to consider all the theories and work from a position of meta-ethics, awareness of and balancing the core values, we reach better decisions.

To be able to hold a both/and context, we must look at how the two traditions complement each other rather than see only how they are in opposition. Wilber, a constructive postmodern Buddhist writer, provides a key. In his seminal work *Sex, Ecology, Spirituality: The Spirit of Evolution,* Wilber asks, "how can you sympathetically align the traditions with each other."[5] To answer the question, Wilber traces the evolution of individual and collective beliefs. He lays out a matrix containing broad patterns that clearly shows the interrelationship of reflection and action in individual and collective community development. Expanding Plato's *Allegory of the Cave,* Wilber asserts that for the past several centuries the Western world in particular has focused on the exterior side of development.[6] The result is what he calls

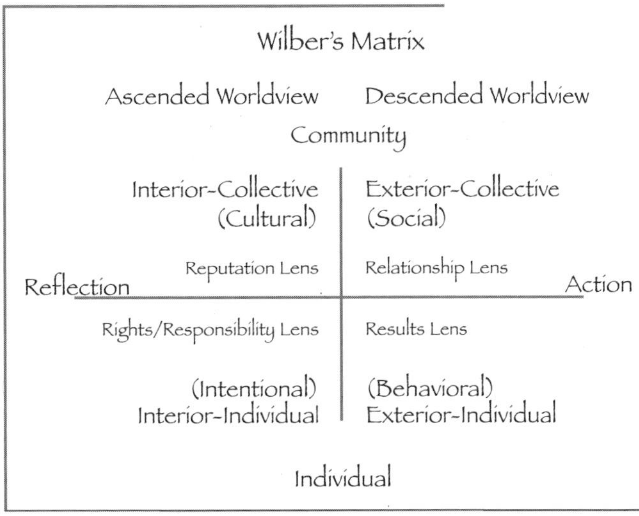

> ...a purely Descended world view. Spirit is simply identified with the Sum Total of exteriors, the Sum Total of the shadows in the Cave. So intent are we on proving that the shadows are one great interlocking order that we never move from these exteriors to the real interior, and thus we never find the genuine superior.

He claims that we need to include the Ascended world view where the self-transcending nature of Spirit is added to the mix.[7]

Two insights emerge from Wilber's matrix. The first is that as we consider the world and then act, we move between action and reflection. The essence of critical thinking (a staple in our educational system) is learning to use the tools of reason to reflect on the authority and tradition of our culture as well as our own experiences after we choose to act. Then when the action creates new data, we reconsider our total world view, modulating our beliefs as needed. Thus, Wilber's horizontal axis moves between interior and exterior — reflection and action — and matches our current best understanding about how to become mature ethical agents.

The vertical axis moves between the individual and the community. Ethics is traditionally defined as an individual's moral standards. This definition masks the observation that, unless we live in a community, we do not have to worry about ethics. A way to put the conversation into sharper focus is to adopt the language of another set of constructive postmodern theorists, Herman Daly (an economist) and John Cobb (a theologian) who coined the phrase "person-in-community." Daly and Cobb assert that "[t]he self that is to be understood is not a bundle of separate aspects, and it has no existence at all apart from its relations to its human and non-human environments."[8] They note further that "[i]n reality political, social, economic, and cultural aspects of human existence are indissolubly interconnected" and so, rather than seeking to divide knowledge into ever tinier boxes, we learn to focus on holistic synthesizing of our knowledge, impelled by the human desire to know.[9]

If in fact we are persons-in-community, then the discipline of applied ethics does not just focus on the principles that individuals choose to adopt as they navigate their path through this world. Rather, the discipline explores the synergy created between individuals and their communities through ongoing conversations which inform and moderate beliefs and actions. Wilber's vertical axis which moves between the individual and collective helps us understand the balancing act that many have instinctively employed in sorting out for themselves how best to live. To be ethically mature, we not only attend to our internal development and external reality, but also to spirit and reason. We also attend to our lives as individuals while considering and enhancing the common good. In the process we have the possibility of moving from an egocentric viewpoint to, in Wilber's words, a "worldcentric or non-ethnocentric", more holistic viewpoint which embraces both historic ethical traditions.[10]

Petrick and Quinn's Matrix

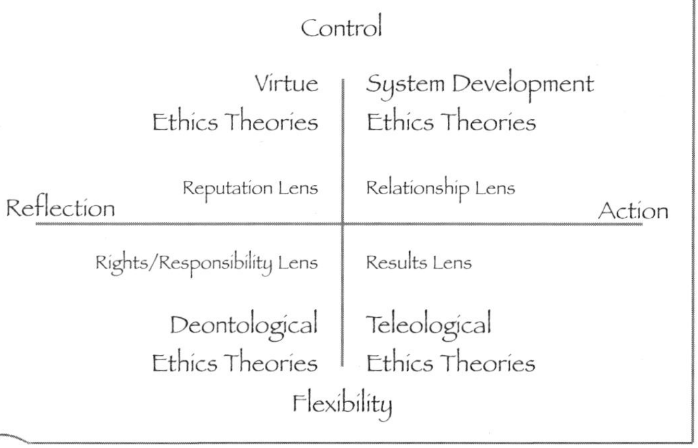

Joseph A. Petrick and John F. Quinn, apparently independent of Wilber, organized traditional ethics into a similar matrix, asking the same question as Wilber, but from a management perspective. Petrick and Quinn mirror Wilber's axis between reflection and action. However, they identify the points of the vertical axis "control" and "flexibility", rather than Wilber's collective and individual.[11]

Petrick and Quinn note that deontology and teleology locate the control for action within the individual, that the two traditions focus on what each of us believes is right action for ourselves. As we cherish flexibility, we nimbly move in community. However, control is needed if the community is going to have stability. Thus, individuals learn to follow the rules of society as they accommodate the collective interests of others. Like Daly, Cobb, and Wilber, Petrick and Quinn argue for a richer understanding of ethics for business leaders, where they use the tools and insights of the traditions to move against "ethical relativism in favor of an enriched but bounded tradition of moral pluralism."[12]

Interestingly, when the representative philosophers (p. 70) are placed in the core ethical frameworks grid, the self-correcting nature of each tradition emerges. The traditional teleological theories of utilitarianism (the Results Lens — seeking the greatest good for the greatest number) and egoism (seeking happiness for oneself) which can lead to acting from expedience are moderated by virtue ethics (the Reputation Lens — developing a good character). As one chooses to act to gain the goods of the community which can lead to expedience (Results Lens), one must reflect on how that action will affect one's reputation in the community and seek excellence (Reputation Lens). Traditional deontological theories (the Rights/Responsibility Lens — asserting individual rights and responsibilities) are moderated by theories of justice (the Relationship Lens — disciplining desire for the common good). As one considers personal entitlement which can lead to selfishness, one must assure that everyone has the ability to exercise the same rights, or at least simular, which lead to procedural justice, sharing, and generosity.

Theoretical Evolution

Aquinas (1226-1274) MacIntyre (1929—) Teleological Reputation Lens	Augustine (340-430) Rawls (1921-2002) Deontological Relationship Lens
Rights/Responsibility Lens Deontological Kant (1724-1804) Plato (427-347? BC)	Results Lens Teleological Mill (1806-1873) Aristotle (384-322 BC)

As each tradition has evolved over our history, it appears that the excess of one generation is moderated by turning the theoretical coin over to see its other face. Thus, we can place the theorists in an evolving spiral around the matrix. The grand sweep of history appears to mimic the balance that many instinctively seek. Plato and Aristotle laid the foundation for modern ethics by focusing on the place of individuals in society. As Augustine and Aquinas rearticulated classical thought in light of Christian doctrine, they emphasized the prerogatives of community, the Church. The perceived excesses of the Holy Roman Empire were moderated by Kant and Mill in the emerging Age of Enlightenment with a reassertion of the rights of individuals to choose how to live. The excesses of individualism are tempered by the voices of Rawls who made a claim for procedural justice and MacIntyre who reclaimed the tradition of virtue ethics.

Wuthnow suggests that these shifts can be seen as the difference between a "spirituality of wandering" and a "spirituality of dwelling." When ideas and institutions are challenged or in flux, we must rely on our own resources to sort out what is true and thus we tend to be more pessimistic about the human condition as we see ourselves as pilgrims in an unfriendly land. During settled times when institutions are strong and the community holds beliefs in common, we tend to be more optimistic and are willing to put down roots as we see ourselves connected to the larger community."[13]

The work of each of these theorists not only addressed the elements of their preferred lens but also included elements of the other lens of the particular tradition. So Mill, while focusing on the importance of individuals choosing what makes them happy, spends considerable time talking about character and virtues, the balancing lens. Kant, while focusing on the rights and responsibilities, foreshadows the work of Rawls as he talks about our responsibility to the larger whole. In addition, each theorist responds to the strengths and critiques of the others. However, as each theorist is placed in the context for which he is best known, the rhythm of the evolving thought comes into relief. As we become skilled in moral pluralism, recognizing all aspects of both traditions, we see the gift of each tradition. As we learn to use the core heuristic question of each tradition, we become more effective ethical actors.

Core Heuristic Questions

As we move from childhood to adulthood, we begin the journey with a set of inherited assumptions. As discussed earlier, our world view is informed by the authorities we find persuasive, the traditions we embrace, and our personal experiences, all of which are mediated by reason and emotion and harmonized by the crucible of the spirit. Our assumptions shape our world view, setting the course for our activities in the world. The center of the Path to Maturity Chart (p.146) posits four heuristic questions (tending to stimulate investigation) that each of us is invited to answer, as we find our place in our community. As youngsters we begin life enmeshed in their family with no separate sense of self. The "terrible twos" represent the move from immersion in our family to the recognition of ourselves as a separate person with desires and the ability to reason. As we grow, we anticipate the larger questions asked by our representative theorists. At each stage of our development and when faced with difficult situations, we ask the questions over and over again, hopefully maturing into a richer set of answers.

Core Heuristic Questions

Who am I?	How do I fit?
Reputation Lens	Relationship Lens
Rights/Responsibility Lens	Results Lens
Why this choice?	What do I want?

Why This Choice?

The question, "why this choice," focuses our attention on our motives and reasons for acting. Although annoying for parents, the primary developmental task of children is to differentiate themselves from their birth family. This transition is signaled by the words "mine" and "no." One of my children has the "Rules of Toddlers" on her refrigerator. The precept is that "everything that is mine is mine and everything that is yours is mine." Parents help children sort out concepts such as private property and virtues such as respect for possessions and sharing by helping them figure out their motive for acting. If parents reinforce the claim that prior rights to a truck can be claimed because the toy is the child's, they plant the seeds of rights, in this case the right to private property. As parents teach their children to pick up after themselves, say "please" and "thank-you," and share with others, they plant the seeds of responsibility.

As adults we learn to examine for ourselves our motives for acting. Kant provides a key restraint on selfishness by asking us to consider whether the reasons we are using for acting would be equally persuasive if those reasons were used by others in relation to us. Many writers assert that we cannot be held morally accountable for an act that turns out badly but which was done with good intentions. Of course, what counts as good intentions is also contested. For example, is a good intention to act to maximize shareholder value ethically acceptable if this policy results in many of the employees not having sufficient resources (salary, health care, leisure) to live relatively good lives?

What Do I Want?

The question, "what do I want?" requires that we choose among competing goods. One of the most frustrating characteristics of being human is that we can not have it all: every choice precludes other choices. Robert Frost's poignant poem "The Road Not Taken" which opened Chapter Four, tells of a person making choices along life's way, promising to come back while somehow knowing that the path will never be traveled again. By asking this question, each of us has the opportunity to follow our heart's desire.

Mill's articulation of utilitarianism, which invites us to choose for ourselves how to live, is compelling because he asserts that we should not be locked into certain vocations or life circumstances simply because of our family history, birth order, or the family business. The lack of social and economic mobility in Europe and the promise of the New World accelerated the crumbling of the feudal age where the first born got all the property and the business (or, if a woman, married to someone with property to manage the family fortunes), the second son was sent into the military service, and the third son (and sometimes daughter) was sent into the service of the church.

This new notion of self-determination was intoxicating. At the time in England, when licenses to do business were inherited, the promise of a market economy, where people could make their own choices about what services they wanted and what price they wanted to pay, was heady stuff indeed. While clearly some unintended consequences flowed from the move to a market economy, on the whole the founding fathers of America found the trade-off worthy.

How Do I Fit?

The question "how do I fit?" reminds us, in the words of John Donne, that "No man is an island. All are part of the promontory."[14] Because we are persons in community, determining how we fit is critical. While the image of the tenacious entrepreneur or independent pioneer fashioning a living in the wilderness is a compelling part of the American mythology, individuals, whether in the new economy or on the frontier, depended on each other in myriads of ways. The trappers needed customers for their pelts and suppliers of goods. Those on farms and in the towns needed goods as well as security from those who would threaten. Wuthnow notes that as settlers and immigrants came to the United States, they built their communities with churches and institutions which provided a place for them to be and familiar rituals and celebrations which gave them a sense of belonging.[15]

Bill Convery, an historian who did a stint as a guide in one of Colorado's Ghost Towns, states that a persistent question asked by visitors (after inquiring at what altitude elk become deer — really!) is where the gun fights were held. Convery patiently explained that the frontier towns did not see much action as "guns are bad for business."[16] The first thing the town fathers did was to pass laws, elect a sheriff, put up a jail, and prosecute those who did not fit into the community.

The story portrays businesses' persistent ambivalence towards government. While many in business prefer to be free from government regulation, they also depend on a legal system to assure that contracts are enforced, debts paid and that their goods get to market without being stolen. Thus, business and government have always had an interesting relationship: business asks government to protect it while asking that they also be left to run their affairs at will.[17]

Determining how and where we fit into the workplace is also an interesting question. Our parents settled into their jobs with the expectation that they would keep the same job for a lifetime. The rhetoric often masked the reality of changing economic needs. My father worked for Boeing as a chemist. Noting the pattern of layoffs during economic downturns, the family sardonically affirms that Dad retired after 25 years — only it took him 30 plus years to get his retirement pay.

Students are currently told that they should expect to change jobs five to seven times over a lifetime; clearly the expectation for finding a community at work is different. As not only blue-collar but also white-collar professional jobs which used to be filled by Americans are outsourced to other lands, a result of the emerging global economy, answering the question of what exactly creates a community becomes ever more important. Peering through the glasses of business owners, investors, and consumers, a global economy sounds pretty nifty. Looking through the glasses of an employee or a citizen, the picture may not be quite as rosy. We forget that, depending on our particular role at a given time, all of us look through both sets of glasses which makes determining where we fit even more challenging.

Who Am I?

The final question, "who am I?" is one of identity. As children we take our identity from our families: "Daddy's little girl" or "Mommy's muffin." We learn that members of our families do certain things — we chew with our mouths closed, say please and thank-you and do not terrorize our younger siblings. We learn that we are expected to do well in school, excel in sports, or continue the family tradition in the arts or police work. While we usually think of identity as being positive, our families and community also can create a negative self-image. Children who are the scapegoats for all that is wrong for the family or who belong to an ethnic group which is not fully accepted have different issues surrounding their identity than those who are raised in a loving, accepting family.

One of the most disturbing cases I ever had as a juvenile defense attorney was representing three high-school students who happened to live in my upper-middle class professional neighborhood. Two of the students found themselves in the wrong place at the wrong time, breaking into the local elementary school and stealing the computers. The third, the master-mind, had a father who fenced the stolen goods for the boys. The notion of an upper-middle class parent encouraging his child to engage in illegal behavior which would jeopardize that child's life and well being was incredibly discouraging. That child received praise from his father for stealing; the twig was bent.

Another example of the power of identity comes from Michael J. Sheeran, who was raised in segregated Kansas City. He tells of discovering at the age of nine the world of those who were not able to be part of his life. He was at a BBQ joint and needed to use the restroom. To get there he had to go through the "colored only" section of the restaurant.[18] Even at age nine, he knew that all humans were worthy of respect. The realization that some people were not free to go wherever they desired based only on race profoundly shaped his sense of justice and deeply influenced his work to make sure that, in the words of Martin Luther King, Jr., "all little boys and all little girls will be judged not on the color of their skin, but on the content of their character."[19]

As intimated by the examples above, each of these four questions leads to an ethical framework where we can explore the implications for being effective persons-in-community. Each question has intrigued successive generations of theorists and activists who have worked to find just the right balance among the competing values. For each of us, the opportunity is to learn to be responsible ethical agents by intentionally engaging in the questions and then carefully choosing a course of action.

To see our personal trajectory of growth and to find our preferred tradition, we must go back to our cultural roots. This journey helps us understand both our own world view and the way that we move through society. To make effective ethical decisions while living in our pluralistic community with its contested core assumptions, we must determine where we stand and where we want to go. As we embrace a holistic approach to ethics, we will have the opportunity to claim our own truth which will guide us as we face difficult questions in a complex world. In the process we can become fully functioning adults who nourish our reason, our emotions, and our spirit.

The Ethical Map

For those accustomed to using the terms ethics and morality interchangeably, separating reason and emotion may seem artificial. However, the implications of the historical division between the world of ethics (which uses the mind to find the rules of life) and the world of morality (where we explore how we use our emotions to develop empathy) profoundly impact our understanding of ethics. Aided by the invention of the printing press (1436), as the Protestant Reformation (beginning in 1518) and the Age of Enlightenment (1700s) unfolded, the key impetus for individual rights emerged as ordinary people learned how to read, question, and reason. As people were expected to determine for themselves first their religious views and then their political views, the ability to read the Bible and discern its truth was viewed as crucial. However, because the notion of Divine Right of Kings was still in play, the religion of the leader determined the religion of all in the community. In Europe. wars raged in community after community in Europe as the battle between Protestantism and

> **The World of Ethics**
>
> Disciplining the mind through reason to find the rules of life.

Catholicism took its toll.[20] As the political and religious agenda of the Protestant Reformation took hold during the 1500s, the politics of a given city depended on the religious persuasion of the leadership. If the leaders were Catholic, the established religion was Catholicism, and the economic and legal benefits went primarily to Catholics. Likewise, if the leaders were Protestant.[21] The political changes were fueled by religious convictions and were accompanied with much bloodshed. To help end the carnage, the Enlightenment philosophers posited that through reason alone one could determine the rules for living. Descartes' famous dictum "I think, therefore I am," introduced the notion of doubt as to the nature of reality as a beginning for the search for truth.[22] With reason as the litmus test for truth, the authority of a church father or political leader could not substitute for careful thought and reasoning in a situation. As much of the fighting was fueled by religious zealots fanning the emotions of the people, philosophers, such as Kant in particular, extolled reason for decision making and declared the passions as untrustworthy.

Thus, most traditional ethics texts focus on critical thinking to help us discipline our minds, as we use the tools of reason to determine the rules of life which we will follow. Using reason, we apply ethical principles and criteria to a problem which helps us choose the most ethical act. As we explore the traditions further, patterns emerge and we see how the theorists approach the four core questions. One part of each tradition focuses on individual action; the other side highlights our responsibility to society. Because we are complex individuals who live in community, and because we are also self-centered like the "little girl with the curl" from nursery rhyme days — "when she was good, she was very, very good, and when she was bad she was horrid" — we need both sides of each tradition. To make an ethically mature decision, we must consider the problem from all angles to balance the tendency to excess which is present if one ignores the complementary and corresponding parts of the ethical traditions.

Deontology (the study of duty) inspired by idealism, directs our attention to the perfection to which we should aspire. This strand of ethics focuses on our duty to ourselves and our community. Kant, who is commonly associated with this school of thought, asks the question, "why this choice?" while Rawls explores the question, "how do I fit?" The tension between

> **The Deontological Balance**
>
> The rights and responsibilities of individuals moderated by systemic concern for the least advantaged.

the individual and the community is explored through the lenses of personal rights and responsibility (Kant) and our obligation to assure that the least advantaged are considered in the distribution of power and privilege (Rawls). Kant and others who emphasize personal responsibility call us to consider our own obligations rather than blindly following the dictates of tradition, whether religious or political. Rawls and others who focus on themes of justice invite us to see how, with the roll of a die, we could be unable to care for ourselves and become disadvantaged. Thus, we need to consider what limits the community should place on individuals.

As discussed earlier, the second tradition, teleology (the study of goals and results), is grounded in realism which directs our attention to the here and now. This strand of ethics focuses on goals and outcomes. Mill, a seminal author, asserts that the answer to the question, "what do I want?" is for individuals to be happy. A second voice is that of MacIntyre who asserts that the key to knowing which outcomes to choose is to ask "who am I?" in relation to other community members in light of the core virtues which are expected of people as they live out their various roles.

In the teleological tradition, the tension between the individual and the community is explored through the process of selecting actions that result in happiness and the development of good character. Mill and others who invite us to consider the consequences of our actions exhort us to do what makes us, not someone else, happy. MacIntyre and others who explore the role of character encourage us to pursue virtues such as integrity, justice, and courage so we are not seduced by expedience and forget excellence.

In addition to the assumptions behind each of the traditions being contested, *e.g.,* not agreed upon by all theorists, a related question is which theory is prior to the others — whether the principles or rules from which we live (deontology) or the goals we choose (teleology) determine our choices. As the theorists grappled with the two traditions, they gave their theory priority based on what comes first. In making the case for deontology trumping teleology, Kant notes that we need to consider the consequences, but he believes that they are secondary to doing our duty. Mill and other

> **The Teleological Balance**
>
> The individual pursuit of happiness moderated by development of a virtuous character.

consequentialists argue that we can only determine our duty by considering our goals and what makes us happy.

The question becomes a version of the classic chicken and egg conundrum: do we begin by figuring out our responsibilities and let the consequences fall as they might, or do we consider the consequences and from there determine duty? Or, in philosophers' terms, is "the right prior to the good...in that its principles are independently derived" by reason, or do we first determine "final human purposes or ends...conceptions of the good" and then choose to act.[23] That conversation will probably never be definitively resolved.

Core Ethical Frameworks

Community/Reflective Who am I? Reputation Lens	Community/Action How do I fit? Relationship Lens
Rights/Responsibility Lens Why this choice? Individual/Reflective	Results Lens What do I want? Individual/Action

In a practical sense, we tend to get a better result if we consider both sides of the coin before acting. Using the four core ethical frameworks with their heuristic questions helps us formulate the context of our world view and decide how we should act in given situations. Each of the frameworks encompass a particular set of theorists and traditions which informs our process. Thus, each lens has a particular content — principles or goals — which help people determine the best answer for a particular ethical dilemma. Each framework also has a process which helps us hone our analytic skills and correct for bias which may be present in the other part of the ethical tradition. Those who engage in the field of applied ethics — taking abstract principles and goals and applying them to concrete situations — find that the criteria of either tradition can give a good result. The key is to use at least two of the four lenses in any analysis to compensate for the inherent distortion embedded in each lens.

The Moral Map

The world of emotion, which had been marginalized by the emphasis on reason during the Age of Enlightenment, moved to center stage in the mid-twentieth century. Many different strands of research led to a reassertion of the importance of our emotions. Biologists began doing research on the physical effects of emotions on our bodies as well as on our thought processes.[24] Sociologists and historians noted that the atrocities of the Holocaust in Europe, of Stalin's Purge in Russia, and of slavery in the United States which treated people as property and separated families, resulted from a strict attending to reason without seeing the others as fully human.[25] As we dampened our feelings of empathy for others by not seeing them as fully human, we cruelly imposed rules which destroyed relationships and deeply wounded human lives.[26] The discovery that a well-disciplined mind does not necessarily have a clue about how to build satisfying relationships was popularized in the whole "Mars vs. Venus" dialogue about the differences between men and women.

> The World of Morality
>
> Disciplining emotions through empathy to nourish relationships.

Another strand of research during the last half of the twentieth century focused on how individuals make ethical decisions. Kohlberg, who studied the ethical development of humans, demonstrated that, through learning how to reason more effectively, people could make better ethical decisions. One of Kohlberg's important insights is the notion that ethical development continues over the course of a lifetime and is not finished at the knees of our mothers. As Kohlberg's research continued, his evidence seemed to indicate that women were less ethical than men: when faced with a difficult decision, women tended to try to preserve relationships rather than choosing actions dictated by rules which might damage rapport. According to Kohlberg's scheme where reason was king, this tendency showed a lack of ethical maturity.[27]

Women scholars took a measure of exception to the notion that women are ethically inferior to men. As research continued, Haan demonstrated that, while men tended to be taught to discipline their *mind* through the tool of reason, women tended to be encouraged to discipline their *emotions* using the tool of empathy.[28] Haan constructed a model of ethical development where preservation of relationship was key. The steps to ethical maturity paralleled Kohlberg's as people moved from considering only the implications of the individual to including systemic consequences.[29] The two strands of thought were brought together by the work of Bandura, a psychologist who taught that to be a fully functioning adult in this world, one needs both rational and emotional maturity.[30] Ethical decision-making is like playing a beautiful fugue: the melody line, our mind, is made whole by the counterpoint, our emotions. Effective decision makers have both skill sets.

Gillian's work *In a Different Voice* put forward the idea that an ethic of relationship as historically exercised primarily by women is as valid as an ethic of rules which tends to be embraced by men.[31] Another seminal writer, Noddings, calls the ethic that emerges from relationship an ethic of care. Noddings invites us to augment Kant's notion of the ethical act as the one where we do our duty with empathy and commitment. The counterpoint to "why this choice?" is "as you exercise your rights and responsibilities, respond to the other with care and commitment."[32] Just as an ethic of care which comes from emotional maturity tempers the excesses of individualism, an ethic of compassion and mutuality tempers excesses in the teleological tradition where people are tempted to operate from an ethic of expedience rather than embracing an ethic of excellence.

> What Should I Choose?
>
> As you choose that which makes you happy, respond to the other in mutuality.

Haan asserts that while happiness is important, one must also pay attention to the moral balance between people so that all may have a chance to achieve their goals.[33] For this framework, the key is to choose goals which will also support others in also reaching their goals. Lonergan reflects this approach by asking us to always seek the highest good, that good which addresses the complex, interdependent goals of many in the community.[34] Thus, we are invited to think systematically about the ways we support others in achieving their dreams and how best to reach our own.

Theorists concerned with emotional maturity also explored the question of "how do I fit." The claims of justice articulated by Rawls expanded from concern about an individual's ability to fairly negotiate a complex system to an awareness of how we are all profoundly connected to all people and nature. The study of ecosystems by Frederick revealed that healthy natural systems require cooperation in addition to competition according to the rule of survival of the fittest. Management theorists began speaking of an ethic of cooperation to nourish and sustain the ecosystems of the workplace.[35]

> How Do I Fit?
>
> As you create just (fair) systems, respond to the other cooperatively as an integral part of your community.

The ethic of relationship expanded into exploring the ways that we are all connected, which underscores our obligation to care for the whole community. So, the counterpoint to "how do I fit?" is "to create just and fair systems and respond to the other cooperatively as an integral part of the community.

The final question of "who am I" focuses on what constitutes a good character. Psychologist Charles Shelton states that the answer can be found as we each assert that "I am a moral person" and explore what that identity means for us. While developing ethical virtues is important, for Shelton being moral, which involves emotional maturity, is the critical characteristic of being human. Shelton asserts that we become moral by exercising our conscience and developing empathy, the ability to walk with another in life.[36] Shelton and other developmental psychologists maintain that the self-regulation of our emotions is essential for ethical and moral behavior because reason does not attend to the feeling side of life. Emotions have the potential to give valuable information to our minds as we reason through problems or to cast us into a maelstrom of feelings. Through disciplining our emotions, we come to heed their wisdom and not be overwhelmed by them. By listening to our minds and our hearts, we can become morally mature and have the tools to maintain moral balance. So the answer to the question "who am I?" includes "I am an ethical person with a good character and a moral person with a well developed conscience."

> **Who Am I?**
>
> As you are a virtuous person of good character, respond to the other with empathy and a well-developed conscience.

While a morality of the heart complements an ethic of the head, the picture is not complete. Neither the world or morality nor the world of ethics, alone or together, provides a sufficient answer to the conundrum of how to find and navigate a path leading to "success." Neither of these worlds alone or together provides hard and fast guidelines for determining the rules to follow, choosing goals that are satisfying, learning how to build good relationships with difficult people, or developing a good character. The worlds of ethics and of morality help us live a satisfying external life, moving effectively in our professional and personal life. However, neither of these world views addresses our internal life, the place where we find meaning. To address our interior life, we must turn to the third level, the spiritual realm. The third strand of questions, which arise in the crucible of spirit, ask whether it is it possible to intentionally blend the interior world of spiritual maturity with the exterior world of emotional and intellectual maturity as we seek to be ethical and effective in our professional lives. The answer turns out to be yes.

The Crucible of Spirit

Bookstores are rearranging their shelves to make room for whole new sections about spirituality at work, and courses are flourishing in major universities which explore the gifts that both Western and Eastern spiritual traditions bring to the table. The time is clearly ripe for a conversation about how spirituality influences the world of business. As business ethics is about how we treat ourselves and others in the workplace, exploring the realm of our deepest desires makes some sense. A careful review of the literature shows that each of the core heuristic questions has caught the attention of different authors. Thus, looking at the world through a spiritual lens reveals intriguing answers to the perennial questions with the added twist of how to tend to our souls as we embrace the worlds of ethics (reason) and morality (emotion).

> The Crucible of Spirit
> Discipline of the soul through love to achieve integration.

Even though philosophers attended to reason during the modern period, most people in the Western community identified themselves as Christians or Jews. Thus, the value structure of Christianity permeated the business world. However, in light of the post-modern shift that changed the face of ethics and morality, people tend to make conversations about spirituality independent of conversations about theology. As Wuthnow notes, "[a]t the start the twentieth century, virtually all Americans practiced their faith within a Christian or Jewish framework...Now, at the end of the twentieth century, growing numbers

The Crucible of Spirit

Sacred Essence "I am special... just like everyone else." Who am I?	Sacred Creation "I am part of all that is." How do I fit?
Why this choice? Sacred Will "I delight in my work."	What do I want? Sacred Imagination "I am co-creator of what is."

of Americans piece together their faith like a patchwork quilt. Spirituality has become a vastly complex quest in which each person seeks in his own way."[37]

This individual journey has two different implications for the world of business ethics. First, given that the two primary needs for human beings are to work and to love, our spirituality, the meaning we give to the whole of our lives, profoundly affects both what we see as our role in the business world and how we then fit into the whirlwind of commerce. Second, spirituality has ethical and moral components in that our spirituality determines what rules and goals constrain our behavior and what virtues are appropriate as we discern how we can best act with love. So, as we acquire wisdom, the content of our ethical and moral beliefs is nuanced by the shape of our spiritual beliefs and practices.[38]

Spiritual reflection is the process by which we both take a stand for what we believe as well as search our own soul to find our biases and interests.[39] Theologian Mark McIntosh states that spirituality becomes "a discovery of the true 'self' precisely in encountering the divine and the human other — who allows one neither to rest in a reassuring self-image nor to languish in the prison of a false social construction of oneself."[40] With this definition, McIntosh reminds us that through blending theory and practice, one is transformed. Our work life, no more than our personal life, can become the crucible for growth and change and in the process more than an inconvenient interlude where we get the resources we need to live. By weaving the thread of spirituality through our work, these resources can help us discover what it means to be fully human and find our personal center which is essential for effective leadership. For each lens the spiritual polish provides a nuance — not a replacement — for the answers to the core questions revealed through the worlds of ethics and morality.

Spiritual maturity requires that we reason with skill, relate to others with care, and that we integrate the two through love — first by loving ourselves and then by loving all of creation as we love ourselves. Every spiritual tradition teaches that as we explore "why this choice?" we can become aware and learn to love and serve ourselves others with delight. Then, as we go to our work, we can go with a spirit of joy rather than with grumbling with discontent or discouragement. Imagination and creativity help us answer the question "what do I want?" Much of the literature on the spirituality of work invites us to envision a world where all are able to thrive as full human persons and then act to make that world a reality. As we take responsibility for creating our own work life, or at least creating our response to it, we can find meaning in even difficult situations.

For example, a woman who works to teach young adults who have just been released from detention facilities how to read finds much that is discouraging. The skills of the students are far below par, their lives hold little hope, and their circumstances are grim. Yet, the teacher takes comfort in the fact that maybe one of her students, as he or she is treated with dignity and respect, will find the way out of the box and acquire the skills to be a participating member of our community. That possibility keeps her going to work even as her students move in and out of the penal system.

As we consider "how do I fit?" spiritual teachers encourage us to notice that we are not separate from each other but are part of the whole. This insight has interesting and complex implications as we consider whether we should focus on local or global concerns, giving rise to the popular slogan, "think globally and act locally." And finally, in response to the question "who am I?" the spiritual literature entreats us to consider that we are part of the Sacred, the Divine, just like every other person.

The spiritual also calls us to accountability for what Carl Jung calls our shadow side, that part of us which, according to many spiritual traditions, is driven by fear rather than by love.[41] All of the ethical, moral, and spiritual frameworks has a challenge and risk which are subtle variations on a theme: I do not have to account to anyone. This hubris, arrogance which often comes from pride, has led to the downfall of many an executive.

Those whose ethical home is in the Rights and Responsibility quadrant are especially prone to believing that they can operate by themselves. Isolating themselves from the discipline of a community, they can become self-righteous and judgmental, finding excuses why they do not have to play by the same self-imposed rules as everyone else. Those whose home is in the Results quadrant begin to believe that their way is the only way, their goals are the only goals. They end up making inconsistent

Hubris Inherent in the Frameworks

I am special... So I'm entitled	I know the truth... So I'm exempt
Who am I?	How do I fit?
Why this choice?	What do I want?
I can do it alone... So I'm excused	My way is the best... So expedience is fine

choices between long- and short-term goals, reducing everything to a cost/benefit analysis. In the process they live by expedience rather than excellence, doing whatever is required to meet their self-directed goals.

Those whose ethical home is in the Relationship quadrant may over-identify with their group, and begin to believe that they know "The Truth." As a member of the group they can become authoritarian while believing that they are exempt from the community norms. Those whose home is in the Reputation quadrant often believe that they are special and thereby entitled to indulgence, favoritism, and leniency. A contemporary example of this hubris is seen with the sentencing requests of Andrew and Leah Fastow, who, after being convicted for their role in the Enron scandal, argued that they needed to serve consecutive jail terms so their children would not be without a parent. Many who are less advantaged do not have the luxury of tailoring their jail sentences to their children's needs. [42]

The headlines of the business pages trumpet stories of highly respected business executives and those in the lower ranks who did not temper their preferred ethical approach with awareness and moderation. Blinded by their own hubris, they ended up being the antithesis of what they desired while becoming that which they feared: unreflective, unfulfilled, isolated, and broken. As we use the disciplines available through the crucible of the spirit, noting where we are not whole and complete, we at least can militate against disaster.

At its core, spirituality is the drive to wholeness. Employing a wide range of practices which are primarily found in the world's religious traditions, we each ultimately find meaning for our lives. The difficulty is that while work is one of the two essential functions of being human, many of us find that, in the words of William F. Lynch, our employers only want our technical selves, that part of us which does our work carefully and well.[43] Our employers may not want our whole selves, that part of us which has families, worries about our children, lives in a community, and values clean air and water, and has a spiritual practice. Thus, we must each be ever mindful of the tensions which call us to park our minds, emotions, and spirits at the entrance of our offices. Those of us in positions of power must also be mindful of the choices we are giving our employees and suppliers who may not have the bargaining power that we do. As we consider fully what it means to find meaning in our work, we will create business environments where all cannot only survive, but thrive.

The Opportunity for Maturity

The spiritual journey requires that we all walk an individual path while we do our own work in community. Not surprisingly, the claim of many spiritual teachers is that, as we do our work, we will move beyond a focus on ourselves to a larger picture, one that includes all and compels us to compassionate action. Shaped by our response to core heuristic questions about the nature of the world and the people in it, our core beliefs and commitments give our lives meaning and provide the rationale for our actions. Our core beliefs inform the way that we hold the core values in balance and how we manifest the virtues associated with those values. Further, because our core commitments are those ideas which we hold with affection which impel us to action, we often respond to the circumstances of our lives based on whether or not the events match our preferred world view and whether or not we believe that we can make a difference — our perceived personal power, or self-efficacy.

Those who believe that they have power often work to strengthen those institutions and situations with which they agree. Thus, if we believe that we are employed by an ethical company *and* we believe that what we do shapes that company, we proactively work to strengthen the core values and assure that the choices made mirror those values. In situations with which we do not agree, with perceived self-efficacy we begin to implement strategies for change. Sometimes we find that we only need to alter our perception of an event. Other times we are moved to actively work to change the beliefs and actions of people in an organization or community. Those who do not believe they have any personal power to make a difference (or choose not to exercise the power they have) can become apathetic, tacit participants in a system with which they either basically agree or disagree.

Possible Response to Our Circumstances

	Match world-view	Do not match world-view
Believe I have power	Work to strengthen	Work to change
Believe I have no power	Apathetic agreement	Perceive self as victim

We see this tendency when Boards of Director's offer CEO's very high wages and stock options, stating that the market demands this level of compensation to get the "brightest and the best." Rather than making an independent determination that the salaries are out of line with those in the rest of the organization, CEO's accept the pay as a modern version of "the devil made me do it." In situations we do not like where we believe we have no power, we become passive-aggressive participants, giving lip service to the existing structures while doing our best to undermine them. We also can see ourselves as victims, powerless to do anything and demanding that others make our circumstances better.[44]

Clearly, commitment to our core values and their associated virtues both defines us and has the potential to energize and transform the self and community. The quest for self-knowledge has at its center the task of identifying core beliefs, determining whether those beliefs are in fact accurate and worthy of shaping us as persons, and then identifying the opportunities and barriers before us as we try to make consistent choices based on our beliefs about the right treatment of people, the right use of property, and the appropriate use of power. Theorists in both traditions provide their understandings of the how the virtues which are embodied in the core values provide the overlay for our key position about how best to live. This patina colors our ethical beliefs as well as our political (conservative or liberal), economic preferences (capitalism or communitarianism), social (independent or interdependent), and spiritual (exclusive or inclusive) preferences.

None of these positions is black and white: they are tendencies on a continuum. However, the hardest questions are those which require that we choose between two competing actions, each of which will have a different bad result. In these situations, our core values will determine the outcome. We know that people who abuse alcohol may injure themselves or others at work. On one hand, we may value autonomy, the right of each person to choose how to live. Thus, we might not intervene in the situation even if the person might cause damage to the company. On the other hand, we may value the well-being of the community and demand that all persons be subject to strict rules about drinking (limits of alcohol at lunch and company gatherings), even though the vast majority of people do not abuse alcohol. Unfortunately, rather than carefully looking at the underlying core values and virtues which drive the decisions, many people choose actions based solely on perceived threats of possible legal liability.

Ironically, giving our power to corporate counsel (or any other external party) does not absolve us from responsibility for making an unethical decision or going against our core values. Rather, as we explore our own core beliefs, see how they square with the prevailing beliefs in our community, and then act in consonance with our best understanding of how to reach our desired goals, we become responsible ethical participants in our community. As we take our desires and values — our ethics, morality, and spirituality — to the workplace, we soon learn that no one path is the only way to mastery.

In this day of ethical, moral. and religious pluralism, no one tradition has a prior or privileged claim on truth. Each tradition offers a theory or belief which guides those in that tradition to wholeness. Each tradition has a corresponding moral content, an emotional response to the reasoning of the mind. And each tradition has a set of spiritual practices which assist us in becoming integrated human beings. The multitude of approaches are variations on a theme: we are all part of the sacred fabric called life and participate in weaving the next segments of the cloth, our civilization.

However, ethical and religious pluralism does not absolve us from the responsibility of living morally aware and spiritually enhanced lives. Digesting the traditions and theories underlying the worlds of reason, emotion and spirit, we develop the skills to become masters in our business, professional, and personal lives. As we do our work, we can embrace life as a *process* with a series of *practices* which lead to integration rather than an *answer* to be found through pursuing goals or following a set of *rules.* With practice and grace, we can become comfortable and skilled in moving between the immanent world, where all is profoundly connected, and the transcendent world, where ideas are forms which are first imagined and then brought to reality.

The promise is that as mature individuals who have mastered the tools of reason, empathy, and love, we can give joyously back to the community and fashion a world where all can thrive. This promise does not just apply to our family and friends. This promise does not apply only to our social and community lives. This promise also applies to the cloth of commerce, the world of work where we earn our living and make our contributions to the whole. The question we each get to explore is how we will contribute to the fulfillment of the promise of achieving integration and integrity in the office and shops in which we work.

Conclusion

As we engage in practices which make us more effective ethical agents, more aware moral persons,while seeking wholeness in the crucible of Spirit, we change as people. We take our changed person with its expanded world view, back to the workplace and see the problems and opportunities of the day through a more perfect lens.The world where goods and services are bought and sold is a world of reason, governed by ethics. The world of customers and co-workers is a world of emotion, governed by morality. The crucible of Spirit is a place where we find our center. Placing our personal crucible within the blast-furnace of the business world, we creatively and imaginatively transform the iron of the world of reason and the carbon of the world of emotion to create organizations with the beauty, strength, and durability of steel.

And as we let joy, compassion, and gratitude permeate our soul, we find that the world of business turns out to be not quite so frenzied. Doing the right thing becomes just a bit easier, and we reveal ever more in the person we are. By using the same tools for our common professional lives that we use for our personal journeys, we learn to respect the path of each person and walk together with integrity and towards wholeness. Celebrating our professional lives as a process which leads to ethical, moral, and spiritual maturity, we hear what questions to ask to create a healthier business community.

Continuing the Conversation

1. As you reflect on your own ethical belief system, how would you answer each of the four core heuristic questions? What experiences and decisions about yourself have shaped your answers to those questions?

2. Does the distinction between ethics as a discipline of reason and morality as a discipline of emotions make sense to you? Do you agree or disagree with that distinction? Why or why not?

3. As commentators were evaluating the high profile case of Martha Stewart which dominated the press in 2004, one made the comment that Ms. Stewart could not accept the fact that she made a mistake. Thus, instead of settling for a civil penalty to the SEC, she went to trial and was convicted of perjury. As you look at other high-profile cases dealing with breaches of business ethics, what was the hubris of those executives? Where did they believe that they would not be held accountable to the community?

The Rights/Responsibility Lens

Conceptual Map

Concepts	World of Reason	World of Emotion	World of Spirit
Key Question	What are my motives? To whom do I owe what?	What is the emotionally mature, caring response?	What is my relationship to the sacred?
Theory	Rights/ Responsibilities	Self-organizing pathways; ethic of care	Sacred Will; discipline of desire
Representative Author	Immanuel Kant W.D. Ross	Carol Gillian Nel Noddings	Ronald Rolheiser Anthony DeMello J.P. deCussade
Tools and Practices	Reason; research	Awareness; self-soothing	Individual piety; reflection
Key Phrase	I am responsible	I am caring	I delight in my work
Goal	Set of principles to determine duty	Ability to evaluate emotions and respond with care	Awareness of participation in sacred will
Gifts	Autonomy; responsibility	Commitment to caring for others	Live fully in the present; humility; love of God and self; faith; trust
Challenges	Legalistic; judgmental; ideologue	Accuracy of matching data	Busyness
Risk	Autocratic	Overly emotional response; co-dependence	Spiritually dry
Hubris	Excuses	Knowing what is best	I can do it alone
Vice	Judgmentalism	Martyr	Self-righteous
Crisis	Alienation	Exhaustion	Emptiness; isolation

Knowing others is intelligent;
knowing yourself is true wisdom.
Mastering others is strength;
mastering yourself is true power.

If you realize that you have enough,
you are truly rich.
If you stay in the center
and embrace death with your whole heart,
you will endure forever.

From the Tao Te Ching — 33[1]

Chapter 7

Rights/Responsibility Lens

The first ethical lens comes from a long tradition of ethicists who focus on the decision maker's rights and responsibilities. Drawing upon the idealist traditions of Plato, St. Augustine, and Luther, the earliest theorist in the modern era who focused on the rights and responsibilities of the individual is Immanuel Kant [1724-1804]. As the history of modern ethics has unfolded, Kant is the philosopher most people name as marking the beginning of the Age of Enlightenment as well as the voice which determines the trajectory of the deontological tradition in the Modern Era. Working from the central concept that the ideal for ethics is to find the core rules by which we should live, the Rights/Responsibility Lens requires that each of us determine for ourselves what prerogatives and duties we have as adults in community. Kant

Core Questions

- What are my rights /responsibilities?
- What is a caring response to this situation?
- What is my relationship to the sacred?

and other Enlightenment philosophers broke from the medieval traditions where the church, or some other authority, defined the privileges and obligations for each person. Thus, they resisted being seen as one of many and demanded to be seen as an individual, a person with rights and responsibilities — just like every other person in the community. Of course, it has taken more than 250 years for every person to be given those rights. But the theories of Kant provided ethical ammunition for the abolition of slavery, the emancipation of women, equal employment opportunities for all, and supports the current quest by homosexuals for full inclusion and rights within the community.

The other major shift heralded by Kant's approach was using the tools of reason (and by implication the scientific method of testing assumptions) rather than the authority of scripture or proclamations of the monarchy or church, to determine the validity of any particular ethical principle. This shift laid the groundwork for the end of the notion of the divine right of kings as well as the eventual separation of church and state.

As with any enduring writer, Kant engages us in the perennial conversation about duty and inclination (or preference), obligations and virtues — in short, what emphasis is to be given to the various strands of thought which weave together in the tapestry we call ethics. Although Kant's theories may not get us to universal truths which will hold for all people, the template he laid out for determining individual rights and responsibilities endures. As the tradition has matured, various ethicists such as W.D. Ross [1877-1971] have proposed a definitive list of duties. Even though all may not agree with the specifics of any given list, the *reflective process* by which we determine what core principles should govern our lives remains fresh and relevant.

From the vantage of individuals reflecting on our place in the community, we can use strategies of critical thinking to consider what rights and responsibilities we can claim. The sticking point for many is that whatever rights and responsibilities (which tend to come in matched sets) are asserted for any one person need to be given to everyone else in the community as well. Thus, Kant's theories (and others writing in the same tradition) provide support for the idea of autonomy — we all get to choose how we wish to live and use our own resources.

Characteristics of the Rights/Responsibility Lens

Definition

An action is ethical if I fulfill my duties and do the right thing as I claim my individual rights.

This lens focuses on whether the means or the principles used to achieve our goals are appropriate, not whether the goal or the result is ethical. From this perspective, an ethical person acts from motives which can apply to all persons in all situations. The criteria for ethical action do not focus on whether the result is desired. A moral person is one who carries out his duty with care for the other person. Thus, as we act responsibly and exercise our rights, we need to always remember that others are also persons with intrinsic human dignity. As we treat people with care and respect, we can carry out our duties with integrity and grace. As we seek transformation within the crucible of spirit, we can discipline those desires which can lead to asserting rights which are not appropriate and to shirking our responsibilities. In the process we find joy in our work and community.

> Definitions
>
> - An ethical act is one which fulfills the rights and responsibilities of the agent.
> - A moral person is one who does the right thing with care and concern for the other person.
> - The crucible of spirit allows us to discipline our desires — to find balance and joy in life.

Questions for Determining Right Action

- *Motives:* What are my motives in advocating one solution rather than another?
- *Principles:* What ethical principles are present in the conversation? Which of these principles should take priority and why? What are the criteria for determining which principles should take priority in this particular situation?
- *Autonomy:* How does this decision protect individuals from unwarranted interferences from government and/or other people in the exercise of that right?
- *Caring:* How does this ordering of principles demonstrate a caring attitude and respect for others?

- *Accountability:* How does this ordering of principles assure that I have held myself accountable for my reason for acting?

- *Balance:* How does this ordering of principles contribute to balance and joy in my life?

Virtues Which Flow from These Theories

- *Life and safety:* Individuals have the right not to have their lives or safety unknowingly and unnecessarily endangered.

- *Truthfulness:* Individuals have a right to not be intentionally deceived by another.

- *Privacy:* Individuals have a right to do whatever they choose outside of working hours and to control information about their private lives.

- *Freedom of conscience:* Individuals have a right to refrain from carrying out any order that violates those commonly accepted moral or religious norms to which they adhere.

- *Free speech:* Individuals have the right to criticize conscientiously and truthfully the ethics or legality of organizational actions as long as the criticism does not violate the rights of other individuals within the organization.

- *Financial transparency:* Individuals who invest in companies and others to whom the firm has a fiduciary duty have a right to a fair, accurate reflection of the financial status of the firm.

- *Right to contract:* Individuals have a right to enter into contracts according to the terms that each party to the contract find agreeable.

Nuances of Theories of Morality

Noddings in her seminal work, *Caring,* asserts that the source of moral behavior is twofold: a sense of caring directly for the other and a sense of feeling for and with our own best self. As we learn to care for others, we can also accept and sustain the feeling of being cared for. In describing the ideal, Noddings states that we move toward "our best picture of ourselves caring and being cared for."[2]

In response to being cared for by others, we commit ourselves to acting on behalf of the one for whom we care. We learn to care for others as we notice that concrete situations of caring and being cared for are good. Noddings and others in this tradition argue that, as we care for others, we are acting from a universal ideal: maintenance of the caring relationship.[3]

The theories of morality also call us to responsibility. Hans Jonas and other advocates of the common good note that, since we as humans have the power to destroy the environment and other nations, we must carefully consider the ramifications of our acts. Jonas asserts that we must consider public policy as well as our individual responsibilities when we act because our actions can affect the very existence of our planet and civilization.[4] For example, as we soberly realize that scientists have demonstrated that the climate changes which come with global warming are the result of human action, we must carefully weigh the goal of productivity and economic growth against the possibility of leaving our great-grandchildren a legacy which is on a trajectory to extinction.

The Crucible of Spirit

Many people ask whether it is possible to delight in our work, to find work which has meaning and is satisfying. One of the problems with a Kantian approach to life is that we can do the right thing, care for others, and still be miserable. Sometimes our work becomes so segmented that we have no sense of how it fits into the whole or how it makes a shred of difference in our world. Many times we take on more and more responsibility at work, which leads to our lives being out of balance, putting more of our heart and soul into our work than into our family or community lives. As we learn to discipline our desires and seek what is really important, we can put our seemingly conflicting responsibilities into perspective.

A common refrain among my students is that they do not want to see their work as a life sentence, as they perceive their parents did. Thus, they seek some way to find joy in their work. This anecdotal evidence was borne out by the research of Nash and McLennan who found that people "want to live a life of meaning, they want to be more effective at problem solving, they need connection to other people; through it all they optimistically assume that in discovering this sacred, authentic self, they will find that it can be a rather noble self."[5] For some the choice is to follow their own heart's desire in selecting their careers rather than living out expectations of their family. Others look for ways to serve rather than trying to climb to the top of an organization or make as much money as possible. Still others find meaning and satisfaction as they are caring and civil to those in their workplace. Others find happiness by making the lives of their co-workers a bit easier as they work together to accomplish the goals of the organization.

The first question that writers in this tradition ask is how we can blend responsibility and joy. If the goal of life is to love and to work, as we find work which satisfies us, we can be happy. John Eldredge states that "[d]esire, both the whispers and the shouts, is the map we have been given to find the only life worth living."[6] Roland Rolheiser reminds us that "[s]pirituality is, ultimately, about what we do with that desire." Our spirituality is what we do with our longings, how we handle the pain and the hope they bring.[7]

Whyte, a poet who explores the intersection between spirituality and the corporate life, asserts that if we try to plan our lives, the young innocent heart of desire may turn all of our efforts to naught. Whyte found in his work that if our desire is not given its due, "our personalities can work all the hours God sends to no avail, pushing water upstream on a project which is destined to die no matter what we do...[t]he unawakened yet youthful soul is so entangled with the world and so physically alert...that it need not to keep track of every detail in order to find its way in the world."[8] As Whyte describes the intersection of the wily mind and the innocent soul, when we are following our heart's desire, he finds that we work out of "sheer joy," that which we love gives us the energy to do the hard work. Thus, as we find ourselves in the crucible of spirit, we can "make an equal place in the psyche for both strategy and soul."[9]

The second question writers in this tradition ask is whether we are willing to become sufficiently disciplined to know ourselves and reach our heart's desire. As we engage in the individual/reflective process, we have to be ruthlessly honest with ourselves. We have to develop habits of awareness to avoid excessive self-preoccupation and excessive focus on work, achievement, and the practical concerns of life which can drain us of all our energy.[10] Thus, our workplace spirituality is the discipline by which we "both access that energy and contain it."[11] We have seen many good business people who, unable to contain the drive for power and greed, have self-destructed — often taking their companies with them. In the American culture where the mantra is often "[h]e who dies with the most toys wins," learning self-discipline as we follow a path which makes our hearts sing feels counter-cultural. Our mentors on these paths are few. Yet, if we look carefully we can find those who found meaning in their work and satisfying relationships without getting seduced by power or sidetracked by greed.

Using the Rights/Responsibility Lens

The theorists who are representative of this ethical lens, Kant and W.D. Ross, invite each of us to consider what rights and responsibilities we have as individuals in community. When we have to choose among good options, this process helps us identify and prioritize competing values.

The theorists at the beginning of the Age of Enlightenment asserted that individuals as individuals have the right to self-determination. Ironically, the notions of autonomy were grounded first in the Protestant Reformation. As Martin Luther protested the abuses and excesses of the Holy Roman Empire, he asserted that individuals could determine for themselves what scriptures said and thus they were responsible before God alone for their salvation. A corollary to spiritual self-determinism was that people could also decide for themselves how they were to be governed.

The work of early Lutheran lawyers and other seminal thinkers laid the foundations for the theory of social contract where each of us has the right to negotiate with each other to determine the shape of our community.[12] The source of individual rights for the theologians was the belief that all persons are created in the image of God and thus are entitled to being treated with respect and dignity. This theme was carried forward in the Protestant tradition by theologians such as John Calvin and Richard Hooker. Theologians such as St. Ignatius Loyola who were part of the Catholic counter-reformation articulated many of the same themes.[13]

Philosophers assert that we have individual rights and the right to self-determination because adults, unlike children or the animals, have the ability to reason. Those who agitated for equal rights for women and the abolition of slavery (as well as those committed to the goal of universal human rights today) used the core belief of the ability of humans to reason as the primary persuasive tool.

Those in power (in the United States free white males) made the argument that, because women and Negroes lacked the ability to reason and to be taught, they should not be granted the political and economic autonomy they sought. Those who were charitable considered women and slaves as children who needed protection; those who were uncharitable considered, particularly the slaves, non-human and thus not entitled to any rights. Ironically, at the same time slave owners, in particular, asserted that their slaves could not reason, laws were passed prohibiting teaching any slaves to read or write.[14]

The responsibilities we embrace provide a tight corollary to our rights. The gift of self-determination means that we also are entitled to all of the consequences which come with that gift, including not being able to blame anyone else for what happens to us. If, in fact, we are able to exercise our rights of political autonomy, we get (in the words of political pundits) what we deserve. If we can make our own choices about our economic well being, then we get whatever goods come to us as a result of our actions. Thus, we cannot demand more from others to make up for the shortfall of our own resources. Instead we need to work harder, make better bargains, or be content with our lot in life. The freedom both to succeed and to fail granted when we embrace the notion of individual rights and responsibilities gave rise to the wonderful pithy folk exhortation — you made your bed, now sleep in it.

At the end of any analytical process, we have to explain why a particular option was chosen and why others were not. The following set of questions helps us identify the rights and responsibilities which govern our ethical choices. As we become more skilled, the analysis will become easier, and we can begin to identify the core values which, for us, trump other competing values. However, even when we think we know the answer to the question, the discipline of working through the process can help clarify our thoughts.

To help understand the process, an abbreviated version of a real problem will be given in a set of text boxes. The particular problem which will be used in all four of the theoretical chapters came from an actual ethics committee in Colorado for a Preferred Provider Organization (PPO), a healthcare network. In the late 1980s, this PPO worked through an issue involving whether or not to disclose to patients that, if they tested positive for HIV, their names would be placed on a registry with the state. After we look at the problem four times, the answer will be obvious. However, the committee debated for over an hour as it worked through the problem from every angle.[15] In each of the chapters, an abbreviated version of the analysis will be presented in the text. These examples will give us a feeling for the tools of each theory.

Step 1: Be Attentive

▶ *Identify the ethical actor*

The first step is to determine who is responsible for making the decision. Each of the theorists has a different understanding of the self, the ethical actor who is going to engage in the ethical decision. As Kant was striving to find universal principles, he knew that the ethical agent needed to be removed from the everyday circumstances of life. For Kant this means that "the notion of a subject [ethical agent] which is prior to and independent of experience, such as the deontological ethic requires, appears not only possible but indispensable, a necessary presupposition of the possibility of self-knowledge and freedom."[16]

> **Ethical Actor**
>
> The ethics committee of a PPO is charged with setting protocols for all the physicians who are part of the group.

This self, called a "transcendental subject," a self which is "the something 'back there', antecedent to any particular experience that unifies our diverse perceptions and holds them together in a single consciousness."[17] Kant invites us to move ourselves out of the particular circumstances in which we make the decision — the people, the times, the place — and determine principles which hold for all times and places. Using this approach, the universal principles then determine our actions. This approach has the value of leading to consistency, as the ethical agent treats all persons who are similarly situated the same.

▶ *Determine the stakeholders*

The next step is to identify the stakeholders — the people who will be affected by the decision. As we consider the stakeholders, we need to attend to the agreements among the parties. Those who use the Rights/Responsibility Lens presume

> **Stakeholders**
>
> - The committee: which has to make the decision.
> - PPO: with whom the ethics committee has a contract to act in the best interest of the PPO.
> - Physicians: with whom the PPO has employment contracts to provide services.
> - Patients: with whom the PPO has contracts to provide care.
> - Citizens of the state: with whom the PPO has a social contract to follow the law.

that individuals with equal power will be negotiating with others who also have autonomy. Thus, the contracts between the parties help determine the ethical obligations. Often the agreements are explicit: the price set for goods, a certain number of hours to work. Just as often the agreements are implicit: grading papers fairly, treating all students alike. In a financial setting we expect the information on balance sheets to be accurate and complete without entering into an additional agreement.

In completing this step, we must examine the agreements with every constituent and determine what our responsibilities are to each. How we *feel* about the people involved is irrelevant. The strength of the process is that we do not make decisions based on whether we like another person or whether we feel like doing a particular act. The litmus test is whether we are following the maxim, the required principle for acting.

As Kant sorted out our responsibilities to the various stakeholders, he asked us to consider whether (1) the duties are perfect or imperfect and (2) whether we are assisting people in making the best decisions they can. Many ethicists distinguish between perfect duties — those we have explicitly agreed to undertake — and imperfect duties — those actions which we could take but are under no obligation to do so. For example, a physician only has an obligation to those patients he has agreed to treat. Even though many may need help, until the physician has taken a particular person on as a patient, she only has an imperfect duty to the general public.

As ethical actors, our primary duties are to those with whom we have express and implied agreements: we have a *prima facie* ethical obligation to honor the terms of our contracts. Often, however, we also owe a duty to people with whom we are not in direct contractual relationship. Thus, companies that trade on the stock market have a fiduciary duty to make sure the financial information is accurate. This duty, which arises out of an obligation of trust, flows to both those who sell and buy stock. We may also have an obligation to those with whom we are in relationship because of the social contract not to act in a way which will adversely impact our ability to live and thrive. For example, increasing numbers of people are asserting that companies have an implicit duty as citizens not to put toxic materials into the air or water in order to assure that members of society do not become ill. Each successive level of duty — those with whom an actor is in contractual relationship, those who will be directly affected by the action of the company, and those who are indirectly affected by the action of the company — moves along a continuum from perfect duties to imperfect duties.

► *Attend to the context*

As the Enlightenment philosophers established the primacy of reason over tradition or emotion, Kant spent much of his time exploring the role of reason in determining the shape of the law. *Critique of Pure Reason*, one of Kant's seminal texts, asserts that through reason we can discover the universal principles of life, the ethics by which we should all live. Thus, if "an action is really moral, it will not only accord with a law; it will be done because a law is acknowledged as absolutely and universally binding...it will be...'ethics based on pure reason'."[18]

In arguing for using reason as the final arbiter of what is right rather than personal inclination, Kant was aware of the fact that various people have different skills and interests. Kant taught that we have a responsibility to help others develop their own skills of analysis which would lead to autonomy. He also instructed that we should not act from our passions, our emotions, as those can be misleading. One of the most troublesome examples that Kant gives of this concept is when he asks whether a husband who deeply loves an invalid wife and thus cares for her is more or less virtuous than a husband whose love has become cold and who nevertheless stays with his wife to assure that she receives the care she needs. Kant asserts that the one who stays from duty is more ethically meritorious than the one whose actions are motivated by love. While many may disagree with that particular standard, Kant gives the example to underscore that we should carry out our duties even when the action is uncomfortable, inconvenient, or financially disadvantageous. The ethical person lives by the principles, or maxims, which reason reveals.[19]

Kant argued that through reason we could find the universal principles of life which would guide our actions. While Kant's claims are subject to much critique, asking the questions demanded by the categorical imperative helps us determine the overarching principles of life which form our core personal values as well as those of our community. The principles are then applied to the specific situations to determine what we should do. In specific situations the cultural context can be considered, though the context itself should not drive the final choice.

Step 2: Be Intelligent

▸ *Pinpoint the Issue*

What central problem is to be resolved? As we phrase this issue as a question, we need to focus on the conflicting rights and responsibilities which are present. The intriguing part of ethics is that each lens uses a different set of criteria to scrutinize any given question. The Rights/ Responsibility Lens focuses our attention on becoming a fully functioning adult who acts from a sense of duty.

> Issue
>
> Given that the state requires that health care providers report all persons who test positive for HIV to a central registry, should we tell people before we do the blood work that a positive test result will be reported to the health department?

▸ *Explore the values-in-conflict*

In a Kantian setting, conflicts can arise on several fronts. We may have conflicting duties with different stakeholders. For example, we may have a duty of loyalty to one person which would preclude meeting the requirement of truthfulness and integrity with another person. We may encounter a person who asserts rights but does not embrace the accompanying responsibilities. As Kant encourages us to assist others to become responsible adults. Kant would expect us to hold those persons accountable, as each of us is to act responsibly. Further, Kant would probably not raise an eyebrow if we found ourselves upsetting people with whom we are in relationship in order to meet our obligations. As we meet the requirements of the categorical imperative, people who expect favoritism will most certainly be annoyed.

> Values-in-Conflict
>
> The two values-in-conflict are autonomy for the individual and safety for the community. Patients have been told that their relationship with the doctor is confidential, thus we want to assure that we maintain the privacy of our patients. The patient-physician privilege is important to the medical profession to assure that the physician gets full information prior to beginning treatment. On the other hand we want to assure that a highly infectious disease does not spread further. Our commitment to the community requires that we do all we can to minimize the spread of disease.

▸ *Identify options for action*

The next step is to identify the options. Clearly one can choose whether to carry out an action or not. More interesting is finding complex solutions which meet as many of the core values as possible and which also reveal systemic solutions. Working through a problem which on its face looks unethical is intriguing. Sometimes we notice that an option which appears to not meet any of the requirements of the template is the best.

Options for action

1. Tell the patient about the reporting requirement before doing the blood work.

2. Do not tell the patient about the reporting requirements before doing the blood work.

Step 3: Be Responsible

▸ ***Hone critical thinking skills***

For Kant, the point of critical inquiry was to honestly articulate the reason for acting. To begin the process, we are asked to determine the motives we have for choosing each option. Kant believed that, by examining our reasons for acting, we could identify our rights and responsibilities and begin to formulate key principles for life. When considering our reason for acting, it helps to think in terms of the virtues associated with all of the core values. Is the reason for this option so people will have autonomy, to be able to make a decision with full information about the choices they are going to make? Is the reason part of the cluster of virtues surrounding sensibility, making sure that the organization's resources are used appropriately?

As Kant explains the notions of the categorical imperative, reason helps us determine the right act. The universal rule which is identified through use of the categorical imperatives is an *imperative* because it is a command of reason, a command which tells us what we ought to do. A categorical imperative is one which directly commands a person to engage in certain conduct which is objectively necessary without reference to any other purpose or end.[20] For example, a categorical imperative would be to respect human life, even if the end or the purpose might result in the abolition of the death penalty or the cost of a product being increased in order to assure that it is safe.

Reasons for Acting

Option 1 — Full disclosure: The reason for making full disclosure before the blood work is to assure that the patients are fully informed of their options and the consequences of choosing blood work should they test HIV positive.

Option 2 — No disclosure: The reason for not disclosing is to assure that those who are HIV positive are identified and receive proper treatment. If people know about the testing requirements, they may choose not to be tested and thus infect other people.

Kant contrasts the categorical imperative, that which we do because our reason tells us the act is our duty even if we do not like the results, and the hypothetical imperative, that which we do as long as we like the results that we get. An example might be a company which manufactured baby clothes with a coating that was supposed to retard flames. After testing, the company discovered that the product did not retard flames, but rather increased the likelihood of the sleepers catching on fire. The product could not be sold in America because of the laws concerning safety. However, the laws of Europe did not restrict the sales. If the categorical imperative tells us that we should always act in a way that respects human life, then the company would not sell the product in Europe, even though it could. If we were operating against the hypothetical imperative, the ethical rule might be that the company will act in a way that respects human life as long as the financial consequences are not too high and it does not violate the law (or will not get caught). Selling the baby clothes in Europe might pass the hypothetical imperative, because the financial consequences for not selling the clothes are high and no law prohibiting the sale or establishing liability exists in Europe.

In framing the reason, we work to get to the highest reason possible, a reason that reflects the best of human action and understanding. If my reason for hurting you is to watch you squirm in pain, the action would be, by definition, unethical. Most of us are unwilling to be hurt by another person who only wants to see how we respond to pain. However, if I am a physician and to remove a tumor I must also inflict physical pain, the reason for inflicting pain being to assure greater health and preserve life. We are generally willing to let a physician inflict pain to assure that we have greater health. Thus, the physician's motive for hurting me would pass ethical muster.

From time to time people in charge want to say, "the reason is because I said so and I'm in charge." Those in leadership positions should use the prerogatives of authority with care. Using authority and loyalty as reasons for acting will chill any conversation about the best reason for a firm to act as well as discourage others from engaging in their own reflective process.

▸ *Apply ethical content*

To apply ethical content, we ask four questions which are embedded in Kant's categorical imperative and Ross's *prima facie* duties. These questions help us sort through the competing rights and responsibilities which individuals claim because they are members of the community.

▶ *First Question: What would happen if everyone adopted this reason for acting?*

As Kant developed his theory, he articulated two categorical imperatives which assist us in finding the principles by which we should live. The first categorical imperative is *universalizability:* the person's reasons for acting must be reasons that everyone could act on, at least in principle.[21] The notion is that, as we reflect using the tools of reason, we should only adopt maxims or principles which are not inherently self-contradictory. The principle of universalizability challenges us to consider those universal rules which all persons can follow without the rule becoming inconsistent.

Kant illustrates this maxim by asking whether, when we have our backs to the wall and we do not like the anticipated consequences of telling the truth, we can make a promise that we do not intend to keep. As Kant explores this situation, he concludes that we would not be content if everyone operated on the rule "I will make promises but only keep them if it turns out that the consequences are consequences that are acceptable." Kant rightly notes that the proposed universal rule would destroy itself as soon as it became the law: if I keep only those promises which turn out to have good ends, no-one will know whether or not my promise would be kept. Thus, the whole idea of promises and contract would dissolve.[22]

On the other hand, one could universally adopt the rule "when I make a promise, I will keep it regardless of whether the anticipated or unanticipated consequences are those which I prefer." Thus, everyone would keep promises once they were made. The popular version of this rule is seen in the notion of business by handshake. The highest compliment of a person's integrity in our community is that a complex deal is discussed and sealed with a handshake — and then honored. Even if later, the market changes or the legal analysis shows that parts of the deal may not be advantageous, if we have adopted this principle, we consider our word to be our bond. We would not try to use legal loopholes to escape the obligation that we made.

As Kant laid out the criteria of what he called universalizability, he invited

Universalizability

Option 1 — Full disclosure: Everyone could adopt the reason for making full disclosure, in actuality and in principle. If we know all of the ramifications of our choice before we act, we can make sound contracts and agreements.

Option 2 — No disclosure: Everyone could also adopt the reason for not disclosing, in actuality and in principle. If we know that a person may not be giving us all the information, we can ask questions which will give us the information that we desire. A presumption with this option is that even though disclosure may not be voluntary, the physician will give the truth when asked.

us to move into systemic thought rather than merely look at the impact of our decision on ourselves. While we are relatively certain that no reason for acting will ever be acceptable to all people in all cultures, asking this question helps us think about overall systems, not just the act.

For example, if we have superior knowledge in a situation, we may be able to use our position of power to press an advantage against a client or customer. While acting from superior knowledge and power seems to be a compelling motive for our choice, we need to consider what would happen if everyone drove an advantage in a negotiation based on superior power and knowledge. A recent example was seen as EchoStar took on Viacom for what EchoStar called extortion in order to increase the price to be charged to carry the station in areas where the Columbia Broadcasting System (CBS) did not have local affiliates. The two companies went into a face-off to see who would blink first as the negotiation for the royalties to be paid broke down. Viacom believed that it would be able to control the negotiations as EchoStar's customers would not tolerate disruption in their service. EchoStar, even though it was a smaller company with seemingly less power, believed that their customers would support their efforts to keep prices low. Within 48 hours of EchoStar pulling the plug on Viacom's programming, a new unpublished contract was signed, with both companies declaring victory.[23]

Kant would invite us to consider what happens if the power of knowledge is consistently used to take advantage of others. The result in American culture is lack of trust, increased transaction costs, and lawsuits. If a business person has a reputation for always being a sharp dealer, then every transaction will be carefully examined by lawyers and accountants to make sure no advantage is taken, which drives up transaction costs. The next consequence is an increase of litigation because we do not trust each other. Thus, rather than each of us taking individual responsibility for a deal gone sour, the one taking advantage of power will quickly blame the other person for the bad result. The line between strong market power and coercion is fine. Living on the edge of that line may cause overall systemic damage which may mean that pressing an advantage, just because you can, may not ultimately be a good way to do business.

- <u>*Second Question:*</u> *Am I willing to have someone else use this reason in deciding how they will treat me?*

The second part of the first categorical imperative is *reversibility:* our reasons for acting must be reasons that we would be willing to have all others use, even as a basis of how they treat us.[24] Thus, the second litmus test we use when adopting a reason for acting is whether we would be willing to have another person use this reason which justifies our action to determine how that person treats us. If we articulate a reason for acting and are not willing for someone to use that reason in how they treat us, then the option is by definition unethical. Reversibility is a variation on the Golden Rule. We tend to say that we are to treat others in the way that we would want to be treated. If we are not careful, however, we focus on the *result* of the action rather than the *reason* for the action.

> **Reversibility**
>
> Option 1 — Full disclosure: I am willing to have the reason for giving me full information, protecting my autonomy, before treatment be the reason for how I am treated when I go to the doctor. Further, I want to preserve the tradition of physician/client confidentiality.
>
> Option 2 — No disclosure: I am not willing to have the reason for not giving me full information, protecting the community, be the reason for requiring that I be proactive in asking questions about the ramifications of having various treatments.

An example of this principle in action comes as we look at people treating some people differently than others, based on gender, race, nationality, or economic class. In deciding who is going to get a particular contract, would I be willing for the *reason* that a contractor signed a deal be that the contractor felt more comfortable playing golf with one vendor rather than with me? Given that the social aspect of business is important, would I be content with the reason for someone else receiving a contract being that the contractor wanted to assure that the vendor was a person who not only had a good product but was also accepted at the country club? Said another way, am I willing to have the reason a contract is denied to me be that the contractor had always done business with the family of the one who got the bid?

Many of us who seek competitive advantage are willing to use whatever tools and resources we have to get a contract. If that means being cheerful when we are crabby or sociable when we want to be alone, we would try to meet the needs of the contractor. However, in the final analysis, most of us want to be judged according to the requirements of the contract. Most of us would prefer that the reason for a contract going to another person be that the product or price is better, not that we play golf badly, are a boring dinner companion, or that our parents are not members or the right — or any — county club.

Many students miss the point of this step of the process by focusing on the *result* of the action rather than the *reason* for the action. Kant never expected people to necessarily like the result of the action — they just had to be willing for others to use that reason in how they were treated. For example, when I ask someone a question, do I prefer the unvarnished truth or a polite lie? Given that I make decisions about what I am going to do based on accurate information, I would welcome a hurtful critique if the reason for giving the data is to assure that I have complete information. If the reason for the hurtful information is to make me feel badly or for retaliation, I would prefer that the person keep her counsel. This step of the process is very black and white. If I am not willing for the reason to be used in how I am treated, then the option is not ethical. Once the motive for acting is determined and the test of reversibility is applied, the path of action becomes clear.

- *Third Question: If I adopt this option, am I treating people the way they have freely consented to be treated? Am I assisting them in their own process of becoming fully functioning adults who can make their own choices?*

This question asks whether we are acting from selfish reasons alone or to fulfill our duty to another. While Kant expected people to examine their motives and follow their own lights in determining individual rights and responsibilities, action always is taken in community. Thus, if I have to cause you misery in order to fulfill my duty to you and others, then the action would be considered ethical. If I have to have a deadline for accepting papers to meet my obligation to the university and other students and I refuse to accept a paper after that deadline, then my reason for acting is not just for the selfish reason of easing my load but to assure that I treat both the student and the university as they have agreed to be treated. The second categorical imperative states that an action is morally right for a person if, and only if, in performing the action, the person does not use others merely as a means for advancing his or her own interests, but also both respects and develops their capacity to choose freely for themselves.[25]

Kant was absolutely committed to the notion of autonomy and the value of the human person. In making this point, Kant talked about the difference between everything having a price or having dignity Kant asserts that if we treat people as means to our own ends, we assume that people are interchangeable commodities who do not have dignity or value in themselves. If, however, we look at people as ends in themselves, we accord them dignity and respect, regardless of their monetary worth.

This tension is seen poignantly in the health care debate. When a child is born at 26 weeks of gestation, six weeks before full term, what resources should be used to keep that child alive? If the child has dignity and value as a human person, then the life of that person should not be measured in terms of how expensive it will be to preserve life. However, we also know that even if we use the very expensive technology we have available, the prognosis for the person ever being mentally and/or physically independent is very grim. Many premies who survive have diminished mental and physical capacities which drain the health care resources of the community and profoundly affect the lives and resources of the family. Does treating that baby as a person in its own right require using every available resource to keep that person alive? Or would treating that baby with dignity be the way one of my students was treated who was born several weeks premature. Her grandmother wrapped her in a blanket, placed her in a shoe box by the fireplace, and waited to see if she would breathe and survive. The thought was that if the baby was strong enough to survive, they would feed and care for her.

> ### Treating People As Ends
>
> Option 1 — Full disclosure: Telling people before the blood test the consequence of the test treats people as they have freely consented to be treated. We have agreed to the implicit contract of informed consent which requires fully disclosing all ramifications of the treatment before proceeding.
>
> Option 2 — No disclosure: Not telling people before the blood test the consequence of a positive HIV test violates the implicit contract of informed consent. In addition, it does not develop the capacity for people to choose for themselves by educating them to make a sound decision.

We also see this tension in how people are treated at work. Many times it seems that employers really do not care about us as people, about the totality of us as full human beings. Thus, many people believe that they are being treated as means for the employer to make lots of money rather than as ends, people who have value as human beings. If someone else can do the job more cheaply, perhaps by outsourcing, or an immigrant, a non-documented worker, or one who has less experience or qualifications, we are replaced — like cogs in a machine. Of course, if we shift the vantage slightly to consider our obligation to assure that others who are very poor have an opportunity to have an income, the act may in reality be ethical. For Kant, the reason for an act is key in distinguishing between ethical and unethical acts.

This problem is amplified in that employees who embrace their role as an agent for the company tend to see their interests as the same as the employers and thus do not notice the pattern. Without thinking systemically, we identify with the owners — the stockholders — of the businesses that are our employers rather than seeing ourselves as workers in solidarity — persons with the same interests as other workers. Many times our concern is first preserving shareholder value which often translates to giving the workers as little as possible while driving them to be as productive as possible. Ironically, advocating such policies leads to small raises for ourselves or the outsourcing of our jobs to other nations. The categorical imperative becomes an interesting lens: are we willing to be fired or to take lesser compensation because others are willing to do the same work for less?

My personal discomfort about this tendency only to consider the owner or shareholder of a company when making a decision was eloquently explored by William F. Lynch, S.J., in *Images of Hope* when he asserted that:

> [t]he usual form of citizenship created by these exclusive cities of man is that of the ideal or the beautiful self we have earlier described. But the form of citizenship created by the technological cities of exclusion is that of *the useful self*...Only the useful part of the human self gets into the kind of community we will describe by the name of formal or mechanical organization.[26]

Using the work of Christopher Argyris, a leading management theorist, as his foil, Lynch goes on to describe how American management theory glorifies strategies where managers assure that the worker is convinced that any discontent is the problem of the worker and not the nature of work which is provided by the firm. Lynch asserts that "[i]n addition to the usual charges that workers are lazy and lack goodwill, those on top respond with every measure save the kind that will nurture responsibility, autonomy, and, I would add, the good taste of the human self."[27]

Troubled by Lynch's indictment of American business, I began probing to see whether my students had bought into the notion of the "useful self" as the ideal for the business world rather than the "beautiful self." One telling exercise came as I was exploring the notion of gratitude and trying to dispel the notion of the self-made person with my seniors in a seminar on Economic Justice. I asked my students to list all the people who were responsible for their being in class that glorious September day. They listed parents, former teachers, and mentors in the community. One student even went back to the Mayflower and was grateful for his forebears who crossed the stormy Atlantic. Not one of them listed the people in the cafeteria who made their breakfast, the cleaning staff who assured that the room was vacuumed and the chalk boards were washed, the grounds keepers who mowed the lawns and tended the roses, the library staff who facilitated the research for the paper due that day. To my students, all of those people who were necessary for their success at school were, in fact, faceless *instruments* — valued only for the services they provided, people who were a useful means to the end of an education and a diploma.

Conversations about the right treatment of workers, conversations which began with an invitation to actually *see* those who provide the infrastructure for our success, often are quickly marooned on the shoals of relative ethics. This tendency is an unintentional fallout from the nascent postmodern ethos which seems to permit students to embrace the philosophy that anything goes as long as I am able to autonomously seek my goals.

This conversation leads to the next implication for Kant's theory, the sanctity of contracts. One of the ways that we treat people as ends is by treating them in the way they have freely consented to be treated. Thus, if you and I negotiate on the price of my services or the goods I am selling, once we have agreed, no one else should be able to second guess the contract. This understanding of contracts presumes that we each have roughly equivalent market power and have the ability to walk away from a contract. In reality, many people do not have that kind of market power and thus an inquiry into fundamental fairness and justice becomes important.

A preliminary step in determining whether we are treating people as they have agreed to be treated is identifying the agreements we have with each other, which was part of setting the context. So, we must examine the implicit and explicit agreements with each constituent and determine what responsibilities we have to each. A corollary to the agreements is whether, in making those agreements, we acted in good faith and did not abuse our power. Acting in good faith requires that we give people the information they need to enter into fair, appropriate contracts. If we keep information from each other, we cannot make good agreements. Not abusing power means that we must be sensitive to forced agreements, where in truth people cannot make good choices. We are fond of saying that we embrace the notion of contract at will, that employers can lay us off when they desire and we can leave when we wish. However, we know that for the vast majority of workers, finding a job is much more difficult than being replaced. Thus, especially in a non-unionized setting, employers have a great deal more market power than employees.

When power is out of balance, we often are using the other person as a means to our preferred goals rather than treating the person as an end, a human being with autonomy and choice in how to live his life. The classic example is the medical experiments with the Tuskegee Airmen where testing was being done concerning syphilis. The Airmen were told that participating was part of their patriotic duty. The conversations happened in the Airmen's home churches, giving the experiments an even greater imprimatur of authority. Even after the researchers determined that a cure for syphilis existed, the tests continued (which included no treatment for the disease) to document the physical results of syphilis, to the great detriment of the Airmen. In this case, the researchers used the men as a means to their goal, or end, of compiling more data.

A final consideration asks whether we are helping people make the best decisions possible. To accomplish this, we need to help people realize that they are rational human beings who can determine for themselves the best way to live. One indicator of a person's autonomy is the balance of power among the various stakeholders. If either party abuses power, which can result from an imbalance of information, education, or financial resources, then the other party may not be able to freely choose what she wants to do. Another indicator of balanced power is the presence of real options. A person who has no access to health care cannot choose to be treated for illness. Thus, for this step we look for balance of power and options.

- *Fourth Question: How does this option meet the requirements of traditional and personal ethical principles?*

Many people assert that we all instinctively know the principles — the rules by which we should live. The difficulty is that unexamined instincts often lead to bad results. Thus, considering the concrete duties which become clear as we consider the categorical imperatives is useful. While we may not agree on the list or the priority to be given to each rule, reviewing the lists of traditional duties as outlined by ethicists such as W.D. Ross can be instructive in the process of balance and prioritizing our options. While Ross does not assert that the following list is exhaustive, reviewing the commonly accepted duties can help us assure that we are being responsible.[28]

- *Duties of fidelity:* telling the truth, keeping actual and implicit promises, and not representing fiction as history.

▷ *Duties of reparation:* righting the wrongs we have done to others.

▷ *Duties of gratitude:* recognizing the services others have done for us. Being thankful for our lives and our community.

▷ *Duties of justice:* preventing someone from distributing pleasure or happiness that is not in keeping with the merit of people involved (people should not give good things to bad people).

▷ *Duties of beneficence:* helping to better the condition of other people with respect to virtue, intelligence, or pleasure.

▷ *Duties of self-improvement:* bettering ourselves with respect to virtue, intelligence, or other skills.

▷ *Duties of non-maleficence:* avoiding or preventing an injury to others. Not hurting other people.

Again, this list is most helpful in identifying the duties which seem to make sense for members of our community after people have attempted to identify universal principles. The list can help us assure that our core cultural duties have been considered before we act.

► *Overlay the moral content*

As we reflect on the options, our next task is to consider whether that option can be carried out in a way that demonstrates caring for the other person. Ethical actions have two dimensions — what we do and how we do it. Modern theorists consider primarily what we should do and do not focus on method. When we use the Rights and Responsibility Lens, the question becomes which option will fulfill the prerogatives and duties which we have voluntarily taken on in our community. However, if we are not careful, we can carry out an ethical option in a way that is hurtful to others.

The postmodern viewpoint invites us to consider the context of the situation and to look at those affected by a decision as whole persons with feelings and emotions. We are not expected to violate our duties and responsibilities, but rather to carry out those duties in a way that acknowledges the essential humanity of the persons affected by the decision. In an era of downsizing and firing, many employers decide to give people 15 minutes to clear out their desks and escort them to the door. Others choose to give people time to say goodbye, help with résumés, throw a party, and let the grieving/celebrating run a course over several days. Those companies that dismiss people with integrity and care, fulfill their responsibilities while the dignity of the person is maintained. The moral lens turns our attention to caring for others as we invoke our rights. This overlay does not require that we act contrary to our rights and responsibilities. Rather we are asked to consider how we can accomplish our duty in a wholly rational way while we see others as humans and treat them with respect and care.

> **Act with Care**
>
> The only option which passes the Kantian ethical test is informing the persons before the test of the possibility of being reported to the state if the person tests positive for HIV. However, in giving this information, the physician or nurse should be aware that the patient might be afraid and not want the notoriety. Thus, even though time is precious, sufficient care should be given so that the one who may be affected feels like a valuable person who is faced with a difficult choice. The nurse or the doctor giving the informed consent should resist the tendency to rush through the process in record time while using "legal language."

Step 4: Be Responsible

▸ *Rank the options from least preferred to most preferred*

Having determined the reasons for acting and then evaluated the options against the criteria of (1) can everyone act on this reason [universilizability]; (2) would I be willing for someone to use this reason in how they treat me [reversibility]; (3) am I treating people as individuals with value [ends and not means to an end]; (4) the core ethical principles/rules; and (5) whether I can carry out this option in a caring manner, we can then rank the options from least preferred to most preferred.

As the options are ranked, summarize why the ranking of options was made and demonstrate the primacy given to autonomy: (a) because each person is valuable in his or her own right, each person can choose how best that person wants to live; (b) but once having freely chosen, a person is obligated to fulfill those responsibilities.

> **Rank the Options**
>
> In this case, the only option which meets the ethical and moral litmus test is giving the information before the test. Whether the information is given orally or in writing, the person getting medical treatment is respected as an adult who can make choices. The choice is hard — not being tested and running the risk of not being treated or being treated and risking notoriety. However, the choice should be in the hands of the person with the disease, not the health care provider.

▸ *Correct for bias*

While the individual/reflection lens provides us with the gifts of autonomy and responsibility, if our actions are not tempered with compassion, we can become autocratic. If we believe that *we* have found the right principles and the preferred priority and others have not, we can become judgmental and legalistic. Many times those who prefer this lens want to impose their own understanding of the principles on all others. Thus, we have to assure that we listen to each other and subject our pet ideas to a healthy dose of skepticism.

Correct for bias

The tension is to avoid the hubris of the belief that we as health care providers know best. While we believe that people can make good choices, in many cases educating them is difficult and they seem to make bad choices and then want us to pick up the pieces. Further, working with people takes time — time that we do not have in a managed care environment. We also do not want the disease to spread. Yet, our commitment to informed consent is higher than the ease of "playing God."

A corollary is that as we criticize and punish others for not obeying the rules, we have all kinds of reasons why we are exempt from following the very same principles. As the press revealed the hubris of top business executives at the end of the 20th century, all had myriads of reasons why they did not have to follow the accounting rules or provide financial transparency for their stakeholders. Even while they required people in the firm to be careful with resources, they lived lives of excess, believing somehow that the wealth was deserved and was their prerogative. While they paid themselves exorbitant salaries and bonuses, they forced vendors to deeply discount prices and paid employees as little as possible to demonstrate the company's commitment to efficiency and the bottom line.

California Pacific Gas & Electric (PG&E) provided a stark example of this hubris when it awarded $83 million in bonuses in January and $89 million in bonuses in July of 2004. The startling part was that in addition to being a regulated monopoly, the company emerged in April from a three-year stint in Chapter 11 bankruptcy following the energy crises in California. While the rank and file received performance bonuses at 11% of their base salary, the seven top execs received up to 70% of their base salary. The Chairman received $1.7 million in the first round and $10 million in the second, while the CEO received $906,000 in the first and $10 million in the second. A spokesman defended the bonuses as the due of the executive team for the work they did to bring the company out of bankruptcy. The spokesman, John Nelson, added "it's not like customers' power bills would be lower if PG&E stopped handing out millions in bonuses. It's the profits of the company," he said. "We earned it."[29]

A final concern with this lens is that the perspective does not address the inequities which come from a difference in the original position — the discrepancy in wealth and power between those who are born with access to resources and privilege and those who do not have that access. Neither Kant nor the theorists who rearticulate his position in the 20th century, most notably Robert Nozick, advocate for a redistribution of resources based solely on need. For Nozick, the current distribution of goods in our community is the result of myriads of legitimate transactions over time and thus the discrepancies in wealth are fair. Arguing for a minimal state (which is important because governments are responsible for the transfer of wealth through taxation and redistribution), Nozick argues that "[w]hatever arises from a just situation by just steps is itself just."[30]

This position articulates what some philosophers call a principle of negative rights: we are entitled to whatever we get either because of our original position (the resources of our family) or because of how we choose to use the resources we inherit or have earned. Thus, if we agree to employment which pays minimum wage with no benefits, that transaction is fair because we had the freedom of contract to either take or leave that job. Again, the conversation becomes stark when we consider health care. Is it ethical for a parent to take a child to the hospital for care if the parent knows that he cannot pay for the care? Those who advocate for negative rights would state that we should not incur any obligation which we are not able to pay, including debts for health care. Those who believe that every person is entitled to adequate health care disagree vehemently with limiting access to health care based solely on the patient's ability to pay. Those who are in the philosophical camp of Nozick argue for limiting governmental regulations concerning our contracts (minimum wage, wage and hour laws, laws concerning safety) and reducing taxes. Those advocating for a minimal government believe that people should be responsible for their own well being and not have any expectation of protection from bad agreements or from being on the public dole. Those who advocate for more government involvement to assure the well being of members of the community believe that the public policy positions of those who argue for a minimal state are meanspirited and selfish.

This conversation will be revisited in Chapter 9 when we look at Rawls' theory of justice (Relationship Lens) which states that we have an obligation to transfer resources and care for the least advantaged. Nozick does not agree with Rawls. Nozick states that "[j]ustice is determined not by the patterns of the final outcome of distribution, but by whether 'entitlements' are honored."[31] Rather than including health care, education, food, and shelter as positive rights to which all persons in a community should have access, the only positive right which Nozick recognizes is the "right to acquire and transfer property."[32] Thus, he advocates protecting the right to private property, which is a bedrock for a market economy. Nozick's mantra is "[f]rom each as they choose, to each as they are chosen."[33]

> **Attend to the Common Good**
>
> At first blush the common good would seem to require that we act without telling people the consequences. We would expect that the needs of the community would outweigh the desires of the individual. However, in this case the physician has much more power than the patient. The physician has the power of knowledge, information, as well as status. Achieving the common good requires that we work to balance power. In this case, maintaining the protocol of informed consent works toward balancing power.

▶ *Attend to the common good*

While this lens focuses on the rights and responsibilities we as individuals claim, we must note that all others in the community are entitled to the same rights. Of course, the difficulty is that we do not always notice that we must have a modicum of personal and financial power to exercise rights. To correct for the bias of assuming that all have the same opportunities and resources, as we rank the options, we should focus on balancing between achieving individual rights and responsibilities against the rights and responsibilities of the stakeholders. If the rights and responsibilities of any party are to be compromised, we should compromise on the side of the one who has the least power and the least ability to gain access to power.

▶ *Act with courage*

Because most of the work in ethics is persuasion, we should be able to articulate clearly both what choice we have made and why that choice meets the requirements of the lens. After giving some background information to set the stage for the problem, we can frame the statement so that we answer the core questions of this particular lens. What are our *reasons* for choosing this action? Having examined our motives, how are our *duties, rights, and responsibilities,* both our own as the ethical actor and all of the other of the stakeholders, fulfilled? How does the way that we propose to carry out this action demonstrate *caring* for the stakeholders involved?

> **Statement of Action**
>
> After consideration, the ethics committee will recommend that the protocol of informed consent be maintained, even when the patient is just getting blood work. Because one of the ramifications of the test is that people who test HIV positive will be reported to the state, the ethics committee believes that patients should have full knowledge of the law before that choice is made. We cannot second guess the desires of the patients. While we would hope that no one would choose to not be tested and thus not be treated, we know in the final analysis, each person is responsible for his or her own health care, regardless of our preferences.

Step 5: Return to Awareness

After we describe our resolution of the problem, we next consider whether the ethical analysis made sense. Did we like the result? What were the problems with the process? What are the sticking points with the process? How was the process enhanced or modified by adding the world of emotion or caring?

▶ *Continuous improvement*

The process of continuous improvement involves evaluating the result of the action. As we act in our life based on the Results/Responsibility Lens, we can watch for intended and unintended results. Also we should watch for new questions or answers that were not complete. The trajectory for maturity is not necessarily smooth, but as we attend to our rights and responsibilities, we can get there. As we treat people with respect and dignity, we consider to what degree autonomy can be respected. This process will call us to accountability for paternalistic and autocratic behavior while caring for those who legitimately cannot care for themselves.

▶ *The Crucible of Spirit*

As we are called to balance, we need to address whether we are being overly responsible or not responsible enough. As we learn to live fully in the present, attending to our own desires and our inner child, we can avoid the problem of busyness for the sake of busyness or becoming self-righteous as we try virtuously to meet all of the spoken and unspoken requirements of the community. If we do not attend to our spirit as we do our work, we risk becoming bitter and brittle. Duty without joy provides naught but dry bread and water for sustenance. As we seek tastier fare, we can learn how to be responsible while treating ourselves and others with compassion.

Conclusion

The Rights/Responsibility Lens invites us to consider how to live a responsible life. Beginning with the ethical key phrase, *I am responsible,* we learn to be adults who consider our motives as we act. To avoid becoming legalistic and autocratic, we learn to be compassionate, or in the words of the moral key phrase, *I am caring.* As we learn to use both our heads and our hearts, caring for others while assuring that they too are granted autonomy, we can *delight in our work.* Balancing rights and responsibility with caring and autonomy requires careful thought. With practice and discipline, we can act with discretion and wisdom when faced with difficult choices.

Continuing the Conversation

1. Using either the first problem in the GG Ethics Game or another fact pattern, analyze the situation using the Rights/Responsibility Lens. Was the problem easy to resolve, indicating that this might be your preferred method of working ethical problems? Was the process difficult indicating that this may not be your ethical home?

2. Read an op ed piece in your local paper or a national paper and find examples of an author using the Rights/Responsibility Lens. In what ways did the author appeal to the right of contract and negative rights (solutions requiring no transfer of resources/money from one to another)? What distinctions were made between rights and equality of opportunity for all people? How did the author explore the motives of those making the decisions and taking action?

3. Review the conceptual map of the Rights/Responsibility Lens paying special attention to the gifts of this tradition. Considering both your own life as well as two others who make decisions using this tradition, what are the strengths of the Rights/Responsibility Lens? Give examples of situations in which you have seen excellent results as someone used the viewpoints and processes of this lens to make a decision.

4. What strategies can you put in place to strengthen your own mastery of this lens? How can you help the organizations in which you work, whether paid or volunteer, to ask the core questions (p 173) to help them make better ethical decisions?

5. Again, review the chart which opened this chapter, this time attending to the weaknesses of this tradition. Considering both your own life as well as others who make decisions using the vantage of this tradition, what are the weaknesses of the Rights/Responsibilities Lens? Give examples of situations in which you have seen problematic results as someone used the viewpoints and processes of this lens to make a decision.

6. What strategies can you put in place to help you recognize and attend to the imbalance which comes from an inappropriate appropriation of the Rights/Responsibility Lens, whether concerning abuse of power or hubris in your personal and professional life. How do you know when you are improperly using the tools of this lens? How can you help the organizations in which you work, whether paid or volunteer, to ask the core questions to help them avoid imbalance or hubris?

The Results Lens

Conceptual Map

Concepts	World of Reason	World of Emotion	Crucible of Spirituality
Key Question	What are good results?	What are mutually good results?	How can I be a partner in creating a better world?
Theory	Utilitarianism — greatest good for greatest number	Complex harmonizing of goods for greater good	Sacred Imagination
Representative Author	John Stuart Mill Jeremy Bentham	Bernard Lonergan Frederick Ferre	William Lynch Rosemary MacNaughton
Tools and Practices	Experience; action/reflection	Awareness; self-efficacy	Imagination
Key Phrase	I have choices	I am consistent	I am co-creator of what is
Goal	Identify the goals of life	Creatively imagine solutions which lead to higher goods	Awareness of participating in sacred plan
Gifts	Self-directed choices	Respect for others; ability to live with ambiguity, Integrity	Optimism; enthusiasm; flexibility; hope
Challenges	Inconsistent choices between long- and short-term goals	Maintaining consistency between actions and self-view	Anger
Risk	Reduce all to cost/benefit	Non-attention to imbalance of power	Attachment (lack of detachment)
Hubris	Expedience	Assuming that one is identical with the other	My way is best/only way
Vice	Greed	Freeloading	Pride
Crisis	Failure	Guilt	Discouragement

Dream Deferred

What happens to a dream deferred?

Does it dry up like a raisin in the sun?
Or fester like a sore? And then run?
Does it stink like rotten meat?
Or crust and sugar over — like a syrupy sweet?
Maybe it just sags like a heavy load.

Or does it explode?

Langston Hughes[1]

Chapter 8

Results Lens

The next ethical lens comes from the tradition which focuses on the decision maker's goals and objectives. Because the emphasis is on each individual person choosing to act in a way which makes him or her happy, the lens is called the Results Lens. Drawing upon the works of Aristotle, St. Aquinas, and St. Ignatius Loyola, the earliest theorists in the modern era who focused on the right of people to pursue the goals that make them happy are John Stuart Mill and Jeremy Bentham. Dubbed utilitarianism, the notion is that the ethical action is that which provides the greatest good for the greatest number. In this quest, all people are to be included so that members of the local and now even the global community do not have to live with dreams deferred. Although many have taken issue with the theory, the underlying

> Core Questions
>
> - What results do I want to achieve?
> - What are mutually good results for all in this situation?
> - How can I be a partner in creating a better world?

concept is that we each get to choose how we will live and pursue the ends that make us happy. This particular tradition has had much criticism for not attending to concepts of justice as well as the deontological tradition does.[2] However, the *reflective process* by which one determines what key goals are important and worthy of pursuit for individuals and how to preserve the goals for the community remains fresh and relevant.

Working from the central concept of an ethical act being a goal or result which will create the most happiness for the most people, the Results Lens invites each ethical actor to determine what goals are worthy of pursuit. This school of thought matured as Mill and other Enlightenment philosophers were breaking from the medieval traditions where the church, or other authority, told each person what his or her role would be based on the family structure, economic status, and gender roles. Mill and Bentham put forward the notion that each of us has the right to choose what makes us happy, which will then lead to happiness for the whole community. While the foundations were laid in the 1800s, it has taken more than 200 years for us to come into a fuller appreciation of the right of individuals to choose how to participate in the community based on their own preferences rather than an assigned role.

One stark example of the tendency to limit women's participation based on role was sketched by Linda Kerber as she traced the history of women being able to fully participate as citizens in our community. One of the chapters in her seminal work, *No Constitutional Right to be Ladies,* traced the history of women's attempts to be systematically included on juries, one of the last barriers to full civic participation. Kerber recounts the following conversation which took place in the U.S. House of Representatives in 1966:

> Emmanuel Celler of New York — who had been supporting women's voluntary service for many years— rose in the House of Representative to assure Martha Griffiths of Michigan that he was willing to support compulsory [jury] service for women if he could be reassured on one issue: "Frankly, I am caught between the urging of the gentlewoman from Michigan and a male constituent, who expects a hot meal on the table when he returns from work. Is it the gentlewoman's desire to come between man and wife?"[3]

Not until 1975 did the Supreme Court find that to meet the constitutional requirement of "a jury of peers," women needed to be systematically included in jury panels, even if that meant that they may not be home to prepare dinner.[4]

Mill, who ardently supported the rights of both women and men to be full participants in the community, articulated a theoretical basis for each of us to follow our own dreams rather than those dictated by roles. Intriguingly, many times we all choose to embrace traditional roles; however we must always be careful to assure that the choice is our own. Mill reminds us that even though we are part of society, we are not just one of many but individuals with dreams that should not be deferred.

In the process Mill reminds us that we cannot only satisfy the desires of the moment. Mill also invites us to seek the ideal goals, such as liberty, equality, and democracy. We are sometimes asked to put aside our individual preferences for the higher good. As anyone who has stayed inside on a beautiful day to finish a paper or project knows, we sometimes have to endure short-term pain for long-term gain. In a similar vein, those of us with access to power may be required not to press our advantage in order to allow those with less power to realize their dreams.

The theories of utilitarianism also provide the foundation for our market economy. Just as we can each choose what we want to do, each of us can choose how we wish to use our resources. Classic liberal economic thought finds that individuals are the basis of our community. As each of us rationally maximizes our self-interest (presuming full information of our options and opportunities) and does that which makes us happy, the market reaches equilibrium. The notion is that when we have access to all the data, we will not pay more for something than it is worth to us (including employee's wages), nor will we work for less than we think we are worth. Thus, Smith and the economists who have followed in this tradition use the philosophical foundations of utilitarianism to justify their political and economic theories and policies of what has come to be known market economy.[5]

Characteristics of the Results Lens

Definition

An action is ethical if good ends — good results — come from the action. In particular, an ethical action will assure that the greatest amount of ideal goals and/or results (happiness) is reached for the greatest number of people.

In this tradition, a moral person is the one who works to harmonize her goals with those of others. Knowing that relationships with others are alive with feelings, as we make choices which bring us happiness or as we notice that our goals and dreams are thwarted and so change direction, we work together to move toward the common good.[6] As we mature we come to terms with the need to choose among competing goods, choices that mean that one good path must be chosen over another equally good path. Each choice requires change. Even if, after reflection, we rechoose the same goal we are satisfied. If we choose another path, we have new opportunities for happiness. In the process we use our spiritual energy to fuel the process of change while maintaining the integrity of the societal structures of which we are a part.[7]

Definitions

- An ethical act is that which creates the greatest happiness for the greatest number.
- A moral act is one which moves toward the greater good, resulting in complex harmonizing satisfactions for many.
- Spiritual balance is maintained as we use our imagination to work for mutually supportive goals.

Questions for Determining Right Action

- *Goals:* How does this result help my long-term self-interest while allowing for concern about the well-being of others?
- *Greatest good:* How does this result produce or tend to produce the greatest amount of satisfaction for the greatest number of stakeholders?
- *Ideal goals:* How does this result promote or tend to promote those goals which are part of human happiness (*e.g.* health, wealth, friendship, knowledge)?
- *Harmonized goals:* How does this result move toward harmonizing goods for other individuals in the community?
- *Responsible choice and creative change:* How does this result support responsible choices and move toward creative change?

Virtues Which Flow from These Theories

- *Maximizing satisfaction:* The ethical agent should work to maximize the satisfaction of all the organization's stakeholders.

- *Efficiency:* The members of the organization should use every effective means to achieve the goals of the organization, in the attempt to attain its goals as efficiently as possible by consuming as few resources as possible and minimizing the external costs which the agency imposes on others.
- *Loyalty:* The employee should should act in the best interest of the organization and not act in a way which would jeopardize the goals.
- *Avoid conflict of interest:* The employee should not get into situations where personal interests conflict significantly with the goals of the agency.

Nuances of Theories of Morality

As each of us learns that we can live our lives the way we choose, we might become heady with the freedom of autonomy. Thus, we must note that we make our choices in a matrix of personal relations, a community which cooperates and is bound together by its own goals and a drive to move toward the common good.[8] These relationships are not isolated and theoretical. Rather they are infused with the whole range of emotions that come as one member embraces a dream, works to make that dream a reality, and then finally succeeds or fails. Along the way we discover that some goals give us as individuals a particular good. Then we learn that we can work with others to harmonize our individual goods so that others may also attain their heart's desire. This shift may be from making sure that I have a job to making sure that others are employed as well. Another example may be noticing that I had good mentoring to learn how to do my work and thus want to put in place programs to assure that all new members receive an orientation to the organization which will enhance their ability to succeed.

Constructive post-modern theorists point us to the common good by asking us to consider how to move to greater good. Frederick Ferré asserts that self-interest encourages us to survival. According to Mill, choosing to survive and be satisfied is even better. The best is to find a way to survive with "complex, harmonized satisfactions."[9] Ferré believes that, as we seek to maximize the good for all members of the community, we begin to mitigate the problem of evil. As individuals limit their vantage to only their personal happiness rather than the overall happiness of a community, we wind up focusing only on narrow self-interest rather than taking a systemic approach, attending to the interests of the whole. Working towards these complex, harmonized satisfactions is the goal of good leadership. Goleman identifies one style of leadership as coaching, where the leader helps people identify their strengths and weaknesses then works with them to harmonize their individual goals with the goals of the organization.[10] Effective coaches manage themselves by being emotionally aware, empathetic, and authentic. Then they are able to work with others without either micro-managing or putting the goals of the organization ahead of the goals of individuals.

Lonergan asserts that one of the results of our unrestricted desire to know is a yearning to also seek the good. This desire propels humans into a quest for the good which is

> dynamic...[with] its own normative line of development, inasmuch as the ideas of order are grasped by insight into concrete situations, are formulated in proposals, are accepted by explicit or tacit agreements, and are put into execution only to change the situation and give rise to still further insights.[11]

For Lonergan, the practical, concrete trajectory for ethical growth begins by acknowledging the provisional state of our knowledge. The ideal ethical person acts bravely with imperfect knowledge, exploring in the here and now how to live a life that is fully human and offers others in the community the opportunity to do the same. Considering how to find our own happiness while developing empathy for others as they find happiness is the focal point of the moral component of the Results Lens. As we act, we consider not only ourselves but also others.

The Crucible of Spirit

The crucible of spirit allows us to creatively find ways to meet both our own goals as well as others. Pheobe Snow, a folk singer, laments in a song called *Harpo's Blues*, "I hate to be a grown up and live my life in pain." Many people think that as we pursue our goals, the most we can hope for is survival — keeping body and soul together. If Lonergan is right that the goal of being human is to know and to learn, we progress not only by seeking the individual goals of survival, but also by moving toward those "terminal values" which parallel Mill's ideal goals.[12] Terminal values allow us to think beyond ourselves and our projects, to become in the words of the theorists "self-transcending," because we choose goals which move not only ourselves but also our co-workers and compatriots on the path toward maturity. As we learn to see beyond the pain of the day toward the larger good, we come to realize that what look like failures may in fact be gifts.

A young man who was nervous about his work recently asked my husband how being fired can be good. My husband recounted a situation of being "fired" while serving in the Air Force which involved a reassignment. While he was devastated at the moment, he realized some five years later that, but for the reassignment, he would never have received his next promotion. Thus, what seemed like a bad result was exactly what was needed in the larger picture of his overall career. He thus learned that one can never be sure what is success and what is failure. Being committed to the terminal value of integrity resulted in what looked like a set-back but was ultimately a step forward on his desired path.

This tale is told on a larger stage as we consider the flash point of the Civil Rights Movement in America when a young worker, Rosa Parks, refused to move to the back of the bus. The segregation laws in Alabama required that African-Americans sit in the back. Parks was active in the National Association for the Advancement of Colored People (NAACP) and worked with Dr. Martin Luther King, Jr. The local NAACP chapter was considering how to highlight the effects of discrimination. While the event itself was not planned, the emotion galvanized the local Black community. Hundreds of African-Americans joined in the boycott, putting aside their own goals of riding to work on a bus to seek the greater good, the core value of equality manifesting in the virtues of liberty, dignity, and equality.[13] In the process the national community was compelled to face its own goals and the way that it treated its neighbors.

Progress of the sort described above is not inevitable. Only as we learn to keep our egos in check by thinking that our goals are the only ones worth considering, we can avoid deluding ourselves into believing that our self-centered actions and goals are the only ones that count. If we do not learn to moderate our seemingly unsatisfiable need for "more" as we seek higher salaries and more perks, we do not learn to temper our greed. If we use the tools of reason to justify inaction and personal acquisition, we blind ourselves to the long-term consequences of our policies and choices.[14] Only as we come to terms with our very human frailties of greed and pride, do we move beyond expedience caused by reducing everything to a cost-benefit analysis and turn towards excellence.

Using the Results Lens

As we use the template for the Results Lens, we are asked to consider what makes us happy. Those who write in the utilitarian tradition focus on what makes an individual happy while also considering what provides the greatest aggregate happiness for all. If the focus is on each individual maximizing his own happiness, we see ethics mimicking Adam Smith's invisible hand, which is the bulwark of a market economy. The underlying assumption is that each of us makes choices based on what will lead to our happiness. An example can be seen by looking at students in an MBA class. While many think that learning for the sake of learning is pretty exciting, most people who give up their time and money to get an education are deferring the happiness of a fat bank account an active social whirl, or the chance to make a different contribution, to acquire new information, a better job, and/or another credential. As choices are made, if people believe that an MBA will be a stepping stone on the way to their dream, they will sign up for classes and the program will thrive. If, however, people no longer value a Masters in Information Systems degree because the jobs in the IT sector are drying up or moving off-shore, then the classes disappear because of lack of interest.

One temptation is to reduce this Results Lens to a cost/benefit analysis. While financial issues are important, other goals of life which are harder to define are, according to Mill, more important to consider. Thus, the joy of a cultivated mind or freedom to make choices cannot be reduced to cost. Elections are expensive, but the right to participate in a democracy is seen as bringing greater happiness than reduced taxes. Thus, we agree to tax ourselves (and make contributions) to pay the expenses which are needed to guarantee free elections. Another temptation is to focus only on short-term happiness, pleasure, and pain, which is called "hedonistic" utilitarianism. Mill and Bentham ask us to focus on ideal goals or ends such as truth, beauty, or freedom. The school of thought which seeks the ultimate goals of life is known as "ideal" utilitarianism.[15] As we seek that which is truly important and embrace long-term ideals, we find ourselves avoiding expedience to reach short-term financial gains. To help understand how this lens is used, we return to

Ethical Actor

The ethics committee of a PPO is charged with setting protocols for all of the physicians who are part of the group. They are concerned with the decisions that are the best for this particular group with their specific patients.

our ethics committee at the PPO trying to decide what to do with the question of informed consent and HIV.

Step 1: Be Attentive

▸ *Identify the ethical actor*

As always, the ethical agent is the one with the authority to act. However, for this lens th actor is a person who lives in a particular time and place with specific desires and goals and a particular decision. Rather than the transcendental person of Kant, Mill brings us into the rough and tumble world of reality. One of the primary differences between the deontological tradition, which focuses on ideal persons and situations, and the teleological tradition is the focus on the real circumstances and desires of a specific community.

▸ *Determine the stakeholders*

For this analysis, we focus on two elements of the stakeholders — the number of them in any given category and the impact that our decision will have on them. The reason for identifying the number of persons in each stakeholder group is to determine the group's influence factor. To the degree that individuals concur about what makes for happiness, people will make the same choice. With the criterion being to maximize overall good, those groups with the largest number will determine what is ethical. This number is more about the difference in size than about precise data. Thus, if one group has 10 people and another group has 100, that which makes the 100 happy will eclipse the happiness of the 10. For those who are Star Trek afficionados, Mr. Spock was the quintessential utilitarian. Facing his own death, a death caused by bringing the main engines back online in a radiation-filled section of the *U.S.S. Enterprise* in order to save the lives of his shipmates, Spock states, "It is logical. The needs of the many outweigh the needs of the few." The line was finished by Kirk, "Or the one."[16]

Calculation of Influence Factor (IF)

Stakeholders	Number in group	x Impact (1.00)	= IF
Committee	1	.2	0.2
Physicians	100	.3	30
Patients	100,000	.395	395
State	4,300,000	.005	21,500
PPO	1	.1	0.1

To determine the influence factor of any particular group, we begin by establishing the approximate number of people who are affected by the action over a specific span of time. In the example with which we are working, the time frame is a year. Each of the 100 physicians in this particular practice saw approximately 1,000 patients per year, for a total of 100,000 patients being served by the PPO. Next we determine the impact of each particular decision on each of the stakeholders based on our best knowledge (see the third column of the chart on page 213). So the weighting of the impact is fairly distributed, when we add up the impact factor for all of the stakeholders, the total impact is always 1.00. The impact includes the strength of the group's economic and political voice, as well as any direct impact to their well-being. As stated above, at the end of this step, the numbers in column three, the impact column, need to add up to 1.00. Finally, the influence factor is calculated by multiplying the number of stakeholder in each set by the impact factor. The difficulty in a utilitarian analysis is that a decision which has tiny impact for a large group may outweigh the interests of a few. Of course, the impact factor can be adjusted to change this result.

For example, one student considered whether technical climbers should be able to put permanent bolts in the rocks in national parks. Currently, the United States has 281 million citizens, each of whom has a tiny interest in preserving rock faces in national parks. Even considering that maybe 50,000 people are technical climbers, the minute indirect interest of the citizens in keeping those rocks intact will far outweigh the more direct interest of the technical climbers in putting permanent bolts in the rocks. Thus, an analysis of the problem revealed that no bolts should be allowed in the rocks in national parks. The only redeeming consideration is that large groups are not monolithic. Some portion of citizens will value pristine parks. Others may find the sport interesting and thus be perfectly willing for fixed bolts to be in the rocks as long as one set of bolts is made to serve all technical climbers. These citizens argue that because the ordinary person cannot see the bolts, their enjoyment of the park will not be compromised. Thus, we may need to divide the groups into smaller sub-groups to reflect shared values.

The whole point of market surveys and polls is to try to get a sense of the interests of different stakeholder groups in a population. If the information of a company or political group is wrong, they will not get support for their product, policy, or candidate. One only has to think of the legendary Ford Edsel, built without noticing a change in the buying habits or needs of car owners, and thus a marketing failure. If a group contains stakeholders with very different goals, who would divide the group. So, in the case of climbing in the national parks, citizens who are not climbers would be divided into those who support technical climbing, and have the same interests as the climbers themselves, those who are not climbers, and those who really do not care. Again, good data help us identify what groups to include.

As the United States began reconsidering security policies after 9/11 when airplanes were flown into the World Trade Center in New York City, the question about the needs of the many outweighing the needs of the few came into sharp relief. The issue was whether American citizens who are of Middle Eastern descent or have Arabic surnames should be automatically subjected to greater scrutiny as they boarded airplanes than others with a different ethnic heritage. One school of thought said that, because those who masterminded the hijacking of the planes were from the Middle East, subjecting all who were part of that ethnic group, in effect engaging in racial profiling, made perfect sense and was ethical. Others said that all citizens should be subject to the same level of scrutiny because terrorists come from all different races, as evidenced by a Caucasian American bombing the Federal building in Oklahoma City. In any event, the security concerns of being able to fly safely clearly outweighed the interest of any one citizen not to be subjected to the annoyance of a thorough search of shoe soles and luggage. The rules, however, are subject to constant tweaking based on the tolerance and concerns of the flying public.

▶ *Attend to the context*

One characteristic of the teleological tradition is that the theorists emphasize that we are born into a community and shaped by that society. Because we are social beings, Mill asserts that we each want to have harmony between our feelings and goals and those of our fellow humans.[17] Thus, we find ourselves attending to the community in which we participate to see what are considered noble goals and consequences worthy of pursuit. Mill, like all seminal theorists, expects members of the community to continue to think and grow as they mature. While the temptation may be to look only at what gives immediate short-term pleasure, Mill encourages each of us to work for unity, which is the motivation and strength of the utilitarian ethic, as we build communities and advance civilization.

Step 2: Be Intelligent

► *Pinpoint the Issue*

What is the central problem which must be resolved? As we phrase this issue into a question, we must focus on what will create the greatest happiness for the greatest number of people. The theorists for this lens assert that because each of us desires to be happy, as we make choices which lead to greater happiness, we will be ethical.

> Issue
>
> Given that the state requires that health care providers report all persons who test positive for HIV to the a central register, should we tell people before we do the blood work that a positive test result will be reported to the health department?

► *Explore values-in-conflict*

In a utilitarian setting, the conflicts arise with competing goals, each of which is expected to lead to someone's happiness. One set of conflicts arises when people focus on short-term rather than long-term happiness. Mill never allows us to wallow in our own selfish notions of happiness. Mill advocates attending to the long view. Mill also asserts that the community is always happier when people have cultivated a noble character. In addition, we are to look at the whole fabric of our lives, not just individual moments. Mill believes that the qualities of self-consciousness and self-observation will assist us in determining the rules of behavior which will allow for all persons, if not all creation, to find happiness.[18] Conflicts may also arise from different ideas about what makes an ideal community. Honest communication and dialogue help uncover the differences and point to how we can resolve seemingly conflicting values.

While engaging in the exercise of speculating about what makes people happy might seem pointless, any time an ethical agent makes a decision, the other stakeholders, either ratify the decision or not. Generally, people do not give us notice about their choices and preferences; rather, they "vote with their feet." If they are unhappy with choices made by the leadership, they leave the firm, choose other products, or find other suppliers. The more accurate we are in evaluating the stakeholder's criteria for happiness, the more likely it is that we will also get the results that we want.

> Values-in-Conflict
>
> The two values-in-conflict are autonomy and predictability or safety. The patients want to receive health care at the same time that their privacy is maintained. The physicians want to make sure that patients receive health care at the same time that they care about assuring that a highly infectious disease does not spread further. Our commitment to the community requires that we do all we can to minimize the spread of disease.

► *Identify options for action*

Having surveyed the problem, the ethical agent has to come up with a beginning array of possible options. While the evaluation of the problem will almost certainly lead to refinement of the options and of the precise action that moves toward harmonized goods. The process of decision-making requires that we to test our possibilities against the abstract principles and values revealed through the perspective of the lens. One characteristic of those who are more ethically mature is that they look for options which not only satisfy individuals but which also make the system as a whole function better. Thus, the more skilled a person becomes in ethical decision making, the more nuanced the resolution will be. Some negotiated options look like compromise for the sake of compromise, where everyone gets a little something but the overall result is not good. However, skilled mediators teach us to listen for the goals of each person affected by the decision and then to fashion an option which meets as many of the needs as possible. Thus, the result is not a naked compromise but, in current management parlance, a "win-win" solution where every party gets what is important at the same time that the integrity of the overall system is maintained.

> **Options for Action**
>
> 1. Tell the patient about the reporting requirement before doing the blood work.
> 2. Do not tell the patient about the reporting requirements before doing the blood work.

Step 3: Be Reasonable

► *Hone ethical thinking skills*

One critique of utilitarianism is that it supports a mindless calculation of pain and pleasure. Bentham, who was of a methodical bent, proposed a system of calculation where we add up points for what makes us happy and then subtract the points for pain to determine what we should do. While it is tempting to dismiss the process as arcane, most of us do a cost/benefit analysis as we work through tough decisions. The analysis does not always include only financial considerations but also quality of life values, balance of our happiness with that of others in our family, and concern for the community. Whether we choose not to take a promotion because we would have to be away from our families too much or choose to work in a non-profit setting to assist those who are less fortunate, we are weighing the relative value of our choices. The appeal of this theory is that those who may not understand why we would choose to minimize financial wealth while seeking happiness in other quarters, are themselves free to find happiness where they will.

Mill invites us to thus consider both qualitative happiness and quantitative happiness. Mill was absolutely committed to the notion of a strong society where people were free to choose how best they wanted to live. The notions of liberty and personal independence were central to his thoughts about the greatest good for the greatest number. He was a visionary in the areas of women's rights, for example, advocating that when *all* people are free to manage their own property and be responsible for their destiny, all of us are happier. He also advocated sacrificing for others as long as that sacrifice resulted in a greater sum total of happiness for the community. Mill would advocate that each of us limit our power in order to assure the well-being of the collective interests of the community. In making leadership decisions, CEOs and others can move from only considering how to maximize shareholder value to being a good citizen while attending to the well being of employees, consumers, the community, and the company.

One executive director of a non-profit which was part of the health care system was advised by a consultant to include greater health care benefits for the top three employees of the company than for the rest of the employees. The rationale was that all of the executive directors and CEOs of other organizations were doing it. This ED refused. He asserted both to the consultant and the board of directors that the culture of their organization was built on all people being valued the same and thus being treated equally. By all people having the same health care plan, those at the top remained aware of the changing health care costs and coverage, and those in the heart of the organization knew they were valued. The leadership exhibited by this ED means that in tough times employees will be willing to sacrifice for the good of the company. All have a sense of being valued as they work together to make the organization successful.[19]

▸ *Apply ethical content*

To apply the principle of the greatest happiness for the greatest number, we have to determine what, exactly, makes each of the stakeholders happy. In this particular sense, the goals to be sought are those ends which make people happy in light of their core values. Each of us must balance our core values in terms of personal goals, the goals of the community as a whole, and our own tolerance for pain. Some of us are willing to tolerate great pain because of the adrenaline rush (think of your favorite stock broker) while others prefer a more sedate life and are risk adverse.

After identifying the stakeholder who will be affected by the decision, another task is to determine what makes them happy. The first criteria to consider are the deal breakers. For each constituent, we need to determine what ideal goals are non-negotiable. If we are lucky, the constituent will be self-aware enough to identify wht is non-negotiable. Most of us are not that aware and so we have to listen to each other to determine what is important.

Next consider those goals which are preferred but not necessarily deal breakers. Most of us have a set of personally important goals that we try to achieve. The more resources and personal power we have, the more we are able to reach those goals. However, when we cannot reach our goals, we compromise. In these situations, the ethical agent must be aware of what has come to be called the tipping point. At some point the unhappiness of a given person or group reaches critical mass. Something becomes the proverbial "last straw that broke the camel's back." The example given earlier in the chapter of Rosa Parks is an example of a tipping point which ignited the national Civil Rights Movement. For Rosa Parks, the tipping point came when, exhausted after working all day, she was asked to give up her seat in the front of "colored" section of a Selma bus for a white person. That unjustified request galvanized the Black community to action with a bus strike which ultimately led to the end of segregation.

Many of the ethical scandals over the past three years came when the cumulative actions of CEOs and boards of directors, which resulted in greater and greater opacity of financial dealings rather than transparency, reached the breaking point.

Criteria for Happiness

Stakeholder	Criteria
Committee	1. Consistent process 2. Happy physicians who will not leave for another plan
Physicians	1. No malpractice actions 2. Easy process to inform
Patients	1. Full information before treatment 2. Confidentiality of treatment
State	1. Stop spread of AIDS 2. Accurate information
PPO	1. Consistent process 2. Protect physicians 3. Protect patients

Then, when the floodgates opened and people got a sense of the tremendous amount of money and jobs which were put at risk by aggressive accounting techniques and greed, people demanded a much greater accountability from business executives.

If either the good citizens of the South or those with financial power in American business had attended to what made for the greatest happiness for their stakeholders, they would have moderated their own quest for personal happiness. Through self-sacrifice and restraint, both groups could have avoided Congressional intervention. Had those in power worked to assure that African-Americans fully participated in the economic life of America, the Civil Rights Act of 1964 would not have been needed. Had the financial moguls of the late 20th century attended to well-identified financial best-practices, the Sarbanes-Oxley Act would not have been passed. A it happens, the cost of compliance with the law is much higher than the cost of being ethical in the first place.

For ease of calculation, a technique has been developed to calculate happiness. Assume that all constituent groups get 10 units of happiness. Economists call a unit of happiness a "util." So each constituent group begins with ten utils of happiness. As we review the options, we decide how happy each option will make each group. The scale runs from 1 util — very unhappy — to ten utils — blissfully happy. We need to remember to look at both the identified deal breakers and tipping points. So, as we calculate the utils of happiness generated by any given decision, we begin by assuming that if one is blissfully happy, the option will generate 10 utils of happiness. We deduct utils of happiness to the extent that an

Calculate Happiness Utils (out of 10)
Option 1: Do not notify before blood work

Stakeholder	Utils	Rationale
Committee	5	While the process is consistent, physicians will not be protected and thus might leave.
Physicians	4	The process will be easy, but not notifying the patients of the effect might expose them to malpractice action.
Patients	5	Most will not be affected by the policy. However, even when informed of the state policy, most are willing to compromise their privacy to stop spread of the disease. Those few who are impacted may feel betrayed as they value their privacy more than release of information to the state.
State	8	Most will be happy as the information about AIDs will be available.
PPO	5	The process will be consistent. Physicians and most patients are protected.

option does not make us happy. The rationale for the allocation of points is as important as the allocation itself. A person reviewing our calculations should be able to see the relationship between the identified criteria for happiness and the utils of happiness any given option generates. Calculate the happiness points for each option under consideration. While the process may feel arbitrary, make your decision based on your best understanding of the goals which advance the virtues embodied in the core values of the stakeholders. The task is to be objectively subjective. By using the best data we have available and then making a calculated estimation of what people value, we will get to a good policy. If we are wrong, we will find out sooner or later and, hopefully, be able to correct it.

Lest we think that no-one goes through this process, we can think of every market survey in which we have participated or every opinion poll which is conducted. An effective market survey measures what people value and anticipates a public policy or business decision will be supported with market choices, votes, or other action. If someone launching a product is wrong about what customers need and/or want, the product will fail. If we misread an employee's tolerance for invasion of privacy or moving jobs off-shore, we will have people walking out or protesting in other ways.

Finally, do the math to determine which option generates the most utils of happiness and leads to the greatest good. This involves multiplying the influence factor (IF) by the number of utils generated in the previous two charts to calculate the weighted utils of happiness. Finally, add the weighted totals for each stakeholder group to get the grand total of weighted utils of happiness for this option. The process of calculation is repeated for

Calculate Happiness Utils (out of 10)
Option 2: Notify before blood work

Stakeholder	Pts	Rationale
Committee	8	The process is consistent, and the physicians will be protected and will not leave. However, some people might not get treated for the disease.
Physicians	7	The process will be not be as easy as no telling, but they will not be exposed to a malpractice action.
Patients	9	Most will not be affected by the policy but may be inconvenienced. Everyone will have the opportunity to choose what they want to do from full information.
State	6	Many will be unhappy because they will fear the spread of an epidemic. Those who value freedom of choice will be happy.
PPO	9	The process will be consistent. Physicians will be protected and most patients informed.

each option. For the demonstration problem, given the assumptions of the ethical agent, Option 1 — not telling patients about the list — is more ethical than Option 2 — full disclosure.

Calculating the Greatest Good
Option 1 compared with Option 2

Stakeholders	IF (x)	Utils	= Weighted Total Option 1	utils	= Weighted Total Option 2
Committee	0.2	5	1.0	8	1.6
Physicians	30	4	120	7	210
Patients	395	5	1,975	9	3,555
State	21,500	8	182,000	6	129,000
PPO	0.1	5	0.5	9	0.9
Total weighted utils			184,096.5		132,767.5

This process is a hybrid between the calculus of Bentham and the idealism of Mill. The reason the process is effective is that it forces each of us to consider the interests of the stakeholders as separate from ourselves. We often believe that everyone has the same interest that we do when in fact their interests are very different. The other point of this exercise is to show the tyranny of the majority. If the majority considers only its narrow self-interest as it acts, it can trump the minority concerns every time.

▸ *Overlay moral content*

As we reflect on the ethical options, we can ask whether we are treating people with inherent dignity. Are we moving toward the greater good, which means moving from our own self-interest into the greater good for the community? This process is different from compromising. It requires the hard work of listening to each other and finding ways that each person's desires can be met. Often what people initially say they want is just a cover for a deeper desire. By entering into a process of discernment where we ask questions to uncover the root dream, we can come to individualized solutions.

Act Toward Harmonized Good

While protecting the few is tempting, the importance of protecting the physician-patient relationship and confidentiality is more important than reporting information without disclosure. If we treat our patients with respect and know that their goal is also to receive treatment, we can find a way to assure that the community is protected at the same time that the patient is respected.

For instance, having a good paying job may be important either for status or for providing for a family. A very high paying job may be required to meet the goal of status, whereas a more moderate income may meet the goal of providing for a family. Accomplishing harmonized goals may require that we think outside of the box to come up with innovative solutions. However, in the process we become co-creators of our destiny and discover that being an adult does not necessarily mean that one has a life sentence to live in pain.

Step 4: Be Responsible

▸ *Rank the options*

Having determined the utils of happiness generated by the weighted good, we can see which option truly does generate the greatest good for the greatest number. As the options are ranked, summarize why the ranking of options was made, and demonstrate the primacy given to not only individual happiness but also the good of the community. Sometimes options will generate very close numbers. In those situations, the ethical agent can choose whichever option she prefers. In other cases, while one option may generate the highest number, another option may be chosen which is perceived to better meet the harmonized goals of the community.

> **Rank the Options**
>
> After calculating the utils of happiness, at first blush not disclosing the information about the list maintained by the government provides the greatest happiness for the greatest numbers. Those who care may ask whether physicians can maintain their role of healer and counselor. Because the list does exist, the citizens can find out who is infected. However, for the vast majority of people, knowing that those infected with the disease are treated and educated not to spread the disease is the result that is wanted. Thus, the harmonized goal is in fact putting in place strategies to stop the spread of the disease, not a process which might embarrass some folks. Adding a process of thoughtful informed consent does reach the goal of the greatest good for the greatest number.

▸ *Correct for Bias*

The temptation at this level is to rationalize toward expedience rather than pursue excellence. Thus, we must seriously ask whether we are embracing excellence rather than seeing ourselves content with expedience. In the process we must not be blinded by our own selfishness or greed, which often is realized at the expense of others. Another bias is considering only cost. While the financial side of the conversation is important, we must attend to overall happiness and goodness, not just the bottom line.

- ▹ *Efficiency* judges people in terms of the acquisition of riches, power, status, and prestige while *excellence* judges people against community established virtues such as awareness, maturity, and competence.

> **Correct for Bias**
>
> As we give the informed consent, we need to be sure that we take the time to explain fully what the process is and listen to the fears of the patients. Because of the conditions under which the HIV virus is spread and the bias in the community, we will have to be particularly attuned to those who would hide because of shame or fear.

- *Efficiency* requires only that a person act to maximize satisfaction of his own wants and needs while *excellence* requires that a person seek goals in light of the virtues embodied by the community.

- *Efficiency* requires that a person identify the strategies to acquire goods and become skilled in using those strategies to get ahead while *excellence* requires that a person continue to progress in reaching the ideals of the community and recognize what is the highest perfection.

- *Efficiency* requires only that a person follow the rules of justice until the rules change while *excellence* can be defined independent of the current rules.

Thus, people who are efficient may not have any personal moral standards while people who strive for excellence have personal moral standards which are harmonized with those of the community at large.

▸ *Attend to the common good*

The chapter began with a poem by Langston Hughes concerning the disappointment of "dreams deferred." Mill asserts that everyone has the right to seek what makes him happy — not just those with power or privilege. We forget that as we have people who help us and thus, we need to help others. We may forget that we are building on the hopes and dreams of our parents and grandparents and thus need to attend to the hopes and dreams of our children, all of our children. We need to attend to systemic barriers which keep people from being able to find happiness resulting in deferred dreams.

> **Attend to the Common Good**
>
> At first blush the common good would seem to require that we act without telling people the consequences. However, as we work toward complex, harmonized goals, we must realize that most people desire health. The question is what to do to give us the best chance of healing. Thus, telling people what the consequences of their blood tests might be and working to find solutions which will make both the patient and the community happy attends to the common good.

▸ *Act with courage*

After we make our choice, drafting a short statement that could be placed in a memo to others in the company or a press release helps to articulate our ethical decisions so that we answer the core questions of the Results Lens. How does the selected option make the stakeholders happy and meet their individual goals? Having attended to the whole person of those who are affected, how have we attended to feelings and basic dignity? How do we move toward the greater good for all the community, not just myself? Again, the purpose of the statement is to explain our action at the same time that we both educate and seek buy-in because the goals of the individual members of the group are met.

> **Statement of Action**
>
> After consideration, the ethics committee will recommend that the protocol of informed consent be maintained, even when the patient is just getting blood work. Because the greatest good for the greatest number requires that all people know the ramifications of a medical procedure, we will assure that a careful process be implemented. We will also work with all of our patients to assure that in the case of illnesses which may impact the larger community, educational policies are in place to minimize the spread of disease.

Step 5: Return to Awareness

After we describe our resolution of the problem, we next consider whether the ethical analysis made sense. Do we like the result? What were the problems with the process? What are the sticking points with the process? How was the process enhanced or modified by adding the world of emotion and attending to the common good?

► *Continuous Improvement*

The process of continuous improvement involves evaluating the result of the action. As we take action based on the calculus of the process, we are cautioned to watch both for intended and unintended results. We also need to attend to new questions or answers that were not complete. The trajectory for maturity is not necessarily smooth, but as we attend to the goals, harmonized values, and our ideals, we can get there. As we take responsibility for our own self-directed choices as well as respect the choices of others, we learn to live with ambiguity and integrity. In the process we learn how to maintain consistency between our actions and our self-concept.

► *The Crucible of Spirit*

As we are called to balance, we must address whether we are being overly attached to our goals or whether we are detached from our every-day lives enough to see the bigger picture and attend to the higher good. As we become aware of being part of a larger community, we become optimistic and enthusiastic about participating in the community as a whole. We become aware of our tendencies toward pride and control, believing our way is the only way, and being attached to our own desired ends. We make sure that in the community we carry our own weight and do not freeload on the good will of others. If we do not attend to our spirit as we do our work, we risk becoming angry and discouraged. Finally, as we notice where we have power to help others reach their dreams, we discover the joy of helping others rather than attending only to ourselves.

Conclusion

The Results Lens invites us to consider how to live a productive life. Beginning with the ethical key phrase, *what are good results,* we learn to make responsible choices which will help us survive and thrive. To avoid becoming greedy as we seek ever more toys, and accolades, we learn to seek *mutually satisfying results.* As we use our imagination, we see ourselves as *partners in creating a better world.* With detachment, caring more about the people and the process than the result, we help all to have a shot at realizing their dreams.

Continuing the Conversation

1. Using either the second problem in the GG Ethics Game or another fact pattern, analyze the situation using the Results Lens. Was the problem easy to resolve, indicating that this may be your preferred method of working ethical problems? Was the process difficult, indicating that this may not be your ethical home?

2. Read an op ed piece in your local paper or a national paper and find examples of an author using the Results Lens. In what ways did the author appeal to the "greatest good for the greatest number" as a justification for the policy direction? How did the advocated policy balance the goals of those in power against those who do not have as much opportunity to reach their goals?

3. Review the Conceptual Map of the Results Lens which opened this chapter, paying special attention to the gifts of this tradition. Considering both your own life as well as two others who make decisions using this tradition, what are the strengths of the Results Lens? Give examples of situations in which you have seen excellent results as someone used the viewpoints and processes of this lens to make a decision.

4. What strategies can you put in place to help strengthen your own mastery of this lens? How can you help the organizations in which you work, either paid or volunteer, to ask the core questions (p. 203) which can help them make better ethical decisions?

5. Again, review the chart which opened this chapter, this time attending to the weaknesses of the tradition. Considering both your own life as well as that of others who make decisions using the vantage of this tradition, what are the weaknesses of the Results Lens? Give examples of situations in which you have seen problematic results as someone used the viewpoints and processes of this lens to make a decision.

6. What strategies can you put in place to help you recognize and attend to the imbalance which comes from an inappropriate appropriation of the Results Lens, whether concerning abuse of power or hubris in your personal and professional lives? How do you know when you are improperly using the tools of this lens? How can you help the organizations in which you work, whether paid or volunteer, to ask the core questions which can help them avoid imbalance or hubris?

The Relationship Lens

Conceptual Map

Concepts	World of Reason	World of Emotion	Crucible of Spirituality
Key Question	What is a fair system?	What is the appropriate subordination of my rights to those of the group?	What is my place in the web of life?
Theory	Justice Ethics Communitarianism	Moral Ecology	Sacred Creation
Representative Authors	John Rawls, Amitai Etzione	Robert Bellah, William Frederick	Robert C. Fuller
Tools and Practices	Tradition, group activities	Ability to evaluate and respond to the emotional climate of group	Commitment to Justice, service
Key Phrase	I am part of a tradition	I am part of the group	I am part of all that is
Goal	Set of processes to assure a just/fair community	Correct evaluation of event based on group response	Awareness of place in sacred community
Gifts	Participation in economic ecosystem	Connection to persons in community	Awe of all that is, generosity, forgiveness; balance independence and interdependence
Challenges	Balance between equal opportunity and equal outcome; respect of individual rights	Finding appropriate emotional response to event	Exclusiveness
Risk	Authoritarian	Entrainment	Over-identification with group
Hubris	Exempt	I do not have to evaluate	I have the "Truth"
Vice	Ambition; abuse of power	Group-think	Elitism
Crisis	Separation	Guilt and shame	Lack of meaning; isolation

Let justice
roll on like a river,
righteousness like
a never-failing stream!

The Prophet Amos[1]

Chapter 9

Relationship Lens

The third ethical lens calls us back to the deontological tradition where we look at the decision maker's rights and responsibilities. However, the question now moves from consideration of the individual to seeing how that individual fits into the community while determining what responsibilities we all have for assuring that the community and its supporting institutions are healthy. Drawing upon the idealist traditions of Plato, St. Augustine, Luther, and Kant, the theorist on the edge of the postmodern world who began to move us toward a consideration of the community through a moderation of individual rights is John Rawls (1921-2002). Rawls places himself in the modern tradition of those who consider the social contract as foundational for our community.

Core Questions

- How do I fit into my community?
- How do I balance the group's and my own interests?
- What is my place in the web of life?

However, he critiques the Hobbesian notion that we subject ourselves to the community because of a self-serving desire for security. Hobbes argues that "if a citizen in a relatively secure state desires to commit an illegal act and is confident that he can avoid detection" there is no reason for him either ethically or morally to refrain from acting on that desire.[2]

Rawls argues that meeting our agreements should not depend on our particular situation. The core of Rawls' theory is twofold. First, we should be committed to social agreements regardless of our original position, the position of our birth — our nationality, gender, race, and economic position. As we consider the claims of others to the resources needed to thrive, we make commitments which last in perpetuity, beyond our own particular interest. Second, that our ignorance about the intricacies of a particular rule should not govern whether we follow it. Rather, as we learn more about our responsibilities to the community, our commitment to the underlying social contract will grow.

Working from the central concept of ethics as finding the correct process by which decisions should be made and our rights and responsibilities exercised, the Relationship Lens focuses our attention on what social agreements we would make if we didn't know who we were in the community and wanted to assure fundamental fairness for all persons. Rawls asks us to make our decisions from an impersonal position as an *ideal observer* where we choose to act without knowing anything about ourselves or others in the community. In that role, we are called upon to consider whether the agreements we make would satisfy us if we found ourselves as the least advantaged in the community. Rawls thus anticipates the postmodern approach to ethics where the process by which the rules of the community are decided is more important than the actual rules themselves. Rawls understands that while the rules may change, the process will help us to avoid acting only out of self-interest.

As we apply the template for the Relationship Lens, we use our mind and the tools of reason to see how we fit into our community and what relationships are important to sustain. The sticking point for many is that whatever process upon which we agree is to be applied equally to all persons in the situation. Rawls also entreats us to consider the whole community, and in particular the claims of those who are least advantaged, as we make choices about how best to live.

Characteristics of the Relationship Lens

Definition

An act is ethical if it supports a framework for continuous systemic ethical improvement for both the organization and the institutions supporting it.

In this tradition, a moral person is one who deeply understands that he or she is a member of a community and thus must work within that community in order to have healthy institutions. A society depends on institutions such as schools, churches, hospitals, and businesses to thrive. Those organizations provide continuity for the people in the community as well as a safety net for those who are having a hard go of life. Often, supporting our core institutions means being shaped by them and being held accountable to them. Rather than just going off on our own, we find that we need the support and love of others to work through the difficult time. Our spiritual balance is maintained as we find our place within the web of our community. At times we need to share from our abundance; at other times we must receive from others as we do not have particular resources. At times we need to move into leadership roles; at other times we need to be served by others. At times we need to teach others and hold them accountable for their agreements; at other times we need to be taught by others and be reminded of our obligations. As we move through life, spiritual wisdom lets us know how we fit at this particular time into the on-going fabric of society.

> **Definition**
>
> - An ethical act is one which sustains integrity-building environments.
> - A moral act is one where we act as members of the community to support healthy institutions.
> - Spiritual balance is maintained by knowing how we fit into the web of our community.

Questions for Determining Right Action

- *Process:* How does the process is used to implement the decision assure that all stakeholders are considered and heard in this choice?

- *Healthy institutions:* How does this decision support my responsibility for assuring that the community and its institutions are healthy and effective?

- *Support of the organization:* How does this decision enhance the achievement of the organization's goals, responsibilities, and values?

- *Enhancement of relationships:* How does this decision enhance the relationship of my organization to the community at large?

Virtues Which Flow From These Theories

- *Fair treatment:* Persons are to be treated in accord with the social agreements that have resulted from our analysis as an ideal observer. Those who are alike in relevant respects should be treated similarly; persons who differ in some respect relevant to the job they perform should be treated differently in proportion to the difference.

- *Fair administration of rules:* Rules should be administered consistently, fairly, and impartially.

- *Fair compensation:* Individuals should be compensated for the cost of their injuries by the party who is responsible for those injuries.

- *Fair blame:* Individuals should not be held responsible for matters over which they have no control.

- *Due process:* The individual has a right to a fair and impartial hearing when he or she believes that personal rights are being violated.

Nuances of Theories of Morality

While Rawls calls us to consider what an ideal observer would do in a given situation, Bellah and Frederick invite us to personalize the conversation. Rather than taking a position which is removed from the hustle and bustle of the real world, those who are part of the communitarian movement invite us to consider not just our individual acts affect us but also how those acts support a healthy community and vibrant institutions.

Bellah and Frederick both use the concept of moral ecology to call us to greater responsibility for the community. Ecology, in sociological terms, is the study of the relationships and adjustments of humans to their geographical and social environments.[3] For Bellah, moral ecology is the notion that we should understand that "the individual is realized only through community" so we should consider how to build and maintain healthy institutions which are the matrix from which healthy character is formed.[4] Frederick reminds us that corporations must attend to those life-conserving virtues such as fairness, unselfishness, and restraint which both create and sustain human collective life.[5] The moral component of the Relationship Lens invites us to see ourselves as part of an ongoing web of life where our business systems and institutions support the community.

This lesson was learned by one of my students who was an ardent individualist, believing that he did not need anyone else to make it in this world. He was absent from class for several weeks and then came to me with an explanation and an apology. He had been very ill. But for a close friend who nursed him through the illness and put his physical interests above her own needs, he literally would not have survived. He said that as he lay on his bed, he thought about his assertion in class that he (and by implication, everyone else) could make it on his own, and realized that he was wrong: he needed the larger community to thrive.

As we consider the Relationship Lens, the first of the two lenses that call us to accountability for the community, the first reaction of many is that any sharing of resources or providing opportunities to those who are disadvantaged is communism or socialism and thus to be avoided. Ironically, many who make this claim are people of deep faith who do not explore how the Judeo/Christian tradition (or the traditions of other faiths) call us to responsibility for others. In the Jewish community, practices such as gleaning (leaving part of the harvest) to provide for the poor or prohibitions against usury to assure that lenders did not gouge borrowers were woven into the fabric of their lives together.

The Christian community began with sharing their resources to care for each other and the poor. Much of the New Testament focuses on our financial responsibilities to each other. In the basic economic unit of our community, the family, resources are shared according to need not contribution (otherwise children and college students would have a difficult time). As the communal life of the early church unfolded, they discovered that an essential element of those economic choices, however, is trust among the members and people contributing what they can to the well-being of the community. Thus, many families embrace sharing their resources with each other, children receiving assistance in accordance with their need rather than their contribution. However, once the circle expands beyond the immediate family, we do not seem to trust that others truly need the resources or that they will use them appropriately. At that point many become miserly in their sharing with others.

As the United States embraced the radical individualism that was a logical outgrowth of the theories of Kant, Mill, and Hobbes, whose theories deeply informed our Declaration of Independence and governmental structures, we adopted the philosophies of the Rights/Relationship Lens and the Results Lens and often chose to put in place structures to help those who were less advantaged. The idea was that people could use their brains and their brawn to provide for themselves and their families. Any needs in the community could be provided by the extended family or the religious and charitable organizations. The structure of the economic and social institutions were not to be regulated by the government; rather, we would use our power of contract to moderate the excesses of the institutions.

In the beginning of the 20th century, a tipping point was reached and society began to tilt toward the perspective of the Relationship Lens. As businesses grew during the Industrial Revolution (1850), many began to acknowledge the powerlessness of the every-day person to bargain with business organizations. The religious community joined with those in the Labor Movement and called upon businesses to temper their power by providing appropriate wages, safe working environments, and setting fair prices. As business leaders believed they deserved to push for their own economic advantage, they resisted those changes unless the bottom line was enhanced. The response was an increase in governmental regulation after the stock market crash of 1929 to assure that the excesses of businesses were tempered and some mechanisms for caring for the disadvantaged were put in place.

At the beginning of the 21st century, we are seeing a renewed call for businesses to be socially responsible, as the questions of a hundred years ago are revisited in terms of health care, living wages, and holistic work conditions. Added to the current mix are issues related to environmental responsibility. Members of the community are asking what responsibility an organization has to provide for the needs of its workers, including health care and sustained employment? What is the responsibility of an organization to assure that it does not damage the environment or community? What responsibility does an organization have to help the community in which it finds itself? How do we balance between the need to stay in business and the responsibility for caring for all of the stakeholders, including the community?

As explored in Chapters 2 and 3, polarizing the conversation into advocating for only an unregulated market economy or pushing for absolutely all resources being shared is not useful. Rather, Rawls and Bellah call us to consider how to balance the needs of individual autonomy and responsibility to ensure that our institutions and organizations remain robust, while assuring that all members of the community, and the environment itself, can survive and thrive. Different communities find that balance in various ways; thus, conversation and commitment to both the individual and the whole are acknowledged to be essential.

The Crucible of Spirit

Those who are committed to justice for all find themselves part of the ethical tradition which emphasizes systemic integrity and control. In the United States, the religious groups which have been responsible for raising these issues are the historic justice communities, the Quakers and Mennonites, those who are part of the Catholic Social Thought community, the Baha'is, and the Black churches, which champion the call for civil rights. As we listen to voices from these faith communities, we come to realize that all of humanity is profoundly connected, and we are each part of all that is. At that point the differences among us begin to dissolve, and we understand that if our brother or sister hurts, we hurt as well. We are then called to consider the subtle connections of dependence, independence, and interdependence.

Healthy dependence comes when we acknowledge our needs, whether as children, the physically or mentally challenged, or the elderly who cannot provide for themselves. Those of us who seem fully capable still need mentors and teachers to help us navigate new situations and community structures to make our lives enjoyable. Roads, sewer systems, judicial systems, schools, and parks ought to be maintained by all, based on ability to pay, for the community to thrive. Unhealthy dependence comes when we do not take responsibility for doing what we can to improve our situation and care for the whole. Healthy independence flows when we are as responsible as possible for ourselves both physically and economically. Unhealthy independence comes when we do not acknowledge that we cannot survive on our own. Often we ignore the claims of those upon whose work we depend, such as janitors, technicians, and farm workers. We ask them to work to make their lives better as we scheme to pay them as little as possible for their efforts.

Those who embrace interdependence know that we all need each other. At the same time, we each are responsible for assuring that we carry out our own part of the bargain as well. Thus, as we seek interdependence, we acknowledge when we need others and when we must act on our own. Recalling the image from outer space of the blue globe we call our home, no boundaries are present, no nations are seen — we know we are all one. As we learn that the environmental changes of one continent affect the environment of another, we realize how we are all profoundly connected. As we then commit ourselves to work for others, in addition to ourselves, for the good of the whole, we can stand in awe of our wonderful life together. In the process we learn to receive and give the gifts of generosity and forgiveness.

Using the Relationship Lens

Rawls invites us to consider what processes and procedures we would put into place in our community if we did not know our original position (*e.g.*, our economic class, gender, race, health) or what our role (*e.g.*, worker, parent, professional, laborer) in the community would be. Rawls is concerned with ethics as fundamental fairness, a call to justice in distribution of the burdens and benefits of the community. Rawls also invites us into a process which he calls "reflective equilibrium" where we constantly balance the needs of individuals against the needs of others in the community. As he lays out his theory, he asks us to be careful to consider those who are least advantaged, those without access to power and privilege.

At the end of any ethical analysis, we have to explain why a particular option was chosen and why others were not. The following analytic process helps us work through each of the options using the Relationship Lens. As we become skilled, the analysis will become easier as will identifying the core values and virtues which, for us, trump other competing values and virtues. However, even when we think we know the answer, the process can help clarify our thoughts.

Ethical Actor

The ethics committee of a PPO is charged with setting protocols for all of the physicians who are part of the group. As you think about the problem, you realize that you do not know if you are the physician, the patient with AIDS, or the person who might be infected through any number of means. You realize that you might be any number of persons connected with this situation. Thus, you care both about how the individual is treated as well as the overall system in which the care is given.

Step 1: Be Attentive

▶ *Identify the ethical actor*

Imagine that we are the subject of a science-fiction movie. We are hovering in space, not connected to our bodies, and looking down at a business setting. We have a vague notion that we know something about that setting, a situation where people are scurrying around trying to solve some difficult problems. We also have a sense that we might be one of those persons — but we do not know which one. We know that we are looking at a business, an organization which manufactures something to sell or which provides services for people. We know that in this business, people sometimes get along and sometimes they fuss with each other. We have a sense that if we cooperate, we might get better results. We also know that people measure success by how much money they make, and so we have some understanding about economic theory. Basically, we know enough about this situation to make some intelligent guesses about how people will respond to the options chosen for the problems they face.

Watching further, we notice that people do not particularly care about what other people do; they are *mutually disinterested.*[6] If someone says they want to get ahead in an organization, people will support her in that decision. If another person wants to slow down a bit to care for his family, people will generally support that decision as well. People tend to be *rational*, in that they want more of the basic goods of life and are willing to do what is required to get more of the good things, whether products or additional leisure time.[7]

We also notice that when they cooperate, they seem not to be *envious*, preferring to gain primary goods even if others gain more than they do.[8] We are a bit skeptical about this last assertion: we remember reading somewhere that people who are envious prefer that no one get a particular good if they can not have it.[9] Many of us have seen Michael Douglas and Kathleen Turner in the movie *War of the Roses* and know that in divorces people will go to the death swinging on a chandelier rather than share their resources. We have also watched business people take each other down rather than amicably divide the resources after dissolving a partnership or corporation. We know that we have to make a decision that will affect all of these people — and we do not know who we are. How will we make a decision that each of us is willing to embrace whether we turn our to be the CEO or the groundskeeper?

The above scenario plays out the notion of being an ideal observer who operates behind a veil of ignorance. Rawls asserts that if we focus only on our own self interest, we in fact do not attend to the needs of the community as a whole. Going behind the veil of ignorance is difficult. However, if we step outside of our reality and put ourselves in another's shoes, we can make decisions which move toward a systemic solution rather than achieving happiness for only those in the privileged or fortunate groups.

▸ *Determine the stakeholders*

The next step is to identify the stakeholders — the people who will be affected by the decision. Building on the notion of being behind the veil of ignorance, Rawls invites us to consider which stakeholder is the least advantaged in the situation. In our community we obtain power from three sources: access to autonomy, knowledge, and economic resources.As we determine what social and economic inequalities are present, we are called to rank the stakeholders from the most advantaged to the least advantaged in terms of inequality in access to resources which variations results in inequality of power.

Persons who are autonomous feel free to speak up and have their voices heard. They believe that they are independent actors who in some measure control their destiny.To the degree people are marginalized or silenced, either because they do not believe that they have a right to speak or because they are not invited to the table, they will lack autonomy. in the process we need to remember that access to resources includes both knowledge and money.

People who know what resources are available, what systems are in place to access the help, and how to negotiate the various systems of our community have a great deal of power. People who have knowledge are better able to obtain the goods which are important to them. Knowing what opportunities are available helps people get ahead. Public libraries provide those with limited economic resources with crucial access to knowledge. Economic resources also open doors. Those access to economic resources have

Stakeholders — from most to least power

- Physicians: with whom the PPO has employment contracts to provide services;
- The ethics committee which has to make the decision;
- PPO: with whom the ethics committee has a contract to act in the best interest of the PPO;
- Citizens of the state: with whom the PPO has a social contract to follow the law;
- Patients: with whom the PPO has contracts to provide health care who may not know the law and who need to be treated for their illness.

both flexibility and the freedom to make a variety of choices in their lives than those without.

People who do not have autonomy and resources lack power. A touchstone for a just act is how well it cares for those without power. A key concern for ethics is assuring that we do not abuse our economic or personal power as we carry out our work. Images of firemen hosing innocent children rather than allowing schools to be integrated in accordance with the law seared the minds of many and added fuel the Civil Rights Movement. While we know that the work of police officers is dangerous, we cringe when we hear of an officer who, rather than using a search warrant, uses brute force to intimidate a person into a search of his premises.

▶ *Attend to the context*

Rawls requests that we evaluate the stakeholders in light of each person's access to autonomy, knowledge, economic resources and their consequent power. We are asked to determine who is the least advantaged in a situation and then work our analysis from there. We have to be careful because the least advantaged person may not be immediately obvious. One director of human resources related a conundrum where a woman came to him and wanted to report an incident of sexual harassment. The woman asked that the conversation be confidential; the HR person knew that he had an obligation to the company to report sexual harassment, and discipline the person who was responsible. Initially the woman appeared to be the least advantaged. However, by requesting that the HR executive violate the company rules and put the company at risk in exchange for the information, she actually was wielding considerable power. The director was the least advantaged: he had to decide whether to help the victim who did not want to operate within the protocols of the company or put the company at risk. Thus, as we consider the context in which the decision has to be made, we must attend to the resources available to all persons and the nuances of power which attend the situation.

However, we also must be careful not to make the middle manager the one who is usually the least advantaged. Everyone is pressured by various stakeholders to meet their needs and desires. Often, those in the middle of

> Issue
>
> Given that the state requires that health care providers report all persons who test positive for HIV to a central registry, should we tell people before we do the blood work that a positive test result will be reported to the health department?

organizations believe that if they do not accede to the pressure of the people at the top they will lose their jobs; and, in fact, our record of how we treat whistle-blowers in our community would seem to indicate that the fear has some validity. However, those in the middle of organizations have power of position and conviction which can help them shape the system and the processes to assure that justice is done. When, attending to justice requires that we hold those in positions of power responsible for their actions and call them to accountability, wisdom and the counsel of others help us navigate the difficult situation. We must remember, however, that Rawls does not ask that we just protect ourselves, but that we also look out for those who are truly without personal power.

Step 2: Be Intelligent

▶ *Pinpoint the Issue*

What is the central problem which must be resolved? As we look at the problem, Rawls wants us to consider the systemic issues as well as the individual issues. We are called to attend to processes which create or perpetuate injustice. Rawls asserts that if we reach procedural fairness, then we will have substantive fairness.

▶ *Explore values-in-conflict*

Etched deep into the American consciousness is the notion that as individuals do well, the community will prosper. However, as Bellah reminds us, as he gives a long description of the game of Monopoly, an unrestrained market economy leads to those with power being able to leverage that power into more resources and more power. As Bellah notes "[a] game that begins with equality of resources among all players ends with only one winner and the rest dispossessed."[10] Thus, given the rules of the free market game, those who are rich get richer and those who are not suffer.

The difficulty is that those of us raised in our liberal market economy

> **Values-in-Conflict**
>
> The two values-in-conflict are autonomy and predictability or safety. Patients have been told that their relationship with the doctor is confidential; thus, we want to assure that we maintain the privacy of our patients. The patient-physician privilege is important to the medical profession to assure that the physician gets full information prior t beginning treatment. On the other hand, we want to assure that a highly infectious disease does not spread further. Our commitment to the community requires that we do all we can to minimize the spread of disease.

are used to considering our economic gains and losses as individual rather than seeing them as part of the fabric of the whole. However, in addition to a plethora of legislative enactments, we depend upon an independent judicial system to uphold the integrity of contracts and to arbitrate among competing claims when someone has been physically or economically damaged. Identifying the spoken and unspoken agreements that are maintained by the various institutions is not always easy. We need to also acknowledge the way that the community as a whole exercises its shared power through government action which establishes and protects our prerogatives.

For example, as the United States established its claim to the western part of the nation, those who moved West relied upon an institution called homesteading in which the government promised that the settlers would get the title to the land by living on it and farming it for five years without attending to the claim of the land by Native Americans who were already living on or using the land's resources to survive. We have systems of subsidies (reduced fees for grazing, logging, and drilling for oil and gas on public lands), we have protections for property (copyright and patent laws), we have protections for people (minimum wage laws, unemployment insurance, and safety requirements).

All of these policies arise as we correct for abuses in application of the Rights/Responsibility Lens, to prevent individuals with power not considering the claims of the community and its institutions in the distribution of resources and economic benefit. In the Relationship Lens, questions arise such as when should we subordinate our own desires and goals in order to assure that the community as a whole may flourish? When can we legitimately make a claim against community resources and when should we depend on what we have provided for ourselves? What processes should be in place to make sure that justice is in fact accomplished? How can we assure that autonomy and access to resources are appropriately balanced among groups and individuals in our community? Rawls theory thus becomes a valuable resource for determining public policies as we navigate the shoals of determining how best to share resources and allocate responsibility. The challenge is to appropriately balance between equal opportunity and equal outcome.

▸ *Identify options for action*

Again, the ethical actor determines an array of options. Many times our intuition provides us with a good first cut of available choices. As we seek guidance from others and see how different people have handled similar situations, our option set becomes richer. As you choose, look for options which address the processes and systems in place and that highlight the tension between supporting a healthy community, its institutions, and the individuals who are part of that community. Rawls requires that we look at the system as a whole, both its spoken and unspoken processes which are established to enforce the community norms (*e.g.*, requiring that an endangered species not be disturbed, even though alternative solution exists; requiring identification for voting even though some may not have resources to pay for an identification card). In framing options, observe what macro- and micro-systems are in place and how they need to be changed or maintained. Remember that the lack of specific processes, as well as informal (as opposed to written) processes to enforce community norms, is a system.

> Options for Action
>
> Option 1 — Full disclosure: Require that the patient know about the reporting requirement before doing the blood work.
>
> Option 2 — No disclosure: Does not require that the patient know about the reporting requirements before doing the blood work.

Step 3: Be Responsible

▶ ***Hone critical thinking skills***

Identify the least advantaged and then determine how the interests of the least advantaged can be balanced against those of the advantaged. Rawls does not focus on rigidly determining the principles which we are supposed to follow or calculating happiness as a guide for what we should do. Rather, Rawls suggests that in complex situations we need to balance among the competing claims of the stakeholders. He advocates using a process which he calls "reflective equilibrium."[11] After we have considered the situation from behind the veil of ignorance, we identify principles which will lead to justice. As we test those principles against the concrete situation in which we find ourselves, just results can emerge. When we deliberate about what to do, we consider what tweaking is needed, either by pruning the rules or stretching the protocols, or by changing the

> Reflective Equilibrium
>
> The interests of the community have to be balanced against the interests of the person who is potentially infected with AIDS virus. We need to protect the least advantaged, the patient, without unduly burdening the most advantaged, in this case the physician, by requiring lots of paperwork or making the physician ultimately responsible for the situation.

stipulations about the original positions. Rawls advocates a back and forth method of testing, in which "eventually we shall find a description of the initial situation that both expresses reasonable conditions and yields principles which match our considered judgments duly pruned and adjusted."[12]

As we practice reflective equilibrium, we become skilled at both attending to situations where the least advantaged have not been considered and noticing nuances in the context which before were not seen. This skill requires wisdom and discretion. Leaders in our community are expected to exercise discretion as they carry out their responsibilities. Discretion carries with it the expectation that we will be prudent in our decisions and carefully consider the implications of action. This critical thinking skill enables us to make better decisions.

▸ *Apply ethical content*

Rawls' process asks four questions which we can use to evaluate our options.

▹ *First Question: What are the basic liberties to which every member of the community is entitled?*

Rawls writes from the tradition of democracy and so is interested in assuring that his system of ethics upholds the basic principles of a free, self-determining society. The first task is to define what basic liberties all persons should have because they are part of our community. Rawls asserts:

> Each person is to have an equal right to the most extensive total system of equal basic liberties compatible with a similar system of liberty for all.[13]

This statement is much more narrow than it first appears. The notion is that everyone has exactly the same access to rights as everyone. When we think of a list of rights, we tend to think of what are called positive rights — rights to food, shelter, education. But no one has the same amount of any of these things. We do not even have access to the same amount of air: those who live high in the mountains do not have as much oxygen as those at sea level. Those who live in industrial settings have lots of pollution in their air.

Basic Liberties

- A primary liberty is the right to notice, to have information about one's life from which one can make deliberate choices.
- Health care is not a basic liberty. Different amounts of health care are given to people based on ability to pay, extent of illness, and other factors. As a community we choose not to give each person exactly the same amount of health care, so this benefit is distributed unequally.

The rights that all of us can claim are procedural rights. Thus, we have a right to notice and participate in the decisions that affect us. When Rawls talks about a "total system of equal basic liberties," he invites us to assure that the process by which decisions are made includes everyone. As we design processes for determining what action will be taken, actions which affect the well-being of our stakeholders, we must assure that people have a right to a voice and to a vote. We need to remember that the right to participate is not a right to a veto. Rather, it is a right to notice, to comment, and to have a meaningful voice.

This right to notice and having a voice is the bedrock upon which democracy is formed. As we all know, pure democracy where everyone has a right to participate is burdensome — whether in a political or organizational setting. To alleviate some of the time-consuming requirements of pure democracy, we often opt for representative democracy — making sure that a representative of various stakeholders is present at the table when decisions are being made. Those of us who are asked to represent the interests of a group ought to remember that we speak for others and not just ourselves. Thus, our personal biases and concerns cannot override the interests of the group for which we speak. One mistake that is often made is not including the interests of every constituent in the decision making process. We assume that those of us with resources and power know the issues and concerns of those without resources. We assume that those of us with power can voice the fears and desires of those without power.

For an option to be ethical, it must include a process of comment for all individuals and/or groups who will be affected by the decision. If the option does not include a meaningful process for assuring that all have a voice in the decision,the process for decision-making needs to be changed to assure full participation. Adding a process for notice and voice may make a decision which first appears unethical, in fact, ethical, if all are willing to embrace the same option that the decision maker presented.

- *Second Question: Does this option meet the "just savings principle?"*[14]

We are able to meet all of our needs in the immediate time, but meeting those needs and desires may result in an irreversible depletion of our resources. When we are viewing the problem from the position of the ideal observer, we do not know to what generation we belong. We may be our own children or grandchildren.

The Western states are in the middle of a vigorous conversation about water. As communities in Colorado, New Mexico, Arizona, and California grow, a fierce battle rages for who is going to get what water for what uses. The mantra of growth fuels conversations about drilling more wells or finding ways to bring water across mountains. However, we are finding that the water supply may not stretch to meet all of our desired needs. The Ogalalla aquifer is not being replenished as quickly as water is being taken out. The Colorado and Rio Grande rivers are at all time lows, urban,environmental, recreational, and agricultural uses all need to be balanced to sustain our way of life. Given the precariousness of our water supply, is it appropriate for local governments to issue building permits when a developer can identify a five- to ten- year source of water, or should a longer trajectory be taken? Should we protect the jobs of builders and satisfy our need for large, individual homes when the land may not be able to support that kind of development? Should we buy water from farmers and leave the land fallow rather than assure our own food supply?

> Just Savings Principle
>
> Both options meet the requirement of the just savings principle in that none of our children's resources are required for either option.

These questions are incredibly complex as people in disparate communities with differing interests advocate for alternate solutions. As individuals in community, our reflective process and subsequent action can benefit from the constraint of the just savings principle advocated by Rawls. This principle claims that if an option does not adequately provide for our children and grandchildren, is not sustainable, that option is unethical. We must assure the good of future generations as we attend to our own needs and preferences.

- ***Third Question:*** ***Does this option arrange the social and economic inequalities so that they are attached to offices and positions which are open to all under conditions of fair equality of opportunity?***[15]

This question is also a process question: is everyone informed about the opportunities and so are able to make choices about whether to participate? With this criteria, Rawls wants to make sure that we move to equality of opportunity rather than focusing on equality of result. Some are confused by Rawls' use of the term "offices." He does not limit the word to political offices, but is talking about all of the roles that we have — from employment opportunities, to seats on Fortune 500 boards, to slots in prestigious universities, to parenthood. The term is broad, reaching to all of the possible opportunities we have.

The Civil Rights Act of 1964 (Title VII) is a poster-child for this principle in action. The law was passed as Congress was made painfully aware of the systemic barriers which kept African-Americans out of the mainstream of political and economic life.[16] An African-American colleague recounts that, before Title VII was passed but after the Supreme Court declared segregation unconstitutional in *Brown vs. Topeka Board of Education,* Blacks were routinely placed in trade classes and not in college-prep courses nor were they counseled about preparing for college. Thus, he didn't hear about the Scholastic Aptitude Test (SAT) which was required for admission to universities. He saw a sign in the hall and decided on a lark to take the test to get out of a half-day of school. He received a score of 1600 — a perfect score. He then received offers for scholarships and ultimately earned a Ph.D. in psychology. But for that sign, he would not have known of the opportunity and requirements for a college education.

Equality of Opportunity

Option one — Full disclosure: telling the patient does give the patient equality of opportunity. By knowing what the options are and the consequences of choices, the patient can make his own determination about the risk that he wants to take.

Option two — No disclosure: not telling the patient does not give the patient equality of opportunity. By not knowing the risk of being reported (which for many people is a small risk), the person does not have the choice of determining how he would prefer to proceed.

As companies and schools determine whether they have met the requirements of the law, they have to ask whether they have made the information available to all who might want to apply. Are the criteria for hiring applied the same to all persons? Once people get jobs, do they have the same opportunities for advancement? The emphasis is not on mindlessly filling quotas but rather assuring that those who wish to advance have the opportunity to do so.

The systemic barriers can be subtle. A young woman who was a trade representative to an agricultural association went to the national meeting. She had taken golf lessons so that she could fully participate with the men, who were the vast majority of those at the conference. When she went to sign up for her tee time, she was told that women had never played golf with the men at this meeting and would not be starting now. She was more than welcome to play with the women, but the "wives" tournament was scheduled for the same time as the business meeting at which she was presenting. As a young executive, she was not prepared to face this level of subtle systemic discrimination. At one level golf is only a game. However, all who are familiar with business in America know that much gets accomplished on the links, if nothing more than cementing important relationships which facilitate business transactions. If women are systematically excluded from the social events, they will not be able to do their jobs as well.

Rawls does not expect a quota system nor does he require cranking numbers to assure equality. While looking at the spread of people in particular jobs or income brackets might be instructive as to how well the goal of equal access to opportunity is met, we are asked also to carefully look at the stated and structural barriers to equality.

- *<u>Fourth Question:</u> Does this option arrange the social and economic inequalities so that they are to the greatest benefit of the least advantaged?*

Even when we attend to the systems and make them as fair as possible, inequalities still exist. In these situations we are asked to reconsider two previous questions. The questions to be addressed are: who are the least advantaged? What kinds of policies must we put in place to assure that the inevitable inequalities of life do not unduly disadvantage the least advantaged? As we recollect life behind the veil of ignorance, we have to ask whether we would be willing to be that person and take our chances at getting the good things in life. At this point we should revisit the difference between negative rights and positive rights. The Rights and Responsibilities Lens emphasized negative rights: the community would provide certain goods as long as no transfer of wealth was required. Any other goods that we purchased would be with our own nickel.

Rawls invites us to consider the role of positive rights, where assets are to be transferred from the most advantaged to the least advantaged in order to give them a fair opportunity in this life. The system which considers only negative rights assumes that all of us begin with about the same resources, sort of like the proverbial Monopoly game where we all start with a die and $200 in the bank. The notion is that those who were strongest, smartest, and the most ambitious will then rise to the top,

Social Inequalities

Option 1 — Full disclosure: having a system which gives the patient th information, does tip the balance to the least advantaged, the patient. The patient is between a rock and a hard place — getting treatment and possibly being placed on a "list." By giving full information, the patient can make a choice that makes sense to the patient.

Option 2 — No disclosure: a system which does not require giving the patient the information, does not tip the balance to the least advantaged; rather, the physician keeps the power balance by making the choice for the patient or waiting to see if the patient thinks to ask the question.

like cream. Those who rise to the top will do so on merit, not by an accident of birth or privilege. The Darwinian notion of survival of the fittest meshes well with this ethical philosophy.

The difficulty is that we all know in our heart of hearts that we may not the brightest and the best — everyone has gifts and talents as well as flaws and weaknesses. First, we know that we are born into a specific family. The very way our body gets put together depends on whether our mother took good care of her body while she was carrying us and on our family genetics. We have no control over whether we are born into a family where the mother was healthy, took all of her prenatal vitamins, and had access to good health care; or whether we are born into a family where the mother was an alcoholic; or whether we lived in a rural area with limited health care. In this situation, because the baby has no ability to care for itself, it is the least advantaged. If any of us were behind the veil of ignorance, we would want the best shot at health. Thus, many people support transferring community wealth to provide prenatal health care for pregnant women and well-baby care for newborns.

As adults we know that our ability to care for ourselves depends on both receiving good care when we are children and a solid education. Thus, we might advocate transferring wealth for pre-school and quality K-12 education for all people. Not only does each of us need the best education possible, but the community must assure that well-trained, productive people who will carry on when members of the current workforce are no longer able to work. In each stage of life, some do not have access to either the physical, intellectual or monetary resources to have a shot at getting the good things of this life.

Thus, we see that the process of attending to the least advantaged both invites us to consider where we need to pool our resources as well as notice where life is most fragile. Rawls reminds us that the decisions always have to be made in dialogue with those who are affected by the decision. We must consider the tradeoffs necessary to assure that each of us has enough incentive to work and to care for ourselves at the same time that all persons have an opportunity to become self-sufficient adults.

▸ *Overlay the moral content*

We must next determine which of the remaining options contributes best to an ecology of care, a value which notes that we are all deeply interconnected. As we look at an ecology of care, we note that this is perhaps the place where

Americans are the weakest. We have been so careful to assure autonomy that we fail to notice that our very institutions become frayed if we do not pay attention to them.

Frederick (see Chapter 3) took the lessons of biology and the emerging study of environmental ecology and applied them to business organizations. He noted that, while the notion of survival of the fittest is true on the margins of biological systems, within the ecosystems themselves, rich interdependencies allow many different species to survive. Whether one looks at the remora, tiny fishes which clean the backs of dolphins, or plants and insects which are mutually interdependent, we see that no species is radically independent and able to survive by itself. We also notice that those ecosystems which lose their diversity are in fact weaker than those teeming with a variety of life. If one species gains preeminence over the others, the entire system weakens.

A parallel is seen in business life. Our antitrust laws are based on the economic notion that our economy does better when we have a variety of products and choices. However, each person really hopes to be the next Bill Gates and corner a particular market. The lessons of nature play out in the computer world as we track the viruses which attack the Microsoft products while ignoring Apple products. If all of us have the same operating system, we are as vulnerable as a forest which only has one kind of tree. Thus, we need to nurture diversity and cooperation within our communities. As we apply the moral lens, we decide which option (and if necessary with appropriate procedural modifications) best accomplishes the following ecologizing virtues:

- *__Linkage:__ those connections which give life, provide shelter, and create safety nets.*

"Linkage extends the realization of genetic potentialities...permits an efflorescence of life forms...nurtures collectivities of organic beings...and regularizes and patterns the interactions that life units have with and within their oftentimes threatening environments."[17] Many times the institutions of our society provide

Ecology of Care

Fully disclosing the information to the patient best supports an ecology of care. If the physician takes the time to explain the options, educating and supporting the patient during the difficult decision, an ecology of care can be maintained. The physician can empathize, considering times where she would want a safety net and be connected to the community. If the patient is at risk, connecting the person with support groups or others who can help with not just the physical needs but also the emotional and financial needs will help assure that the whole person is cared for. At the same time, the physician should attend to the needs of the community and assure that, as far as possible, the community is safe.

the connections which support life. Institutions provide the such as families, churches, social organizations, professional groups, and book clubs provide places where relationships are nourished. If we are lucky, the institutions in which we work provide us with a support structure where we grow and mature, learning our craft and becoming more effective in our work. Our task then is to assure that we support and strengthen those institutions which nourish us.

- *Diversity: created by options which support variability and a diverse life web, a diverse context.*[18]

Many of us like to clone ourselves at work. We want to have people around us who think like we do, have the same values, and make us comfortable. What we know, however, is that if only one voice is heard, other vantages are lost and other options are foreclosed. As difficult as listening to other people may be, both the organization itself as well as the individuals within it do better when many different cultures and ideas are represented.

We also want to the skill we have well. What diversity teaches, however, is that multiple approaches to the same problem may result in a better solution. The tension is between "sticking to our knitting," as management guru Tom Peters advised, and looking at a variety of ways to accomplish our goals.[19] Many universities are facing this situation as more students want their education delivered in multiple ways. On-line education, accelerated classes, and community-based learning are starting to make the model of a professor in front of a room obsolete. Each method of delivering education has strengths and concerns. None is by definition more legitimate than another.

- *Homeostatic succession: a process of change that occurs within continuity.*

How well does the option allow for the ongoing evolution of the community?[20] As we attend to diversity, we also have to attend to change. The most healthy organizations are those which understand the life cycle of a business and a product. As one product is reaching maturity, another is being nurtured and brought on line. As one set of senior executives is reaching its peak, another set is being mentored so leadership continues. Change that is too rapid disorients people and often has disastrous results. No change leads to stagnation with concomitantly disastrous results. An excellent leader has a vision of change and gradually changes the culture, putting structures in place to achieve that change. Like a rafter leaning into the excitement of riding rapids, a skillful leader facilitates change while maintaining enough constancy to comfort folks.

- *Community: created by options which are able to achieve the necessary degree of integration and cooperation to make life tolerable.*[21]

We are social creatures. Whether we gather around water coolers or giggle in cubicles, each of us needs to be wanted and included. One strategy used by slave owners to maintain control on the plantations was to forbid their slaves to communicate, fearing that through communication they would strategize for freedom. Enslaved African-Americans learned to build community through their songs and quilt patterns which transferred essential information about how to reach the North as well as strategies for emancipation. The seemingly innocuous folk song encouraging people to "follow the drinking gourd" was shorthand for following the North star to freedom.

The worst punishment in our jails is isolation. The worst working conditions in our companies and factories are those which expect us to be automatons rather than full human beings who are part of a community. As cheesy as company functions may seem to those who are introverts, the T-shirts, parties, and motivational seminars and workshops promoting excellence, provide opportunities for people to play as well as work together. We get a sense of belonging to a community which then enriches our work life.

Step 4: Be Responsible

- ***Rank the options from least preferred to most preferred.***

Having determined what liberties are essential (right to voice, right to notice, and right to participate) we rank the options from least preferred to the most preferred based on which option best assures that (1) the basic liberties are met, (2) our children will have an inheritance, (3) the positions are available to all, (4) the least advantaged receive the benefit, and (5) the ecologizing values and virtues are included. As the options are ranked, summarize why the ranking was made and demonstrate the primacy

> **Rank the Options**
>
> Telling the patient of the legal requirements is the preferred option. This one meets every requirement of the community, from caring for the patient and balancing that care with the needs of the community. Not telling the patient, according to this lens would not be ethical. The patient does not have an opportunity to make choices, and, as the least advantaged, is denied his basic liberties.

given to justice and community: (a) because we can only thrive if we have systems in place which will assure a fair process, and (b) we need strong communities and institutions in order for individuals to thrive.

► *Correct for bias*

The risk that we run as we use this lens is that we will become authoritarian and paternalistic. While we need to attend to the institutions, we must avoid embracing the notion that "father knows best." Assuring full participation assists in this process. This balance is difficult because we all want someone to tell us what to do — as long as they also have the responsibility for the outcome. One management trainer describes this shift of accountability as the monkey on our back. When people become paternalistic and take responsibility for directing the actions of others, they have taken on the "monkey." A key responsibility of leadership is placing responsibility and accountability on appropriate shoulders.

I once gave an assignment to a class to practice shared decision making — to give responsibility for a decision to those who were actually affected by the decision. One student, a retired Army sergeant, was absolutely convinced that the process would not work. He was the manager of a company that manufactured seat belt buckles. The company was getting new equipment and had to decide how to rearrange the plant. To humor the instructor, he created a committee and had them meet in his office. Two of the senior women who were on the assembly line commuted together. They kept working at solving the problems and then talked to everyone else in the plant. Thus, when the committee was finished with its work (which did take longer than it would have had he made the decision), the decision was better than the one he fashioned, and he already had buy-in from all of the employees. He was (reluctantly) converted.

Correct for Bias

The physician will have to be careful not to coerce the patient into a treatment that is not desired. While the physician wants to assure that patients are treated, we all have the opportunity to reject treatment — and take the consequences. The physician needs to listen carefully and not turn to guilt or shame to force the patient to do something against the patient's desires. Those in the health care system also have to look for any tinge of homophobia or bias against someone who happens to carry the AIDS virus.

Another bias is entrainment, where we all get caught up in the excitement and do not ask hard questions for fear of squelching enthusiasm. While we all like team players, many a disaster has happened because people didn't believe that they were able to speak up in the face of impending crisis. Another opportunity for entrainment occurs when it is not politically correct to question the party line. As we track the demise of companies at the end of the 20th century, many in the organization believed that they would either be silenced or ostracized if they did not parrot the party line. Thus, no one really pushed the question of whether the accounting practices of Enron were appropriate. No one questioned whether cutting health care benefits was right. No one challenged million dollar bonuses for those at the top while those at the bottom were not earning enough to pay rent, let alone care for their families. Avoiding group-think at the same time that one is a good team player requires wisdom and attention.

▸ *Attend to the common good*

The Relationship Lens invites us to look at individuals — but not in the same way as the Rights and Responsibility Lens. With this lens we are asked to focus on those without power, those without a voice. As those of us with power learn to share our power, to assure that all have an opportunity to participate in our community, we will find ourselves strengthened.

▸ *Act with courage*

Because ethics is also about persuasion, we must be able to articulate clearly what choice we have made and why. After giving a bit of background information to set the stage for the problem, we can frame the statement so that we answer the core questions of this particular lens. We should formulate the announcement so that we show that we value the system as a whole, as well as the individuals within the system, attending both to assuring a fair process and the needs of the least advantaged. A reader should be able to discern how we used the process of reflective equilibrium to reach the result.

Step 5: Return to Awareness

After describing our resolution of the problem, we consider whether our ethical analysis made sense. Did we like the result? What were the problems with the process? What are the sticking points? How was the process enhanced or modified by considering emotion or caring?

> **Announcement**
>
> The ethics committee has decided to assure that all patients get full informed consent, even if they are carrying communicable diseases such as the AIDs virus. Patients will be told of the reporting requirement so that no one is surprised by the results. To assure that the patients are treated with dignity, physicians will be asked to assure that the process of informed consent happens in a setting where the concerns of patients can be addressed.

► *Continuous improvement*

The process of continuous improvement involves evaluating the result of our action. The Relationship Lens requires that we carefully balance between the prerogatives of individuals and the needs of the community. One trial attorney described the process adjustments over time for making sure that settlements for personal injury cases were appropriate. If the settlements were tracked, the pattern would look like a sine curve. When the insurance companies are too miserly with their offers, attorneys take the cases to trial. If they demand too much, insurers take the cases to trial. Going to trial is always a risk because neither party can predict what a jury will do. However, cases which are litigated reset the calibration as both the results of the case and the rationale given by juries reflect the values of the community. Those who are in the business also constantly calibrate their antennae, noticing where on the curve the current settlement offers are. In this way, the interests of those who are injured are balanced against the need to place appropriate blame and the need to shoulder responsibility.

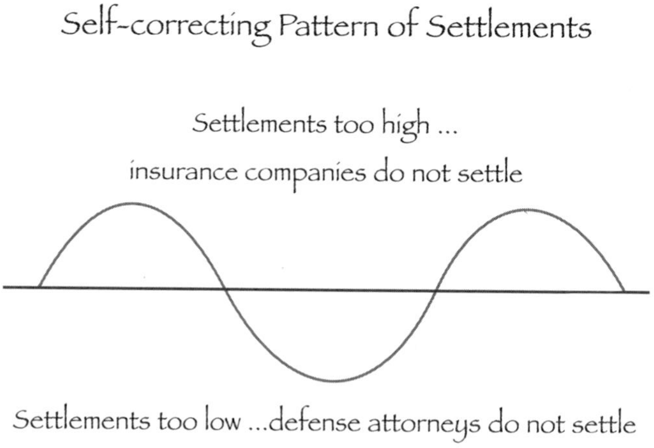

► *The Crucible of Spirit*

As we are called to balance, we ought to make sure that we do not over-identify with a group to the exclusion of an individual. As we realize that none of us, neither individuals nor communities, has a corner on "The Truth," we can make sure that we attend to the good of the whole without trampling on the needs of the few. A mark of spiritual maturity is moving from following a process for the sake of process while demanding that our own needs are met to joyously serving others while being committed to justice. If we truly serve others, we will put aside our own ambitions and needs for power to make sure that the least advantaged have a possibility of getting the good things of life. In the process, we will find joy in our work and meaning for our lives.

Conclusion

The Relationship Lens invites us to consider how to live life in relationship with others, how to be a person-in-community. The focus for this lens is always fundamental fairness — what is required to thoughtfully balance the needs and prerogatives of society against the needs and prerogatives of the individual? As we ask that question, we can move beyond technical fairness to genuine fairness, learning when we ought to subordinate our own individual rights to those of the group or when the group should celebrate personal idiosyncracies. One key to this conundrum is noticing what annoys us. Often, if we are not threatened by the individual behavior of a person or celebrate the demands of the group, we have resolved the underlying issues and concerns and can fit into the web of life. However, when we find someone very annoying rather than just different, we are usually encountering questions or concerns we have about ourselves and how we belong to this group. When we accept ourselves — both gifts and flaws — we fit easily into different groups and find our own niche in the ongoing web of life.

Continuing the Conversation

1. Using either the third problem in the GG Ethics Game or another fact pattern, analyze the situation using the Relationship Lens. Was the problem easy to do, indicating that this might by your preferred method of working ethical problems? Was the process difficult, indicating that this may not be your ethical home?

2. Read an editorial in your local paper or a national paper and find examples of a justice emphasis. In what ways did the author appeal to the fairness of the process assuring notice and voice for those affected? In what way did the author explore whether the needs of the least advantaged were considered? How did the author balance the needs of the organization and institutions against the needs and desires of individuals?

3. In light of issues raised by the Relationship Lens reflect on ways that you attend to imbalance which comes from an inappropriate use of the Relationship Lens, whether concerning abuse of power or hubris in your personal and professional life. How do you know when you are improperly using your personal power? How do you know when your life is not in balance? What strategies do you have to bring your life back into balance?

The Reputation Lens

Conceptual Map

Concepts	World of Reason	World of Emotion	World of Spirit
Key Question	What is a good character?	What is a healthy, functioning conscience?	Who is my neighbor?
Theory	Virtue ethics	Morality of the heart; emotional IQ	Sacred essence
Representative Authors	Alasdair MacIntyre	Charles Shelton Daniel Goleman	Parker Palmer
Tools and Practices	Personal reflection; community conversation	Empathy; gratitude; self-awareness; and self-management	Fellowship; intimacy; attention
Key Phrase	I am virtuous	I am moral	I am special... just like everyone else
Goal	Cultivation of virtues; placement in a tradition; coherent narrative	Ability to empathize; ability to integrate emotion and intellect	Awareness of sacred identity
Gifts	Cultivation of personal virtues while being an integral part of community	Compassion; conscience; emotional maturity	Gentleness; empathy; long view of life
Challenges	Lack of awareness	Lack of accurate self- assessment	Perception of being special
Risk	Righteousness	Failure to manage emotions	Overwhelm; spiritually dry
Hubris	Entitlement	Unrealistic self-esteem	I can do it alone
Vice	Hardness of heart; self-righteousness	Unreflective action	No commitments
Crisis	Being misunderstood	Loss of authenticity	Losing the center of meaning

I have a dream that someday little black boys and little black girls will not be judged by the color of their skin but by the content of their character.

Martin Luther King, Jr.[1]

Chapter 10

Reputation Lens

The fourth and final ethical lens focuses on the virtues that a society believes should be cultivated by a good person; thus, the Reputation Lens requires that we explore the world of character, virtue ethics. An integral branch of the teleological tradition, with this lens our focus spirals back to the teachings of Aristotle and St. Thomas Aquinas who emphasize our charge to become a person of good character as we live out our role in the community. Those who write about virtue ethics remind us that becoming a person of good character embraces our whole life and can become a quest which occupies us until our death. This tradition distinguishes itself by focusing first on moral actors and their lives. The Reputation Lens does not dictate specific motives or duties, as seen with Kant who invites individuals to focus on their duties and prerogatives

Core Questions

- What is a good character?
- What is a healthy, functioning conscience?
- Who is my neighbor?

using the Rights/Responsibility Lens. Neither does the Reputation Lens mirror the work of Mill and ask individuals to actively pursue their goals for happiness using the Results Lens. Finally, although virtue ethics has a community focus, the goal is not to determine how to act in community as seen in Rawls' invitation to fashion a just community using the Relationship Lens. Rather, the Reputation Lens invites us to reflect on how we want to be viewed by others in the community and what qualities are essential to be a good citizen.

The core questions associated with the Reputation Lens direct our attention to what kind of person we want to be, what we want our character to be, and how we want others to see us — in essence, our reputation. This lens compels the ethical actor to determine for herself what human qualities are important.[2] Clearly, as we determine what virtues we will embrace, obligations follow and specific goals will be chosen. The question is what process comes first and receives emphasis: examining the character from which the action flows or choosing actions which then determine character.

Virtue ethics, or character ethics as it is often called, focuses on the key qualities which are required for us to fulfill our obligations in the community. Given that we are born into a community and take on certain responsibilities, we naturally strive to develop the virtues which are required by our various roles. The tension in defining ourselves by our roles is to assure that we can meet the requirements of excellence without becoming defined by our roles rather than by who we are as people.

This balance is delicate; who we are is shaped profoundly by the roles we assume. None of us has an unrestrained choice in the matter. Some are limited because of perceived or real constraints created by gender or nationality. Our access to resources and opportunities makes a difference. Finally, we are influenced by our personal dreams, preferences, and choices. At the height of a career, a person who is trained in the law but teaches is different than that person would have been had he chosen a life in the courtroom; the skills and the character requirements for an effective teacher are different than of a good litigator. Thus, as we choose roles and modify our actions based on our preferences and the response of others, we attend to our character and reputation. The Reputation Lens invites us to consider our own sense of who we are and how we are viewed by others, both as individuals and in our roles, and not judge ourselves only by our accomplishments.

Working from the central concept of ethics as attending to the development of our character, the Reputation Lens invites us to determine for ourselves what kind of a person we want to be and how we want to be seen by others. The conversation centers on how we define ourselves in light of the expectations that our community has for a "good" person. Essential to this process is that we see ourselves as moral and strive to meet the criteria of ethical behavior which we have for ourselves as well as that which is expected by the community. This tradition reflects the essential optimism of the teleological tradition, which says that, as people are placed in community they will respond to love and acceptance by becoming good people. We also are required to to hone our reflective skills to become emotionally mature and flexible. A person who is comfortable with her place in the community, manages herself at the same time that she understands and empathizes with others.

Characteristics of the Reputation Lens

Definition

An act is ethical if it is consistent with the habitual development of sound character traits including habits of thoughtful reflection, good intentions, and noble human virtues. Using the Reputation Lens, a moral person is one who makes decisions or judgments based on his conscience, an internal sense of "oughtness" about how one should live or what one must do, and based on one's core beliefs. As we develop a good conscience, we embrace the qualities of a good character deeply within our person and not just wear the virtues as a mask which can be shed when we believe that others are not watching. Then, rather than being motivated by what others think of us, we can be motivated by our core commitments — notions or ideas that are held with affection which result in passion or action. These commitments defines us and have the potential to energize and transform us and our community.[3] By focusing on the core commitments of our life, we make choices about

> **Definition**
>
> - An ethical action is a virtuous act which is consistent with a good character.
> - A moral person is one who fosters an awareness of the interplay of mind, emotions, and meaning in deciding what one "ought" to do.
> - Spiritual balance is maintained by knowing our neighbor as we learn that we are special — just like everyone else.

what path we want to follow rather than be swayed by those around us. Asking ourselves what is important and what we would be willing to go out on a limb to pursue is essential. While zealots may make us uncomfortable, if we do not have *any* commitments which inspire us to action, we miss an opportunity to leave our footprint on the sands of time. The spiritual balance is found by asking "who is my neighbor." Having attended to the core question of identity, the Reputation Lens invites us to consider those with whom we share this glorious planet. Many religious teachings emphasize that all human beings are our neighbors, and thus we have some responsibility to those persons. In the process of meeting those in our neighborhood, we discover that we are special — just like everyone else. All people love their children and want the best for them. All people have relationships which are important to them. All people want to make a difference in their world. As we see the sacred essence of each person, we learn to live with gentleness towards ourselves and others as we each walk our personal path.

Questions for Determining Right Action

- *Essential qualities:* what are the qualities that a good human being should have?

- *Core virtues:* what respected human virtues are demonstrated by this right action (*e.g.,* courage, moderation, justice)?

- *Role requirements:* how does this decision demonstrate the virtues of a person who is respected in this role (*e.g.,* competence, loyalty, diligence, fairness)?

- *Professional virtues:* how does this decision demonstrate the qualities of a person in this profession (*e.g.,* commitment to public service, self-regulation, trust, integrity)?

Virtues Which Flow from These Theories

- *Integrity:* A person should develop habits of truthfulness.

- *Justice:* A person should seek to do that which will promote the fair treatment of people in terms of compensation for work done or contribution to the community. A just person also assures that the resources of the group, both opportunities and assets, are distributed fairly.

- *Courage:* A person should embrace the opportunity to demonstrate the highest qualities of the individual or profession even if others choose another path.

- *Civility:* A person should always behave in a way which respects the inherent dignity of people and encourages their development as persons.

Nuances of Theories of Morality

We become a moral person as we develop an internal sense of oughtness that is the result of a life history that incorporates "who we are, who we are becoming, and who we desire to be" in light of the virtues and a healthy conscience.[4] Further, we become moral persons as we develop self-awareness (emotional self-awareness, accurate self-assessment, and self-confidence) as well as self-management (demonstrating emotional self-control and exercise of core virtues, such as transparency, adaptability, and optimism).[5]

As we come full circle in studying all of the primary theories of ethics, one quality is implicit in each of the theories — that we each ought to take personal responsibility for who we are and what we do. If we are ruled only by laws, we check to see who is watching over our shoulders and aim for compliance in the letter of the law rather than celebration of the spirit of the rule. As we mature and become grounded in our core beliefs, we learn to do what is right because it is right, not to avoid getting caught or punished. A morally mature person embraces self-regulation and self-efficacy. Self-regulation, choosing to be self-disciplined and directed by a carefully considered internal sense of values, gives us the ability to be guided and motivated to do those things we know ought to be done. Self-efficacy, knowing that we have the tools to be effective, gives us the confidence that we need to act effectively and make a difference in our world, providing an essential link for the continuity of our community.[6]

The Crucible of Spirit

In one scene of the popular movie *Romancing the Stone,* a novelist who is trying to rescue her sister is stranded with an ex-patriate American who is following his dream. He describes his passion, a sailboat. As he goes on about his life in Columbia where he is working by himself to reach his goal, she says to him, "That sounds lonely, Jack T. Colton." As we follow our individual dreams, we find that we are back where we started — in community. In America in particular, with our mobility and our busyness, it becomes very easy to become lonesome because we have not put the time and energy into being part of a community. Rather, we strive to get it all for ourselves. As we learn to see ourselves as part of the larger whole, realizing that we do not have to do it all, and that there is plenty of work for everyone, we can be gentle with ourselves and savor the joy of working with others. This book began with Cain's question to God, "Am I my brother's keeper?" It turns out that to thrive as a person-in-community, we need to see each other as neighbors and friends: we are indeed our brother's — and our sister's — keepers.

In a business world where we cut our teeth on competitiveness, seeing each other as neighbors and thus responsible for each other may seem farfetched. However, we can have healthy competition at the same time that we recognize that we are profoundly connected, that no one is more special than anyone else, and that we must work together and care for each other. With this realization, we can give up our fear of failure and settle into enjoying the work we have been given to do. We can develop healthy relationships and networks as we each follow our heart's desire. In the process we find our spiritual center which keeps us in balance when the world goes crazy and helps us maintain the long view, the perspective which keeps us from being overwhelmed by all of the changes of life.

Using the Reputation Template

While many contemporary authors write about virtue ethics, Alasdair MacIntyre in *After Virtue* is a paradigmatic philosopher in this tradition. MacIntyre describes the history of this ethical tradition and provides a contemporary process which guides us in the conversation about what is a virtuous person. Evaluating an ethical option using MacIntyre's process requires a conversation between the ethical actor and the community.

After looking at the history of the strands of both deontology and teleology (including consequentialism, a form of utilitarianism), MacIntyre asserts that the way out of ethical relativism is to have people develop a sound character by embracing the core values of humanity. When toward the middle of the 20th century philosophers began to quietly admit that the Enlightenment Project which sought to use the tools of reason and science to find the certain foundations for truth appeared to have failed (a claim with which many perceptive scientists agree), it seemed that no criteria for ethical action could be established. MacIntyre claims that as we embrace our roles and seek to become people of virtue, we find our ethical bearings. This action is not done in isolation; none of us gets to decide on our own the shape of our role in the community nor how we will exercise the virtues. Rather, we shape our understanding of our roles and expectations in community, everyone learning from the other. In conversation and dialogue, we each determine how best we should live.

MacIntyre also states that those who are part of a particular practice are responsible for maintaining the integrity of the work. Because MacIntyre sees institutions as potentially corrupting, those of us in a particular profession must work together to assure that the virtues are embodied and celebrated in our personal and professional lives. The integrity of any profession depends on individuals to maintain and demand excellence rather than succumbing to the subtle pressures of expedience and hubris. Thus, a primary value of the Lens is that it mitigates our basing decisions solely on the bottom line, doing whatever is required to reach the goals which are desired.[7] Rather, as we seek the goals of life, we are invited to consider what a good person in our role would do and seek excellence.

As we make our choices, each of us is asked from time to time to explain why a particular option was chosen and why others were not. To demonstrate how to accomplish this task with integrity, the same problem and overall template will be used as with the other ethical lenses, but the ethical content will come from MacIntyre and others in the virtue ethics tradition. The reason for the repetition of process is the belief that the more we practice, the more our skill increases, with the process of analysis becoming easier. As we look at problems from different angles, we learn to balance between what we believe are the attributes of a good person and the expectations of the community while honoring our own personality. As we "exercise our conscience" and strive to be the best that we can be, our reputation for excellence is enhanced.[8] However, even when we believe that our character is sterling and our reputation is stellar, the process assists us in correcting for personal bias and self-delusion.

Step 1: Be Attentive

▸ ***Identify the ethical actor***

For this analysis the role of the ethical actor is key. As we choose to act, we ask what qualities we expect a person in this role to demonstrate As we return to our ethics committee, the focus shifts slightly. The committee must first identify its role in the problem at hand. This ethical tradition asserts that each of us is defined by our role. The legal profession illustrates this concept well. In a criminal case, three attorneys are involved — the prosector, the defense attorney, and the judge. Each of them bring forward different virtues based on their role. The trial attorneys must zealously present their case to the court. The judge must evenhandedly assure that the rules of the courtroom are followed and the law is fairly applied. The judge (and by extension members of the jury) cannot go on a quest to find evidence; that is the role of the prosecution and defense. Each player in the mini-drama has a role which is clearly defined by the practice of law.

Ethical Actor

The ethics committee of a PPO is charged with setting protocols for all of the physicians who are part of the group. In this role, the ethics committee is the clearing house for ethical dilemmas faced by employees of the PPO and is also responsible for determining the protocols that the members of the PPO must follow.

Every profession has similar role constraints and expectations. Thus, as an ethical actor assumes responsibility for deciding a course of action, the agent must determine what core ethical values should be brought forward in light of the core virtues which should be cultivated by persons in community in that particular role. One of the key questions each of us must eventually confront is what kind of a person we are: what exactly *is* our character and our reputation in the community? Because none of us likes to think ill of ourselves, learning to seek and hear the unvarnished truth can be difficult — but enlightening. The truth may even save a career.

▶ *Determine the stakeholders*

As the conversation evolves between us, the ethical actor, and the stakeholders who are impacted by our decision, we need to consider what our stakeholders expect of a good ethical actor in this situation. Thus, as we list the stakeholders, we must include a description of the competencies that the stakeholders expect the *ethical agent* to bring to the table. In framing this conversation,

Stakeholders

- ▶ The committee which has to make the decision;
- ▶ PPO: with whom the ethics committee has a contract to act in the best interest of the PPO;
- ▶ Physicians: with whom the PPO has employment contracts to provide services;
- ▶ Patients: with whom the PPO has contracts to provide health care;
- ▶ Citizens of the state: with whom the PPO has a social contract to follow the law.

we must remember that the stakeholders do not always expect to be happy, but they do expect the agent to act within the constraints of the role. Thus, if a good teacher is fair and impartial, a student will understand and accept getting a low grade for a paper that is inferior.

► *Attend to the context*

MacIntyre asserts that three conversations inform the context of an ethical decision. The first is the practice in which we engage. That concept will be developed later. The second is what MacIntyre calls the "narrative order of a single human life."[9] One of the gifts of feminist and postmodern scholarship is the notion that each of us has the ability to construct for ourselves a life based on the stories we tell about ourselves. Mary Catherine Bateson opened the door to the conversation in *Composing a Life* by noticing that each of us not only has different seasons of our lives, but that we also define who we are by the way we talk about our lives.[10] To see what is important, listen to the strands of conversation when you tell people about yourself. Are you strong or pig-headed? Are you deliberate or slow? Are you a leader or a team-builder? As we look at an ethical problem, we must attend to our own narrative as an ethical agent as well as the narrative of the people and companies with whom we are working.

Listening to the stories, the narratives, people tell about themselves is fascinating. One person may come from a family of strong-minded women — just ask. This family believes that being fiercely independent, economically independent, and a bit "uppity" are marks of strong, fine women. Thus, she may highlight in her narrative those times when she went against convention, was able to move with ease in a "man's world," and took care of herself. Another person may come from a family which values civic service and see himself as "pulling himself up by the bootstraps." He may spin a story about how he walks in the steps of the men in his family who toughed it out on the prairie, were "pillars of the community" as they served on school boards, and were successful in business. A useful exercise is to reflect on the stories of both one's family as well as those of the community. Seeing which story lines are incorporated into one's script for life can help us sort through our core values and commitments as well the subtle and not so subtle messages about what is expected of us in the roles we embrace.

Organizations also have a narrative, a story about the characteristics and virtues which are important to them and the values which they hold dear. Often the personality of the founder forms the central story of the organization. One example is seen in the book *Pour Your Heart Into It* by Howard Shultz, founder and CEO of Starbucks.[11] The chapters lay out his corporate philosophy. One telling story underscores why the company provides health care for all employees who work ten hours a week or more. Shultz remembers when his father was injured on the job, had no health care, and the family almost did not make it. Shultz vowed that if he got the opportunity, no one who worked for him would ever be in that situation. This story is often part of the narrative told at employee orientation as one joins the "Starbucks family."

MacIntyre states that the third conversation involves identifying and steeping ourselves in the moral tradition which shapes our life. As we examine the four central ethical lenses which inform both our personal and business ethics, we note that each comes from a moral tradition which purports to assist us in knowing what is right action. The lenses focus several thousand years of conversation for us, as people consider the nature of humans, the goals for the community, and how we should best live in community. Each lens has (a) content, certain beliefs which define them, (b) a set of practices or exercises that help us understand the lens, and (c) advocates in the community who support us as we learn how to be better ethical agents.[12]

While the lenses give us a chance to view different ways of looking at problems, if we are not careful, exploring the different traditions becomes an excuse not to grow. To become mature ethical agents, we need to find a community which can support us in our growth as we go deep into the practices of that group. Traditionally, churches, mosques and synagogues provide the structure and support for us to mature as we learn to balance the gifts of the four lenses. Currently others find that support groups and seminars provide the structure needed to explore their strengths and weaknesses. Additionally, our workplaces and relationships provide a proving ground for our lessons and show us where we've grown and where we need to focus next.

Thus, if the quest for justice is one of our core commitments, we may choose to be formed by traditions that are informed by teachings on economic and social justice. If we find a particular religious tradition meaningful, we will steep ourselves in those thoughts and practices as we learn to be a good person. While no one path is the only way to find truth and achieve ethical adulthood, people who seek to grow in moral maturity often find that they need to go deep into one tradition and have their hearts and minds transformed in the crucible of a particular set of beliefs and practices while being sensitive to the perspectives and requirements of other traditions.

Step 2: Be Intelligent

▸ *Pinpoint the Issue*

What is the central problem to be resolved? As we shape the issue into a question, we need to focus on the conflicting role expectations of the players in this situation. As stated above, the Reputation Lens encourages us to see what a good person, a person of virtue, would do in a particular role.

> **Issue**
>
> Given that the state requires that health care providers report all persons who test positive for HIV to a central register, should we require that physicians tell people before they do the blood work that a positive test result will be reported to the health department?

▸ *Explore values-in-conflict*

Virtue ethicists highlights three arenas of difficulty. The first is a conflict in expectations associated with the role itself. Different people may have different expectations for a person in this role, and, so we must clarify what exactly a person in this role *should* do. The second is a conflict between excellence and expedience: we are often called to do that which is expedient, which will get a result quickly or with the greatest return, even if the virtues of the ethical agent or the organization are compromised. The Reputation Lens calls us to focus on excellence. The third problem that may arise may be a conflict between the role expectations and our vision of ourself as a good person, or a good member of the larger community. Virtue theorists remind us that, at the end of the day, who we are as a total person is what matters.

> **Values in Conflict**
>
> The two values in conflict are autonomy and predictability or safety. Patients have been told that their relationship with the doctor is confidential; thus, we want to assure that we maintain the privacy of our patients. The patient-physician privilege is important to the medical profession to assure that the physician gets full information prior to beginning treatment. On the other hand, we want to assure that a highly infectious disease does not spread further. Our commitment to the community requires that we do all we can to minimize the spread of disease.

▸ *Identify options for action*

Again, we must act, even in the face of difficulty and lack of clarity about the outcomes. In framing options with this lens, the focus will be on the role expectations for the ethical agent. One task is determining whether the decision is within the purview of the ethical agent. Then we choose options within the purview of our role. While our framing of the options should not include value language, being attentive to the vantage point with which the ethical lens will examine the problem helps.

Options for Action

Option 1 — Full disclosure: tell the patient about the reporting requirement before doing the blood work.

Option 2 — No disclosure: do not tell the patient about the reporting requirement before doing the blood work.

Step 3: Be Reasonable

▸ *Hone critical thinking skills.*

MacIntyre gives an elegant process for determining the virtues which mark an ethical person. Envisioned as a conversation between individuals and society, he begins by defining a "practice" as

> ...any *coherent and complex form* of socially established cooperative human activity through which *goods internal* to that form of activity are realized in the course of trying to achieve those *standards of excellence* which are appropriate to, and partially definitive of, that form of activity, with the result that *human powers to achieve excellence*, and human conceptions of the ends and goods involved, are systematically extended. *(Emphasis added)* [13]

The first seminal concept is that a practice is a coherent and complex activity. To illustrate, MacIntyre distinguishes between tic-tac-toe which is easy to learn and has little strategy, and chess which is complex with many rules. An individual event — making a sale — is not a practice. However, the discipline of learning how to be a sales person and embracing the qualities of sales person is a practice. So, we need to distinguish between doing something sporadically and plunging into the practice to learn the rules and master the skills that mark true mastery.

As each of us looks at our own profession or role, we must seek the macro-definition, the big picture of whom we are and what we do. Each one of us has times where we fail as we strive to do better. Because our practices are complex, we can always improve. Thus, we never really completely master a practice; we just continue to get better as we intentionally hone the skills which are the hallmarks of the practice. Rather than getting caught in the micro-minutiae of daily living, we learn to keep our eye on the ultimate goal, a life which has meaning and purpose and is lived out within the context of our roles.

The second integral characteristic is that a practice is socially established and cooperative. All theorists in this tradition emphasize that we cannot in isolation determine the qualities that mark a good person in a particular role. Rather, our practice is continually nuanced in the lived conversation among members of the community. An interesting observation is that we may have a practice which is exercised in the privacy of our home but is still socially established.

For example, one who loves blues piano learns to play music in a particular way with certain rhythms and the distinctive walking bass which marks the movement of the piece. That person may never presume to play outside of the confines of his own music room but is still shaped by the masters of the practice, pianists who define the essence of what it is to be a blues pianist. A corollary is that sometimes we either are not good enough or others do not value our practice enough to pay us to do it. Thus, restaurants are classically staffed by starving artists who are honing their disciplines while supporting themselves by serving others.

We all have multiple practices — parent, child, employee, citizen. We are called to consider what to do when the requirements of one practice conflict with the requirements of another. A perennial problem for many of us is balancing the demands of our work against the demands of our families. Thus, a pressing question for many young parents is when they should cut back on professional demands in order to attend to the needs of their children. Negotiating the boundaries and balance between professional and family responsibilities involves both the parents and their employers. Conversations such as availability of flex-time and day care begin to sort through the tangles of this issue.

The definition of our practices is refined through dialogue and experience. As we listen to the wisdom and stories of others, the expectations that we and others have about the obligations and characteristics of our practice become more clear. As the needs of a discipline change, the role expectations are also modified. Thirty years ago managers were expected to be in charge and direct the life of the company. Currently, managers are seen as facilitators of a team, accountable to the whole company and individually responsible for carrying out their part of the organization's mission. Continually attending to how the practice is evolving helps us remain fresh in our work and current in our skills.

From time to time we find that we cannot live within the constraints expected of us in a particular role. We have to ask two separate questions as we chafe against the stated role requirements. The first is whether we are fundamentally unsuited for the expectations of the role. Those who hate conflict do not make good supervisors. Those who hate pressure should not seek out jobs on Wall Street. Those who cannot manage deadlines should not get a job as a reporter for a newspaper. As we learn to know ourselves, our talents, and our limits, we can seek roles which enable us to flourish and thrive rather than thwart us in our work.

The second question considers whether the role constraints themselves are inappropriate. If the role does not allow for all who wish to engage in that practice to be welcomed, we must be willing to challenge the parameters of the role. The long line of litigation to assure not only access to a practice (such as women and minorities demanding to be admitted to professional school) as well as equality within the practice (such as lawsuits for equal pay and/or equal opportunity for promotion) remind us that pioneers of courage have challenged traditional boundaries in order to gain access to practices.

Sometimes the role requires that we go against our core ethical commitments. This situation is perhaps the most difficult for each of us as we struggle to clarify whether the role requirements are in fact appropriate: should we fight to change the practice or leave it altogether? For example, being a soldier may require killing another person. Those who are fundamentally opposed to killing have the opportunity to become conscientious objectors and fulfill their obligation to the community through other forms of service. Those who are absolutely committed to financial transparency may bristle at a rule that says that pay rates of all employees should not be shared across an organization. We must remember that even leaving is a conversation with a community.

Tip

Work the process in two parts. First eliminate the options which do not meet the threshold competencies. Then prioritize the remaining options based on the virtues and desired unity of life.

Many people who find themselves doing unethical things justify their actions by saying "I'm just doing my job." In these situations, we may be like the frog placed in cold water who boiled to death as the water was slowly heated rather than jumping out as it would have had it been placed in hot water. One management theorist states that each of us needs to write our own ethics exit card. What he means is that we must to know our core values so well that, when we are asked to go against those commitments, we decline, if necessary, and leave. His assertion is that if we do not know our own personal bottom line — what we absolutely will not do under any circumstance — we are in fact unethical because we have no guiding principles or values by which to live.

▸ *Apply ethical content*

When the meaning of MacIntyre's complex sentence which defines a practice is (in the words of the philosophers) unpacked, we see a set of basic steps which help us to determine proper ethical action. The conversation always begins with the ethical agent who determines the contemporary shape of the practice which has been developed by others through history.

▹ *Determine the components of the practice, as defined by the ethical agent*

MacIntyre invites us to determine the core competencies of the practice in light of four elements: (1) standards of excellence, (2) rules, (3) internal goods, and (4) external goods which define and partially constitute the practice. Many ethicists assert that our primary ethical obligation is to be competent — to meet the threshold requirements of our work. The criteria developed by MacIntyre help us determine competence in our practice. We come into roles which have been established and designed by the community. We then add our own proficiencies, expertise, and vision. Thus, in conversation and community, the ethical actor and stakeholders continue to shape the practice and move it toward excellence.

▷ *Standards of excellence: what are the standards of excellence which mark the practice of the ethical actor?*

To learn the standards of excellence in our chosen practice, we begin by

> **Standards of Excellence**
>
> The PPO is committed to assuring that it provides quality health care to those members it serves. As part of its commitment to excellence, the PPO has committed itself to a program of continuous quality improvement, assuring that the very best care is given within the constraints of medicine. Part of quality care is treating all patients with dignity and respect, even those who otherwise might be looked down upon or be otherwise marginalized by the community at large.

looking to other practitioners in the field to see the benchmarks. MacIntyre encourages us to look at two faces of excellence, that of the finished product and that of the performance or skill needed to create that product. The conversation about the quality of a product can be related to the current trend to identify best practices and standards in our field and engage n continuous quality improvement. As we adopt strategies of continuous improvement, we are part of a conversation for excellence. For example, the bar has been raised for professional presentations by the emergence of technology and PowerPoint presentations. Through graphics, presentations can be much clearer than those which are just spoken or rely on earlier forms of technology, such as an overhead projector. If we choose not to use the technology, our oral presentation must be even more compelling than was previously required so that we can meet the new community standards.

Excellence of performance can be seen in the quality of research and the care with which a presentation is constructed. We want to avoid having a beautiful, technology-enhanced presentation that has no content. Skilled presenters know that they must have a great deal more background information than they can ever present. A test of excellence is how many questions can be fielded before the expert gets to the end of her knowledge.

As noted, perennial task in the quest to be as good as we can be is to differentiate between excellence and expedience. MacIntyre explored the parameters of virtue, he sharply distinguished between excellence, which is the hallmark of a master, and expedience which may involve cutting corners and result in shoddy work. One set of distinctions was laid out in Chapter 8 during the discussion of utilitarianism. Another, more nuanced version, is below:[14]

If we reduce utilitarianism to a cost-benefit analysis rather than retaining the richness of ideal goals as envisioned by Mill, we find ourselves in the trap of expedience. The temptation to slide into expedience is very strong when companies are judged on short-term results rather than long-term returns. However, the quest for excellence cannot be achieved if we have a knee-jerk reaction and change course based on the vicissitudes of the stock market. By constantly attending to the tension between expedience and excellence, we discern when we need to relax the quality of our work just a tad to get a product out because we can never achieve perfection and when we need to be ruthless in our attention to detail.

Excellence is judged in terms of standards established within and for some specific form of systematic activity and is best thought of in terms of role in community.	*Expedience* is judged in terms of the acquisition of riches, power, status and prestige — goods which can be and are objects of desire by human beings before they consider excellence and independent of any desire to excel.
Excellence inherently strives for progress in achieving those qualities which mark excellence and also for progress in identifying our ideas and recognition of the highest perfection.	*Expedience* inherently strives to identify those means which will be effective in securing the goods and becoming effective in using those means to secure the goods.
Excellence defines justice in terms of merit and what we deserve, using the same standards for all.	*Expedience* defines justice in terms of reciprocity of effective cooperation with the other person.
Excellence recognizes that someone who breaks rules generally hurts himself.	*Expedience* believes that someone who breaks rules generally hurts other people.
Excellence is a virtue which is definable independent of and before the establishment of enforceable rules of justice.	*Expedience* is a virtue which is defined as following the rules of justice until the rules change and thus has no independent ethical content.
Excellence has, as a reason for acting, the goal of achieving excellence and being subject to the virtue of justice.	*Expedience* finds the reason for acting to maximize the satisfaction of its own wants and needs.

▷ *Rules of the practice: what are the rules which we must follow?*

The first category of rules is those which define the practice. For example, one who plays jazz uses a certain set of scales and rhythms which are different than those of Mozart's concertos. The second category of rules which limit the practice, consist of codes of ethics, professional codes, or laws. Sometimes we want to challenge the professional codes or the law because they are (arguably) unjust. If the preferred option requires civil disobedience, going against these rules, we must to count the cost and assure that we are responding to a higher or more complete understanding of ethical behavior and not simply just rebelling or demanding our own way. Often what poses as civil disobedience is a person trying to play the edge and not get caught.

Rules of Practice

▶ A health care provider must first of all assure that the standards of good medicine are met, which includes both contractual agreements and implied cultural agreements. In this context, full informed consent before any procedure is expected by the community.

▶ The provider is accountable to the state, that licenses and regulates the provider, as well as to the physicians and other professionals who must maintain their licenses to practice.

Every practice has implicit and explicit rules. Building on the example of public speaking, a good presentation has a coherent outline, cogent examples to illustrate the points, and good supporting data. As people learn the rules of the practice of public speaking, they master skills such as pacing, voice quality, and organization. A presentation may also be subject to external rules — length of time, appropriate content, depth of research. Those who choose to flaunt the external rules often have to be very, very good in order to get past the expectations of the audience and the gatekeepers of the practice. Anyone who has ever tried to change the way a practice "has always been done," knows that innovation is simultaneously encouraged and discouraged. On one hand, people say that they like innovation to keep a practice fresh and people engaged in the work. On the other hand, meeting the requirements of the practice means that one must be sensitive to the historical character and requirements. Walking the tightrope to remain true to the practice while bringing in fresh ideas is difficult.

▷ ***Internal goods: what array of internal goods — satisfaction, feeling of a job well done, ability to make a difference — is important to us in this situation?***

Internal Goods

People go into medicine in order to facilitate the healing process for others. No one is more vulnerable than those who are ill. Those in medicine also have a soft spot for those who are rejected by others, who find themselves ill with diseases which many in the community misunderstand. Thus, physicians get satisfaction from not only healing their patient's bodies, but also by attending to the whole person. Finally, in this case, the physician also wants to help the community and contain the spread of a highly contagious, social disease. By finding ways to assure that people who are infected are treated with respect and given good health care, the community as a whole can thrive.

A person who is not skilled at public speaking but who actually gets through the presentation will feel very good about the accomplishment, regardless of the opinion of others. We each have areas where we are stretching to become better as we perfect our practice. One of the questions we must ask as we seek to improve at a practice is whether we are committed excellence in the practice enough to be marked as a master in a field or whether we will be content to be a journeyman or even an amateur. For many, being "good enough" is sufficient as they work for mastery of a set of skills. The excitement of the youngsters who participate in the Special Olympics makes us realize that transcending personal limits is often as satisfying as being recognized as the very best in a given arena for the proverbial fifteen minutes of fame.

Much personal satisfaction comes with noticing where we are on the leading edge of our own practice as we define our personal trajectory of excellence. Thus, being able to confront our fear and make a set of cold calls to launch a career in sales may seem to a veteran marketer like a baby step, where for a new person the achievement is monumental. Our mentors and coaches help us see where we need to fine tune our work to become even better at what we do.

- ▷ *External Goods: what array of external goods — title, prestige, financial rewards — is important enough to be sought and protected?*

Those who excel at a practice are in demand. Those who are very good in highly valued practices command a high salary and get status. In the process of choosing which practice to pursue, each of us has to carefully critique our own talents and abilities to determine what will bring sufficient external goods so that we support ourselves and meet our own ego needs. We may engage in practices which we thoroughly enjoy but which do not have enough value in the community to provide us with our desired standard of living. For example, we may need to carefully explore whether our need for security is too high to make us willing to risk all to possibly become a very successful entrepreneur. We may need to acknowledge when our need for status through title or education is important enough to make us forego other opportunities as we seek our certifications and diplomas. As we each make these decisions, we have to know ourselves very well.

One effective manager stated that he was able to foster excellence in his employees by giving them the external rewards that they wanted rather than trying to give everyone the same thing. One young father valued salary more than perks, so he received bonuses for his work. A widow valuedtraveling more than money, so he rewarded her work by

> **External Goods**
>
> Physicians have a great deal of status in the community, which is important to maintain. Remaining licensed so that the practice as well as the physicians get paid is also an important external good.

sending her to conferences and appropriate training so she could travel throughout the United States. Another person wanted to move ahead in his profession, so he was allowed to do *pro bono* work for local charities in order to strengthen his professional networks and raise his profile in the local community. Attending to the internal and external goods which are important to employees contributes to an excellent organization.

People always ask whether excellence can be taught. Experience seems to indicate that one who has a modicum of talent can become a good "B+" practitioner but may not be able to bridge the gap to become a good "A" practitioner. Those who through innate talent are good "A" practitioners, with practice and work, can become an "A+," although they may choose to function at the "A" or even "B+" level. Clearly, we all have different talents and gifts which we honor and hone. At the same time, we need to recognize the bittersweet truth that, by choosing to pursue excellence in one practice, we may need to forgo excellence in others for which we have equal aptitude. Many of us are confronted with the challenge of the proverb, "[b]e not a Jack of all trades, but a master of one."[15]

- ***Community expectations:*** *what does each member of the community consider to be the core competencies of the ethical agent.*

For this stage, we join in conversation with others to ascertain whether our determination of the core competencies match those held by other members of the community, particularly those who are acknowledged as masters in the field. To complete this phase, we consider the expectations that each constituent has for a competent ethical agent. In determining what makes a good person in this role, we need not focus on what makes us happy but rather on what kind of person we want to become. A good teacher is fair and demanding,

Stakeholders

- PPO: with whom the ethics committee has a contract to act in the best interest of the PPO. They expect the committee to balance the needs of all stakeholders to assure that quality, ethical care can be given.
- Physicians: with whom the PPO has employment contracts to provide services. They expect the committee to put processes in place that will enable them to give good care while maintaining their license to practice medicine.
- Patients: with whom the PPO has contracts to provide health care. They expect the physicians to care for them and let them know what the best course of treatment is. They also expect confidentiality.
- Citizens of the state: with whom the PPO has a social contract to follow the law. The citizens want to assure that the AIDs virus is contained and that people are not infected through irresponsible behavior.

stretching the mind of students. Sometimes students say that they would be happier in a class that is not hard. However, often those teachers who give soft classes are also not seen as good in their profession — both by their students and their peers.

As we consider the concerns of the stakeholders, we need to remember that the stakeholders do not get to veto the chosen option. The goal is to assure that the competencies as we have defined them and the considered opinion of the stakeholders are met. This is where a conversation about the requirements of the practice might help. As we talk with others to define excellence in a role, we begin by meeting current professional expectations. Perhaps with time we can participate in raising the bar, both as we sharpen our own sense of excellence as well as clarify the expectations others have for people in this role. Often we have vague ideas about what a good professional is but do not really know how to evaluate the professional or sort through our own conflicting desires. A skilled ethical agent will listen to what the stakeholders want, modify the practice where appropriate, and educate the stakeholders in the trade-offs and requirements of the practice where needed. At that point, we make a preliminary determination as to the proper ethical action. As we review our choices, we evaluate the options against our own stated competencies and standards. If the option does not meet our own threshold expectations of competency, then the option is not ethical. Only options which meet the core requirements of the practice are considered in the next three steps. Thus, if an option does not meet the threshold requirement of demonstrating competency in the field as determined by the individual practitioner, others in the field, and the key stakeholders, the option is, by definition, unethical.

▸ ***Evaluate each option which meets the requirements of the competencies against the core virtues: (a) integrity; (b) courage; (c) justice; and (d) civility. Include a working definition of the content of those virtues so that points of agreement and disagreement can be determined.***

Evaluation Against the Competencies

1. The option of telling the patient that, if he tests positive for HIV, his name will be reported to the state, meets the requirements the majority of the stakeholders. That option meets the agent's core competencies as well as those of everyone but the citizens. However, while the citizens want the epidemic to stop, as individuals they also want to be treated with respect. Thus, as long as the names are recorded, the majority of the citizens will be content.

2. The option of not telling does not meet the competencies of the ethical agent, and it does not meet the requirements of the stakeholders. Making sure that the patient is responsible for his own care is core to the practice. Further, the patient expects the physician to give him the information necessary to make good choices. Thus, this option is not ethical.

Once an act meets the requirements of the core competencies, it is judged against the virtues. MacIntyre chooses the core virtues of courage, honesty, and justice. However, he does not claim that his list is exhaustive. As he defines a virtue, MacIntyre is very clear that pursuit of the virtues is essential for the good life. Thus, a key critique of our culture is that we have abandoned the quest for virtue and thus find the good life illusive.

A virtue is an acquired human quality, the possession and exercise of which tends to enable us to achieve those goods which are internal to practices and the lack of which effectively prevents us from achieving any such goods.[16] According to MacIntyre, while we may receive all of the external goods of a practice, unless we attend to the virtues, we will not have any of the internal goods such as satisfaction, joy, and peace in our work. Whether from our own experience or as we watch the media clips of executives in hand-cuffs doing the "perp-walk" as they go to trial or to prison, we see that achieving the brass ring of financial success alone will not guarantee long-term satisfaction.

A critique of MacIntyre is that he does not describe the ethical content of the virtues nor tell us how to clarify what elements are part of each virtue. For example, while MacIntyre is clear that truth-telling is essential both for our own sense of well being and the preservation of practices, he neither tells us what constitutes a life of integrity nor how to get there. Thus, to begin to understand the content of the virtues as extolled in our chosen tradition, we draw upon the wisdom and learning of the other theorists as we determine what behaviors and attitudes are essential marks of the virtues we choose to embrace.

- *Integrity is what truth needs to be told so we are true to ourselves and the practice can retain its integrity in the face of the corrupting influence of institutions?*

As we consider how to be true to ourselves and as we work to assure that other people have the information they need to make good choices, the Rights/Responsibility Lens might be useful in helping us remember what commitments we have made. Whether looking at the broad agreements which are part of our social contract or the specific agreements which are part of our particular relationships, the questions posed by Kant help us explore our motives and our obligations which shape the virtue of truth-telling. Attending to integrity will also help us remember to treat each person with dignity and inherent respect.

The Relationship Lens helps us remember to step back from the situation and ask what information we would want if we didn't know who we were in a particular situation. We can borrow the veil of ignorance concept from Rawls to help us determine what is essential for a well functioning system and move away from only considering our small part in the puzzle. We then attend to instituting and refining processes which assure that the practice is true to itself.

MacIntyre departs from Kant by asserting that the codes of ethics may change from culture to culture. Thus, MacIntyre repudiates the notion of universal principles which Kant posited and moves rather to the notion of universal virtues. MacIntyre states that while the norms of the community, especially their application in specific circumstances, may change from time to time, every community must value certain core virtues if the community is to flourish.[17] Again, as we see the call to a return to ethics in our business community, the argument can be made that rather than attending to the core virtue of integrity, we began to tolerate deception and chicanery in our business leaders, as long as our bottom line — our salaries and our stock portfolios — became fat.

- ***Courage*** *is the "capacity to risk harm or danger to oneself. This virtue has a role in human life because of its connection with care and concern.*[18]

In today's business climate, courage is required not only for individual acts but also to hold those who are responsible for our institutions accountable. The exercise of personal courage involves engaging in the hard work of learning about ourselves and holding ourselves accountable, even when it is not convenient. As we have gone through each of the lenses, the hubris attached to each lens has been articulated. Hubris is that quality which allows us to avoid accountability for meeting the norms of the community either through arrogance, pride, or passion.

As discussed in Chapter 6, failing to facing our own tendencies to hubris, the places where we do not want to be accountable to ourselves and our communities, causes a deep tear in the fabric of our community. Many who study history assert that

Evaluation Against the Virtues

The option of telling the patient that, if he tests positive for HIV, his name will be reported to the state demonstrates integrity in that the patients are treated honestly and given the information needed make good decisions. The option also demonstrates courage in that the physicians have to trust the patients to make the right choice, to be willing to risk notoriety in order to be treated. If the physician treats the patient with grace, then the patient will be able to face this difficult prospect. This option also supports justice in that the least advantaged, the patient, is considered first. The community is also honored in that the physician will work to minimize the spread of the disease.

when a society which has achieved excellence loses its moral fiber, that society begins a decline and risks losing all it has accomplished. In our business community, the ultimate act of courage is whistle-blowing. Even after being extolled in the press for extraordinary courage, those who hold their leaders accountable often find that they are unemployed and blackballed. Thus, while we say we value the courage it takes to confront the system and expect that individuals will hold the organizations accountable, those who actually speak up may find their careers derailed.

▶ *Justice requires that we treat others according to uniform and impersonal standards.*[19]

Justice is a more complex conversation. At its core, justice is the study of appropriate relationships in the community. The question becomes how one looks at the right treatment of people, the right use of private and public property, and the proper exercise of power. Different ethical traditions have varying understandings of the way that individuals and the community should use their power and property. Examining a traditional way of organizing the themes of justice may be useful. Four categories of justice help us understand the conversation.

▷ *Contributive Justice:* how do we assure that people get a measure of the goods and services in the community based on what they have contributed? People who take very high risks and have high exposure in the community tend to get more financial rewards than those who live more conservative lives and make measured choices.

▷ *Retributive Justice:* This conversation assures that people are appropriately punished for violating the rules of the community. Paul Tillich, a contemporary theologian, asserts that if we err too far on the side of mercy, not holding people accountable for their actions, we in fact keep them as children and deny them the opportunity to be adults who are responsible for themselves — the greatest gift we have in this life.[20] Thus, in the business community, we have to assure that people who engage in fraud, theft, and dishonesty are held appropriately accountable for the effects their actions have on our economic life.

▷ *Distributive Justice:* The process of determining who should get what goods and services in the community forms the content of the conversation about distributive justice. One problem is that we have different criteria for distribution of goods based on what goods are being distributed.[21] The primary categories are *merit*, what we earn through our work and effort; *need*, the threshold necessities such as food, housing, and education, which we deserve because we are part of a community; and *market*, what we buy because we have the resources. In conversation, members of the community make decisions about who gets what and how those goods should be distributed.

▷ *Restorative Justice:* An emerging conversation about justice invites us to consider how we restore community when someone has violated our trust. Begun as a way to help juveniles who had engaged in petty crime see that their acts impacted people's lives, the whole conversation about restorative justice has merit for businesses. As we learn to rebuild relationships which have been frayed by technology and mobility, principles of restorative justice can help businesses, individuals, and the communities which they share find ways to work together for common goals.

Each lens has a different slant on what is considered a just act. Because the claim of members of the community is so strong, each theory has addressed the various components of justice as the use of power and impact of influence profoundly shapes our choices. In each case, the claim of justice requires that we subordinate our interests to those of the other, people who also lay claim to an opportunity for the good life. As we look at the particular focus of each lens, we see that, as we are called to justice, we begin to limit the prerogatives of individuals and institutions while working to avoid the vices which beset us as human beings in a contingent, flawed society.

For the individual focused lenses, we are asked to limit personal power so that the community can flourish. For the community focused lenses, we are asked to limit collective power so individuals can thrive.

Core Justice Frameworks

A just act is where I honor and respect the integrity and courage of others.	A just act is where the community limits power so individuals can flourish.
Reputation Lens	Relationship Lens
Rights Lens	Results Lens
A just act is where I only claim rights I'm willing to grant to others.	A just act is where I limit my choices for the well being of all.

Again, through careful balance of the interests of all, justice can be achieved. Many businesses find that they want to give back to their communities, and so within the constraints of their fiduciary responsibility to their shareholders, subordinate their financial interests to build the common good. Employees volunteer to help in myriad ways and companies support the efforts. By working with others in the community, the people who otherwise would be faceless statistics become real human beings with lives and dreams. As we work with the people whose lives our business decisions impact, we become aware of the ripple effect that our decisions have in our communities. Many businesses also find that they want to nurture individuals in their organizations, assuring that each is treated with justice and dignity. True leadership emerges as one skillfully balances between the needs of the individual, the organization, and the community at large.

▸ *Civility requires that we treat others with respect and dignity.*

While MacIntyre did not include civility in his list of virtues, in a world where shouting at each other has become the norm and road-rage is commonplace, considering the contours of civility is important.

First, civility embraces the notion of ordinary good manners — please and thank-you. These seemingly tiny acts of civility provide the social glue which helps us remember that the persons with whom we interact are humans who are to be treated with dignity and respect. Actually seeing those who work with us and serve us in varying capacities reminds us that all work is useful and that none of us make it in this world alone. Many times we do not even see those whom we consider unimportant, thus rendering them invisible.

Secondly, civility embraces the notion of treating those with whom we disagree or are in conflict with respect and dignity. In an age where being right is more important than being thoughtful, we polarize every conversation and insist on portraying people, their motives, and their actions as the purist of white or the darkest of black. While finding middle positions is often derogatorily condemned as playing in the muck of shades of grey, we need to remember that, to the artist working with pigments, white is the absence of all color and black is the presence of all color. All of the hues of the rainbow are possible only because of differences. As we track political conversations, we notice the tendency to demonize each other rather than listen for points of convergence and search for a meaningful resolution which satisfies both.

Shouting, rather than listening, becomes the norm. Pulling data out of context and magnifying tiny parts of the puzzle rather than seeing the whole substitutes for careful thought and analysis. In an age where change and insecurity has seemingly caused us to lose our center, whole new career fields are emerging to help us manage our conflict and resolve our differences.

Finally, civility includes the notion of building trust and reciprocity which are needed for healthy communities. Robert D. Putnam in *Bowling Alone* charts the reduction of social trust in the United States as he reports sociological data tracking the decline of reciprocity and civility.[22] Putnam interprets the data to show that, as we have become more anonymous, as we do not think that we will see each other again, and as we do not have a face to put on our actions, the need to be kind to one other diminishes. The social cost for a loss of civility is an increase in preventive lawyering and litigation. When business people knew that they would see each other not only in board rooms but also in church and in civic organizations, their need to maintain civil relationships was much higher. With larger and more complex communities, we never know when or if we will be in relationship with a particular person again, so it does not matter how we treat her. Thus, having a reputation for integrity and courage does not matter — because no-one knows anyone well enough to know the other's reputation.

As we no longer have webs of relationships where we see each other in multiple settings, many believe that they have no good reasons to develop social trust and social capital through cooperation. Rather than sealing deals with hand-shakes, to protect ourselves we resort to putting everything in writing. Rather than being kind to a stranger, trusting that a stranger will at some point be kind to us, we eye everyone suspiciously and turn our backs. In the process we forget that embracing the virtue of civility not only makes the world a better place, but also enables us to have strong webs of relationships, even with strangers, which enhances our businesses, strengthens our community, and lowers our legal bills. However, to accomplish this goal, we must be willing to embrace the virtue of civility for the sake of the virtue itself, not to gain any ulterior reward. In the process the thin trust which we bestow upon strangers can nourish a rich community which is ultimately not only more safe but also more enjoyable.

▸ ***For each option that meets the requirements of the virtues, determine which one will best support the actor's requirements of unity of life.***

After an act is judged against the virtues, it is measured against our unity of life, that which gives meaning and purpose to our life and supports our becoming a moral person rather than one who does a series of ethical acts but who may not have a coherent world view. As we rank the options from the most preferred to the least preferred, we remember that this step invites us to consider the ultimate newspaper test — would we want this decision on the front page of the local news. As we consider the end of life, it is helpful to focus on what we want be, do, and have. Each of us has particular virtues we want to cultivate. We have certain things that we want to do. We also have goals we want to achieve, which may include staying in business. As each of us strives to find meaning in life, we also shape our own life's story. A useful exercise might be to consider what we would want written in the company's annual report or what the comments at our retirement party would reveal. The unity of life question invites us to consider our lives as a whole, not just as a set of separate, unconnected actions.

Evaluation Against the Unity of Life

The option of telling the patient that, if he tests positive for HIV, his name will be reported to the state will assure that the PPO stays in business in that all of the agreements with the core constituencies will be met. By exercising the virtues, the PPO will also enhance its reputation in the community and thus be known as a place which provides excellent service. This option also allows the PPO to assure that both individuals and the community are served, that their interests are balanced so that each person is treated with grace and dignity.

▸ ***Overlay the moral content***

The Moral Lens demands that we carefully assess not only our intellectual strengths but also our emotional health. Thus, the final step in the analysis is determining which of the remaining options best meets the requirements of our conscience and our core beliefs. As discussed earlier, a core belief is a notion or idea that is held with affection which results in passion or action. Actions which are consonant with our core beliefs are marked by a commitment that defines us and has the potential to energize and transform both us and the community. Thus, each of us needs to see what kinds of commitments have emotional energy behind them — a passion which makes our heart race or our voice become strident. Hopefully, each one of us has a commitment which causes us to get on a soapbox to persuade the whole world of the value of that commitment.

MacIntyre asserts that as we begin cultivating the core virtues, we will be able to shape an ethical life for ourselves. His final provisional definition of a virtue is

> those dispositions which will not only sustain practices and enable us to achieve the goods internal to practices, but which will also sustain us in the relevant kind of quest for the good, by enabling us to overcome the harms, dangers, temptations and distractions which we encounter, and which will furnish us with increasing self-knowledge and increasing knowledge of the good.[23]

While this definition begins to move us from the notion of seeing ourselves as ethical if we accomplish a set of discrete moral acts to striving to have the habits of thought and action of a moral person, MacIntyre does not ever directly address the issue of emotions and the human spirit. To fill this gap, other authors investigate the role of our emotions and the life of the spirit in the shaping of the human person. To provide a perspective on this facet of our lives, we turn to the work of Shelton, a psychologist who studies the formation of conscience. As he explores the contours of conscience, Shelton begins with the core teleological assumption that we as humans strive to be good in the roles we embrace.

Evaluation Against the Moral Criteria

The option of telling the patient that, if he tests positive for HIV, his name will be reported to the state is part of a habitual decision to assure that people will have good information. This option also helps the physicians avoid the temptation of paternalism, asserting that they know what is best for the patient. Finally, full disclosure also allows the physician to treat the person with compassion and love. While the easy way of running people through the office might be a way to avoid the difficult tasks, taking the time to be with the patient and explain the consequences of a routine procedure makes lots of sense.

Like MacIntyre, Shelton finds that each of us must take responsibility for placing ourself in a life history, or narrative, which shapes and give meaning to our lives. As we determine how we fit into the history of our particular world and find for ourselves the meaning of our lives, Shelton asserts that we need to explore who we are, who we are becoming, and who we desire to be. One useful tool may be to ask questions which help us clarify the requirements of our conscience and help us develop a good conscience. Shelton poses these questions as "exercises for the conscience" to help us become a good person.[24] How does this option:

- *support our moral beliefs* and commitments?
- *support our own notions* of self-respect, respect for others, and a realistic look at who we are and others?

- ▸ *support our ideals*, our moral vision, and hope for the community?
- ▸ *assure that we do not think* of ourselves as better than we are or appropriate for ourselves prerogatives which we should not have?
- ▸ *meet the criteria* of empathy, compassion, and love?
- ▸ *mitigate our personal defenses* which allow us to cope in this world and function?
- ▸ *support our emotional health* and acknowledge the complexity of our lives?

Each of these questions provides a lodestar for helping us determine a virtuous course of action. As we learn to habitually ask these or similar questions while making both simple and complex decisions, we cultivate the habits of the heart which Robert Bellah and others, who write in what is known as a communitarian tradition, state are essential for a healthy community.

Our sense of who we are as business people absolutely determines how we will behave in our work community. A person who is disgruntled and sees herself exploited by her employer will behave very differently than one who sees himself as an integral part of the community. The ability to correctly assess our skills and talents, our strengths and weaknesses, is critical for identifying who we are. "Who we are becoming" is decided by the myriad of choices we make. A person who chooses to go to law school and practice law becomes a very different person than one who chooses to get a Ph.D. in English and specialize in the novels of Charles Dickens. Each of our career choices, as well as the way we choose to deal with the specific incidents in our lives, shapes us as people and contributes to the narrative of our lives.

"Who we desire to be" is an essential component of our life story. Our mentors, our guides, our heroes help to determine the trajectory of our lives. As we begin to see possibilities for our futures and choose not only actions but also habits of thought and being, we participate in our own transformation. For example, Shelton asserts that those who cultivate habits of gratitude are healthier and happier than those who see the world through a dark, misty fog of resentment.

Goleman in *Primal Leadership* asserts that one must have self-awareness, knowledge of one's emotions as well as one's reason, exercise self-management, where one is able to keep disruptive emotions under control, and display a full array of virtues in order to be an effective leader. As one tends to both the emotional and rational sides of the person, one can be and become a virtuous person, a leader and mentor in the business community.

Step 4: Be Responsible

▶ *Rank the options from least preferred to most preferred*

Having determined the elements of the practice and then evaluated each option against the criteria of (a) the ethical actor's understanding of the core competencies; (b) the stakeholders' understanding of the core competencies; (c) the virtues; (d) the ethical agent's dreams for unity of life; and (e) the whisperings of conscience, the next step is to rank the options from least preferred the most preferred. As the options are ranked, we summarize why the ranking of options was made and demonstrate the primacy given to the virtues, the character of the ethical agent.

▶ *Correct for bias*

The Reputation Lens allows us to cultivate our personal virtues within a coherent personal narrative while we are an integral part of the community. However, if we use this lens without the balance of other viewpoints, we become self-righteous. As those of us who are especially privileged cultivate the virtues, we somehow believe that we are entitled to the blessings of our lives if we are not aware of the contributions that others have made which allow us to be who we are. A colleague once quipped about a politician born into privilege who seemed blind to the needs of the less advantaged, that "he was born on third base but thinks he hit a triple."

As we work to become "all that we can be," we need to remember that we are special — just like everyone else. As we look at ourselves with clear eyes and engage with others with compassion and emotional maturity, we avoid the hubris which comes from a sense of entitlement and unrealistic self-esteem. As we take a final look at our choice, we should assure ourselves that our action comes from our commitments and a sense of ourself as people wearing all of our varied hats — employers, employees, consumers, and citizens. As we resist the temptation to view our choices from only one narrow perspective, we become people of virtue and choose that which meets both short-term needs and long-term goals.

▸ *Attend to the common good*

As many voices explore how we are going to fashion our emerging history, a new note is starting to be heard, the inclusion of the spiritual. Not tied exclusively to any particular religious tradition, members of the community invite us to question what Rosemary Haughton calls the "taken-for-granted separation between the material and spiritual, between physical and mental, [as] we struggle to express in that language the disintegrating conclusions of quantum physics and "field" theory, in which there are no 'things' at all, but only relationship, information, movement."[25]

All of us who work in business need to explore what our professional ethics will look like in a world not defined by individual action, facts, and stability, but by the fluid situation Haughton describes where our only lodestar is what we believe responsible human beings should do to build a community in which all can thrive. As we begin to see ourselves as whole humans, we can resist taking only our useful self to work. If we only come to work with a skill set that will enhance the bottom line and guarantee the well-being and success of the organization, we will deny whole segments of who we are as people and breed "passivity, submissiveness and dependence."[26] The emerging academic and popular inquiry into spirituality at work addresses the question of how we take our whole selves to work and contribute to the life of the economic community.

In these fluid times, freedom comes from our ability to imagine what we would like to become and what we want our businesses to be, and then to deliberately choose a particular direction while we work to make that dream a reality. To act from a thoughtful consideration of the specific situation rather than mindlessly responding to a determined world, we must be willing to take responsibility for ourselves and our community, including the community that manufactures goods and provides services — the world of business.

▸ *Act with Courage*

Because most of the work in ethics is persuasion, we should be able to

Announcement

The PPO will be implementing a protocol which assures that even for a routine procedure like drawing blood, full informed consent as to the possible consequences of drawing blood will be given, e.g., that if the person tests positive for HIV, their name will be placed on a central registry with the state. While this protocol will not affect many people and thus may be seen as an inconvenience, we want to assure that those who might be affected by the policy have full information and are treated with respect and dignity. In this way we will maintain our reputation for being patient-centered, putting their interests first.

articulate clearly what choice we have made and why. After giving a bit of background information to set the stage for the problem, we frame the statement so that we answer the core questions of this particular lens. As we fashion the statement, we should attempt to allude to the virtues which are important as well as the unity of life of the organization. Remember that these announcements become part of the narrative of the organization. As such they are instrumental in demonstrating which traditions are important to the organization and assure that a tradition of excellence is continually reiterated. We write the statement in such a way that we answer the core questions: (1) What respected human qualities and virtues are demonstrated by this decision (*e.g.*, courage, moderation, justice, *etc.*)? (2) How does this decision demonstrate the qualities and virtues that a person who is respected in this role has (*e.g.*, competence, loyalty, diligence, fairness, *etc.*)? (3) How does this decision demonstrate the qualities of a person in this profession (*e.g*,. commitment to public service, self-regulation, trust, integrity)?

Step 5: Return to Awareness

After we describe our resolution of the problem, we next consider whether the ethical analysis made sense. Did we like the result? What were the problems with the process? What are the sticking points with the process? How was the process enhanced or modified by adding the world of emotion and attending to the virtues which are essential for all of us to be effective in our world?

▸ *Continuous Improvement*

The process of continuous improvement involves developing strategies to assure accurate self-assessment. In many spiritual traditions, the process of self-assessment involves neither thinking better nor worse of ourselves than we should as we learn to be content no matter what our situation. We hear inspiring stories of people who were incarcerated in the German concentration camps and were able to be gentle and thrive. Viktor Frankel recounts that part of his secret was to see the guards as human beings. The German guards knew how to interact with people who gave up their humanity, but were thrown off balance by those who retained their humanity and saw their captors as fully human as well. As we attend to developing the virtues essential for our varying roles, we are cautioned to watch for intended and unintended results. We also need to attend to new questions or answers that were not complete. The trajectory for maturity is not necessarily smooth, but as we attend to our character while supporting others in their journey, we can get there. As we take responsibility for our own self-development while respecting the path of others, we will learn to live with gentleness, grace, and maybe even a dollop of frivolity. In the process we will learn how to live from our center while we find meaning for our lives.

▶ *The Crucible of Spirit*

As we are called to balance, we need to address whether we are being overly attached to our own sense of entitlement and self-righteousness in our need to be "special" or whether we are detached from our situation enough to begin to develop compassion and empathy for those with whom we live and work. As we become aware of being part of a larger community and celebrate the amazing diversity of choice and experience, we begin to take the long view and, with gratitude, celebrate our lives. We will become aware of those places where our fear overwhelms us so that we are not able to notice the gifts of others. We will also be aware of our tendencies toward unrealistic self-esteem, not accurately seeing both our gifts and our challenges, which keep us from being effective while walking gently in this world. If we do not attend to our spirit as we do our work, we risk losing our center, the core of our being which allows us to act from certainty and authenticity. We will also notice where we have power to help others judge members of their community by their character rather than external characteristics. In the process we will become aware of our own sacred identity.

Conclusion

The Reputation Lens invites us to consider how to attend to our character and embrace the virtues which allow us to become effective leaders in our community. Beginning with the ethical key phrase, *what is a good character,* we learn to develop the habits of personal reflection as we seek the counsel of others in the community who will help us become virtuous while becoming an integral part of the community. To avoid becoming overwhelmed with either self-righteousness or fear, we learn to continually attend to developing a *healthy, functioning conscience.* As we embrace the spiritual focus, we turn from attending only to ourselves as we ask *who is my neighbor?* With detachment, seeking to see the spark of the divine in each person, we seek excellence rather than expedience in all that we do — and in the process become effective leaders.

Continuing the Conversation

1. Using either the fourth problem in the GG Ethis Game or another fact pattern, analyze the situation using the Reputation Lens. Was the problem easy to do, indicating that this might be your preferred method of working ethical problems? Was the process difficult, indicating that this may not be your ethical home?

2. Read an op ed piece in your local paper or a national paper and find examples of virtue ethics thinking. In what ways did the author appeal to the competencies of the practice? What virtues were described as important for this particular practice?

3. Review the Conceptual Map of the Relationship Lens which opened this chapter, paying special attention to the gifts of this tradition. Considering both your own life as well as others who make decisions using the vantage of this tradition, what are the strengths of the Reputation Lens? Give examples of situations in which you have seen excellent results as someone used the viewpoints and processes of this lens to make a decision.

4. What strategies can you put in place to strengthen your own mastery of this lens? How can you help the organizations in which you work, either paid or volunteer, ask the core questions to help them make better ethical decisions?

5. Again, review the chart which opened this chapter, this time attending to the weaknesses of the tradition. Considering both your own life as well as that of others who make decisions using the vantage of this tradition, what are the weaknesses of the Reputation Lens? Give examples of situations in which you have seen problematic results as someone used the viewpoints and processes of this lens to make a decision.

6. What strategies can you put in place to help you recognize and attend to the imbalance which comes from an inappropriate appropriation of the Reputation Lens, whether concerning abuse of power or hubris in your personal and professional life? How do you know when you are improperly using the tools of this lens? How can you help the organizations in which you work, whether paid or volunteer, ask the core questions to help them avoid imbalance or hubris?

The highest good is like water.
Water gives life to the ten thousand things
and does not strive.
It flows in places men reject and
so is like the Tao.

In dwelling, be close to the land.
In meditation, go deep in the heart.
In dealing with others, be just and kind.
In speech, be true.
In business, be competent.
In action, watch the timing.

No fight: no blame.

From the Tao Te Ching ... eight[1]

Chapter 11

Life with Integrity, Grace — and a Dollop of Frivolity

Greed is good! So declares Gordon Gekko, the hero/villain of *Wall Street*, the 1987 block-buster movie which reviewer Jeff Stone notes "perfectly embod[ies] the Reagan-era credo" of unbridled ambition as Gekko entices the young Bud Fox into his lair with promises of power and privilege. Stone comments that the movie "grabs your attention while questioning the corrupted values of a system that worships profit at the cost of one's soul."[2]

At the end of the 90's, with almost monthly exposés of companies and their leaders who clearly violated the law as well as societal norms, people at cocktail parties and journalists asked whether those who were hauled before grand juries and then trundled off to prison were a few bad apples who needed to be plucked from the barrel of commerce before all the contents were spoiled or whether they represented the whole crop, signaling that something was deeply wrong with our community. The answer is probably "yes" to both.

Many of those who became household names pushed the envelope of accepted behavior. As long as the stock prices kept going up, no one asked too many questions, because we had a matrix of expectations and practices which allowed the behavior to be both tolerated and celebrated. Lester Thurow reminds us that

> [c]rony capitalism exists everywhere. Examine the end of any financial boom in American history and one finds scandals...The Enrons, Worldcoms, and Mercks are not abnormalities in a basically sound system. They are completely normal, common garden variety events...At the end of a boom the pressure to keep the good times going just a little longer is enormous.[3]

After watching *Wall Street*, the question was asked how Gekko knew that Fox would be a good candidate to be drawn into his web of greed and destruction. Fox sent the first signal: he brought Gekko a box of smuggled cigars for his birthday. Through that first act, Gekko intuited that Fox's desire to advance was greater than his commitment to the community norms and the law. Faced with a set of desires and goals that were complex and conflicting, the young stock-broker found that his drive to succeed according to Wall Street's definition was greater than his willingness to live by the values and norms which would lead to personal satisfaction and allow the community as a whole to thrive.

Can't We Just Return to the Good Old Days?

Evaluating the status of business ethics at the beginning of the 21st century, one is tempted to longingly yearn for a return to some mythological Camelot where community ethics were strong and individuals and businesses were able to thrive. However, those days probably never existed. Each era has both challenges and celebrations as it plays out its act on the grand stage of history.

As we take a long view back, determining that other periods of time were more or less ethical becomes difficult. Different periods of time have ever changing expectations and definitions of the right use of people, property, and power. Thus, whether observers accept the overall set of practices which define the business climate of a community as ethical, depends on how congruent business ethics are with community ethics.[4] When the personal values of community members are mirrored in the corporate behaviors, businesses are touted as ethical partners in the community. However, when the shadow side of business comes to the fore and expectations for financial transparency and fair dealings change, we claim a crisis in ethics and scramble to find ways to regulate behavior and shame the practitioners into addressing the new problems. Looking at the three broad areas where we evaluate our ethics helps us put our history in perspective.

Right Treatment of People

In one sense, our businesses are more ethical than they have ever been because we have an ever increasing commitment to human dignity and respect. Our founding fathers boldly proclaimed in The Declaration of Independence that

> [w]e hold these truths to be self-evident, that all men are created equal, that they are endowed by their Creator with certain unalienable Rights, that among these are Life, Liberty, and the pursuit of Happiness...[5]

Over the past two-hundred and fifty years of our existence, members of the United States have worked relentlessly to make that dream a reality.

In terms of relationships between employer and employee, at this time in American history, men and women, both minorities and those in the majority, have greater opportunity for access to positions and privilege than ever before. Those with physical and mental handicaps, and those of different races and gender, enjoy more opportunity for participation in the wider community.

In terms of the relationship between producer and consumer, our products are safer than they have ever been. We have ever increasing mandates for safety (with some asking when a product should be considered safe enough). We also have for quality improvement as seen in the Baldrige Initiative and Sigma 6. The transparency between producer and consumer is also greater than ever. We have information about the products and services available to all — including nutritional information on products. Magazines and websites give the vitals for equipment, cars, and machinery.

At the same time we have seen an erosion in personal privacy in the name of security and safety. Alcohol abuse and drug use are not tolerated as random drug and alcohol screening are accepted as *de rigueur*. During the 1960s and 1970s, sexual harassment was named and then not tolerated. The treatment of women which was accepted even thirty years ago is no longer welcome in the workplace. Monitoring one's use of computers at work is expected. Finally, the use of global positioning devices to keep track of employees is gaining in use. Some companies are even putting GPD's in their employees' badges to their every move can be tracked. While knowing where one's employees are in the event of disaster might be useful, most people find "big brother watching" a bit unnerving.

While we continually calibrate our practices, working to appropriately balance among the four core values, in both expectation and performance, we continue to reach towards the ideal. While we have not yet arrived, that trajectory to include all in the American Dream continues to be a hallmark of excellence in the United States.

Right Use of Property

The hallmark of American capitalism is the right to private property — using one's own resources in the way that one chooses. Traditional property law provides that within the boundaries which mark the land, one owns rights to the core of the earth and the dome of the sky. However, those property laws have historically not addressed what happens when toxins leave your property and enter your neighbor's. Those laws also did not address what happens when resources became scarce.

One of the most amazing shifts in the past fifty years is the commitment to cleaning up the environment. No longer are company's allowed to transfer the cost of environmental degradation. Public land and water are to be preserved. Finding the proper balance between the unregulated use of private property and protection of the environment as a whole is difficult. However, the conversation has moved to the forefront of public discourse. Thus, in our treatment of the land, air, and water, our ethical benchmark has been raised.

Technology is challenging our traditional understanding of property. While ownership of a coat or a book is clear-cut, ownership of electronically transmitted data is more problematic. One of the ironies of the day is that young Republican students, while aligning themselves with the party which historically has defended the right to private property by asserting the primacy of negative rights, vigorously defend their right to download music and make copies of movies. While staunchly maintaining the right to use their physical property as they see fit, they do not seem to notice that taking someone else's cyber-property is theft. A related question is the right protection of copyrights and patents which protect innovation. As the cost of pharmaceuticals increases, those who need the drugs ask whether a company has a right to set prices so high in one market (*e.g.*, the United States) that those who need the medications cannot afford them while the cost is less in another national market (*e.g.*, Canada), And yet, even those lower prices makes medication unattainable in a third world county in Africa. As the costs for payment are shifted to third parties in the form of insurance, the traditional regulators of the market do not work.

Right Use of Power

We must be ever vigilant to assure that greed and the quest for power greed don't corrupt individuals and organizations. While a market economy appears to be the best economic model for maximizing the wealth of individuals and for increasing the well-being of the overall society, unregulated capitalism has the power to economically destroy many individuals while benefiting a few. A key critique of the ethical theory of Mill and the corresponding economic model of Smith is that issues of distribution of resources are not considered.

Ethics and public policy constrain the individual acquisition of wealth and power to assure that the whole community can thrive. As we work to maintain the proper calibration between individual initiative and socially imposed restraints, we need to remember that American capitalism is just one expression of this economic model. As public policy experts work to find the best way to harness the benefit of capitalism while moderating for its excesses, we can learn from the other economic models which are tailored to assure that cultural differences are acknowledged while the various economies flourish.[6]

Even in light of the different versions of capitalism, Alice Rivlin, former vice chair of the Board of Governors of the Federal Reserve System and director of the White House Office of Management and Budget, notes that three tensions make public policy in a capitalistic economy difficult (1) if markets are to work, agreed upon rules must be in place to govern the right use of people, property, and power, (2) social, environmental, and other public policies must be in place to keep people and companies from shifting the cost of business from themselves to others, and (3) we have public goods such as "armies and navies, police, roads, parks, and public health services — that private investors operating on their own will not provide."[7] Rivlin reminds us that we must constantly tinker with our policies as conditions change. To effectively manage the process, as individuals in community we must attend to the overarching goal of our community: working to assure that individuals can thrive while the community remains strong. Rivlin notes that at this particular time in history we have three dilemmas:

> First, how do we make capitalism work better for people in the bottom quarter or third of the distribution of skill, education, income, and luck?...Second...[i]rresponsible behavior and corporate excesses abuse trust in egregious ways — not just trust in one company, but trust in the whole system...If [people working hard for low wages] come to believe that the system is corrupt, that the bosses lie and cheat and make out like bandits at the expense of hard-working folks, something very fundamental is lost...Third, [how do we assure that] our commitment to private decisions and the profit motive [doesn't get] in the way of recognizing that there are things we need government to do or at least to organize.[8]

Depending where we are in the boom-bust economic cycle, one of these three perennial dilemmas will move to center stage while the others might be in the shadows.

Mirroring Rivlin's concerns, when asked whether companies are more ethical or less ethical than they were fifty years ago, many point to the imbalance of salaries and benefits between those at the top of the corporate ladder and those in the middle and the bottom as a prime indicator of business ethics out of skew. During the 1970s, the difference in salaries between the top and the bottom of organizations was the narrowest that it has ever been. Interestingly, that period also was the high-water mark of unionization. While in the 1970s inequities existed between the salaries of women and minorities, the difference between the top and bottom for white males was often a variable of thirty or less. Thus, the CEO of an organization would make no more than thirty times the salary of the lowest paid person in the organization. Currently, for many companies the variable is exponential.[9] Thus, even though the gap between men's and women's salaries is shrinking, that overall reduction in differential is caused by a general decrease in men's salaries rather than an increase women's.

The issue is not simple. When we only look at the economy of the United States we have concerns about eroding salaries and soft jobs as employment opportunities are moved overseas. When we look at the global resource distribution, we realize that by comparison, virtually all of us in the United States are very wealthy indeed. The conundrum of appropriate balance between individual initiative and equality of opportunity and result becomes even more difficult to solve.

Increasing Complexity as We Move to a Global Economy

At the beginning of the Industrial Revolution (approximately the 1850s), organizations were small and thus easy to manage. Because family-based businesses are not complex, congruity between individual and community values and business practices was simple. Further, because the communities were also small and mobility was low, people knew each other, and so the social relationships provided constraints on unethical business practices. While we had international trade, the scale was relatively small and information about different markets was very limited.

By the beginning of the 20th century, corporations became more complex as they began to reap economic gain from realizing economies of scale. The number of employees grew and the financial structures became more intricate. In order to manage the changes, the discipline of scientific management was developed which increased efficiency but had the unintended result of depersonalizing workers. As the economic well-being of the United States began to increase, given our comparatively unregulated market, we continued to outpace other national markets in terms of overall economic growth. Two landmark pieces of legislation militated against the tendency toward greed and kept the power relationships among key stakeholders in balance: the antitrust legislation of the 1890s and the legislation legitimizing and regulating unionization of the 1930s.

Equilibrium was reached in the 1950s and 1960s as the power relationships between employers and employees equalized as unionization and industrialization matured. World War II had given us an opportunity for unprecedented economic growth. With the industrial decimation of our primary competitor Europe, we had two decades of near global monopoly power. However, three interrelated events threw the US out of balance. We found ourselves mirroring the events and the disquiet of the emergence of the Industrial Revolution, that period called the Gilded Age and populated with Robber Barons and huddled masses.

First, in the early 1990s we had the information and technology revolution. Whole new industries came to the fore which were not anticipated and thus not regulated. With personal computers, e-mail, the Internet, and wireless telephones, people had the ability to connect almost instantaneously to all corners of the world, to all information sources, and to all markets. With video telephones, news and images moved in matters of seconds across the globe. The ability to track prices and market fluctuations on Wall Street and international markets revolutionalized the interconnectivity of the world economy. Advances in medicine meant that we were able to militate against disease and death in ways that were absolutely unforeseen. The expectations and policies which were in place for an industrial economy did not meet the needs of the new wired community.

Second, the monopoly status of the United States was challenged by the growth of the manufacturing capacity of other countries. After World War II, Japan began the challenge as it embraced technology and a commitment to quality. As other Asian countries have developed their manufacturing and technical capabilities, jobs have started moving off-shore to take advantage of the lower wage scales. The tension is palpable: as consumers we love keeping prices low; as employees we mistrust the insecurity of competition with a global workforce.

The fluidity of information provided by technology radically increases the availability of both a global workforce and marketplace. When x-rays can be digitally sent to India to be read overnight with results back in the offices of American physicians the next business day, defining the norms of business ethics becomes challenging. As patients we love having good information available for our doctors at a lower price; if we are the workers who have been displaced, we are not as sanguine about the turn of events.

Finally, access to the stock market became democratized. In 1952 only 4% of Americans owned stock, either directly or through mutual or pension funds. By 2000, 48.8% of all families owned corporate stock.[10] Further, even those in who made less than $10,000 per year increased their ownership from 5.4% in 1995 to 7.7% in 1998.[11] Stock ownership for African-Americans grew from 26% in 1998 to 37% in 2001, while ownership for Anglo-American families remained relatively flat at 51%. Even though African-Americans are still less likely to invest than White Americans, clearly the trend indicates a growing interest in investments.[12] With an increase in stock ownership, much of it in pension funds, the need for financial transparency became even greater.

At the end of the 20th century, burgeoning technology created new sources of wealth, which mirrored the increase of wealth which came as steel mills, the Tin Lizzie, and electricity burst upon the scene at the end of the 19th century. The scientific breakthroughs of the early 20th century changed our understanding of the physical as well as our social world and paved the way for the technological innovations that transformed our world at the end of the century.

Our new Einsteinian world view opens for us a world that is more complex than that of our great-grandparents. Thus, we must rearticulate the norms and traditions of the past as we create the narrative of the present to learn to live effectively. We have to find new ways to balance the four core values to restrain greed and abuse of power — but this time in a global context. Like learning to see a fractal emerge from a random data set, we must learn to see the beauty of complexity in the seemingly random chaos which surrounds us.

Embracing Complexity and Moving Toward Wisdom

Those who are uncomfortable with the ambiguity of complexity want to return to what seemed to be the certainty of the principles by which our fathers and mothers lived, the perceived glory days of America. However, as seen above, even a cursory review of our economic history reveals that the "good old days" weren't quite as good as we would like to believe.

One proffered solution is to reduce everything to rules — when we have a perceived breach of ethics, we just enact more rules and regulations to tell us what to do. However, as noted in the earlier chapters, the law and its enforcement mechanisms are not designed to answer every question. In addition, we also know that because the world and its values are pluralistic, no one set of rules or norms will be acceptable to all. We also find evidence, even in the annals of recent human history, that excessive regulation will stifle economic and technological progress. The other extreme, letting everyone do what he or she believes is best is also not the answer. Both individuals and organizations need to know the size of the sandbox in which they play: what boundaries constrain acts and what behavior is not acceptable. As we have seen in our romp through ethics, the size of the sandbox is established in ongoing conversations about how we should calibrate the balance among the four core value sets.

Our current conversation thus becomes a variation on an old theme, a conversation introduced into Western thought by Plato and Aristotle. One set of individuals believes that we just need to find the ideals, those timeless principles which endure for all people at all times. Another set believes that we have to use our reason and skill to solve the concrete problems of this life. Both conversations are useful in determining what to do with the difficult decisions that lie before us as we determine how best to live and thrive in the emerging global economy.

Whether we must deal with the employee who manages to fight with everyone, the cantankerous consumer who buys a prom dress on Friday and returns it soiled on Monday claiming that "it just doesn't fit," or training our replacement from China, most of us need *both* principles to give us ethical touchstones for our lives *and* prudential judgment to help us apply those principles to an ever changing kaleidoscope of circumstances. As we learn to exercise sound ethical discretion, we take the best of our ideals and test them against the situations in which we find ourselves. In the process, we learn the habits of thinking and patterns of acting which help us live out our dreams for ourselves, our organizations, and our world.

The goal of ethical maturity is the ability to know when to absolutely follow the rules and when to bend them a tad and exercise mercy. Reviewing the tensions implicit in our core value sets, we note that the wise leaders of our community are those who know how to appropriately and effectively balance between autonomy — the needs of individuals, and equality — the needs of the group. When making decisions, those who are deemed wise use the resources of rationality — their minds and tested principles, as well as sensibility — their emotions and prudential judgment.

Principles and Prudential Judgment

Beginning with the law as the threshold, our society has stated that these statutes and proscriptions cannot be violated without substantial penalty. We have one set of laws which articulate seemingly universal principles, *e.g.*, thou shalt not murder, thou shalt not steal. For these laws, the question is in what limited circumstances violating these norms might be excused or justified. We have another set of laws which define the rules of the game — what taxes we have to pay, what limitations to impose on polluting, what structure is permissible for organizations. For these set of rules, business people often effectively play the edges between acceptable and unacceptable behavior. Drawing on football, one of our central metaphors for business, many believe the adage, "No harm, no foul." At the public policy level, society acting through our representatives, determines the balance among the non-negotiable norms of the community, the tweaking of rules and goals to meet changing circumstances, and the establishment of conceptions of the core values to respond to totally new paradigms.

Another level of decision making concerns the range of legal activities which have unequal ethical gravitas. The most difficult ethical choices are between two or more options, all of which are legal. In these cases, which have been the focal point of this book, the core values and resulting commitments need to be carefully weighed as choices are prudently made.

For these decisions, business ethicist Robert Spitzer distinguishes between the silver rule — the ethical minimum, and the golden rule — the ethical maximum. The silver rule defines our ethical boundary, which often mirrors the legal requirements. This set of ethical rules is proscriptive — "thou shall not..." By following these rules we aim to minimize the harm we do to others. The mantra for the silver rule is "Do not do unto others as you would not have them do unto you." The golden rule is the ethical maximum. This set of rules are prescriptive — "thou shall..." By following these rules we seek to maximize the good we can do. The mantra for the golden rule is "Do the good to others that you would want them to do to you."[13]

In exercising prudential judgment, the first step is to know the parameters of the silver and gold rules. The logical requirements of each determine the boundaries for the available, appropriate ethical options. Then, depending on the circumstances and the resources available, we choose an action which meets the requirements of the silver rule while reaching toward the golden rule. Depending on the problem before us and the constraints of an organization, we may opt for the silver rule as a way to assure that the needs of the majority of the stakeholders is met. For other times we may find that the golden rule is more appropriate as we are able to be generous and proactive to meet the needs of the community. In the process we use both the ideals and intuitions of the deontological tradition and the reality and insights of the teleological tradition in assessing our options and making a prudential judgment about which of the available ethical options we will choose.

The Interplay of Intuition and Insight

A persistent conversation in ethics is whether our intuition is useful in making our ethical decisions. This conversation was initiated by Plato who asserted that humans intuit the ideal forms which then provides guidance for ethical decision making. The counter-point was provided by Aristotle who asserted that empiricism and logic were the fountainhead of knowledge for ethical decisions. Aristotle asserted that our minds "alone gave man the intuitive capacity to grasp final and universal truths."[14] As this conversation has evolved over the ensuing 2500 years, no resolution is in sight. However, for purposes of applied business ethics, both schools of thought are useful.

The first role of intuition is sensing that something may not be right. While all of us have different thresholds of ethical sensibility, we need to assure that our antennae are always tuned to the ethical implications of an act. As our community continues to mature, behaviors which were acceptable yesterday may not meet ethical muster tomorrow. Part of having a well-honed sense of ethics is noticing what is on the horizon — where are the norms about to change. A commentator noted that at the time that Ken Lay and other Enron executives engaged in their creative financing, close to 95% of what they did was perfectly legal. As the implications of the edge of the law became manifest, the edge moved. Now, under the requirements of Sarbanes-Oxley, the behavior is no longer legal.

Once we sense that something may not be right, we can use the tools of our reason to sort out whether or not our instincts are in fact accurate. Using the spiral of Lonergan's process, we can work through what we know and begin to inventory what we know and ask good questions. At the point that our mind no longer has answers, if we wait quietly, we get what Lonergan calls "insight" — in a sense informed intuition. We see connections that we did not see before; we understand the world in a way that we could not before.

Once we have an insight, the cycle begins again. Our intuition is informed by a new experience, and we see new data and have other pieces of information which do or do not fit. We have a novel situation that requires a new ethical analysis. We come to this decision with the information from the past. Nothing is lost, but with the new decision another layer of wisdom and understanding is added.

As we thoughtfully and intentionally move back and forth between intuition and insight, we learn to live with integrity and grace. We are able to have a sense of our core identity and know both the principles that we will follow and the goals that are important to us. We are able to see that we sometimes do the right thing and sometimes we miss the mark. Hopefully, in the middle we learn to laugh at ourselves and at the wonder and mystery of life. The world of business is the place where we buy and sell goods and provide services to each other. In the marketplace our gifts are recognized and we contribute to the well being of the planet while we grow in wisdom and understanding. In our scurrying for wealth, power, and prestige, many of us take ourselves much too seriously and forget to live our lives with joy. One of my favorite definitions of vocation is that place where our heart's desire meets the world's greatest need. As we move from seeing our work as just a job to embracing it as vocation, we find great joy and the world can become just a tad bit better.

Conclusion — The Wisdom of the Tao

As we bring our journey to a close, the Tao Te Ching 8 provides a marvelous metaphor for the world of business and summarizes nicely the paths we have walked.

> The highest good is like water.
> Water gives life to the ten thousand things and does not strive.
> It flows in places men reject and so is like the Tao.

As we look at the history of business, we see that civilization grew along the trade routes. In the process of buying and selling, people traveled through wonderful new lands and encountered different ways of living and contextualizing the world. The world of business is not the world of conflict; it is the world of friendship. Business does not particularly care about national borders — it goes where the money is green and people have needs and desires that can be met. Business thrives on friendly competition and networks of relationships, not asking about religion or politics if the deal would be jeopardized. Yet, business, like water shaping the land, powerfully molds our culture. We enjoy the products, revel in the technology, and our lives are never again quite the same.

> In dwelling, be close to the land.

One of the observations about Ken Lay and company is that they forgot that they were selling energy. Rather than focusing on their core competencies, they got excited about moving money around and seeing if they could sell the proverbial "blue sky." Many companies have failed because it forgot to attend to their customers — they moved away from "the land." The tension is staying tuned to the present while anticipating the future. The Tao reminds us to live in the present as we attend to our business and stay connected with both our product and our community.

> In meditation, go deep in the heart.

One of the critiques of business is that we have made each other objects rather than people. As we go deep into our hearts, we notice the essential humanity of each person and cannot treat either ourselves or those with whom we work as invisible cogs in a machine. Psychologists have opined that the heart attacks of executives that seem to plague those who are in their 50s and 60s are caused as much by the shutting down the emotions as well as the physical stress. Denying their connection to their deeper selves and to the rest of the community, the heart seizes as it breaks.[15] As we learn to go deep within our hearts we find the balance that keeps us sane in the frenzy of the business world.

> In dealing with others, be just and kind.
> In speech, be true.

Every ethical theory has at its core the admonition of the Tao. While our situations are complex, a handful of core principles often provide the necessary lodestars. When Robert Spitzer is invited to consult with corporations about ethics, he works through a process where the participants reduce their own and organization's principles to four or five key questions that they ask in every difficult situations. These questions often deal with justice, kindness, and integrity. Each of us should have a concrete sense of when we would rather be unemployed than do something which goes against our core ethical values.

In business, be competent.
In action, watch the timing

No fight: no blame.

The first step towards becoming an effective ethical actor is to continuously become better at what we do. As we exercise prudential judgment, we notice when to act and when to become silent. Aikido is one of the most effective forms of martial arts because practitioners are trained to deflect an attack rather than meeting it straight on. By watching the opponent and then moving to throw him off balance, the athlete both conserves energy and is victorious. In the world of business as we learn to know ourselves, be clear about our principles, and move intentionally toward the greater good, we become masters of ourselves and leaders in our communities. In the process we find that ethics is about how we live every day. We then are able to make hard choices in a complex world with integrity, grace, and a dollop of frivolity.

Continuing the Conversation

1. Do you think that business as a whole is more or less ethical than it was fifty years ago? What do you see as evidence that it is more ethical than it was in the mid-1950s? What do you see as evidence that it is less ethical than it was in the mid-1950s?

2. How do you see the balance between the silver rule and the golden rule of business? Find an example in contemporary business where choices were based within the parameters of each of these rules. Does the balance chosen by the company make sense to you?

3. Do the words of the Tao Te Ching 8 resonate with you? How do you see your own journey either mirroring or contradicting the wisdom of the Tao?

Appendices

Appendix A Core Ethical Frameworks 309
Appendix B From Ethics to Law 325
Appendix C Rational and Relational Ethics 331
Appendix D Excellence and Efficiency 337

Appendix A

Core Ethical Frameworks

The Rights/Responsibility Lens

Core Questions for Completing an Ethical Analysis using a Rights/Relationship Ethics (Deontological) Framework

- *Core Contextual Question:* What are my rights and responsibilities?
- *Core Ethical Question:* What are my motives? To whom do I owe what?
- *Core Moral Question:* What is an emotionally mature, caring response?
- *Core Spiritual Question:* What is my relationship to the sacred?

Communicating the Decision

As you come to resolution about a problem, consider how your decision will be communicated to those who will be affected by your decision. A useful exercise is to write a short memo that will be circulated to the affected constituents or a press release which will explain your decision. The following questions provide a template for the memo. As the decision is communicated, the reader should be able to tell what criteria were important in your decision.

- *What was the problem?* The reader should be able to tell from one or two sentences what the problem was that the decision maker had to resolve.
- *What was the issue?* The reader should know what particular ethical values were in conflict by the framing of the issue.
- *What choice was made?* The reader should know exactly what action was being taken.
- *What criteria were used in making the decision?* The reader should get a sense of how this decision assures that you meet the requirements of your duties, your responsibilities, as well as embrace your rights. What are your motives? Are you treating people the way that they have agreed to be treated? As the anticipated effects of the decision are shared, the results should be contextualized in light of commonly accepted negative rights and duties. In drafting this statement, see how many of the considerations of the lens can be folded into the rationale.
- *Conclusion.* The report ends with a brief concluding statement which points the group towards consensus.

Template for Complete Ethical Analysis Using a Rights/Responsibility Ethics (Deontological) Framework

- *Be Attentive* (two to three coherent paragraphs)
  - *What was the problem?* In a coherent paragraph, set the context for the problem so the reader knows what the problem you need to resolve.
  - *Who is the ethical actor?* Who or what group will be taking the action in this particular problem?
  - *Who are the stakeholders?* What are the express and implied agreements that you have with each of the constituents?
- *Be Intelligent* (two to three coherent paragraphs)

- ▹ *What is the very specific issue to be resolved?* State the issue in the form of a question. Make sure the question is an ethical question, not a technical question about how to do a job, or a matter of personal preference.

- ▹ *What are the values-in-conflict?* What are the conflicts concerning the right treatment of people? What are the conflicts in the right use of property? What are the conflicts concerning the right use of power (how have your agreements been met)?

- ▹ *What are the options?* Identify the options available to the ethical actor.

► *Be Reasonable* (work the process for at least three options to the problem)

- ▹ *Apply the ethical content.*

    - ▷ *What is the reason* for adopting this option?

    - ▷ *What would happen* if everyone adopted this reason for acting?

    - ▷ *Are you willing* to have someone else use this reason in deciding how they will treat you or your organization?

    - ▷ *If you adopt this option*, are you treating people the way that they have freely consented to be treated? Are you helping them in their own process of becoming fully functioning adults who can make their own choices?

    - ▷ *How does this option meet* the requirements of traditional and personal ethical principles?

- ▹ *Overlay the moral content.*

    - ▷ How does this option demonstrate caring for the other person, both in what you do and how you do it?

► *Be Responsible* (two to three coherent paragraphs)

- ▹ *Explain why you rejected* two of the options which you evaluated. In the process, weigh the relative merits of each of the options and briefly explain why the rejected options did not meet the requirements of this ethical lens.

- *Briefly recapitulate* why the final choice best meets the requirements of the lens. How did you attend to balance and work to avoid the hubris which might be present in the lens?

  - *How does this option assure* that your rights and responsibilities, as well as those of your constituents, are honored?

  - *How does this decision help* people become more effective and responsible persons in our community?

  - *How does this decision assure* that you have corrected for personal bias and avoided acting only from cold reason without attending to the emotional side of the issue?

- *Return to Awareness.*

  - *Discuss whether or not the ethical analysis made sense.* Did you like the result? What were the problems with the process? What are the sticking points? How did you see the process enhanced or modified by adding the world of emotion and conscience?

  - *Consider the spiritual perspective.* As you begin to see yourself in light of the larger community, how can you (and others in the organization) begin to discipline your desires so you can live fully in the present with faith and trust, thus avoiding self-righteousness?

The Results Lens

Core Questions for Completing an Ethical Analysis Using a Results Ethics (Teleological/Consequential) Framework

- *Core Contextual Question:* What results do I want to achieve?
- *Core Ethical Question:* What are good results?
- *Core Moral Question: What are mutually good results for all?*
- *Core Spiritual Question:* How can I be a partner in creating a better world?

Communicating the Decision

As you come to resolution about a problem, consider how your decision will be communicated to those who will be affected by your decision. A useful exercise is to write a short memo that will be circulated to the affected constituents or a press release which will explain your decision. The following questions provide a template for the memo. As the decision is communicated, the reader should be able to tell what criteria were important in your decision.

- *What was the problem*? The reader should be able to tell from one or two sentences what the problem was that the decision maker had to resolve.

- *What was the issue?* The reader should know what particular ethical values were in conflict by the framing of the issue.

- *What choice was made?* The reader should know exactly what action was being taken.

- *What criteria were used in making the decision?* The reader should get a sense of how this decision assures that the choice provides the greatest good for the greatest number, both in terms of short-term needs as well as ideal goals. As the anticipated effects of the decision are shared, the results should be contextualized in light of the ideal goals of the organization, efficiency as well as excellence. In drafting this statement, see how many of the considerations of the lens can be folded into the rationale.

- *Conclusion.* The report ends with a brief concluding statement which points the group towards consensus.

Template for Complete Ethical Analysis Using a Results Ethics (Teleological/Consequential) Framework

- *Be Attentive* (two to three coherent paragraphs)
  - *What was the problem?* In a coherent paragraph, set the context for the problem so the reader knows what the problem you need to resolve.
  - *Who is the ethical actor?* Who or what group will be taking the action in this particular problem?
  - *Who are the stakeholders?* Roughly how many are in each of the discrete stakeholder groups? What will make them happy in this particular instance? What are their non-negotiables? What are the tipping-points which need to be considered?
- *Be Intelligent* (two to three coherent paragraphs)
  - *What is the specific issue to be resolved?* State the issue in the form of a question. Make sure the question is an ethical question, not a technical question about how to do a job, or a matter of personal preference.
  - *What are the values-in-conflict?* What are the conflicts in the goals of the various constituents? What are the conflicts in the right use of property? What are the conflicts concerning the right use of power (what are the considerations in meeting the goals of efficiency and excellence)?
  - *What are the options?* Identify the options available to the ethical actor.
- *Be Reasonable* (work the process for at least three options to the problem)
  - *Identify what will make each group of stakeholders happy.* What are the non-negotiables? What are the tipping points? Be sure to consider both short-term as well as long-term, ideal, goals.
  - *Apply the ethical content.*
    - *Working through each option*, how happy will this option make each constituent group?
    - *Working through each option*, after multiplying the utils of happiness for each group against the influence factor, how many weighted utils of happiness are generated for each constituent group?

- ▷ *What is the total* of the weighted utils of happiness which is generated for this option?

- ▷ *Which option* generated the highest total number of weighted utils of happiness?

▶ *Overlay the moral content.*

- ▷ *Evaluating the options* in light of complex harmonized satisfactions, does the option with the highest utils of happiness also attend to as many of the interests of the constituents as possible? Would a slightly more complex solution meet the needs of more of the constituents?

▶ *Be Responsible* (two to three coherent paragraphs)

- ▶ *Explain why you rejected* two of the options which you evaluated. In the process, weigh the relative merits of each of the options and briefly explain why the rejected options did not meet the requirements of this ethical lens.

- ▶ *Briefly recapitulate* why the final choice best meets the requirements of the lens. How did you attend to balance and work to avoid the hubris which might be present in the lens?

  - ▷ *How does this option* preserve the right of each individual to choose how best to live at the same time that the option meets the greatest good for the greatest number?

  - ▷ *How does this decision* demonstrate the qualities of a creative leader who strives for efficiency and excellence? In a coherent paragraph, indicate how you have corrected for personal bias and used imagination to maintain respect for others while living with ambiguity.

▶ *Return to Awareness.*

- ▶ *Discuss whether or not the ethical analysis made sense.* Did you like the result? What were the problems with the process? What are the sticking points? How did you see the process enhanced or modified by adding the world of emotion and conscience?

- *Consider the spiritual perspective.* Can you see yourself as part of a community, working with others to provide opportunities which allow people to take responsibility for their choices while living with optimism and hope? How can you continue to cultivate the spiritual discipline of detachment, so you can learn to be flexible as you make personal choices and fashion public policy?

The Relationship Lens

Core Questions for Completing an Ethical Analysis Using a Relationship Ethics (Justice Ethics) Framework

- *Core Contextual Question:* How do I fit?
- *Core Ethical Question:* What is a fair system?
- *Core Moral Question:* What is correct subordination of my rights to the group?
- *Core Spiritual Question:* What is my place in the web of life?

Communicating the Decision

As you come to resolution about a problem, consider how your decision will be communicated to those who will be affected by your decision. A useful exercise is to write a short memo that will be circulated to the affected constituents or a press release which will explain your decision. The following questions provide a template for the memo. As the decision is communicated, the reader should be able to tell what criteria were important in your decision.

- *What was the problem?* The reader should be able to tell from one or two sentences what the problem was that you had to resolve.

- *What was the issue?* The reader should know what particular ethical values were in conflict by the framing of the issue.

- *What choice was made?* The reader should know exactly what action was being taken.

- *What criteria were used in making the decision?* The reader should get a sense of how this decision assures that the requirements of procedural fairness as well as substantive fairness were met. As the anticipated effects of the decision are shared, the results should be contextualized in light of the access to information, equal access to opportunity, and attending to the concerns of the least advantaged. In drafting this statement, see how many of the considerations of the lens can be folded into the rationale.

- *Conclusion.* The report ends with a brief concluding statement which points the group towards consensus.

Template for Complete Ethical Analysis Using a Relationship Ethics (Justice Ethics) Framework

- *Be Attentive* (two to three coherent paragraphs)
    - *What was the problem?* In a coherent paragraph, set the context for the problem so the reader knows what the problem you need to resolve.
    - *Who is the ethical actor?* Who or what group will be taking the action in this particular problem?
    - *Who are the stakeholders?* What access to knowledge, resources, and power do each of the stakeholders have? Who is the least advantaged?
- *Be Intelligent* (two to three coherent paragraphs)
    - *What is the very specific issue to be resolved?* State the issue in the form of a question to be answered. The person making the decision must make sure the question is an ethical question, not a technical question about how to do a job, or a matter of personal preference.
    - *What are the values-in-conflict?* Make a preliminary identification of the values in conflict. What are the conflicts in the right treatment of people? What are the conflicts in the right use of property? What are the conflicts concerning the right use of power (how have those who do not have access to information, resources, or autonomy been protected)?
    - *What are the options?* Identify the options available to the ethical actor.
- *Be Reasonable* (work the process for at least three options to the problem)
    - *Apply the ethical content.*
        - *What are the basic liberties* to which each constituent is entitled? Should a process be put in place to assure that each constituent has information as well as a voice in the decision?
        - *How well does each option* meet the requirements of the "just savings principle?"
        - *How well does each option* make sure that social and economic inequalities are arranged so that all constituents have an equal opportunity for success?

▷ *How does each option* benefit the least advantaged?

▷ *Using the tool of reflective equilibrium*, which option gives the best advantage to the least advantaged without unduly burdening those who are the most advantaged?

▶ *Overlay the moral content.*

▷ *How well does each option contribute* to an ecology of care? How does each option assure linkage, diversity, homeostatic success, as well as community?

▶ *Be Responsible* (two to three coherent paragraphs)

▶ *Explain why you rejected* at least two of the options you evaluated. In the process, weigh the relative merits of each of the options and briefly explain why the rejected options did not meet the requirements of this ethical lens.

▶ *Briefly recapitulate* why the final choice best meets the requirements of the lens. How did you attend to balance and work to avoid the hubris which might be present in the lens?

▷ *How does this option* achieve procedural justice - a fair process - as well as substantive justice - a fair result?

▷ *How does this decision* show a commitment to the least advantaged?

▷ *How does this decision* assure that you have corrected for personal bias and avoided "group-think" and entrainment?

▶ *Return to Awareness*

▶ *Discuss whether or not the ethical analysis made sense*. Did you like the result? What were the problems with the process? What are the sticking points? How did you see the process enhanced or modified by adding the world of emotion and conscience?

▶ *Consider the spiritual perspective.* How did this process help you see yourself as connected to the whole web of life? Are you able to understand how you are connected to the other members of the community? How can you continue to practice the spiritual discipline of seeing that all are connected as you embrace generosity and forgiveness while balancing independence with interdependence?

The Reputation Lens

Core Questions for Completing an Ethical Analysis Using a Reputation Ethics (Virtue Ethics) Framework

- *Core Contextual Question:* Who am I?
- *Core Ethical Question:* What are the virtues necessary for a good character?
- *Core Moral Question:* What is a compassionate person?
- *Core Spiritual Question:* How do I celebrate the fact that I am special... just like everyone else?

Communicating the Decision

As you come to resolution about a problem, consider how your decision will be communicated to those who will be affected by the decision. A useful exercise is to write a short memo that will be circulated to the affected constituents or a press release which will explain your decision. The following questions provide a template for the memo. As the decision is communicated, the reader should be able to tell what criteria were important in your decision.

- *What was the problem?* The reader should be able to tell from one or two sentences what the problem was that you had to resolve.

- *What was the issue?* The reader should know what particular ethical values were in conflict by the framing of the issue.

- *What choice was made?* The reader should know exactly what action was being taken.

- *What criteria were used in making the decision?* The reader should get a sense of how this decision assures that the competencies are met, the virtues enhanced, and the end of life goals advanced. As the anticipated effects of the decision are shared, the results should be contextualized in light of the competencies and virtues of the organization. In drafting this statement, see how many of the considerations of the lens can be folded into the rationale.

- *Conclusion.* The report ends with a brief concluding statement which points the group towards consensus.

Template for Complete Ethical Analysis Using a Reputation Ethics (Virtue Ethics) Framework

- *Be Attentive* (two to three coherent paragraphs)
  - *What was the problem?* In a coherent paragraph, set the context for the problem so the reader knows what the problem you need to resolve.
  - *Who is the ethical actor?* Who or what group will be taking the action in this particular problem?
  - *Who are the stakeholders?* What are their expectations for the ethical actor? What do they believe are the core competencies of the ethical actor? What do they expect of themselves?
  - *What is the context and what are the assumptions?* What is the narrative of the organization which needs to be considered in this problem? What are the underlying assumptions which drive the conversation?
- *Be Intelligent* (two to three coherent paragraphs)
  - *What is the very specific issue to be resolved?* State the issue in the form of a question to be answered. The person making the decision must make sure the question is an ethical question, not a technical question about how to do a job, or a matter of personal preference.
  - *What are the values-in-conflict?* As you consider the requirements of your role, what are the conflicts in the right treatment of people? What are the conflicts in the right use of property? What are the conflicts concerning the right use of power (what virtues need to be considered in this decision)?
  - *What are the options?* Identify the options available to the ethical actor.
- *Be Reasonable* (work the process for at least three options to the problem.)
  - *Identify the competencies.* Make a preliminary assessment of your options. Reject any option which does not meet the threshold requirements of competence.
    - *What are the components* as defined by the ethical actor?

- ▷ *What are the standards* of excellence?
- ▷ *What are the rules* of the practice?
- ▷ *What are the internal goods* which are important?
- ▷ *What are the external goods* which are important?
- ▷ *What do the constituents* expect of the ethical actor?

▶ *Apply the ethical content.*

- ▷ *Evaluating the options* in light of the virtues, which option best embodies the virtues, and why?
- ▷ *Evaluating the options* in light of the unity of life, which option best meets the requirements of the ethical actor's unity of life?

▶ *Overlay the moral content.*

- ▷ *Evaluating the options* in light of one's conscience, one's commitment to self-management, which option best meets the requirements of the ethical actor's understanding of who he/she is as a complete person?

▶ *Be Responsible* (two to three coherent paragraphs)

▶ *Explain why you rejected* at least two of the options which you evaluated. In the process, weigh the relative merits of each of the options and briefly explain why the rejected options did not meet the requirements of this ethical lens.

▶ *Briefly recapitulate* why the final choice best meets the requirements of the lens. How did you attend to balance and work to avoid the hubris which might be present in the lens?

- ▷ *What respected human qualities* and virtues are demonstrated by this decision? How does this decision demonstrate the qualities and virtues that a person who is respected in this role has (competence, loyalty, diligence, fairness, etc.)?
- ▷ *How does this decision demonstrate* the qualities of a person in this profession or vocation?

- *Return to Awareness.*

  - *Discuss whether or not the ethical analysis made sense.* Did you like the result? What were the problems with the process? What are the sticking points? How did you see the process enhanced or modified by adding the world of emotion and conscience?

  - *Consider the spiritual perspective.* Where are you prone to not seeing your gifts and when are you tempted to see yourself as more special than others? Is it difficult to consider that you are special...just like everyone else? Are you able to see intrinsic value in each person?

Appendix B

From Ethics to Law: Responsibility and Accountability

Six Levels of Responsibility

Personal Ethical Beliefs and Actions

The first level of responsibility and accountability springs from the personal beliefs and values that I have about what kind of a person I want to be and what I will do. While these are formed in community, in the final analysis we each have a set of commitments and values which we embrace and determine how we will choose to live in community.

Community Ethical Beliefs and Values

The second level of responsibility and accountability flows from the community expectations for me, both as a person and as a professional. These are shared values which can come from the family, religious communities, ethnic and cultural communities, as well as professional communities.

Organizational Codes of Ethics

Rules for members of the organization that are created by a business or legislative body (legislature, city council) which lay out the expected behaviors in key problem areas form the third level of responsibility and accountability. These are often developed by those who are part of the organization and provide the organizational norms which guide the behavior of members of the group.

Legislative Regulations

The regulations that are passed by a local community, state legislature, or Congress or their administrative agencies which all people must follow form the fourth level of responsibility and accountability. These regulations tell people what standards they must follow and work to provide a level playing field for people in the community. These regulations are enforced by the judicial system. These rules have the impact of law but may not exceed the authority of the law passed by the legislative body which gives the administrative agency permission to develop the rules.

Civil Law

The fifth level of accountability and responsibility is found in laws that are passed by a local community, state legislature, or Congress which all people must follow. These also include the common law, rules which are enforced by the state judicial systems which are not written (libel, slander, malpractice, etc.).

Criminal Law

Ordinances and statutes enacted by a local government, state legislature, or Congress which all people must follow form the final, sixth, level of responsibility and accountability.

Content of the Rules

The rules and expectations of each of these diverse groups have different content - the specific behavior which is allowed or prohibited takes different forms. For persons-in-community, the perennial tension is harmonizing among individual values and the restraints imposed by community values. If the dissonance between the individual values of the majority and the rules of the community is too great, the community risks unrest or revolution.

Personal Code	*Community Values*	*Organizational Code*	*Legislative Regulations*	*Civil Law*	*Criminal Law*
Rules, informal/ unwritten rules. Results I want to accomplish. Relationships to nurture. Virtues/character to develop.	Informal or unwritten rules that all should follow. Results we want to accomplish as a community. Relationships that are important to maintain. Reputation which matches the group's understanding of itself and its members.	Mission and vision statements. Organizational and individual goals. Employee handbook which states all of the norms and organizational rules. Property laws safety requirements (OSHA), labeling (FDA), proper land use (zoning).	Laws about people: equal access (American's with Disabilities Act) and treatment (minimum wage laws). Laws limiting use of power: price (utilities) and advertising (FDA and FCC) requirements.	Laws about property: theft, embezzlement. Laws about people: harassment, assault, malpractice. Laws limiting use of power: sexual harassment, intimidation, monopolies.	Laws about property: theft, embezzlement. Laws about people: harassment, assault, murder. Laws limiting use of power: sexual harassment, intimidation, monopolization.

Conundrums:

As we each determine how best we will live as we work and play in various communities, we need to learn how to work with and harmonize the differences. In the process we have some core decisions we must make.

Personal Code	*Community Values*	*Organizational Code*	*Legislative Regulations*	*Civil Law*	*Criminal Law*
Deciding which action matches my moral beliefs and will meet my obligations while achieving my goals. Choosing among conflicting goals and commitments. Deciding what to do when my ethical values conflict with those of the community or employer. Deciding what to do when personal virtues or character conflict with the community or employer.	What action meets predominant community ethical beliefs and values. How to resolve differences between ideas about what is ethical. How to negotiate individual ethics and community values. When to renegotiate public norms when the reputation of the community does not match internal image or self-understanding (e.g. racist, sexist).	Deciding whether one must follow the code of ethics in a particular situation. Deciding whether the particular rule applies to the particular action that one is going to take. Deciding what the rule requires in the particular situation. Deciding what to do if your employer or a constituent requests or requires you to violate the code of conduct.	Knowing what the laws are. These change often and are highly detailed and complex. Keeping up with the regs is sometimes daunting. Knowing what specific behavior will violate the law. Deciding what to do if your employer or a constituent requests or requires you to violate the law.	Knowing what the laws are. Given that these are both part of the common law and change with legislative sessions, keeping up with the changes is hard. Knowing what specific behavior will violate the law. Deciding what to do if your employer or a constituent requests or requires you to violate the law.	Knowing what the laws are. Given that laws can have civil liability and/or criminal penalties, knowing what laws apply and with what consequences is often difficult. Knowing what specific behavior will violate the law. Deciding what to do if an employer requests or requires you to violate the law.

Enforcers

Each set of rules is enforced by various entities. One clear trajectory is that violations of personal codes of ethics are very private whereas the greater the violation of the community norm, the more public and protracted the enforcement. Because the consequences are increasingly severe, the procedural safeguards for each level of enforcement increase.

Personal Code	*Community Values*	*Organizational Code*	*Legislative Regulations*	*Civil Law*	*Criminal Law*
Individuals have a personal set of ethical criteria and norms they will not violate. Our conscience is the primary source of accountability. We also have friends and colleagues who have permission to hold us accountable for our core commitments.	The community enforces its values through such actions as shunning or shaming one who violates community norms. Different communities have appointed people as the guardians of the norms, whether formally or informally.	The board or committee given the responsibility for enforcing the ethical conduct of the members of the community conducts an investigation to determine whether the code was violated. In companies, the HR department is often responsible for the procedural enforcement of the handbook or organizational codes.	The charge is filed by an individual or a state agency which believes an administrative regulation has been breached or a law has been violated. The claim is adjudicated in an administrative hearing or judicial proceeding which determines the validity of the claim.	The charge is filed by an individual who believes a contract has been breached or a law has been violated. The judicial system determines the validity of claims made in a civil lawsuit and the appropriate penalty. In some cases the person charged is entitled to a hearing before a six member jury.	The charge is filed by the state (attorney general, district attorney, or county attorney), after a complaint is filed by an individual or after a grand jury proceeding. The charge is adjudicated by the judicial system in a criminal proceeding. In some cases the person charged is entitled to a hearing before a twelve member jury.

Penalties

The penalty for each level of violation is increasingly severe. While people may hypothesize that others have died (or chosen to commit suicide) because of a guilty conscience, the community itself determines the severity of the penalty. Research into patterns of compliance indicates that, to assure that we follow the law, laws must either be frequently enforced with mild penalties or infrequently enforced with high penalties – large fines or imprisonment. If community norms are infrequently enforced with low penalties, people who do not embrace the norms and are not self-regulating and law-abiding will take the risk of being caught and count on low penalties.

Personal Code	*Community Values*	*Organizational Code*	*Legislative Regulations*	*Civil Law*	*Criminal Law*
Personal sense of failure or guilt. Commitments broken because of short term expedience. Relationships broken because of lack of consistent, ethical behavior. Reputation that does not match what I think is important.	Demoralization of members of the organization. Criticism in the press or among other groups for being "unethical." Relationships broken because of lack of consistent, ethical behavior. Tarnished reputation.	Having disciplinary action taken if the Code of Ethics is violated, including termination. Loss of professional accreditation. Loss of ability to have a contract with the organization.	If found to have breached the regulation or broken the law, a person can have a fine entered against him/her. Loss of license or professional accreditation.	If found to have broken the law, a person can have a money judgment entered against him/her. An injunction (order to not do something) may be imposed.	If found liable, a person can have fines imposed or be sent to jail. If convicted of a felony, one can lose the right to vote and participate in the community. If one is not a citizen, one can be deported upon conviction.

Appendix C

Rational and Relational Ethics

Distinctions Between Rational and Relational Ethics

Lawrence Kohlberg delineated a widely accepted schema for tracking ethical development based on reason - using one's mind to determine the right way to behave in community. Kohlberg's theory was criticized for tending to find that men were more ethically developed than women. Norma Haan, building on the work of Carol Gillian and others, used a different measure for ethical growth and developed a schema for tracking ethical development based on relationship - using one's emotion as a lodestar for how to behave in community. Interestingly, Kohlberg's theories fit nicely with the core assumptions of the deontological theories; Haan's theories fit nicely with the core assumptions of the teleological theories. A comparison of the two theories tends to support a key claim of this text that the effective ethical actor uses both skill sets while moving toward ethical maturity.

* Adapted from Norma Haan, *On Moral Grounds,* p. 55-72.

Content of the Stages of Moral Judgement

The first comparison is the specific content of the two theories. Kohlberg defines the levels by how we respond to the rules of the community; Haan defines the levels by how we maintain social balance between ourselves and others, both individuals and groups.

	Kohlberg - Rules	*Haan - Relationship*
Level 1	*Punishment and Obedience* Right is literal obedience to rules and authority, avoiding punishment, and not doing physical harm.	*A versus B* Vacillates between compliance with others/thwarting others. Balance occurs when self is indifferent to situations, unequal exchanges of good and bad; momentary compromises.
Level 2	*Individual Instrumental Purpose and Exchange* Right is serving one's own or other's needs and making fair deals in terms of concrete exchange.	*Prudential compromises by A & B* Trade to get what self wants; sometimes others must get what they want. Balances of coexistence (equal exchanges of good and bad in kind and amount).
Level 3	*Mutual Interpersonal Expectations, Relationships and Conformity* The right is playing a good (nice) role, being concerned about the other people and their feelings, keeping loyalty and trust with partners, and being motivated to follow rules and expectations.	*A compromises to "good" Bs'; bad Bs rejected.* Emphasis on exchanges is based on sustaining good faith (and excluding bad). Self-interest thought to be identical with others' interests.
Level 4	*Social System and Conscience Maintenance* The right is doing one's duty in society, upholding the social order, and maintaining the welfare of society or the group.	*A and B = AB common* Systematized, structured exchanges based on understanding that all of us can fall from grace. Thus, balances are conscious compromises made by all people including the self (common interests protect the self's interest).
Level 5	*Prior Rights and Social Contract or Utility* The right is upholding the basic rights, values, and legal contracts of a society, even when they conflict with the concrete rules of the group.	*A = B* Integration of self interests with others and mutual interests to achieve mutual, personally, and situationally-specific balances. These balances are preferably based on mutual interests or, if necessary, compromises to discover the lesser of two evils.

Social Perspective of the Stages of Moral Judgement

The next comparison focuses on the different ways that the two theories contextualize the social perspective of the person making the decision. Again, for Kohlberg the focus is on the individual figuring out how to negotiate the community while for Haan the focus is on the individual fitting into the community.

	Kohlberg - Rules	*Haan - Relationship*
Level 1	This stage takes an egocentric point of view. A person at this stage does not consider the interests of others or recognize they differ from actor's, and does not relate two points of view. Actions are judged in terms of physical consequences rather than in terms of psychological interests of others. Authority's perspective is confused with one's own.	People at this stage assimilate their experiences to the self's interest. They have no sustained view of other's interest and no view of mutual interest. The person believes that he or she has unqualified rights to secure his/her own good. Others are objects who compel or thwart self or who can be compelled by self.
Level 2	This stage takes a concrete individualistic perspective. A person at this stage separates own interests and points of view from those of authorities and others. He or she is aware everybody has individual interests to pursue and these conflict, so that right is relative (in the concrete individualistic sense). People integrate or relate conflicting individual interests to one another through instrumental exchange of services, through instrumental need for the other and the other's good will, or through fairness giving each person the same amount.	People at this stage accommodate to the other person's interest when forced. They differentiate the other person's interests from their own concerns but have no view of mutual interests. This person believes that he or she has the same right to secure his/her own good as others have. Other people are subjects who want their own "good" as I want my own "good."
Level 3	This stage takes the perspective of the individual in relationship to other individuals. A person at this stage is aware of shared feelings, agreements, and expectations, which take primacy over individual interests. People relate points of view through the "concrete Golden Rule" putting themselves in the other person's shoes. They do not consider generalized "system" perspective.	People at this stage assimilate their self-interests to other people's to reach common interests. They differentiate other people's interests from their own as mutuality is seen as harmony. They believe that they are moral beings and demonstrate that by goodness, asserting that they have a right to good treatment as do others. Most people are seen as morally good; those who act badly are exceptions, "strange," or outside their moral obligation.

	Kohlberg - Rules	*Haan - Relationship*
Level 4	This stage differentiates the societal point of view from interpersonal agreement or motives. A person at this stage takes the viewpoint of the system, which defines roles and rules. He or she considers individual relations in terms of place in the system.	People at this stage accommodate their self interests to common interests. They assimilate the common interest to their self-interest (self is an object among objects). All persons fall from grace. Thus, this person subscribes to the common regulation to promote my own interests as well as others. Some private self-interests are not subject to negotiation.
Level 5	The stage takes a prior-to-society perspective - that of a rational individual aware of values and rights prior to social attachments and contracts. The person integrates perspectives by formal mechanisms of agreement, contract, objective impartiality, and due process. He/she considers the moral point of view and the legal point of view, recognizes they conflict, and finds it difficult to integrate them.	People at this stage assimilate their self, other and mutual interests. The self, other, and mutual interests are differentiated and coordinated. This person knows that he/she has human vulnerability, weaknesses, and strengths as a moral agent, but also has responsibility to himself, others, and our mutual interest to require that others treat him/her as a moral object. so the moral balance is not upset. Others also have strengths and weaknesses as moral agents therefore he/she must require others to collaborate in achieving and sustaining moral balance. They sometimes need to forgive others for their impositions, given the complexity of situations and the individuality of others and myself.

Observations About Moral Development

The third comparison focuses on the different ways that the two theorists see ethical development. Again, for Kohlberg, one can develop by considering higher levels of thinking, thus reinforcing the cognitive foundations for his theory. Haan asserts that as one experiences moral imbalance one develops ethically, thus reinforcing the interactional or relational foundations for her theory.

As we study the implications of the two theories, we note that for maximum moral growth, we need a combination of theory and practice — we have to know both the various lenses which have been used over time to find the right behavior, and we need experience, either through life or through case studies and simulations to get a sense of how we would really react to real-life situations and practice our decision-making skills.

Aspects of Development	*Kohlberg - Rules*	*Haan - Relationship*
Starting status of the young	Blindly obedient, then egotistically self-serving.	Morally naive but immediately induced to participate reciprocally.
General description of movement	Invariant stage sequence recapitulates the history of moral philosophy.	Gradual progression toward more complex, discriminating dialogical skills.
Necessary condition	Logical development.	Social-emotional experience.
Motivation for development	Comparison with others' higher stage thinking and preference for more differentiated moral thought.	Practical realization that more differentiated exchanges and solutions work better. The need to regard oneself as moral.
Vehicle of change	Cognitive-moral disequilibrium.	Social/intersubjective disequilibrium.
Use of moral tradition	Rediscovers historical moral principles; deductively using these to make decisions.	Uses historic moral principles in own constructions; reinterpreted, creative use of tradition.
Social interchange	A sufficient but not necessary element of development and action.	The necessary but not sufficient element of development and action.
Limiting condition	Lack of exposure to organizationally complex societies.	Human interchanges that prevent participation whether in simple or complex societies.
Recommended educational intervention	Exposure to higher stage moral thought which produces cognitive disequilibrium.	Opportunity to participate in actual and important moral experience.

Differences in Views of Action Between the Two Traditions

The final comparison examines the differences between how the two traditions describe the decision-making process. Leaders who are working on their own ethical development as well as trying to create environments where their employees can make good ethical decisions should attend to both sets of information. The research would indicate that to create ethical environments, one needs to attend both to the individual's ethical maturity as well as the relationships in the organization which foster good decision-making. Thus, our current conversation about whether the problem is a few bad apples or bad systems may need to move to the next level where the answer is both-and - we need people who are equipped to make good decisions and organizational systems which help them make those decisions.

	Kohlberg - Rules	*Haan - Relationship*
Context	Cognitive choices of separate persons drawn from the general rules or principles of their attained stages of development.	Dialogue between persons that considers the particularities of the situation.
Process	Deduction of proper action from previously acquired generalized rules or principles.	Participants' inductive clarification of everyone's self-interests and claims through full and free participation in dialogues.
Critical determinant of action choice	Determination of which general class of rules or principles apply to specific situation.	Determination of the particular agreement that restores or maintains moral balance between participants.
Effects of nonmoral concerns, e.g., emotions	Irrelevant but often distort proper moral action and choice of the right.	Essential conditions that facilitate or deter equalizing moral action.
Capacity for enactment	Persons' achievement of the principled stages or B-substage thinking, or judgment that self is responsible.	Persons' level of moral skill, the public nature of dialogues, participants' mutual expectancies, the inductive discovery of solutions that match situations and thus ought "to work."
Deterrents to action	Development only to lower stage.	Persons' experience of stress and the situation's potential for moral oppressiveness.
Reasons (motives) for acting	Judgment that self is responsible.	To maintain a view of self as moral along with maintaining enhancing relations with others.
Social stipulations that ensure citizen's moral action	Promote higher stage development in individual persons.	Provide opportunities for full participation.

Appendix D

Excellence and Efficiency

Distinction Between Excellence and Efficiency

As we look at ethical action and our character as ethical actors, we are often evaluated against the primary touchstone of a market economy - economic efficiency. While efficiency is valuable, it needs to be moderated with a commitment to excellence. Without that tempering, the virtue of efficiency may morph into the vice of expediency. on the next page is a chart which summarizes the observations of Alisdair MacIntyre in *After Virtue,* 2nd ed. and which helps us identify the distinctions between the moral content and effects of excellence and efficiency.

	Excellence	*Efficiency*
Definition	*Excellence* is a virtue which can be defined independent of and before the establishment of enforceable rules of justice.	*Efficiency* is a virtue which is defined as following the rules of justice until the rules change and thus has no independent ethical content.
Goal	*Excellence* inherently strives for progress in achieving those qualities which are considered excellent and also for progress in identifying our ideas and recognition of the highest perfection.	*Efficiency* inherently strives to identify those means which will be effective in securing the goods and becoming effective in using those means to secure the goods.
Reason for acting	*Excellence* has as a reason for acting, the goal of achieving those qualities which are considered excellent and being subject to the virtue of justice.	*Efficiency* finds the reason for acting to maximize the satisfaction of its own wants and needs.
Evaluation of the virtue	*Excellence* is judged in terms of standards established within and for some specific form of systematic activity and is best thought of in terms of role in community.	*Efficiency* is judged in terms of the goods which can be and are objects of desire by human beings before they consider excellence, independent of any desire people have to excel.
Evaluation of people	*Excellence* judges people in terms of their achievement of community values such as awareness, maturity, and competence.	*Efficiency* judges people in terms of their acquisition of riches, power, status, and prestige.
Ethical requirement	*Excellence* requires that a person seek goals in light of the virtues embodied by the community.	*Efficiency* requires only that a person act to maximize satisfaction of his own wants and needs.
Ethical maturity	*Excellence* requires that a person continue to progress in reaching the ideals of the community and recognize what is the highest perfection.	*Efficiency* requires that a person identify the strategies to acquire goods and become skilled in using those strategies to "get ahead."
Personal moral standards	*Excellence* requires that people have personal moral standards which are harmonized with those of the community at large.	*Efficiency* requires only that people follow the rules of justice until the rules change. Thus, people who are efficient may not have any personal moral standards.
Definition of justice	*Excellence* defines justice in terms of merit and what we deserve, using the same standards for all.	*Efficiency* defines justice in terms of reciprocity of effective cooperation with the other person.
Effect of breaking the rules	*Excellence* recognizes that someone who breaks rules generally hurts himself.	*Efficiency* believes that someone who breaks rules generally hurts other people.

Chapter Notes

Chapter 1 Notes

1. Burke, *The Day the Universe Changed,* 7.

2. The central insight for the organization of the four framework model comes from Joseph A. Petrick and John F. Quinn who wrote *Management Ethics: Integrity at Work* and developed a method for determining which of the primary frames one uses in management settings. A significant difference between their model and mine is that I place the justice theories of John Rawls and others opposite of Immanuel Kant and other deontologists. Petrick and Quinn posit a "systems development ethics," which includes contemporary system theorists, 45-55. I believe that Rawls fits within that general construct. The other difference is that I renamed the ends of the continua. In particular, I see "fidelity" and "charity" as being ethical categories that also relate to economic systems. I believe that the essential conversation for ethics is considering and balancing the competing claims of the individual and the community.

3. Burke, *The Day the Universe Changed,* 7.

4. Berger and Luckman, *The Social Construction of Reality: A Treatise in the Sociology of Knowledge.*

5. For many years the United States Army had the slogan "Be All that You Can Be" which aptly describes the plea of developmental psychologists, theologians, and philosophers who all enjoin us to become responsible, fully "self-actualized" adults.

6. See Keller, *From a Broken Web: Separation, Sexism and Self,* and Shotter, *Conversational Realities: Constructing Life through Language.*

7. Jonas, *The Imperative of Responsibility.*

8. Daly and Cobb, *For The Common Good.*

9. Haan, *et al*, *Moral Grounds*.

10. Neufeldt, Editor in chief, *Webster's New World Dictionary of American English, Third College Edition*, 882.

11. See "Christian Character, Biblical Community, and Human Values" by Lisa Sowle Cahill in *Character and Scripture,* William P. Brown, ed., who distinguishes between ethical acts and moral character. The question becomes whether the ethical person is one who in fact does ethical acts or whether the ethical person is the one whose character has been formed to be predisposed to act ethically, even if from time to time one may miss the mark and act unethically. Perhaps the difference is that those of us who are born predisposed to be ethical resonate with the teleological tradition while those who are born ethically challenged resonate with the deontological tradition.

12. Noddings, *Caring: A Feminine Approach to Ethics & Moral Education.*

13. Shelton, *Achieving Moral Health: An Exercise Plan for your Conscience.*

14. Goleman, Boyatzis, and McKee, *Primal Leadership: Recognizing the Power of Emotional Intelligence.*

15. Lonergan, *Method in Theology.*

16. This model was developed from the work of Jacques Maritain, a Christian existentialist philosopher. See Maritain, *Existence and the Existent: An Essay on Christian Existentialism.*

17. Newberg, d'Aquili, and Rause, *Why God Won't Go Away: Brain Science and the Biology of Belief,* 24-26.

18. Goleman, *Emotional Intelligence.*

19. Golub, *The Limits of Medicine,* 90.

20. Ibid., 53.

21. Goleman, *Emotional Intelligence,* xii.

22. Ridley, *Nature via Nurture,* 92.

23. Ibid., 92.

24. Ibid., 96.

25. Ibid., 96.

26. Reason begins in the lower left corner because it is the question for individual-reflection. The questions spiral around the center counter-clockwise which tends to parallel our own quest for self-knowledge. The placement corresponds to Wilber's model of consciousness which will be explored in Chapter 5. See Wilber, *Sex, Ecology, Spirituality: The Spirit of Evolution,* 2nd ed. *Rev*.

27. The United States has a bias toward individualism, so everything we do tends to be evaluated against the question of whether or not we should limit the rights of individuals. Other cultures, particularly Asian cultures, have a bias toward the community. Thus, when they balance ethical considerations, they tend to consider whether they should encroach upon the prerogatives of the community. This difference leads to much misunderstanding in international business transactions.

28. Those who believe in one God, the Jewish, Christian and Islamic traditions, are part of what is called theistic traditions. Those who believe in the sacred but not one God, such as the Buddhist, Hindu, and Wiccan traditions, are part of what is called non-theistic traditions. Those who believe in human reason and spirit to shape our existence together are part of what is called the humanistic tradition (or pejoratively secular humanism).

29. One of the defining points of the Enlightenment was the mind/body split that emerged from Rene Descartes' notion of consciousness, "I think, therefore I am." This idea, named dualism, led philosophers to explore the reality of the observer and the "external" reality of the physical. As the physical world was subjected to scientific rigor, that which could not be seen, measured, or tasted was perceived as not as real, and by implication, as not valuable as that which could be verified in a science lab. Thus, because the Spirit could not be seen, God was relegated to the wholly transcendent, outside of the affairs of humans. Because emotions were chimerical, they were suspect. On the other hand, monists claim that we are complex persons, comprised of body and spirit, mind, and emotion — all of which are valid and valuable. Monism has been reclaimed by feminist philosophers and those who claim that we have inappropriately narrowed Decartes' teachings. See Tarnas, *The Passion of the Western Mind,* 278-279, and Goldberger, 96-102.

30. Lonergan, *Insight: A Study of Human Understanding,* 90-92.

31. Burke, *The Day the Universe Changed,* 7.

Chapter 2 Notes

1. Lonergan, *Insight*, 311.

2. *Cambodian Genocide Program*. New Haven, CN: Yale University, 2003. http://www.yale.edu/cgp.

3. Daly and Cobb, *For the Common Good.*

4. Op cit., *Cambodian Genocide Program.*

5. Gen. 1:27, 2:21-23 (New International Version).

6. Gen. 4:9 (New International Version).

7. Gen. 4:8-15 (New International Version).

8. See Daly and Cobb, *For the Common Good.*

9. Kirkpatrick, *The Ethics of Community*, 91.

10. See Daly and Cobb, *For the Common Good.*

11. One of the tasks of philosophy is to put concepts into categories — which of these things is just like the other. Ethical and moral qualities are those personal or communal virtues which are embraced and desired. Political qualities, those kinds of things that one can expect in a community, flow from moral qualities. Thus, if autonomy — the ability to choose for oneself how to live — is a desired moral quality, political freedom should follow. Because our popular culture does not separate the two carefully, this text will refer to both traditional moral qualities as well as the political ramifications of those attributes.

12. Kirkpatrick, 92.

13. Ibid., 92.

14. Tronto, *Moral Boundaries,* 28-30.

15. Seuss, *Horton Hatches the Egg.*

16. The rule of law provides the legal underpinning of the United States Constitution. The agreement that we each have made with the rest of our community is that we will follow the laws of the land whether or not we agree with them or whether they benefit us, or we will get caught breaking the law. The social contract we have with each other is based in enlightened self-interest which says that I have a better shot of getting the good things of life if we all follow the same rules.

17. Tronto, *Moral Boundaries,* 35-39.

18. MacIntyre, *After Virtue,* 242.

19. Ibid., 12, 32-33.

20. Todd Wilkenson. "Alaska's 'bridges to nowhere.'" *The Christian Science Monitor.* June 15, 2004. National edition.

21. *Webster's New World Dictionary of American English*, 3rd college ed., s.v. economics.

22. Rose Marie Berger and Brian Bolton. "Coca-Cola or Clean Water?" *Sojourners Magazine,* April 2004 (Vol. 33, No. 4, 10) Between the Lines.

23. Baron, *Kantian Ethics Almost without Apology.* While notions of private property are reflected in the oldest legal traditions, until the end of the Feudal Age much property was held in common or in trust for others in the community. Laws often indicate when the norms are changing. In one German community in the mid-1500s the incidence of theft increased by 1000% over the course of the years. Rather than signalling that the members of the community were scofflaws, the trend indicated a shift from wood being able to be gleaned from the forests of the Lord to the wood being considered private property which could be sold. After several years of strict enforcement, the norm was established and litigation receded.

24. A key question concerning justice is whether fairness requires only that we use the gifts and privileges we inherit appropriately or if, somehow, these gifts themselves must be subject to distribution. Michael Nozick, a theorist in the line of Kant, asserts that a just distribution only requires fundamental fairness from our starting position at birth — no matter how unequal our family wealth or genetic inheritance may be. Rawls asserts that our natural talents should be considered a common asset and thus subject to the claim of the community. Sandel, *Liberalism and the Limits of Justice,* 78-80. This conversation becomes increasingly important as biological research shows that the gap between "haves" and "have-nots" is growing wider in the United States, not just because of systemic injustice but because people of comparable wealth and aptitude for academic and financial success are intermarrying. These families give their children incredible advantage because they have both access to the resources for maximum self-development but also the appetite for self-development which tends to guarantee success in our community. Ridley, *Nature via Nurture,* 90-95.

25. Walzer, *Spheres of Justice*, 21-26.

26. Smith, *An Inquiry into the Nature and Causes of the Wealth of Nations* (1776), cited in Backhouse, *The Ordinary Business of Life: A History of Economics*

from the Ancient World to the Twenty-First Century, 128. Backhouse notes that Adam Smith only used the term "invisible hand" once in each of his major books; however, this phrase, which denotes that as each of us acts the aggregate of actions leads to results that none may have directly desired, was a major contribution to the popular understanding of economics.

27. Greider, *The Soul of Capitalism*, 57.

28. Backhouse, *The Ordinary Business of Life,* 128-129.

29. *Webster's New World Dictionary of American English*, 3rd college ed., s.v. "efficiency."

30. Stone, *Policy Paradox: The Art of Political Decision Making*.

31. Greenleaf, *Servant Leadership*. See also Blackaby and Blackaby, *Spiritual Leadership*.

32. Frederick, *Values, Nature, and Culture in the American Corporation*.

33. Ibid., 25.

34. Ibid., 136.

35. As the full economic impact of the Industrial Revolution emerged in the late 18th century, a persistent question was what to do with unemployment and poverty. One school of thought, advanced by Adam Smith and others, was to just leave the problem alone, subject to the vagaries of the "invisible hand" and moderated by individual acts of charity, almsgiving (see Backhouse, 123-126). The desolation caused by those policies provided much grist for Charles Dickens and other novelists of the time. In the United States, after 150 years of *laissez-faire*, when faced with the economic devastation of the Depression, the government stepped in and over a fifty year period initiated a wide array of federally and state funded programs to provide the poor with a needed leg-up on the economic ladder. The wheel turned again at the end of the twentieth century when a shift was made back to "faith-based initiatives" which were believed to be more effective at eradicating poverty and unemployment than government funded opportunities. Each approach provides its own set of problems and opportunities for abuse — which is why the conversation never seems to be resolved and people cynically echo the words of Christ (although somewhat out of context) "The poor you will always have with you." (Matthew 26:11, NIV)

36. *San Francisco Chronicle*. "Those (expletive) Enron tapes,", June 16, 2004. http://www.sfgate.com.

37. Scott Turow. "Cry No Tears for Martha Stewart." *The New York Times,* May 27, 2004. On-line archive http://query.nytimes.com/gst/abstract.html.

38. Sen, *On Ethics and Economics,* 78-79.

39. Paine, *Value Shift: Why Companies Must Merge Social and Financial Imperatives to Achieve Superior Performance*.

40. Gilpin, *The Political Economy of International Relations.*

41. Ibid, 28.

42. Velasquez, *Business Ethics: Concepts and Cases,* 5th ed., 230-231.

43. Grant Peck, "Mapping a geographical strategy," *The Rocky Mountain News*, June 7, 2004, 11B.

44. Velasquez, 231.

45. Bandura, *Self-Efficacy: The Exercise of Control.*

46. Adapted from McCarty and Bagby

Chapter 3 Notes

1. Tarnas, Richard. *The Passion of the Western Mind,* 278.

2. Ibid., 279.

3. Nelson identified the deontological school of thought with the Protestant tradition and the teleological school of thought with the Roman Catholic tradition. He did so to point to the theological roots of these secular traditions and then noted that at some point what are now called liberal or mainstream Protestants in America rejected their theological roots and adopted the teachings of the Roman tradition. Those in the Evangelical tradition tend to maintain the traditional deontological heritage. I have chosen to remain with the philosophical designations while noting that many times our philosophy is deeply informed by our theology. Further, even though the rhetoric of the Calvinist tradition may be softened where each person is responsible for his/her own salvation and one's position in life indicates how well one is doing, the tendency towards marginalizing the poor and moving toward a powerful central government reemerged at the end of the twentieth century. *See* Nelson, *Reaching for Heaven on Earth*, 16-23.

4. Many public policy feuds could be defused if people noted the different beliefs which ground their decisions. Fortunately, because most public policy solutions are compromise positions, elements of both traditions are part of the formal policies and thus the complexity of the human condition is recognized.

5. Adapted from Nelson, 54

6. Hobbes, Thomas. *Leviathan.* 1651.
http://www.gutenberg.net/etext02/lvthn10.txt.

7. The inspiration for this line comes from Guy Noir, Private Eye, the ultimate existentialist, who was created by Garrison Keillor and whose escapades can be followed on the radio program *Prairie Home Companion*.

8. Kierkegaard, *The Journals of Soren Kierkegaard: A Selection, no. 1395.*

9. Nelson, 54-55.

10. Ibid., 54.

11. The founding of the United States gets its legitimacy from the principles of natural law which come from "the laws of nature and Nature's God" which lead to "these truths [which are] self-evident" and give us the right to be self-governing. The founding fathers asserted in the *Declaration of Independence* :

> When, in the course of human events, it becomes necessary for one people to dissolve the political bonds which have connected them with another, and to assume among the powers of the earth, the separate and equal station to which the laws of nature and of nature's God entitle them, a decent respect to the opinions of mankind requires that they should declare the causes which

impel them to the separation.

We hold these truths to be self-evident, that all men are created equal, that they are endowed by their Creator with certain unalienable rights, that among these are life, liberty and the pursuit of happiness. That to secure these rights, governments are instituted among men, deriving their just powers from the consent of the governed

12. Weber, *The Protestant Ethic and the Spirit of Capitalism.*

13. Greenstein and Barancik, "Drifting Apart." "The growth in the incomes of the richest one percent of Americans," observes the Center on Budget and Policy Priorities, "has been so large that just the increase between 1980 and 1990 in the after-tax income of this group equals the total income the poorest 20 percent of the population will receive in 1990." The gap between the wealthy and the middle class has widened such that "in 1980, the total amount of after-tax income going to the 60% of households in the middle of the income spectrum.was...12% percent greater than the income going to the wealthiest fifth of households. By 1990, however, the income going to the middle three-fifths will be seven percent less than that received by the top fifth...Census data indicate that the gaps between both the rich and the poor and the rich and the middle class are wider now than at any other time since the end of World War II."

14. Weber, *The Protestant Ethic and the Spirit of Capitalism.*

15. Dickens, *A Christmas Carol.*

16. Clayton, Mark, "Environmental Peacemaking," *Christian Science Monitor,* March 4, 2004.

17. Ibid.

18. See the works of John-Paul Sarte and other existentialists.

19. See Heidigger, *et al.*

20. See Grenz, Stanley J. and John R. Franke who in *Beyond Foundationalism: Shaping Theology in a Postmodern Context* give a very coherent description of postmodernism and then assert that assuming the foundations hold is the best way to proceed.

21. Lawrence, Fred. "Lonergan, the Integral Postmodern?" *Method: Journal of Lonergan Studies* 18:2 Fall 2002.

22. Wilber, *Sex, Ecology, Spirituality: The Spirit of Evolution,* 525.

23. Tronto, Joan C. *Moral Boundaries: A Political Argument for an Ethics Care,* 2-3.

24. Wuthnow, *After Heaven: Spirituality in America Since the 1950s,* 162.

25. Ibid.

26. Lonergan, *Insight*, 619.

Chapter 4 Notes

1. Carroll, *Alice's Adventures in Wonderland.*

2. Paine, *Value Shift: Why Companies Must Merge Social and Financial Imperatives to Achieve Superior Performance.*

3. Reuters, "Dissidents scoff at move stripping Eisner as chairman." *Business with CBNBC*, March 5, 2004, http://msnbc.msn.com/id/4455951.

4. Ibid.

5. Lonergan, *Method in Theology*, 9.

6. Kaufman, *In Face of Mystery: A Constructive Theology*, 179.

7. Ibid., 178.

8. Patrick J. Kiger. "Truth and Consequences." *Working Woman*, May 2001, Vol. 26, Issue 5, 56. The lead story features Judith Neal who was a manager at Honeywell in Illinois. She was sent to identify a problem at one of the plants. She discovered that supervisors were falsifying test data, which led to an internal investigation and fines. Neal was eventually marginalized by her employers and her life was threatened. She sued under the False Claims Act and 10 years later received back pay and damages.

9. Winter, *A Clearing in the Forest: Law, Life and the Mind*, 76-85.

10. See Frederick, *Values, Nature, and Culture in the American Corporation*.

11. Conversation with Mark Schlander, employee at IBM, Boulder, CO.

12. Schaef, *Women's Reality: An Emerging Female System in a White Male Society.*

Chapter 5 Notes

1. Frost, "The Road Not Travelled" in Perrine, ed. *Literature: Structure, Sound, and Sense,* 3rd ed.

2. Longergan, *Insight,* 619.

3. Bandura, *Self-Efficacy: The Exercise of Control,* 21.

4. Ibid., 20

5. Greider, *The Soul of Capitalism: Opening Paths to a Moral Economy,* 53-56.

6. Hilberg, "The Nazi Holocaust" in Ermann, *Corporate and Governmental Deviance,* 169-172.

7. Velasquez, *Business Ethics: Concepts and Cases,* 5th ed., 35-37.

8. Goleman, Boyatzis, and McKee, 39.

9. Lonergan, *Method in Theology*, 9.

10. Ermann, *Corporate Deviance*.

11. Kohlberg, "Moral Stages and Moralization: The Cognitive-Developmental Approach," in Lickona, ed., *Moral Development and Behavior: Theory, Research, and Social Issues,* 31-53.

12. Haan, *On Moral Grounds: The Search for Practical Morality*.

13. Hagberg, *Real Power: Stages of Personal Power in Organizations*.

14. Liebert, *Changing Life Patterns: Adult Development in Spiritual Direction*.

15. Loevenger, *Ego Development*.

16. Shlain, *The Alphabet Versus the Goddess: The Conflict Between Word and Image*.

17. Jonas, *The Imperative of Responsibility: In Search of Ethics for a Technological Age*.

18. *SustainAbility*. Corporate Website. 2003. http://www.sustainability.com/philosophy.

19. Conversation with Arja Adair, Executive Director of the Colorado Foundation for Medical Care.

20. Wuthnow, *After Heaven: Spirituality in America Since the 1950s,* viii.

21. Helminiak, *Spiritual Development: An Interdisciplinary Study.*

22. Stebbins, "Mission Across the Curriculum: From Promise to Performance." Paper delivered at Colleagues in Jesuit Business Education Conference, Denver, CO, July 2000.

Chapter 6 Notes

1. Kierkegaard, *The Journals of Soren Kierkegaard.*

2. Philosophy seeks to identify the principles underlying conduct, thought and human behavior using the tools of the mind. Theology seeks to identify the same through studying God and the relationships between God and humans. Many philosophers have a deep theological faith but confine their arguments to those which can be supported through reason and logic.

3. As scholars have traced the lines of philosophical thought, many detours and byways are travelled. For purposes of this book, the traditions are placed under the broad rubrics of deontology and teleology.

4. Nelson, *Reaching for Heaven on Earth*, 20-21.

5. Wilber, *Sex, Ecology, Spirituality: The Spirit of Evolution. 39*

6. As Plato was exploring the notion of Ideals, he said that we were like the person chained to the cave with his back to the light. The person could see the shadows on the wall and mistook the shadows for reality. The task of becoming self aware is to remove the chains and turn around to see life in the light, embracing and realizing the Ideals that are in fact reality. As Richard Parnas states "The Platonic perspective thus asks the philosopher to go through the particular to the universal, and beyond the appearance to the essence...The true structure of the world is revealed not by the senses, but by the intellect, which in its highest state has direct access to the Ideas governing reality." Parnas, *The Passion of the Western Mind,* 8,12

7. Wilber, Insight, 525.

8. Daly and Cobb, *For the Common Good,* 125.

9. Ibid., 127.

10. Wilber, Insight, 239

11. Petrick and Quinn, *Management Ethics: Integrity at Work,* 48.

12. Ibid., 98.

13. Wuthnow, *After Heaven: Spirituality in America Since the 1950s.*

14. Donne, *Devotions Upon Emergent Occasions, Meditation 17.*

15. Wuthnow, *After Heaven: Spirituality in American Since the 1950s.*

16. Personal interview with William C. Convery, III. Convery states that in almost every conversation, someone inquired about elk and deer — no matter how bizarre we might consider the question.

17. See Jane Jacobs, *Systems of Survival,* for a discussion of the different regulatory needs of government and commerce. See also Joel Bakan, *The Corporation: The pathological pursuit of profit and power.*

18. Personal interview with Fr. Michael Sheeran, S.J., President of Regis University.

19. King, "I Have a Dream" speech delivered in Washington D.C., August 1963.

20. Tarnas, *The Passion of the Western Mind,* 225.

21. The same policy governed in the early colonies. Each of the colonies came to be free from established religion and persecution and then promptly established their own faith. The First Amendment to the United States Constitution was to bring an end to the practice of seizing the property of those churches who lost the political leadership battle.

22. Greer, *Mapping Postmodernism: A survey of Christian options,"* 31.

23. Sandel, *Liberalism and the Limits of Justice,* 2nd ed., 2-3.

24. Gilligan, *In a Different Voice,* 21-22

25. Ermann, *Corporate Deviance.*

26. One such chronicle of the suppression of women as full participants in the political and economic structure of America is recorded by Kerber in *No Constitutional Right to be Ladies.* For example, the perceived tendencies of women to be overly emotional were used as a reason to exclude them from juries. Of course, in the words of one jurist, women were also needed to assure that the fabric of our society was kept intact by being home to cook dinner. 217-218.

27. As cited in Velasquez.

28. Haan, *On Moral Grounds.*

29. Appendix D compares the findings of Kohlberg and Haan. One of the most interesting comparisons is what is required for change. Again, both approaches used together get a better result than either individually.

30. Bandura, *Self-Efficacy: The Exercise of Control,* 114-115.

31. Gilligan, *In a Different Voice,* 129.

32. Noddings, *Caring.*

33. Haan, 61-62.

34. Lonergan, *Insight,* 618-624.

35. Frederick, *Values, Nature, and Culture in the American Corporation.*

36. Shelton, *Achieving Moral Health: An Exercise Plan for your Conscience.*

37. Wuthnow, *After Heaven: Spirituality in America Since the 1950s,* 2.

38. Ibid., 184.

39. Ibid., 185.

40. McIntosh, *Mystical Theology,* 6.

41. Christopher Bryant in *Jung and the Christian Way* notes that "Jung calls the rejected elements of the personality the shadow...This shadow element is by no means wholly passive. It makes its influence felt in disconcerting ways, like a child who ignored by grown-ups makes a nuisance of himself in order to attract attention." 73-75.

42. AFP. "Lea Fastow, wife of former Enron CFO, begins jail term." Yahoo! News, July 12, 2004. http://story.news.yahoo.com/.

43. Lynch, *Images of Hope: Imagination as healer of the hopeless,* 224.

44. Bandura, *Self-efficacy: The Exercise of Control,* 45-60.

Chapter 7 Notes

1. Mitchell, Trans. *Tao Te Ching,* 33.

2. Noddings, *Caring: A Feminine Approach to Ethics and Moral Education*, 80.

3. Ibid., 84-85.

4. Jonas, *The Imperative of Responsibility: In Search of Ethics for the Technological Age,* 12.

5. Nash and McLennan, *Church on Sunday, Work on Monday,* 34.

6. Eldredge, *The Journey of Desire,* 13.

7. Rolheiser, *The Holy Longing,* 5.

8. Whyte, *The Heart Aroused,* 168.

9. Ibid., 177.

10. Rolheiser, *The Holy Longing,* 32.

11. Ibid., 27.

12. Witte, *Law and the Protestant Reformation*.

13. John Calvin is known as the father of Calvinism which informed traditions such as the Presbyterians and then the movement known as the Anabaptists (because they did not baptize infants) which was the precursor of the various Baptist and Holiness denominations. Richard Hooker is the father of the Anglican tradition as he systemized the reform teaching of Calvin with the liturgical understandings of the Catholic tradition. The legacy of the Anglican Tradition in the United States is the Episcopal and the Methodist church. St. Ignatius Loyola is the founder of the Jesuit Order. Loyola also focused on the individual's relationship with God as seen in the *Spiritual Exercises* which provides the cornerstone of Jesuit spirituality. See Nelson, *Reaching for Heaven on Earth.*

14. Kerber, *No Constitutional Right to be Ladies.*

15. A bedrock of medical ethics is that prior to treatment, patients will have full disclosure of the impact of the treatment — informed consent. The fact that a room full of medical personnel did not immediately raise the issue of informed consent in this situation, but rather were willing to take the risk that the majority of their patients would not be affected and those who would be affected might never find out, demonstrates the tenuous influence of principles which are supposed to inform our actions.

16. Sandel, *Liberalism and the Limits of Justice,* 9.

17. Ibid., 8.

18. Kant, *Groundwork for the Metaphysics of Morals.*

19. Denise, Peterfreund, and White, *Great Traditions in Ethics,* 207.

20. Kant, 30-31.

21. Ibid, 18.

22. Velasquez, *Business Ethics: Concepts and Cases,* 5th ed., 98.

23. Dan Elliott, "EchoStar, Viacom resolve programming fee dispute, restore channels to DISH network." Associated Press as reported in ContraCostaTimes.com, March 11, 2004. Http://www.contracostatimes.com.

24. Velasquez, 98.

25. Ibid., 99.

26. Lynch, *Images of Hope,* 224.

27. Ibid., 225.

28. Munson, *Intervention and Reflection: Basic Issues in Medical Ethics,* 6th ed., 19.

29. David Lazarus. "Bankruptcy has its rewards for PG&E execs." *San Francisco Chronicle.* July 23, 2004.
http://www.sfgate.com/cgibin/article.cgi?file=/chronicle/archive/2004/07/23/.

30. Nozick, *Anarchy, State, and Utopia,* 151.

31. Lebacqz, *Six Theories of Justice,* 56.

32. Ibid., 56.

33. Nozick, 160.

Chapter 8 Notes

1. Hughes, "A Dream Deferred."

2. For a careful exploration of the critiques of utilitarianism relative to distributive justice, see Karen Lebacqz, *Six Theories of Justice,* 22-32.

3. Kerber, *No Constitutional Right to be Ladies,* p. 218, citing *Congressional Record,* Aug. 1, 1966, 17,769, vol. 112, part 13, 89th Cong., 2nd session.

4. Ibid., 359. In a footnote Kerber discusses *Taylor v. Louisiana,* 419 U.S. 522, 537 (1975) which found systems where women had to "opt in" for jury service rather than automatically be included in the pool to be unconstitutional. "The decision in *Taylor* would be reinforced when, in *Duren v. Missouri,* 439 U.S. 357 (1979), Ruth Bader Ginsburg argued the case of a black man charged with crime in a state in which women had multiple opportunities to claim exemption from jury service on the grounds of sex. *Taylor* overturned "opt in" systems; *Duren* overturned '—opt out' systems."

5. Gilpin, *The Political Economy of International Relations,* 28-29.

6. Lonergan, *Method in Theology,* 50.

7. Haughton, *Images for Change,* 104.

8. Lonergan, *Method,* 50.

9. Ferré, *Living and Value: Toward a Constructive Postmodern Ethics*, 221.

10. Goleman, et al., *Primal Leadership,* 61.

11. Lonergan, *Insight*, 619-620.

12. Lonergan, *Method,* 50.

13. Branch, *Parting the Waters.*

14. Lonergan, *Method,* 53.

15. Lebacqz, *Six Theories of Justice.* 16.

16. *Star Trek II: The Wrath of Kahn* (1982).

17. Mill, *Utilitarianism*, quoted in Denise, *et al,* ed, *Great Traditions in Ethics,* 9th ed., 180.

18. Ibid., 174.

19. Arja Adair, Executive Director, Colorado Foundation for Medical Care

Chapter 9 Notes

1. Amos 5:24, New International Version.

2. Denise, Peterfreund, and White, *Great Traditions in Ethics,* 9th ed., 332.

3. Neufeldt, ed. *Webster's New World Dictionary of American English.* 3rd college ed., 429.

4. Bellah, et al., *The Good Society*.

5. Frederick, *Values, Nature, and Culture in the American Corporation*, 136.

6. Rawls, *A Theory of Justice*, 144.

7. Ibid., 143.

8. Ibid., 143, 148-149.

9. Nozick, *Anarchy, State, and Utopia*, 239.

10. Bellah, *Habits of the Heart*, 83.

11. Rawls, *A Theory of Justice*, 48ff.

12. Ibid., 20.

13. Ibid., 302.

14. Ibid., 284-286.

15. Ibid., 111-112.

16. When the law was passed, "gender" was added as a floor amendment. Thus, the legislative history focuses on the discrimination against African-Americans. It turns out that women were anxious to be rid of their systemic barriers to success as well.

17. Frederick, 136-139.

18. Ibid., 139-142.

19. Peters, *In Search of Excellence*.

20. Ibid., 142-145.

21. Ibid., 145-148.

Chapter 10 Notes

1. King, "I Have a Dream" Speech at Washington D.C, August 1963.

2. Crisp and Slote, eds., *Virtue Ethics,* 3.

3. Shelton, *Achieving Moral Health: An Exercise Plan for your Conscience,* 48.

4. Shelton, 48.

5. Goleman, et al., *Primal Leadership: Realizing the Power of Emotional Intelligence*, 39.

6. Bandura, *Self-efficacy: The Exercise of Control,* 43.

7. MacIntyre, *After Virtue,* 2nd ed.

8. Shelton, 37-38.

9. MacIntyre, *After Virtue,* 2nd ed., 187.

10. Bateson, *Composing a Life.*

11. Schultz, *Pour Your Heart Into It: Building a Company One Cup at a Time.*

12. These support groups (as they have come to be called) have traditionally been our churches and synagogues. While for the past 200 years our ethics have philosophically been

separated from our theological roots, for many Americans, our religious teaching provides the conceptual foundation for our ethical beliefs. Thus, our church and other social communities are often the ones who hold us accountable and provide crucibles for growth.

13. MacIntyre, *After Virtue,* 2nd ed., 187.
14. MacIntyre, *Whose Justice? Which Rationality?*, 35-40.
15. *Columbia World of Quotations,* http://www.bartleby.com/66/6/1706.html.
16. MacIntyre, *After Virtue,* 2nd ed., 191.
17. Ibid., 193.
18. Ibid., 192.
19. Ibid., 192.
20. Tillich, *Love, Power, and Justice.*
21. Walzer, *Spheres of Justice.*
22. Putnam, *Bowling Alone,* 142-147.
23. MacIntyre, *After Virtue,* 2nd ed., 219.
24. Shelton, 38.
25. Haughton, *Images for Change: The Transformation of Society*, 43.
26. Lynch, *Images of Hope: Imagination as Healer of the Hopeless*, 225.

Chapter 11 Notes

1. Mitchell, trans., *Tao Te Ching.*

2. Jeff Shannon, from *Widescreen Review.* http://www.amazon.com/exec.

3. Lester Thurow, "Business Scandals," *Commonwealth Magazine*, July 2002. http://www.ilthurow.com/articles.

4. The difficulty with trying to decide whether businesses were more ethical 50 or so years ago is that the community expectations have changed. Fifty years ago, what we now claim is discrimination against African-Americans and women was just the way that business was done. Before the work of Ralph Nader and others, customers had no expectation of either transparency about the descriptions nor safety in the products which they bought. Before the work of Rachel Carson in her seminal work *Silent Spring,* the effects of corporate pollution were not even noticed. Thus, as the bar is raised, the temptation is to assert that business is less ethical than before. However, taking the long view, we notice ever greater expectations for how people are treated and the transparency with which financial transactions are reported.

5. The Declaration of Independence of the Thirteen Colonies. http://www.law.indiana/edu/uslawdocs/declaration.html.

6. See Charles Hampden-Turner and Fon Trompenaars, *The Seven Cultures of Capitalism: Value Systems for Creating Wealth* and *Building Cross-Cultural Competence: How to create wealth from conflicting values.*

7. Alice M. Rivlin, "Challenges of Modern Capitalism, *Regional Review — Quarter 3 2002,* Federal Reserve Bank of Boston, http://www.bos.frb.org/nerr/rr2002/q3/capitalism.htm.

8. Rivlin, 4-5.

9. Robert Greenstein and Scott Barancik, "Center on Budget and Policy Priorities," Drifting Apart, July 1990; Holly Sklar, Let Them Eat Cake, Z Magazine, November 1998, 29-32. A current push is to narrow the gap between those at the top and those at the bottom. The problem is complex because one of the primary incentives for performance was issuing stock. One proposal is to not allow companies to consider any income to executives over a certain amount — say $1,000,000 per year — as a deductible expense for companies. The thought is that such a proposal will provide a strong incentive for companies to reduce the compensation of the top brass. See also http://www.uwec.edu/Academic/Geography/Ivogeler/w111/greedy.htm.

10. A. Srikanth, "Stock market crashes and bubbles — Why do investors never learn?" *Investment World,* April 23, 2000. http://www.blonnet.com/iw/2000/04/23/stories/0823h011.htm. See also the New York Stock Exchange Report *Shareownership 2000,* www.nyse.com/marketinfo/shareownersurvey.html, as well was the New York Stock Exchange's Historical Perspective, http://www.nyse.com/about/TodayInNYSE.html.

11. Bruce Bartlett, "Stock Ownership is Becoming Widespread," *National Center for Policy Analysis Idea House,* January 24, 2000. http://www.ncpa.org/oped/bartless/jan2400/html.

12. Mark Thompson, "Stock Ownership Increasingly Black and White," June 11, 2001. http://www.socialfunds.com/news/article.cgi/article596/html.

13. Spitzer, *The Spirit of Leadership.* p. 215-230.

14. Tarnas, 60.

15. Whyte, *The Heart Aroused.*

Works Cited

Backhouse, Roger E. *The ordinary business of life: a history of economics*. Princeton: Princeton University Press, 2002.

Bakan, Joel. *The Corporation: The Pathological Pursuit of Profit and Power.* Toronto: Viking Canada, 2004.

Bandura, Albert. *Self-Efficacy: The Exercise of Control.* New York: W.H. Freeman, 1997.

Baron, Marcia W. *Kantian Ethics Almost Without Apology.* Ithaca, NY: Cornell University Press, 1995.

Bellah, Robert N., Richard Madsen, William M. Sullivan, Ann Swidler, Steven M. Tipton. *The Good Society.* New York: Vintage Books, 1992. First published 1991 by Knopf. Page references are to the 1992 edition.

Berger, Peter and T. Luckman. *The Social Construction of Reality.* New York: Doubleday, 1966.

Birkland, Thomas A. *An Introduction to the Policy Process: Theories, Concepts, and Models of Public Policy Making.* Armonk, New York: M.E. Sharpe, 2001.

Blackaby, Henry and Richard Blackaby. *Spiritual Leadership.* Nashville, TN: Broadman & Holman, 2001.

Bok, Derek. *The Trouble with Government.* Cambridge, MA: Harvard University Press, 2001.

Branch, Taylor. *Parting the Waters: America in the King Years 1954-63.* New York: Simon and Schuster, 1988.

Brown, William P., ed. *Character & Scripture: Moral Formation, Community, and*

Biblical Interpretation. Grand Rapids, MI: William B. Eerdmans, 2002.

Bryant, Christopher. *Jung and the Christian Way.* San Francisco, CA: Harper & Row, 1983.

Burke, James, *The Day the Universe Changed.* New York: Back Bay Books, 1995.

Carroll, Lewis. Alice's Adventures in Wonderland. *The Junior Classics,* Vol 5. NP: P.F. Collier and Son, 1938, 1948. Originally published by the Macmillan Company, ND. Page references are to the 1948 edition.

Crisp, Roger and Michael Slote. *Virtue Ethics.* New York: Oxford University Press, 1998. First printed 1997 by Oxford University Press. Page references are to the 1998 ed.

Daly, Herman E. and John B. Cobb, Jr., *For The Common Good.* Boston: Beacon Press, 1989.

Declaration of Independence of the Thirteen Colonies in Congress. July 4, 1776.

Denise, Theodore C., Sheldon P. Peterfreund, and Nicholas P. White. *Great Traditions in Ethics,* 9th ed. Belmont, CA: Wadsworth, 1999.

Dickens, Charles. *A Christmas Carol.* New York: Signet Classic, 1984.

Donne, John. "Devotions Upon Emergent Occasions, Meditation 17," 1634.

Eldredge, John. *The Journey of Desire: Searching for the Life We've Only Dreamed Of.* Nashville, TN: Thomas Nelson, 2000.

Ermann, M. David and Richard J. Lundman. *Corporate and Governmental Deviance: Problems of Organizational Behavior in Contemporary Society,* 5th ed. New York: Oxford University Press, 1996.

Etzioni, Amitai. *The Spirit of Community: Rights, Responsibilities, and the Communitarian.* New York: Crown, 1993.

Faure, Bernard. *Double Exposure: Cutting Across Buddhist and Western Discourses.* Janet Lloyd, trans., Stanford, CA: Stanford University Press, 2004.

Ferré, Frederick. *Living and Value: Toward a Constructive Postmodern Ethics.* Albany, NY: State University of New York Press, 2001.

Frederick, William C. *Values, Nature, and Culture in the American Corporation.* New York: Oxford University Press, 1995.

Frost, Robert, "The Road Not Taken."

Fuller, Robert C. *Ecology of Care: An Interdisciplinary Analysis of the Self and Moral Obligation.* Louisville, KY: Westminster/John Knox, 1992.

Gillian, Carol. *In a Different Voice: Psychological Theory and Women's Development.* Cambridge, MA: Harvard University Press, 1982.

Gilpin, Robert. *The Political Economy of International Relations.* With the assistance of Jean M. Gilpin. Princeton, NJ: Princeton University Press, 1987.

Goldberger, Nancy Rule, Jill Mattuck Tarule, Blythe McVicker Clinchy, and Mary Field Belenky, eds. *Knowledge, Difference, and Power: Essays Inspired by Women's Ways of Knowing.* New York: BasicBooks, 1996.

Goleman, Daniel. *Emotional Intelligence.* New York: Bantam Books, 1997. First printed 1995 by Bantam Books. Page references are to the 1997 edition.

Goleman, Daniel, Richard Boyatzis and Annie McKee. *Primal Leadership: Recognizing the Power of Emotional Intelligence.* Boston, MA: Harvard Business School Press, 2000.

Golub, Edward S. *The Limits of Medicine: How Science Shapes Our Hope for the Cure.* New York: Times Books, 1994.

Greenleaf, Robert. *Servant Leadership*. New York: Paulist Press, 1977.

Greenstein, Robert and Scott Barancik, "Drifting Apart," Center on Budget and Policy Priorities, July 1990.

Greer, Robert C. *mapping postmodernism: a survey of Christian options.* Downers Grove, Ill: InterVarsity Press, 2003.

Greider, William. *The Soul of Capitalism: Opening Paths to a Moral Economy.* New York: Simon & Schuster, 2003.

Grenz, Stanley J. and John R. Franke. *Beyond Foundationalism: Shaping Theology in a Postmodern Context.* Louisville, KY: Westminster/John Knox Press, 2001.

Haan, Norma, Eliane Aerts, and Bruce A. B. Cooper. *On Moral Grounds: The Search for Practical Morality*. New York: New York University Press, 1980.

Hagberg, Janet. *Real Power: Stages of Personal Power in Organizations,* rev. ed. Salem, WI: Sheffield, 1984.

Hampden-Turner, Charles M. and Alfons Trompenaars. *The Seven Cultures of Capitalism: Value Systems for Creating Wealth.* New York: Bantam Double-Day Dell, 1993.

Haughton, Rosemary Luling. *Images for Change: The Transformation of Society: Building Cross-cultural Competence* New York: Paulist Press, 1997.

Helminiak, Daniel A. *Spiritual Development: An Interdisciplinary Study.* Chicago, IL: Loyola University Press, 1987.

Hobbes, Thomas. *Leviathan.* 1651.

Jacobs, Jane. *The Natures of Economies.* New York: The Modern Library, 2000.

______. *Systems of Survival: A Dialogue on the Moral Foundations of Commerce and Politics.* New York: Vintage Books, 1994. First printed 1992 by Random House. Page references are to the 1994 edition.

Jonas, Hans. *The Imperative of Responsibility: In Search of Ethics for a Technological Age.* Chicago, IL: University of Chicago Press, 1984.

Kant, Immanuel. *Groundwork for the Metaphysics of Morals.* Allen W. Wood, ed and trans. New Haven, CN: Yale University Press, 2002.

Kaufman, Gordon D. *In Face of Mystery: A Constructive Theology.* Cambridge, MA:Harvard University Press, 1993.

Keller, Catherine. *From a Broken Web: Separation, Sexism and Self.* Boston, MA: Beacon, 1986.

Kerber, Linda K. *No Constitutional Right to be Ladies: Women and the Obligations of Citizenship.* New York: Hill and Wang, 1998.

Kierkegaard, Soren. *The Journals of Soren Kierkegaard: As Selection, no. 432, 1843.* Alexander Dru ed. and trans. (1938). *The Columbia World of Quotations.* New York: Columbia University Press, 1996.

Kirkpatrick, Frank G. *The Ethics of Community*. Malden, MA: Blackwell, 2001.

Kohlberg, Lawrence. "Moral Stages and Moralization: The Cognitive-Developmental Approach." In Thomas Lickona, ed., (1976) *Moral Development and Behavior: Theory, Research, and Social Issues,* New York: Holt, Rinehart and Winston, 1976.

Lawrence, Fred. "Lonergan, the Integral Postmodern?" *Method: Journal of Lonergan Studies.* Volume 18, Number 2, Fall 2000: 95-122.

Lebacqz, Karen. *Perspectives from Philosophical and Theological Ethics: Six Theories of Justice.* Minneapolis, MN: Augsburg, 1986.

Liebert, Elizabeth. *Changing Life Patterns: Adult Development in Spiritual Direction.* St. Louis, MO: Chalice Press, 2000.

Loeb, Paul Rogat. *Soul of a Citizen: Living with Conviction in a Cynical Time.* New York: St. Martin's Griffin, 1999.

Loevenger, Jane. *Ego Development.* San Francisco, CA: Jossey-Bass, 1977.

Lonergan, Bernard. *Insight: A Study of Human Understanding,* vol. 3 of *The Collected Works of Bernard Lonergan.* Toronto: University of Toronto Press, 1957.

———. *Method in Theology.* Toronto: University of Toronto Press, 1973.

Lynch, William F. *Images of Hope: Imagination as Healer of the Hopeless.* Notre Dame, IN: University of Notre Dame Press, 1974. First printed 1965 by Helicon Press. Page references are to the 1974 edition.

MacIntyre, Alasdair. *After Virtue: A Study in Moral Theory,* 2nd ed. Notre Dame, IN: University of Notre Dame Press, 1984. First printed 1981 by University of Notre Dame Press. Page references are to the 1981 edition.

———. *Three Rival Versions of Moral Enquiry: Encyclopadeia, Genealogy, and Tradition.* Notre Dame, IL: University of Notre Dame Press, 1990.

———. *Whose Justice? Which Rationality?* Notre Dame, IL: University of Notre Dame Press, 1988.

Marion, Jim. *Putting on the Mind of Christ: The Inner Work of Christian Spirituality.* Charlottesville, VA: Hampton Roads, 2000.

Maritain, Jacques. *Existence and the Existent: An Essay on Christian Existentialism.* Lewis Galantiere and Gerald B. Phelan, trans. Garden City, NY: Image Books, 1956. First printed 1948 by Pantheon Books. Page references are to the 1956 edition.

McCarty, F. William and John W. Bagby. *Irwin's Legal and Ethical Environment of Business,* 3rd ed. Chicago, IL: Irwin, 1996.

McDowell, Banks. *Ethics and Excuses: The Crisis in Professional Responsibility.* Westport, CN: Quorum Books, 2000.

McIntosh, Mark A. *Mystical Theology: The Integrity of Spirituality and Theology.* Malden, MA: Blackwell, 1998.

Mitchell, Steven, trans. *Tao Te Ching: A New English Version.* New York: Harper & Row, 1988.

Munson, Ronald. *Intervention and Reflection: Basic Issues in Medical Ethics,* 6th ed. Belmont, CA: Wadsworth/Thomson Learning, 2000.

Nash, Laura and Scotty McLennan. *Church on Sunday, Work on Monday: The Challenge of Fusing Christian Values with Business Life.* San Francisco, CA: Jossey-Bass, 2001.

Nelson, Robert H. *Reaching for Heaven on Earth: The Theological Meaning of Economics.* Lanham, MA: Rowman & Littlefield, 1991.

Neufeldt, Victoria, ed. *New World Dictionary of American English,* 3rd College Ed. New York: Webster's New World/Simon & Schuster, 1988.

Newberg, Andrew, Eugene D'Aquili and Vince Rause. *Why God Won't Go Away: Brain Science and the Biology of Belief.* New York: Ballantine Books, 2001.

Noddings, Nel. *Caring: A Feminine Approach to Ethics & Moral Education.* Berkeley, CA: University of California Press, 1984.

Nozick, Robert. *Anarchy, State, and Utopia.* New York: Basic Books, 1974.

Paine, Lynn Sharp. *Value Shift: Why Companies Must Merge Social and Financial Imperatives to Achieve Superior Performance.* New York: McGraw Hill, 2002.

Palmer, Parker J. *Let Your Life Speak: Listening for the Voice of Vocation.* San Francisco, CA: Jossey-Bass, 2000.

Peck, M. Scott. *People of the Lie: The Hope for Healing Human Evil.* New York: Touchstone, 1983.

Peters, Tom and Robert H. Waterman, Jr. *In Search of Excellence: Lessons From America's Best Run Companies.* New York: Harper & Row, 1982.

Petrick, Joseph A. and John F. Quinn. *Management Ethics: Integrity at Work.* Thousand Oaks, CA: Sage, 1997.

Putnam, Robert D. *Bowling Alone: The Collapse and Revival of American Community.* New York: Simon & Schuster, 2000.

Rawls, John. *A Theory of Justice.* Cambridge, MA: The Belknap Press of Harvard University Press, 1971.

Ridley, Matt. *Nature via Nurture: Genes, Experience, and What Makes Us Human.* New York: HarperCollins, 2003.

Rolheiser, Ronald. *The Holy Longing: The Search for Christian Spirituality.* New York: Doubleday, 1999.

Sandel, Michael J. *Liberalism and the Limits of Justice,* 2nd ed. Cambridge, UK: Cambridge University Press, 1998.

Schaef, Anne Wilson. *Women's Reality: An Emerging Female System in a White Male Society.* San Francisco, CA: Harper & Row, 1985.

Schultz, Howard and Dori Jones Yang. *Pour Your Heart Into It: How Starbucks Built a Company One Cup at a Time.* New York: Hyperion, 1997.

Sen, Amartya. *On Ethics and Economics.* New York: Basic Blackwell, 1988.

Seuss, Dr. [pseud.]. *Horton Hatches the Egg.* New York: Random House, 1940.

Shelton, Charles. *Achieving Moral Health: An exercise plan for your conscience.* New York: Crossroad, 2000.

Shlain, Leonard. *The Alphabet Versus the Goddess: The Conflict Between Word and Image.* New York: Viking Penguin, 1988.

Shotter, John. *Conversational Realities: Constructing Life through Language.* Thousand Oaks, CA: Sage, 2002. First printed 1993 by Sage Publications, Ltd. Page references are to the 2002 ed.

Stone, Deborah. *Policy Paradox: The Art of Political Decision Making.* New York: W. W. Norton, 1997.

Tarnas, Richard. *The Passion of the Western Mind: Understanding the Ideas That Have Shaped Our World View.* New York: Harmony Books, 1991.

Tillich, Paul. *Love, Power, and Justice: Ontological Analysis and Ethical Applications.* New York: Oxford University Press, 1960. First printed 1954 by Oxford University

Press. Page references are to the 1960 ed.

Tronto, Joan C. *Moral Boundaries: A Political Argument for an Ethics of Care.* New York: Routledge, 1993.

Velasquez, Manuel. *Business Ethics,* 5th ed. Englewood Cliffs, NJ: Prentice Hall, 2002.

Walzer, Michael. *Spheres of Justice: A Defense of Pluralism and Equality.* New York: Basic Books, 1983.

Weber, Max. *The Protestant Ethic and the Spirit of Capitalism.* New York: Routledge, 1992.

Whyte, David. *The Heart Aroused: Poetry and the Preservation of the Soul in Corporate America.* New York: Currency Doubleday, 1994.

Wilber, Ken. *Sex, Ecology, Spirituality: the Spirit of Evolution,* 2nd ed. rev. Boston, MA: Shambhala, 2000.

Winter, Steven L. *A Clearing in the Forest: Law, Life and the Mind.* Chicago, IL: The University of Chicago Press, 2001.

Witte, John Jr. *Law and Protestantism: The Legal Teachings of the Lutheran Reformation*. New York, NY: Cambridge University Press, 2002.

Wuthnow, Robert. *After Heaven: Spirituality in America Since the 1950s.* Berkeley, CA: University of California Press, 1998.

Index

A

A Beautiful Mind 13
Adam and Eve 77, 78
Adult
  autonomy 42
  fully functioning 8, 43, 161
  independent
  responsible 39
Aesthetic
  reflection 104
Affirmative action 31
Age of Enlightenment 5, 6, 157
Age of Reason 5
Alaska 50
Amos, the Prophet 227
Anarchy
  abuse of autonomy 42
Anecdotes
  verification for belief systems 123
Apathy
  abuse of equality 44
Aquinas. St. Thomas 70
  Results Lens 202
  theoretical evolution 151
Argyris, Christopher 192
Aristotle 70
  Reputation Lens 255
  Results Lens 203
  theoretical evolution 151
Assumptions
  critical thinking 123
Augustine, St. 70
  Reputation Lens 255
  Relationship Lens 227

Rights/Responsibility Len 172
Austin, Jane 48
Authority
component of belief system 25
core value 41-42
wisdom of 78
verification for belief system 125
Autonomy
abuse of 42
building block 41
condition of society 78
economics and 51
employee concerns 111
neo-mercantile economy 85
organizational concerns 111
Rights/Responsibility Lens 190
stakeholder concerns 112
value-in-conflict 106
virtues associated with 42-43, 111

B

Baby-boomers 96
Baha'is 235
Baldridge Initiative
Bandura, Albert 120, 161
Basic liberties 243
Bateson, Mary Catherine 263
Bellah, Robert
moral ecology 230
Relationship Lens 226
unrestrained market economy 238
Beliefs
core, definition 97
Belief system
change 19
flawed, 21
formation of 13-22
political and economic 72
source of information 22-33
verification for 125
Bentham, Jeremy
calculation of utils 214, 210
Results Lens 202
Berger, Peter 6
Bias
correction for 130
Bible 157
Black Plague 23
Boeing Aircraft Company 155
Buddha
moral maturity 137
Buddhism 73
Buffett, Warren 77
Burke, James 2, 34

C

Cafeteria believers 89
Cain and Abel 40
California Pacific Gas & Electric 197
Calvin, John 81
social contract 179
CalSTRS 100
Cambodia
Cambodian Court Project 39
Carroll, Lewis 93
Categorical imperative 185
Catholic Social Thought 235
Contracts
ethics and law 64
favored over regulation 80
Chaos
abuse of sensibility 49
Character
ethics 256
formation 233
Charity
almsgiving 57
Calvinism and 81
of spirit 48
poverty and 82
Chick-fil-A 27
China, People's Republic of 61-62
Christian
human existence 77
state of human nature 75
Jewish-Christian canon 18

Medieval thought 152
provide for poor 233
value structure 164
Civil disobedience
strategy of 115
Civility
core virtue 289
Civil Rights Act 65, 84, 218
Civil Rights Movement 24, 33, 66, 84, 239
Cobb, John 150
Coca-Cola 50-51
Columbine High School 16
Commitments
core, definition 97
Common good
building blocks 40-50
ethical maturity 137
global relationships 86
Results Lens 222
Rights/Responsibility Lens 199
Competencies 275
Conscience
exercises for 284
internal structure for values 59
natural law 80
Context
establishing 20
narratives as 40
sensibility as 47
Continuous improvement 118
reflective process 139
Relationship Lens 252
Reputation Lens 287
Results Lens 223
Rights/Responsibility Lens 181
Consequentialism 260
Convery, Bill 155
Cordillera del Condor Peace
Transborder Reserve 87
Corporate social responsibility
definition 101
economic interconnectedness 138
Core ethical frameworks 4
Core values 40
building blocks of common good
see rationality, equality, autonomy, sensibility.
prioritize 7
proto-typical 3
Courage
core values 277
Creativity
role in spiritual maturity 165
Critical thinking
analytical pitfalls 124
Crucible of spirit
definition, Relationship Lens 231
definition, Reputation Lens 257
definition, Results Lens 206
definition, Rights/Responsibility Lens 175
Lonergan's method 118
path to maturity 146
Cultural context
core statements 164
path to maturity 146

D

Daly, Herman 150
Darwin, Charles 70
decision making process 10-12
Declaration of Independence 293
deCussade, J.P.
Rights/Responsibility Len 172
Deontological tradition
approach to justice 68
Deming, W. Edwards 139
DeMello, Anthony
Rights/Responsibility Lens 172
Democracy
basic rights 242
Dewey, John 70
Dickens, Charles 83, 284
Dilemmas
ethical, definition 103
Divine Right of Kings 157

Donne, John 154
Douglas, Michael 237
Dualism 6, 48
  Cartesian 28

E

EchoStar 188
Ecologizing
  economic value 56
Ecology
  moral 230
Economic(s)
  balance with ethics 52, 60
  classic liberal 205
  civilization requires 79
  core values and 50-58
  current policies and poverty 82
  God's grace and 83
  growth 59
  law and 62-64
  market economy 13, 59
  neo-mercantile 59
  political organization and 59
  public policy and 84
  representative positions 72
  social-democratic 13, 59
  strategies 62
  technology and 69
  triple bottom line 58
  value-free vs normative 58
Einstein, Albert
  Theory of Relativity 5
Eisner, Michael 100
Efficiency
  contrast with excellence 221
Eldredge, John 178
Emotions
  path to maturity 146
Emotivism 48
Ends
  treating people as 191
Enlightenment
  philosophers 51, 158, 174
  project 28 260
  Scottish 48
Enron 167, 251
Entitlement
  definition of 53
Entrainment 250
Equality
  abuse of 44
  building block 41
  economics and 51
  employee concerns 113
  of opportunity 43
  of result 43
  organizational concerns 113
  stakeholder concerns 113
  value-in-conflict 106
  virtues associated with 43, 112
Ethical act
  definition, Relationship Lens 231
  definition, Reputation Lens 257
  definition, Results Lens 206
  definition, Rights/Responsibility Lens 175
Ethical actor
  definition 99
  Relationship Lens 234
  Reputation Lens 261
  Results Lens 210
  Rights/Responsibility Lens 181
Ethical frameworks
  introduction to core 128
  key questions 160
Ethics
  balance with core values 41
  definition 9, 127, 157
  economics and 50-58
  law and 58-66
  organizing questions 36
  path to maturity 146
  prima facie obligation
  public policy 41
Etzione, Amitai
  Relationship Lens 226

Excellence
compared with efficiency 221
compared with expedience 271
Existentialism 87-88
Expedient
reflection 104
Experience
component of belief system 23
verification of belief system 125
External goods 273

F

Facts
critical thinking 124
value neutral
Fastow, Andrew and Leah 167
Federal Reserve System 295
Ferre, Frederick
constructive post-modernist 207
Results Lens 202
Feudal age 154
Fiduciary duty 45
rationality 109
sensibility 110
Financial transparency 197
Ford Edsel 212
Foundationalism 88
Frankel, Viktor
Frederick, William
economic values 55
moral ecology 249
Relationship Lens 226
Free will
definition 120
Frost, Robert 119, 154
Fuller, Robert C
Relationship Lens 226
Fundamentalism
conflict with charity 48

G

Galileo 20
Garden of Eden 78
Gates, Bill 249
Gillian, Carol 89
ethic of relationship 162
Rights/Responsibility Len 172
Gilpin, Robert
Goals
Results Lens 206
God
transcendent/immanent 74
Goleman, Daniel 9, 15, 17, 208
Reputation Lens 254, 284
Gonzaga University 142
Good
external 269
harmonized 220
internal 269
Greenleaf, Robert 55
Greider, William 53
"Guns and butter" 56
work situations 121

H

Haan, Norma 89
moral maturity 131
relationship as basis for maturity 161
Hagberg, Janet
moral maturity 131
Happiness
calculation of 216-217
Harding, Sandra 89
Haughton, Rosemary 286
Heisenberg, Warren 5, 6
Uncertainty Principle 5, 13, 147
Helminiak, Daniel 140
Heuristic questions
core questions 152
Hobbes, Thomas 70, 78, 228
Holocaust 121, 161

Hooker, Richard 179
Hughes, Langston 222
Humanist tradition 73
Hume, David 48
Hutchenson, Francis 48
Hypothetical imperative 185

I

Ideal
  creating heaven on earth 76
Idealism
  relationship to deontology 158
Idealists
  Rights/Responsibility Len 172
Ideal observer 228
Imagination 21
  role for spiritual maturity 165
Immobility
  abuse of rationality 46
Independence
  community 84
  global 86
Individualism
  radical 232
India
  Kerala 50
Industrial Revolution 232, 297
Inequality
  from restrictions 44
  social and economic 236, 247
  systemic 44
Influence factor 219
Inquiry based method 8
Integrity
  core virtue 276
Interdependence
  community 84
  global 86
Internal goods 272
Intuition 302
Israel 47

J

Jesus Christ
  moral maturity 137
Jewish
  Holocaust 121
  Jewish/Christian canon 18
  providing for poor 233
  spirituality framework 164
Jonas, Hans 177
Jung, Carl
  spiritual maturity 166
Just deserts
  definition of 52
Justice
  core virtue 278
  Reputation Lens 258
Just savings principle 242, 244

K

Kant, Immanuel 5, 70
  A Critique of Practical Reason 28, 183
  compared with Rawls 148
  core ethical framework 128
  duty of self improvement 51
  restraint on selfishness 153
  Relationship Lens 227
  Rights/Responsibility Len 172
  theoretical evolution 151
Kaufman, Gordon 104
Kerber, Linda 204
Kervorkian, Dr. 66
King, Martin Luther Jr 78, 156
  moral pacer 132
  NAACP 209
Kierkegaard, Soren 79
Kohlberg, Lawrence 131,
  rules as basis for maturity 161

L

Labor
  movement 232

revolution 84
Law
anti-trust 249
copyright 241
core values and 59
God, law of 80
human 80
patent 241
relationship to ethics 63
relationship to government 79
Lay, Ken 304
Least advantaged 240
Legal settlements 252
Licenses
inherited 154
Liebert, Elizabeth
moral maturity 131
Litigation
regulation of behavior 63
Loevenger, Jane
developmental stages 132
Logic
rules of 123
Lonergan, Bernard 37
about 10
constructive postmodernist 89
decision model 10-12, 92
Results Lens 202
unrestricted desire to know 119, 208
Loyola, St. Ignatius
Results Lens 203
Luther, Martin 70, 78
Relationship Lens 2276
Rights/Responsibility Len 172
Lutheran
lawyers 179
Lynch, William F.
Images of Hope 192
Results Lens 202
technical selves 167

M

MacIntyre, Alisdair 48, 70-71
compared with Aristotle 148
core ethical framework 128
Reputation Lens 254
theoretical evolution 151
MacNaughton, Rosemary
Results Lens 202
Market economy
liberal 60
unregulated 61
unrestrained 238
Market survey 212
Maturity
path toward 146
spiritual 164-166
Marx, Karl 51
McIntosh, Mark
definition of spirituality 165
McLennan, Scotty 177
Medieval Age 5
Merit
definition of 52
MicroSoft 61
Mill, John Stuart 5, 70
articulation of utilitarianism 154
core ethical framework 128
idealism 220
Results Lens 202
theoretical evolution 151
Mind
path to maturity 146
Modern Age 5
Mohammad
moral maturity 137
Monism 28
Moral
definition 129
ecology 230
reflection 104
Moral act
definition, Relationship Lens 231
definition, Reputation Lens 257
definition, Results Lens 206
definition, Rights/Responsibility Lens 175

Moral tradition
definition, Reputation Lens 257
Morality
definition 9
legislation of 65
path to maturity 146
Mutually disinterested 237

N

NAACP 209
Narrative
definition 40
order of a life 263
personal 285
Nash, Laura 177
Native Americans 241
Natural resources
use of 86
Nazi Germany 121
Nelson, Robert H. 71-72
Newton, Isaac 7
Neo-mercantile economy 60
balance with social-democracy 85
Neutral events 13
noticing 15
Newberg, Andrew 14
Newton, Isaac
Newtonian world view 29
Newtonian physics, 30
Nirvana 76
Noddings, Nel 9
Caring 176
ethic of care 162
Rights/Responsibility Len 172
Nozick, Robert
minimal government 198

O—P

Original position 234

Paine, Lynn Sharp 59,
stakeholders 100
Palestine 47
Palmer, Parker
Reputation Lens 254
Parks, Rosa 209, 217
Pasteur, Louis 15
Patriot Act 66
Peter, Paul and Mary 95
Petrick, Joseph A.
ethics matrix 150
Person
ethical, definition 9
moral, definition 9
self-regulating 12
Person-in-community 9
defined 41
task of 42
Phemonenology 87-88
Plato 4, 70,
Allegory of the Cave 70, 149
Relationship Lens 227
Rights/Responsibility Len 172
theoretical evolution 151
Pluralism
responsibilities of 170
Political structures
models of 60
Poor
Judeo/Christian tradition 233
self-interest an 82
treatment of 83
Positive rights 198, 243
Postmodernism 6, 7
constructive 88, 207
Power
relinquishment of personal 170
Practice
MacIntyre's definition 266
Process
for comment 242
Property
necessity for private 81
Protestant
conception of the human 76
religious war 158

Protestant Reformation 5, 70, 157
values of 51
Protestant Work Ethic 81
Prudential judgment 301
Putnam, Robert D. 281

Q

Quakers 235
Quinn, John F.
ethics matrix 150

R

Rationalism 88
Rationality
abuse of
building block 41
economics and 50
individual concerns 109
organizational concerns 109
stakeholder concerns 110
value in conflict 106
virtues associated with 45, 108
Rawls, John 70-71
basic liberties 243
compared with Kant 148
core ethical framework 128
just savings principle 242**
Nozick and 198
original position 234
reflective equilibrium 234, 240
Relationship Lens 226
theoretical evolution 151
Realism
related to teleology 159
Reason
component of belief system 22
content of 23
find universal rules 45
process of 23
verification of belief system 125
Reflective equilibrium 234, 240
Regulations
relationship to ethics
Relationship Lens
characteristics of 229
conceptual map 226
core questions 227
Reputation Lens
characteristics of 231
conceptual map 226
core questions 227
Resources
fairness of distribution 51
redistribution of 43
Results Lens
characteristics of 205
conceptual map 202
core questions 203
Reversibility 189
Rice, Judge Juanita 39
Rich, Adrien 89
Right action
Relationship Lens 231
Reputation Lens 2584
Results Lens 206
Rights/Responsibility Lens 175
Rights/Responsibility Lens
characteristics of
conceptual map 172
core questions 173
Rights
basic 242
positive 198, 243
procedural 242
Rivlin, Alice 295-296
Role
constraints 268
definition 265
Rolheiser, Ronald
Rights/Responsibility Len 172
Roman Catholic
conception of the human 76
religious war 158
Ross, J.D.
duties 174, 194

Rights/Responsibility Len 172
Rule
of law 45
of practice 271
universal 45
virtue ethics 269

S

Sarbanes-Oxley Act 218
Savings & Loan 64
Shelton, Charles
moral maturity 163
Reputation Lens 254
Shultz, Howard 264
Self
dispersed/unitary 88-89
interest and the poor 82
transcendental 181
Self-discipline
restrain desire 12
Self-efficacy
definition 120
Reputation Lens 2594
Self-regulating person 12
Sensibility
abuse of 49
building block 41
economics and 51
ethical, definition 98
individual concerns 111
organizational concern 110
stakeholder concerns 111
value-in-conflict 106
virtues associated with 47, 110
September 11, 2001 56, 213
Sexual harassment 16, 239
Shaef, Anne Wilson 117
Shareholder
theory of management 100
Sheeran, Michael J. 156
Shelton, Charles 9, 283
Shlain, Leonard 137
Sigma 6 293
Smith, Adam 48
creation of wealth 81
invisible hand 52, 210
Results Lens 205
Snow, Phoebe 208
Social contract
Lutheran lawyers 179
Relationship Lens 2276
Social democracy 60-61
balance with neo-mercantile 85
Soul
path to maturity 146
Spitzer, Robert 301
Stakeholder
definition 101
Relationship Lens 236
Reputation Lens 262
Results Lens 210
Rights/Responsibility Lens 181
theory of management 101
Stalin, Joseph
purge in Russia 161
Standards of excellence 269
Star Trek 211
Statistics
in belief system 125
Stebbins, Michael 142
Stewart, Martha 171
Stone, Deborah
economic core values 54
Stone, Jeff 291
Subsidies 241

T

Tao Te Ching 173, 291
Tarnas, Richard 70
Taxes
democracy 210
redistribution of resources 65
Technology revolution 298u r
Teleological tradition
approaches to justice 68
Reputation Lens 257

Results Lens 217
Ten Commandments 27
Thurow, Lester 292
Tipping point
utilitarian analysis 217
Triple bottom line 58, 138
Tradition
component of belief system 30
common set of 41
verification for belief system 125
Truth
ultimate 7
universal 7
Turner, Kathleen 237
Tuskegee Airmen 194

U

United States
Constitution 107
radical individualism 232
Universalizability 187
Utilitarianism
hedonistic 210
ideal 210
Reputation Lens 270
Results Lens 205
Utils
of happiness 217-218
Unity of life 282

V

Values
terminal 208
Values-in-conflict
core values 105
Relationship Lens 238
Results Lens 214
Rights/Responsibility Lens 184
Veil of ignorance 236, 240
Velasquez, Manuel
ethics of market economy 60
critical thinking skills 123
Viacom 188
Virtue ethics
Reputation Lens 2564
Virtues
acquired human 276
autonomy 118
equality 112
life conserving
rationality 108
Relationship Lens 230
Reputation Lens 258s
Results Lens 206
Rights/Responsibility Lens 176
sensibility 110

W

Wage
minimum/living 83
WalMart 65
Walzer, Michael 52
Whyte, David 178
Wilber, Ken
ethics matrix 149
Winter, Steven 108
World view
competing 61-62
consumer 53
Newtonian 29
producer 54
World War II 297
Workers
temporary 53
Wuthnow, Robert 88
sense of belonging 155
spirituality in America 140
spirituality of dwelling 152

About

CB Resources, LLC

CB Presents is an outgrowth of the work of Catharyn Baird in the area of professional ethics and spirituality at work and a subdivision of the company CB Resources, LLC. An educator for more than 20 years, Catharyn is on the leading edge of academics and practitioners who are exploring the relationship between personal ethical and spiritual maturity and professional excellence. Many of the concepts present in Catharyn's material have been developed in collaboration with Kerry McCaig, whose work focuses on strategies for ethical maturity.

In addition to being an inspiring speaker and gifted writer, Catharyn is a leader in developing and presenting classes in a web-based format. Based on her 10 years experience as a faculty member in Regis University's on-line MBA programs, Catharyn has been intrigued with the notion of offering seminars on ethics and spirituality in a web-based format.

As Catharyn has taught business ethics over the years, many of her students have asked whether the ethics and spirituality part of her classes are available to those who are not part of the Regis MBA program. Based on the interest of a variety of people whom she has taught or who have participated in her seminars, Catharyn began exploring the possibility of offering professional ethics and spirituality in the workplace seminars as stand-alone web based classes. Catharyn shared her dream with her longtime friend and nationally recognized graphic designer, Karin Hoffman, and computer gurus Christopher Riley and Shaun Roach.

Together they began the design process which has led to the launching of CB Resources, LLC, a company committed to assisting people on their journey to ethical and spiritual maturity while fully engaged in the workplace environment. The central premise of the work is that by intentionally engaging in strategies for ethical and moral maturity, one can become more integrated as a person and more effective in the market place.